Amanda Odell-West.

A Neofederalist Vision of TRIPS

A Neofederalist Vision of TRIPS

The Resilience of the International Intellectual Property Regime

GRAEME B. DINWOODIE

ROCHELLE C. DREYFUSS

OXFORD
UNIVERSITY PRESS

OXFORD
UNIVERSITY PRESS

Oxford University Press, Inc., publishes works that further
Oxford University's objective of excellence
in research, scholarship, and education.

Oxford   New York
Auckland   Cape Town   Dar es Salaam   Hong Kong   Karachi
Kuala Lumpur   Madrid   Melbourne   Mexico City   Nairobi
New Delhi   Shanghai   Taipei   Toronto

With offices in
Argentina   Austria   Brazil   Chile   Czech Republic   France   Greece
Guatemala   Hungary   Italy   Japan   Poland   Portugal   Singapore
South Korea   Switzerland   Thailand   Turkey   Ukraine   Vietnam

Copyright © 2012 by Oxford University Press, Inc.

Published by Oxford University Press, Inc.
198 Madison Avenue, New York, NY 10016

www.oup.com

Oxford is a registered trademark of Oxford University Press
All rights reserved. No part of this publication may be reproduced,
stored in a retrieval system, or transmitted, in any form or by any means,
electronic, mechanical, photocopying, recording, or otherwise,
without the prior permission of Oxford University Press.

Library of Congress Cataloging-in-Publication Data
Dinwoodie, Graeme B.
A neofederalist vision of TRIPS : the resilience of the international intellectual property
regime / Graeme Dinwoodie.
p. cm.
Includes bibliographical references and index.
ISBN-13: 978-0-19-530461-9 (hardback : alk. paper)
ISBN-10: 0-19-530461-6 (hardback : alk. paper) 1. Intellectual property (International law)
2. Agreement on Trade-Related Aspects of Intellectual Property Rights (1994)
3. Foreign trade regulation. I. Title.
K1401.D564   2012
346.04'8—dc23   2011026821

3 5 7 9 8 6 4 2

Printed in the United States of America
on acid-free paper

CONTENTS

Preface vii
Acknowledgments xi

    PART I   WHERE WE WERE: THE STRUCTURE OF INTELLECTUAL
                    PROPERTY AND THE HISTORY OF THE TRIPS DEBATE

1. The Challenges of the TRIPS Agreement   3
2. The History and Character of TRIPS: How It Shapes the Contemporary Debate   21

    PART II   WHERE WE ARE: DISPUTE RESOLUTION AND ITS IMPACT
                     ON A NEOFEDERALIST VISION OF TRIPS

3. The Dispute Settlement Understanding: Interpretation of the Substantive Features of the TRIPS Agreement   49
4. Interpretation Continued: The Structural Features of the TRIPS Agreement   83
5. TRIPS and Domestic Lawmaking   115

    PART III   WHERE WE ARE HEADED: INTELLECTUAL PROPERTY
                      LAWMAKING FOR THE TWENTY-FIRST CENTURY

6. The WTO, WIPO, ACTA, and More: Fragmentation and Integration   143
7. An International Acquis: Integrating Regimes and Restoring Balance   175

Notes   205
Index   257

PREFACE

The collaboration leading to this book began almost a decade ago, with an invitation from Jerry Reichman and Keith Maskus. They asked us to contribute to a volume on international public goods and technology transfer under the TRIPS Agreement, an instrument which, at that time, was still rather new. Of course, TRIPS was not the first international intellectual property system—the Berne and Paris Conventions were then more than a century old. However, in shifting international lawmaking from the World Intellectual Property Organization (WIPO), which administered these treaties, to the World Trade Organization (WTO), TRIPS raised the standards of intellectual property protection, particularly for technological advances. For the first time, states were required to operate within a detailed international framework. Moreover, as part of the WTO system, TRIPS obligations were subject to the compliance mechanism set out in the Dispute Settlement Understanding. The system was designed to promote innovation and facilitate global trade. Nonetheless, we recognized that a robust public domain is crucial to advancement, and our first article asked whether states enjoyed enough flexibility under the new regime to maintain an accessible knowledge base in the face of future technological and societal change.

That first article focused on the role of the Dispute Settlement Body (DSB) in interpreting the substantive obligations set out in the TRIPS Agreement. But it became clear in writing that piece that the constraints TRIPS was imposing on WTO members were far more substantial than the text of the Agreement might suggest. In its earliest reports, the DSB had adopted formalistic approaches to decision making that substantially curtailed national policy-making choices. In one subsequent paper, we examined the multipart provisions of the Agreement that permit states to make certain exceptions from protection (in this volume, we call these the "Exceptions" tests), which the DSB read as imposing cumulative conditions on states seeking to enact measures that responded to local circumstances, both creative and social. Not only was this interpretative approach overly restrictive, we found that the panels compounded that rigidity in patent cases by construing a provision on technological neutrality as structural, potentially limiting the ability of states to tailor the law to the diverse demands of the various patent industries. In a third piece, we demonstrated how the discrete approach that the DSB took to domestic lawmaking—a term we used to describe the way in which individual parts of complex legislative schemes were formally dissected and examined individually—narrowed political choices and skewed domestic legislation in favor of ever-stronger protection.

As we wrote these articles, it became evident that maintaining a strongly innovative environment requires more than a set of "leaky" international rules—that is, rules that enable national lawmakers to ensure that protected works eventually enter the public domain. Rather, an effective international system must also permit states to gear their domestic laws to the needs of their local creative sectors and to deal with the distributive consequences of raising the cost of accessing the fruits of humankind's ingenuity. Further, it must furnish states with opportunities to continually readjust the balance among the interests of multiple generations of innovators and the public. This requires a more affirmative conceptualization of the international intellectual property system. In two final articles, we looked at the other institutions created by the WTO: the Council for TRIPS and the General Council, as well as the formal relationship between the WTO and WIPO. We saw in these institutions the potential for developing a stronger system, one that protects the integrity of the trade environment while maximizing national autonomy to ensure appropriate regulation of knowledge-intensive goods.

It is that theme—ensuring a regulatory environment that both facilitates international trade and recognizes the importance of policy choices attuned to changing and diverse national needs and priorities—that animates this book. TRIPS is now routinely invoked strategically to repress efforts to improve and refine national intellectual property laws. The volume begins with the rhetoric used in that effort—the conceptualization of the TRIPS Agreement as a code, a one-size-fits-all regime that imposes a single globally optimal set of incentives to innovate. We reject that notion. To us, it is inconsistent with the historical development of international intellectual property law, potentially destructive of what the international system had achieved, and blind to the demands of legitimacy. We see TRIPS as a neofederalist system in which states retain discretion to experiment with their laws and continually engage in tailoring them to national priorities and local cultural values. This vision of TRIPS reflects an understanding of the essential characteristics of intellectual property laws: laws that balance the interests of different groups, that must constantly adapt to new technological conditions, and that reflect a diverse set of values. There is, in our view, no single global incentive structure; instead, the Agreement aggregates the incentives derived from the national law of each WTO member state, and, through structural provisions that coordinate the global marketplace, TRIPS ensures that innovators and consumers everywhere can enjoy the benefits of these domestic measures. In 1994, the conclusion of TRIPS placed the WTO at the center of the international intellectual property system. Although the institutions of the WTO are not a strong central government in the federal sense, they provide a standing venue for continual discussion of ongoing intellectual property challenges and a mechanism that allows successful experiments to be elevated from the national to the international level.

While maximum coherence might be achieved by consolidating all international intellectual property lawmaking in the WTO, we know that this is not likely to be the case. States dissatisfied with the level of protection in TRIPS will continue to shift regimes—from the WTO back to WIPO, to regional and bilateral arrangements, or to new multilateral organizations. We appreciate the benefits of international regulatory competition. Intellectual property law touches on many other fields: harnessing the expertise of the World Health Organization on medical issues, the experience of the Food and Agriculture Organization with promoting nutrition, the United Nations Conference on Trade and Development's views on development, or the Convention on Biological Diversity's familiarity with conserving natural resources can improve the system overall. But the fragmentation of lawmaking can also produce cacophony: bilateral and multilateral agreements that raise protection can clash with norms intended to insulate states and knowledge goods from further demands for commodification. In an unstable legal climate, innovators and investors may be less willing to devote money and efforts to creative production.

The book therefore ends with a look to the future. It suggests three complementary ways to move forward, to bring a measure of coherence to the system while recognizing the benefits of wide institutional input. One is to integrate norms from other institutions into the operation of WTO institutions. Integration can occur most notably by interpretation, permitting the DSB (consistent with the Vienna Convention on the Law of Treaties) to consider the work of other institutions in construing the terms of the TRIPS Agreement, and most especially, in understanding its normative underpinnings. Second, it can occur in the lawmaking function of the WTO, in the Council for TRIPS, by broadening participation in ways that capture the input of the other organizations that are promulgating intellectual property norms.

A third way to move forward, drawn from our individual scholarship, is to establish what we call an international intellectual property acquis. We borrow the concept of a set of rules that bind a multiplicity of institutions from recent scholarship on global administrative law, which is developing a body of shared procedural norms. We do not, however, believe that procedural changes are sufficient to keep the law attentive to the concerns we have identified; we think that a substantive framework is also necessary. We take the term "acquis" from EU and WTO law, where it signifies the commitments that states undertake upon entering those regimes, as a way of protecting the expectations of all members. As we see it, the acquis would describe the core principles that have historically undergirded national and international intellectual property systems. We believe the acquis would be valuable interpretively, and thus complement the approach of integration through interpretation. More important, it would operate prospectively, to frame the negotiation of future international intellectual property instruments. The acquis would also assist in reorienting international intellectual property law, putting the interests of consumers, follow-on innovators, and competitors on the same plane as those of right holders. Further, the acquis gives explicit international recognition to the concept of balance, which has been a sometimes-unappreciated (and unstated) part of the system since the time of Berne and Paris.

Through advances in communication technology, globalization of trade, and increasingly interconnected geopolitical arrangements, the world is drifting toward a virtual Pangaea. Yet pride of place remains strong: nations differ culturally, socially, and technologically, and thus political borders retain significance. Celebrating diversity and attending to distributive justice require a new paradigm in knowledge governance. We have, in short, reached a new "constitutional moment." We hope that our efforts to identify the components of an international acquis will inspire others to participate in fleshing out its contours and the scope of its operation. It is only by recognizing that we have reached such a moment, and by adapting accordingly, that the international intellectual property system will prove resilient.

Graeme B. Dinwoodie
Oxford

Rochelle C. Dreyfuss
New York City

ACKNOWLEDGMENTS

As the Preface suggests, the project of reforming the international intellectual property system will require the work of many others, building (we hope) upon this book. However, this book itself would not have been possible without a great many people. Most prominently, we are grateful to Nicole Arzt at NYU School of Law, who rescued us from formatting issues and otherwise maintained the manuscript in readable form. Our librarians, Gretchen Feltes and Mirela Roznovschi at NYU, Tom Gaylord at Chicago-Kent, and Helen Garner at Oxford, have supplied us with an incredible array of useful materials. Over the course of our collaboration, we have also benefited from the help of many research assistants. Martin McGuinness (NYU LLM, 2011) and Adrian Loo (Oxford BCL, 2011) were especially important in concluding the work on this volume.

The book would not have happened had we not had the opportunity to sharpen our views through our earlier efforts. Accordingly, we are grateful to Jerry Reichman and Keith Maskus for inviting us to write *Preserving the Public Domain of Science in International Law* and publishing it in their book, INTERNATIONAL PUBLIC GOODS AND TRANSFER OF TECHNOLOGY UNDER A GLOBALIZED INTELLECTUAL PROPERTY REGIME (Keith E. Maskus and Jerome H. Reichman eds., Cambridge University Press 2005); to Jacqui Lipton and Peter Gerhart for the invitation that led us to write *TRIPS and the Dynamics of International Property Lawmaking*, 36 Case W. Res. J. Int'l L. 95 (2004); to Lucie Guibault and Bernt Hugenholtz for allowing us to refine the public domain discussion in *Patenting Science: Protecting the Domain of Accessible Knowledge*, which was published in their book, THE FUTURE OF THE PUBLIC DOMAIN (IDENTIFYING THE COMMONS IN INFORMATION LAW) (Lucie Guibault & P. Bernt Hugenholtz eds., Kluwer Law International 2006); to Brian Kahin for urging us to consider the discrimination issue in *Diversifying Without*

Discriminating: Complying with the Mandates of the TRIPS Agreement, 13 Mich. Telecomm'n & Tech'y L. Rev. 445 (2007); to Greg Vetter for the invitation to participate in the Houston Institute for Intellectual Property and Information Law Santa Fe Conference and publish *Designing a Global Intellectual Property System Responsive to Change: The WTO, WIPO, and Beyond*, 46 Hous. L. Rev. 1187 (2009); and to Carlos Correa for publishing *Enhancing Global Innovation Policy: The Role of WIPO and Its Conventions in Interpreting the TRIPS Agreement* in his RESEARCH HANDBOOK ON INTELLECTUAL PROPERTY AND TRADE (Carlos Correa ed., Edward Elgar 2010). We benefited from the insights of those who participated in the conferences at which several of these pieces were presented, as well as from those who attended presentations of various book chapters at the invitation of Niklas Bruun, Jennifer Rothman, Bhaven Sampat, and Yoshiyuki Tamura.

We have learned a great deal from discussing the issues in this book with colleagues, including José Alvarez, Annette Kur, Larry Helfer, Benedict Kingsbury, and Richard Stewart. And we are particularly grateful to Susy Frankel, Robert Howse, Sungjoon Cho, Ed Lee, and Peter Yu, who read the manuscript and provided us with detailed comments. Rochelle Dreyfuss would also like to thank Justine Pila for providing her with a fellowship at St. Catherine's College, which allowed her to work on the book with Graeme at Oxford, and the Filomen D'Agostino and Max E. Greenberg Research Fund of NYU for financial support. And, of course, we could not have done this without the support of our families, Brian Havel and Robert Dreyfuss.

A Neofederalist Vision of TRIPS

PART I

WHERE WE WERE

The Structure of Intellectual Property and the
History of the TRIPS Debate

1

The Challenges of the TRIPS Agreement

> Quite simply, with regard to intellectual property, TRIPS tells all countries—developed, developing and least-developed—*what* they must do and *when* and *how* they must do it.
>
> —Gerald J. Mossinghoff, *National Obligations Under Intellectual Property Treaties: The Beginning of a True International Regime*, 9 FED. CIRCUIT B.J. 591, 603 (2000) (emphasis in original)

> By the mid-1990s, this patchwork of national [intellectual property] laws and multilateral conventions had given way to a supranational code called the TRIPS Agreement.
>
> —Peter K. Yu, *Currents and Crosscurrents in the International Intellectual Property Regime*, 38 LOY. L.A. L. REV. 323, 442 (2004)

> TRIPS.... basically requires all WTO members to adopt the same level of IPR protection as that which prevails in the industrialized world.
>
> —Kamal Saggi and Joel P. Trachtman, *Incomplete Harmonization Contracts in International Economic Law: Report of the Panel*, China—Measures Affecting the Protection and Enforcement of Intellectual Property Rights, WT/DS362/R, adopted March 20, 2009, 10 WORLD TRADE REV. 23–24 (2010)

> Restricting the scope of gene patents to the disclosed purpose while maintaining the principle of absolute product protection for all other technical fields violates the non-discrimination requirement of Article 27.1.
>
> —Wolrad Prinz zu Waldeck und Pyrmont, *Special Legislation for Genetic Inventions—A Violation of Article 27(1) TRIPS?*, in PATENTS AND TECHNOLOGICAL PROGRESS IN A GLOBALIZED WORLD, 289, 304 (Prinz zu Waldeck und Pyrmont et al. eds. Springer 2009)

The second half of the twentieth century marked the beginning of a radically new era for the creative community. Advances in such fields as electronics, biotechnology, computer science, information technology, materials science, remote monitoring and imaging, digitization, and networking technologies ushered in the so-called Third Industrial Revolution and, with it, a Knowledge Eeconomy heavily dependent on information and science-intensive products.[1] Not necessarily tied to physical objects, the knowledge components of these goods could be widely distributed with exceptional ease. The products soon found ready markets: in the post–World War period, global wealth grew, language skills improved, populations migrated, and the taste for foreign products exploded.

As an expression of the cultural, intellectual, and technological aspirations of a nation, the tradition in intellectual property law is quintessentially territorial: the right to exploit the products of investments in innovation is dependent on the laws and policies of the place where these products are exploited.[2] Accordingly, the protection that an innovator from country A enjoys in country B depends on whether B has intellectual property law, and on whether it is willing to extend its benefits to foreigners. Even before digitization and internet distribution, the knowledge industries were dissatisfied with leaving decisions on protection to individual states, for each nation could gain by providing exclusive rights to local innovators while at the same time allowing its own consumers to enjoy cheap access to foreign products. As trade among nations grew during the nineteenth century, the creative industries were increasingly affected by the distortions that territoriality produced. Not only might profits be unattainable in foreign countries, products (and in the case of trademarks, reputations) flowed back from places where they were not protected to the places where they were, putting downward pressure on the prices that rights holders could charge even at their home. Countries with innovative industries and strong intellectual property laws began to search for ways to prevent unauthorized works from undermining the benefits of their domestic regimes.

By the end of the nineteenth century, these problems were ameliorated by two multilateral instruments, the Berne Convention, for copyrights in works of authorship,[3] and the Paris Convention, for patents on inventions and trademarks on commercial signals.[4] The hallmark of both was national treatment.[5] Members of the Berne and Paris Unions committed to extending to the nationals of other members the same treatment they provided to their own authors, traders, and inventors. Thus, whatever protection B offered to those it considered locals was extended to works from A (if A was a part of the relevant Union). In addition, the Paris Convention created international priority rules to facilitate the acquisition of national trademark and patent rights on a multinational basis,[6] and over time, the Berne Convention prohibited formalities, making protection automatic within its Union.[7]

National treatment alone did not guarantee that a Union member would recognize exclusive rights in creative works, for so long as a country did not offer protection to locals, it was not required to offer protection to foreigners. Both Conventions therefore also established baseline standards of protection. However, the baselines were quite minimal—well below the level that intellectual property producers thought necessary under national law to protect their works and provide a fair return on investments. Renegotiations occurred from time to time, with Berne ultimately raising protection significantly. The administration of Paris and Berne (along with later intellectual property instruments) was consolidated first in the United International Bureaux for the Protection of Intellectual Property (BIRPI) and, in 1970, in the World Intellectual Property Association (WIPO), which became a specialized agency of the United Nations four years later.[8] Although these moves were accompanied by repeated rounds of negotiations and revisions, WIPO did not produce instruments capable of dealing with the new dynamism in cultural and scientific production. Real change occurred only at the very end of the twentieth century, when discussions about a global intellectual property regime were coupled with the Uruguay Round negotiations of the General Agreement on Tariffs and Trade (GATT). In 1995, the Agreement on Trade-Related Aspects of Intellectual Property Rights (TRIPS or the TRIPS Agreement) became one of the framework agreements encompassed by the World Trade Organization (WTO).[9]

This book is concerned with that development—with the role of the TRIPS Agreement in the international intellectual property system and its relationship to domestic lawmaking. Our goal is to determine how the TRIPS Agreement shapes contemporary challenges—how it influences the way that member states can encourage innovation and deal with technological, cultural, and organizational change—and to extract lessons on how to improve future attempts at international knowledge governance. The Agreement is certainly a more comprehensive document than the older instruments. When it was negotiated, it was clearly a more ambitious effort to confront the challenges that the Knowledge Economy presented to WTO members. At the same time, however, if read—as the Mossinghoff, Yu, and Saggi and Trachtman quotations at the beginning of this Chapter suggest—as a "supranational code," instructing countries on "*what* they must do and *when* and *how* they must do it," and as "requir[ing] all WTO members to adopt the same level of IPR protection," the Agreement would hobble WTO members' capacity to cope with current social and economic problems and with future challenges.

We do not subscribe to the supranational code view of the TRIPS Agreement. Rather, we see the Agreement as reflecting a different paradigm in knowledge governance, which we term a "neofederalist regime." In our view, member states retain considerable discretion under TRIPS, but agree to operate within an international framework. This framework is substantially less powerful than the central administration of a federal government. However, it is federalist in the sense that the regime comprises a series of substantive and procedural commitments that promote the coordination of both the present intellectual property system and future international intellectual property lawmaking. Thus, while we recognize that TRIPS negotiators reached a series of compromises among the social and technological policies of countries with different cultures, education levels, and economic needs, we see these compromises not as a code, but rather as defining the parameters of national autonomy. To us, it is equally significant that in addition to these substantive provisions, the negotiators adopted national treatment as the cornerstone of the Agreement and established an institutional structure to facilitate continued discussion, revision, and accommodation. In that way, the Agreement creates an efficient trade regime but allows nations at every level of development to tailor intellectual property laws to their individual creative needs. Furthermore, the Agreement anticipates that over time, social conditions will evolve, technological advances will alter creative opportunities, and the law will need to respond. Most often, this will occur through state experimentation, generating valuable input to the development of international solutions.

Although the WTO will likely be the prime locus of future negotiations to consolidate the insights generated at the national level, we acknowledge that there are many international institutions now operating in this space. Accordingly, we also suggest that the neofederalist nature of the regime could be strengthened by the recognition of what we call an international intellectual property acquis. In promoting the idea of an acquis, we are inspired by a similar concept first developed by the European Union to describe the commitments to which new members of the Union must adhere. The term was later borrowed by WTO adjudicators to connote the body of principles reflected in a treaty regime (even if not always expressed). Our notion of an acquis would similarly recognize principles long established in intellectual property law, in both national and international law, as critical to supporting innovation, creativity, and the full enjoyment of knowledge products. We would consider these enduring commitments as the starting point for interpreting the international instruments generated by these institutions and as the basis for all future negotiations.

This Chapter presents a synopsis of our argument and an example of how differing perspectives on TRIPS would affect the capacity of WTO members to respond to technological change. It ends with a description of how the book unfolds.

I. TRIPS as a Supranational Code

Admittedly, it is tempting to read TRIPS as a comprehensive code of intellectual property law—to understand it as harmonizing the law and as dictating to WTO members exactly how they must protect knowledge-intensive goods. The comprehensiveness of the instrument is unprecedented in international intellectual property law. In addition to its coverage of copyright, patent, and trademark,[10] TRIPS deals with geographical indications (terms denoting products that are distinctive because of where and how they are produced),[11] undisclosed information (trade secrets and confidential material),[12] industrial designs,[13] and the design of integrated circuits.[14] As with Paris and Berne, TRIPS commits members to national treatment.[15] In addition, it furthers the principle of equal treatment of foreigners by importing into TRIPS the most favoured nation obligation found in the 1947 GATT. TRIPS thus supplements the measure of a nation's obligations by including as a benchmark not simply the treatment of locals, but also the terms offered to every foreign national.[16]

As compared with Berne and Paris, the protection afforded under TRIPS is generally higher and more detailed. The patent provisions, for example, raise the level of protection significantly above that required by the Paris Convention. Furthermore, TRIPS expands the reach of patent protection by prohibiting discrimination as to where the invention is made or produced, and as to the field to which the advance contributes.[17] For all intellectual property regimes, the Agreement also differs dramatically from the WIPO instruments in that it specifies not only rights, but also obligations regarding enforcement of those rights.[18] Because more countries belong to the WTO than had been members of Paris and Berne, and TRIPS is a mandatory agreement within the WTO, its geographic reach is far broader than that of the earlier instruments.

In addition, TRIPS establishes new intellectual property institutions. Modifications of the Agreement must be made by the Ministerial Conference and the General Council of the WTO.[19] At the same time, the Council for TRIPS was established to monitor compliance, afford members opportunities to consult, and deal with residual and new issues.[20] As important, TRIPS obligations are subject to the WTO's Dispute Settlement Understanding (DSU).[21] Thus, a member that fails to meet its obligations can find itself involved in a proceeding before an ad hoc panel of the Dispute Settlement Body (DSB), ultimately appealable to the DSB's standing Appellate Body (AB). A country that fails to comply with a decision of the adjudicators could become the target of trade sanctions with the possibility of retaliation in any sector covered by WTO Agreements.[22] In sum, a cursory reading of TRIPS makes it appear to be self-contained: a comprehensive code, supported by an institutional structure complete with a legislature, an administrative agency, and a judiciary.

This reading also likely comports with the intent of many of those responsible for bringing intellectual property within the WTO framework. Actors representing the creative industries sought to commodify information products more completely.[23] Indeed, to some in the technology sector, the Holy Grail has long been "a universal patent, respected throughout the world."[24] A supranational code, binding all member states to high levels of protection, is a move in that direction. From a trade perspective, a comprehensive code may also have appeared to be the objective. As some international lawyers see it, multilateral agreements force nations to internalize the costs that their policy choices impose on other countries. If free riding on other nations' investments in innovation is viewed as an externality, then the goal of TRIPS would be to adopt a single "optimal" level of global protection.[25] Free traders also see the crux of the trade system as the exploitation of comparative advantage: world wealth increases as creation, development, and manufacture are situated in the location in which they are most efficiently conducted. If lowering barriers is an unmitigated advantage, trade hands may have reasoned that raising intellectual property standards is likewise unambiguously beneficial. Interdependent WTO markets also enjoy a geopolitical advantage. As the columnist Thomas Friedman famously observed in 1999, "[N]o two countries that both had a McDonald's had fought a war against each other."[26]

Additionally, it is possible to see this reading of TRIPS in the decisions of dispute resolution panels. To date, there have been (depending on how one counts) seven disputes raising questions of compliance with the TRIPS regime that have been taken as far as a panel decision (with less than half ultimately resolved by the AB).[27] Especially in the early cases, panels tended to treat TRIPS as an intellectual property code, with little sensitivity to the needs of individual states, to the demands of the political process in which national lawmaking proceeds, or even to the dynamics of intellectual production.[28] The AB has taken a somewhat more nuanced approach, which emphasizes the limited nature of TRIPS obligations, and the Ministerial Conference has also made a declaration to that effect.[29] The Ministerial Declaration (the so-called Doha Declaration) was, however, announced in the context of a health crisis; as a general matter, the code perspective continues to pervade policy debates.

Certainly, it is a convenient reading for firms (and lawyers) with strong market positions based on current intellectual property laws in the developed world. They can use TRIPS obligations as a basis for consolidating their gains. As the Waldeck quotation at the beginning of this Chapter illustrates, domestic initiatives to respond to new conditions are often met by the argument that the proposals are not TRIPS-compliant. Sometimes the domestic effect is more than rhetorical: there are structural biases that push protection upward. TRIPS introduces several mechanisms—examples include the most favoured nation provision, the nondiscrimination obligation in patents, and the DSB compliance procedures—that generate momentum tending to raise domestic levels of protection over time. Furthermore, since the standard for reviewing TRIPS compliance can be stricter than the standard for reviewing domestic legislation, any compromise implemented in domestic legislation is vulnerable to unraveling: the legislative choice that favors the intellectual property holder is given deference, but the part of the reform that favors consumers is invalidated as beyond the prerogative of the WTO member.[30] The result is that, under this reading, domestic levels of protection will continually ratchet upward, but the baselines are rigid—they can never be adjusted downward.

II. Intellectual Property as a Complex Regime

The code reading of TRIPS thus envisions the Agreement as establishing a high—and ever higher—level of intellectual property protection. In a sound intellectual property system, however, maximum protection is not necessarily optimal. Intellectual property law is shaped not only by the concerns of innovators, but also by the interests of various other entities, diverse values, and changing events.[31]

A. Balance

From a pragmatic perspective, it is clear that intellectual property laws must look beyond the interests of individual innovators. Richard Posner and William Landes, for example, accept the notion that intellectual property law is needed to spur investments in innovation. However, they argue, the system must also consider second-comers—follow-on innovators who wish to build upon the initial work. Optimal production cannot occur if the cost of inputs exceeds the profits obtainable from outputs; to keep the costs of adaptation and improvement in line, ready access to protected works is necessary.[32] That insight is evident in the arts, where works build upon and reference one another.[33] And it is true in science as well. As Isaac Newton famously wrote to Robert Hooke, "If I have seen further [than certain other men] it is by standing upon the shoulders of giants."[34] Scientists' own understanding can also be perceived in the Mertonian norms of communalism, universalism, disinterestedness, originality, and skepticism,[35] which foster an environment of open science where new work is shared and refined—and, indeed, regarded by scientists as refined because it is shared through, for example, funding and publication processes dependent on peer review. Intellectual property rights can also interfere with other, open, forms of innovation.[36] Empirical studies provide support for the notion that higher levels of protection are not always optimal. While there are surveys concluding that formal intellectual property rights do not always impede scientific work,[37] there is also considerable evidence that these rights can chill progress.[38] Prescriptively, intellectual property thus necessarily constitutes a balance between the interests of proprietors in securing a return on their investments and controlling their reputations, and the interests of followers and the public in a robust domain of accessible knowledge.

Exclusive rights in innovative material can also have a significant impact on health, political expression, nutrition, safety, and the environment. Accordingly, access to knowledge can be conceptualized as an aspect of fundamental human rights.[39] Notably, even within the human rights context, the balance between public and proprietary rights is recognized. For example, the Universal Declaration of Human Rights protects the rights of authors to the fruits of their creativity,[40] but it also recognizes that "[e]veryone has the right freely to participate in the cultural life of the community, to enjoy the arts and to share in scientific advancement and its benefits."[41] Likewise, the human rights instruments require protection of property interests—and also expressive values, health, and education.[42]

A cursory look at any domestic intellectual property regime illustrates the many policy balances that have been struck. National intellectual property systems, including those with highly developed intellectual property laws, contain numerous public-regarding provisions. In the United States, for example, the Copyright Act includes a long list of exceptions.[43] These include detailed provisions that permit unauthorized uses of works for educational purposes,[44] as well as open-ended provisions, such as the fair use defense, which vindicate important expressive and competitive values.[45] Countries in the European Union include provisions permitting research on patentable materials.[46] Most nations define the inventive step in a manner that leaves considerable room for incremental follow-on invention.[47] Almost all trademark laws tolerate expressive, referential, and descriptive uses of protected marks.[48] And since intellectual property rights can monopolize both product and innovation markets, nations also regulate the level of protection from outside intellectual property law. In the European Union, for example, competition law provides an important check on a right holder's power to refuse to deal with follow-on innovators.[49]

B. Diversity

In light of the complex range of values that inform individual domestic intellectual property regimes, it is to be expected that countries with different economic and cultural conditions will adopt different approaches. In this climate, harmonization is thus not always desirable as a normative matter. For example, the WTO includes not only the developed countries (largely of the North) that are currently benefiting from the Knowledge Economy; there are also countries (mainly in the South) that are presently not innovative at world levels but which are nonetheless WTO members.

Many of the Southern countries did not have a comprehensive intellectual property system prior to entry into the WTO. Despite WTO membership, a low level of protection is still appropriate for their internal needs and will likely remain so for a considerable length of time. In some, the population is largely impoverished. By raising the cost of food, medicine, and books, strong intellectual property protection can substantially decrease access to nutrition, health, and education. And because these countries are not operating at the technological frontier, they are unlikely to see many offsetting benefits from enhanced intellectual property protection. Indeed, under a variety of economic models, it is clear that any agreement that creates efficient levels of intellectual property protection, when measured from the perspective of developed countries, will have significant distributive consequences for the South.[50] Even if strong protection were confined to the North, the South might suffer in that intellectual property rights can raise the cost of humanitarian efforts to create products—such as medicines and nutritious plants—that meet the needs of its citizens.[51]

Of course, some countries of the South had recognized various forms of intellectual property prior to TRIPS, but they looked upon the law primarily as a tool of industrial policy rather than as a system of individual property rights. Like the North, their laws were largely structured to reward creators as an incentive to invest and disclose. However, their legislation was also structured to promote technology transfer.[52] For example, to attract technological investment while providing local workers with jobs, training, and the opportunity to learn, these countries granted patents but viewed the failure to manufacture the patented product or to use a patented process locally as a form of abuse. They thus required, as a condition of maintaining exclusivity, that right holders "work" the patent locally (or, in some cases, justify the decision to import).[53] Of course, as countries move to the technological frontier and transition from being net importers of knowledge products to net exporters, their optimal level of protection will change. But at least until it does, a "one-size-fits-all" code that harmonizes the law at levels appropriate for the North is inimical to the interests of the South.

Indeed, a one-size-fits-all code can be inimical to the interests of the intellectual property system as a whole. One potential advantage of adding new countries to the international regime is that it increases the opportunity for a wide range of juridical experimentation. That is, intellectual property laws are a product of a country's theory of innovation, its analysis of the right balance between the interests of producers and users, as well as its political economy; differences in these factors will produce different rules. Thus, countries in the North are most likely to have strong protection. While there may be those in the North who question the expansive direction of intellectual property protection,[54] they are largely overshadowed in the political arena. The creative industries are well organized and well financed; debates over protection are usually resolved in their favor.[55] For example, in recent years and despite considerable opposition, most countries in the North have lengthened the term of copyright protection, expanded trademark rights, and enhanced patent protection for pharmaceuticals.[56] In contrast, in emerging countries, such as Brazil, Russia, India, China, and South Africa (the BRICS), the political dynamic is likely quite different. These countries have a growing creative sector, able to enjoy—and interested in enjoying—the benefits of strong protection. At the same time, however, a significant numbers of residents in these countries suffer from the same access problems experienced by less developed economies. As a result, the countries in the "emerging Middle" internalize the problems of both the North and the South. They are therefore forced to acquire the political will needed to seriously consider the views on all sides of the intellectual property debate. And since many of these countries also have a strong legal culture, they are capable of crafting novel laws that recalibrate the balance between access and proprietary interests and of finding new ways to accommodate clashing agendas.[57] A code approach to the TRIPS Agreement would hamper the ability of these countries to experiment and—perhaps—find better solutions to the problems that plague all intellectual property systems.[58]

C. Historical Contingency

Even developed countries, which have long experience with intellectual property, must continually revise and recalibrate the structure of their regimes. The Knowledge Economy has created new avenues for creativity, altered the business of finding, producing, selling, and consuming innovative products, and given rise to entirely new technologies. For example, when the TRIPS Agreement was negotiated in the early 1990s, use of the internet was not yet commonplace, and its impact was never considered. Similarly, the human genome had yet to be fully sequenced, and genomic medicine was more a matter of theory than of practice. But the creative ecosystem evolves. As it does, so too must every form of intellectual property right. Sometimes the change requires strengthening the level of protection, but there are also instances where recalibration may be needed in the opposite direction.

Consider the copyright domain. Cyberspace, scanning, and digitizing technologies have facilitated new forms of collaboration, such as chain art and fan fiction, and altered the ways in which information products are disseminated and enjoyed. The rules on protection must be adjusted to accommodate these developments and will sometimes require softening the exclusive power of right holders.[59] For example, while copyright owners acquired legal protection for self-help measures, such as encryption and watermarking,[60] European right holders who apply these measures to limit certain guaranteed rights of consumers and users risk losing the right to receive remuneration for private use of their works through statutory levies.[61] Similarly, at the same time that right holders sought to restrain widespread internet distribution by pursuing intermediaries, nations started to devise rules to safeguard the interests of these new business models against unlimited liability for online infringement.[62] And as countries extended the duration of copyright, they exacerbated the problem of orphan works (works whose copyright owner cannot be readily ascertained); some responded with provisions that permit the use of orphan works without the authorization of the copyright owner.[63]

Trademark law has also struggled with the effects of new distribution mechanisms. As with copyright, the law must consider the liability of internet intermediaries, such as online auction sites, for infringements committed by those listing products for sale.[64] More generally, e-commerce introduced new ways of finding and comparing consumer products. Initially, consumers relied on domain names that incorporated trademarks, leading states to augment the rights of trademark holders to accommodate the liberal nature of domain name registration.[65] In time, consumers came to use search engines rather than domain names, causing states to reframe the concept of trademark infringement to reflect the use of marks to generate targeted advertising.[66]

In the patent sector, the pressure on the legal system has been particularly acute. The business of doing science is changing radically. As universities enter the patent system, they push patenting upstream, to cover basic scientific research (such as the structure of genes and metabolic pathways). Because the capacity to exploit these broad prospects can be limited, states are finding it necessary to control the extent to which patent holders can dominate large swaths of technological opportunity and thereby chill progress.[67] Specialized firms, now more prevalent, use patents in new ways: as signals to venture capitalists, as organizational devices to manage shifting alliances and collaborative efforts, and as defenses to rivals' infringement actions.[68] With many more patents occupying technological space, patent offices are overwhelmed with applications and are searching for ways to examine the worldwide load more efficiently.[69] As important, there are many new possibilities for strategic and opportunistic behavior (and also many new opportunists, in the form of nonpracticing entities that make money from enforcing patents, rather than from inventing or manufacturing). The law must be modified to preclude the possibility that entire enterprises will be held ransom.[70] Furthermore, there are significant changes in the marketplace: consumer demand for interoperable and multifunctional products, industries that coordinate through standard-setting organizations, and products characterized by network effects and lock-in. Whereas patents once returned rewards that roughly matched inventors' technical contributions, these developments extend patentees' market power; unless the law is modified, single right holders may be able to adopt claiming practices and use standard setting, network effects, and lock-in to extract disproportionate rewards.[71]

New technologies present a diverse array of challenges to the patent system. In some fields, there is a wide gap between upstream research and commercialization, and patent law must be structured to encourage investment throughout the process.[72] In other fields, upstream research may be almost coextensive with the application of that research in commercial products. In those sectors, patents are less necessary to ensure market penetration.[73] By the same token, there are areas where rights are easily delineated, but in others, indistinct boundaries make patents hard to search, increasing the danger of inadvertent infringement.[74] As Dan Burk and Mark Lemley cogently argue, nations must manipulate the levers of patent law (such as the height of the inventive step, the scope of the claims, or the nature of exemptions) in order to tailor the law to the realities of new technological environments.[75] Importantly, these challenges also create new opportunities, for the need to modify the law simultaneously allows states to identify new ways to promote innovation or to reconfigure the relationship between the public and private domains.[76]

III. TRIPS as Reflecting a Neofederalist Agenda

While it may be good rhetoric for proponents of strong protection to argue that the TRIPS Agreement establishes a comprehensive intellectual property regime for all members of the WTO, the previous discussion suggests that it makes little sense from a normative, descriptive, or pragmatic perspective. Indeed, many TRIPS members are acting inconsistently with the view of TRIPS as a comprehensive code. The BRICS, for example, tend to see the TRIPS Agreement as providing them with a menu of flexibilities.[77] They are working within that understanding to enact what they view as TRIPS-consistent laws, but laws that are different from those of the main proponents of the Agreement. The South is actively pursuing a Development Agenda in WIPO, which, in part, would clarify the extent to which TRIPS creates room to maneuver.[78] For its part, the North is engaged in new discussions in a number of fora to further raise the level of protection. While not inconsistent with the thrust of TRIPS, these initiatives emphasize that TRIPS is not a code; it is far from a definitive encapsulation of global intellectual property norms.

These observations suggest that it is more appropriate to look at the Agreement through a neofederalist lens, to recognize that it comprises many of the elements of a federal system. The decision to couple the national treatment approach of the WIPO treaties with detailed substantive standards and new institutional arrangements gives states autonomy to address the complexity, diversity, and historical contingency of intellectual property law, but it requires them to act within the overlay of a coordinated international intellectual property regime. Admittedly, TRIPS differs from a true federal system in that it lacks express guidance on how to vertically allocate prescriptive authority within this system. It is thus necessary to tease from the Agreement principles for deciding where states have ceded lawmaking authority and where they have reserved power to themselves.

To complicate matters, the international intellectual property system is broader than TRIPS alone. The WTO, while nominally focused on trade, is increasingly influenced by values other than those that traditionally inform trade policy, such as environmental concerns, labor standards, and hygiene. Moreover, in its capacity as administrator of an intellectual property instrument, the WTO inevitably engages with a panoply of other institutions, including the World Health Organization (WHO) on the impact of intellectual property on access to medicine, with the Convention on Biodiversity (CBD) on rights over genetic resources, the Food and Agriculture Organization (FAO) on agriculture, the United Nations Educational, Scientific and Cultural Organization (UNESCO) on education, and with human rights law. Thus, the principles that are developed must do more than allocate vertical authority between the national and the international; there is also a need for rules that address relations horizontally among international institutions. Moreover, there is a need to identify overarching substantive and procedural norms common to all intellectual property regimes. These norms—our international intellectual property acquis—would stabilize the framework within which each of these institutions engages in intellectual property lawmaking and enhance the predictability that is essential to motivating investments in innovation and to promoting the enjoyment of the fruits of creativity.

None of this is to deny that there would be advantages to a global intellectual property code. The neofederalist regime we envision would allow countries to engage in a degree of free riding on other nations' investment in innovation and would thus supply suboptimal global incentives. And it is clearly expensive. Registered rights must be acquired—and examined—on a country-by-country basis, producing redundant costs for both governments and innovators. The expense associated with enforcing intellectual property rights can also be extremely high as there will usually be no one court with adjudicatory authority to resolve a global complaint. Courts will often be required to decide complex choice of law questions, and multiple national adjudications can produce uncertainty, delay, cycling, contradictory decisions, and excessive awards.

While some of these problems would be solved by viewing TRIPS as a supranational code, they would not all be eliminated. The level of worldwide innovation is only partially determined by intellectual property laws; it is also dependent on (among other things) competition law, banking and securities regulations, and tax policy—none of which is fully encompassed by the WTO. Furthermore, the WTO does not, in fact, fully contain externalities. One of the chief ways in which countries with lower protection undermine the policies of those with higher protection is through the export of infringing works. Yet the Agreement and in particular its border measures focus almost exclusively on importation issues and activities within the members' territories.[79]

As important, harmonizing national laws does not eradicate the cost of acquiring and enforcing rights on a territorial basis. Other efforts are also required. Significantly, these could be constructed in a manner that does not require complete harmonization. For example, "bottom-up" efforts are under way by national offices to streamline procedures, adopt congruent approaches to examination, and share workloads.[80] As these initiatives begin to bear fruit, the cost of serial registration will decline. Work is also ongoing to improve the efficiency with which private disputes of a global dimension can be resolved.[81] An appreciation of the advantages of neofederalism—or a better grasp of the limits of TRIPS—would accelerate these endeavors.

The argument that TRIPS is not a code can also be made in a different way. As further elaborated in Chapters 3 through 5, the GATT contains several provisions that permit countries to vary their commitments in response to new challenges and internal demands.[82] Examples include Articles XIX, XX, and XXVIII. TRIPS contains fewer express cushioning devices. And yet it is inevitable that the Knowledge Economy will produce dislocations to which member states will need to respond (indeed, the GATT provisions are partly aimed at protecting the ability of member states to absorb technological changes of the type promoted by intellectual property law). If TRIPS were a code, then the absence of equivalent safeguards would be extraordinary. But their omission is understandable when TRIPS is viewed through a neofederalist lens, as leaving substantial room for states to craft laws in their national interests.

Illustration

The controversy over gene patents exemplifies the stakes involved in looking at TRIPS as a code and, conversely, at the advantage of seeing it from a neofederalist perspective. Genetic information is increasingly becoming subject to patent rights. For example, there are now product patents on isolated genetic sequences (such as patents on BRCA 1 and 2 mutations, which are associated with early-onset breast cancer),[83] as well as process patents on associating a genetic sequence with the propensity to contract a particular disease (such as the association between a mutation and vulnerability to curvature of the spine).[84] Gene patenting began long before negotiations on the TRIPS Agreement were initiated.[85] However, as with the internet, the negotiators did not take the consequences of this development into account when drafting the Agreement. Subsequently, however, it has become clear that patent rights over the fundamental building blocks of life are problematic for patients, doctors, and society as a whole.

At least three comprehensive studies of gene patenting have been conducted, one in 2002 by the British Nuffield Council, another in 2010 by the Secretary's Advisory Committee on Genetics, Health, and Society (SACGHS), which was established by the U.S. Department of Health and Human Services, and most recently, by the Australian Parliament.[86] These suggest that patents can severely restrict access to genetic testing and allow single right holders to dominate significant innovation markets. Exclusive right holders have cleared markets for diagnostic tests, forcing patients to deal with sole service providers, who may be unwilling to accept payment from particular insurers or who will charge exorbitant prices for tests. With only one test facility in the market, doctors cannot acquire second opinions or compare laboratory results in order to conduct proficiency testing. Right holders can also obstruct further research: they stop other scientists from developing more efficient tests, investigating other genetic causes for similar diseases, and identifying pharmaceuticals uniquely suited to particular genetic susceptibilities. Right holders have also been known to refuse to contribute new mutations to public databases, where they can be studied by others.[87] The medical and scientific communities are particularly concerned about what these practices mean for the future. Gene patents are already impeding the development of plants that could help feed starving populations;[88] if a pandemic virus were patented, that patent could be used to prevent scientists from searching for a vaccine or a cure.[89] And because approximately 20 percent of the human genome is patented,[90] thickets of rights could interfere with the development of personalized medicine (that is, treatment tailored to the genetic endowment of each individual patient).[91]

If patents were necessary to support research and commercialization, these costs would be tolerable. However, that is not true for all applications of genetic technologies. In a natural experiment on the impact of patents associated with diagnostics, Robert Cook-Deegan and his coauthors could not find cases in which a patent holder was first to market a genetic test.[92] Patents are not necessary in this arena because it is not expensive to convert an upstream insight into a genetic test. Instead, the work is easily supported by a combination of government funding, clinical fees, and donations by patient advocacy groups.[93] Patents on genes and associated diagnostics therefore represent a situation where the reward available through the exclusive right may be disproportionate to the investment made in innovation.

Nations have adopted a range of strategies to deal with the access problems posed by gene patents. In the United States, there has been some judicial sentiment for invalidating these patents on the ground that they are found in nature, express natural principles, or are overbroad.[94] SACGHS recommended new defenses to infringement liability to protect researchers and diagnosticians and recent patent reform legislation requires the director of the Patent and Trademark Office to conduct a study on ways to ensure the quality and availability of genetic tests.[95] Germany limited the scope of gene patents to their disclosed utility.[96] In *Monsanto v. Cefetra*,[97] the Court of Justice of the European

Union (still better known by its former title, the European Court of Justice, or ECJ) took a somewhat different approach, holding that these patents are infringed only when the gene is functioning in the accused product.

Each of these approaches has benefits—they would all substantially reduce a gene patent's obstructive potential. But they also have weaknesses. Precluding gene patents entirely may impair incentives to invest in the very expensive research necessary to develop gene therapies. Recognizing new defenses to infringement could endanger work on diagnostic tests of greater technical complexity than the ones that Cook-Deegan studied. These defenses might also be problematic if diagnostics were to become subject to the same administrative clearance procedures that make it expensive to bring new pharmaceuticals to market. While limiting scope would reduce the breadth of any one patent, it might encourage more patenting, increase the density of the patent thicket, and further raise transaction costs. Because samples are usually dead when they are used for diagnostic purposes, the ECJ's approach might be helpful with regard to patient access to testing, but not with other uses, such as research. Until each approach plays out in practice, its potential cannot be fully assessed.

The code perspective on TRIPS may, however, make it harder to experiment with these approaches. For example, Kamal Saggi and Joel Trachtman see the instances where the Agreement articulates standards rather than rules not as invitations to states to experiment, but instead as an invitation to the DSB to supply the missing components of an incomplete contract.[98] Presumably, that would require the DSB to insist upon protection for new technologies that mirror the protection available to technologies that existed during the Uruguay Round. And as the Waldeck quotation suggests, any statute that singles out the field of genetics could run afoul of the provision in Article 27, which bars discrimination "as to . . . the field of technology." In the *Monsanto* case, the ECJ relied on Article 30, which permits "limited" exceptions, to suggest its ruling was consistent with TRIPS.[99] However, DSB panels have (as Saggi and Trachtman appear to recommend) interpreted Article 30 narrowly and have refused to tolerate exceptions that affect significant rights.[100] Yet the various approaches states have taken to gene patents are effective precisely because they dramatically narrow the patent right.

Invalidating the patent could avoid the Article 30 problem by relying instead on the notion that genes and associations are not "inventions" within the meaning of Article 27.1 of TRIPS.[101] Gene patents were not, however, unknown at the time TRIPS was negotiated. Accordingly, the code view might see the term "invention" as unamenable to that interpretation. Finally, were the DSB to adhere to its narrow reading of Article 30 but accept the idea that genes fall outside Article 27's concept of invention, states would confront an unattractive all-or-nothing choice—they would be forced to either accept gene patents with all their problems, or forgo protection, eliminate incentives to invest in that field, and endure a competitive disadvantage in an emerging and important technology.

A neofederalist would analyze the application of TRIPS quite differently. Gene patenting presents a situation where there is no obviously correct approach for dealing with the negative side of exclusivity. A view that starts from a position of state primacy would strive to read the Exceptions provision to enhance state prerogatives. Furthermore, it would give states greater leeway in interpreting terms in the Agreement that the drafters failed to define. The concept of discrimination might also be handled differently: rules designed to treat a general problem—in this case the special dangers of patenting in areas where there is no gap between upstream discoveries and downstream applications—would not be regarded as discriminating against any particular "field," even if the problem arose only in specific areas. The result would free every state to serve as a laboratory and try novel experiments to deal with gene patents, without imposing significant risks on the rest of the WTO.[102]

This example illustrates, first, that there is an irony in thinking of TRIPS as both a product of the Knowledge Economy and a rigid code. The dynamic of the Third Industrial Revolution creates new problems, requiring fresh approaches. Second, the neofederalist view makes experimentation an active component of national lawmaking. Allied with the standing institutional structure TRIPS put into place, experimentation at the national level ultimately fuels the development of international solutions to common problems.

Organization of the Book

Our neofederalist approach to TRIPS is informed by its history, its text, its implementation, and the subsequent development of the international intellectual property system. Part I (Chapters 1 and 2) investigates the historical context in which TRIPS arose and was concluded. Just as this Chapter challenged the conception of TRIPS as a supranational code on the ground that it fails to comprehend the nature of innovation and its relationship to intellectual property law, Chapter 2 challenges the conventional account of TRIPS's development as insufficiently reflective of the complexities of the Agreement's negotiation history and the compromises captured in its text.

The next Part (Chapters 3 through 5) focuses on how TRIPS operates in practice and tests the competing narratives of TRIPS as a static code or as a component of an evolving regime. Chapter 3 addresses the interpretation of the Agreement by the DSB and extrapolates from its decisions how TRIPS adjudicators would likely analyze a number of pending national initiatives. We demonstrate that in some respects, the DSB has vindicated our neofederalist view of the

Agreement, but that its reasoning can more often impede the enactment of socially desirable intellectual property laws. These deficiencies flow, in part, from a formalist reading of the text of the Agreement without regard to its overall structure. Chapter 4 shows how an understanding of this structural dimension informs questions on the allocation of vertical authority among the institutions of a neofederalist system. Chapter 5 turns to the question of domestic lawmaking, examining how TRIPS affects the crucial role of national lawmaking in the international intellectual property system.

The first two Parts suggest that nations have considerably more autonomy than contemplated by the conventional wisdom, for one way to facilitate the process of meeting the challenges of the Knowledge Economy is by better recognizing the role of the WTO member states in lawmaking. In the concluding section of the book, Part III (Chapters 6 and 7), we look to the future. We offer proposals that would enhance that capacity and remedy the weaknesses that exist in the present system. Chapter 6 addresses these questions at the institutional level, where a variety of actors are generating a wide range of norms. We explore how this increasingly fragmented system of international intellectual property law can be integrated through our interpretive approach to TRIPS. Chapter 7 shifts to substantive matters. On the theory that a truly neofederalist vision requires both procedural and substantive coordination, it looks at intellectual property lawmaking from a broader perspective and begins the process of identifying a set of normative commitments that transcend any one instrument and any single regime. These norms constitute an international intellectual property acquis, a set of framing principles that can be drawn upon to interpret current instruments (both inside and outside TRIPS), facilitate future intellectual property lawmaking, protect national autonomy, and reorient the system to put the interests of consumers, competitors, and follow-on innovators on a par with those of authors, traders, and original inventors.

2

The History and Character of TRIPS

How It Shapes the Contemporary Debate

> My authorities have instructed me to request consultations with the Government of Brazil pursuant to [the] TRIPS Agreement... concerning those provisions of Brazil's 1996 industrial property law... which establish a "local working" requirement for the enjoyability of exclusive patent rights that can only be satisfied by the local production—and not the importation—of the patented subject matter.
>
> —Request for Consultations by the United States, Brazil—Measures Affecting Patent Protection, World Trade Organization, WT/DS199/1, G/L/385, IP/D/23 (June 8, 2000)

The TRIPS Agreement was a momentous development in international intellectual property law. It extended the geographical reach of protection by imposing intellectual property obligations on all members of the WTO—including many developing countries that formerly recognized no such rights. It raised the standards of protection for even the most developed nations, such as the United States. For the first time in an international intellectual property instrument, TRIPS imposed obligations regarding enforcement. It put teeth into the international regime by making national compliance the subject of dispute resolution through the Dispute Settlement Body (DSB). And it created a new institution, the Council for TRIPS, to monitor the Agreement, study residual issues, and consider new developments.

As befits an event of such significance, there are competing narratives regarding its creation. The negotiations leading to its birth were multinational, highly complex, and at times less than transparent. Accordingly, a single authoritative account is impossible: each participant has his or her own view of exactly what occurred. Historical narratives also reflect the experience and perspective of the narrator. Thus, there is a legal and diplomatic story to be told, and each version may have both a trade and an intellectual property perspective. Finally, histories may be tinged by the purpose for which they are related. As noted in Chapter 1, the apparent breadth of the Agreement has led some to regard it as a rigid—and at the baseline end, a static—international code. Those who favor that view describe WTO members as having engaged in an exchange, bargaining market access for setting in motion a mechanism through which intellectual property standards can become stronger, but will never soften. Those who are skeptical about imposing a one-size-fits-all regime, harmonized at the levels of protection prevailing in the developed world, describe a process characterized by unequal leverage and bargaining power among negotiators, and featuring the disproportionate political clout of producers of information products relative to consumers.[1]

Looking at the negotiation process and the final instrument through the frame of international and intellectual property policy, with the benefit of hindsight, and from the perspective of more than a decade of experience with the Agreement, we see the history differently. We contend that TRIPS was the result of a real debate and the product of genuine compromise. In some instances, the Agreement as it was concluded found substantive formulations to which all the parties eventually agreed. Where, however, negotiators could not identify an optimum rule, or where they found that the diversity of the membership made harmonization impossible, they adopted a different strategy. They left the states with varying degrees of latitude to develop their own rules. In some cases, they gave the states complete freedom to operate; in others, international obligations are triggered only when specific conditions occur; in one situation, an obligation is imposed, but it is not subject to dispute resolution.[2] For all cases, the negotiators also established an institution to assess state practices on an ongoing basis. In other words, our analysis of history confirms our neofederalist vision of the Agreement as open to competing national policies, including nonmarket considerations, and as flexible enough to respond to competing international norms and to cope with the challenges of the future.

In this Chapter, we situate the TRIPS Agreement in the historical context of the international intellectual property system, most notably the development of the Paris and Berne Conventions. There are many excellent detailed accounts of the evolution of these instruments and analyses of their provisions.[3] We focus our discussion on those aspects of the history that explain the structure of TRIPS; its vertical allocation of lawmaking authority; and the approach it takes to the issues of complexity, diversity, and historical contingency discussed in Chapter 1.

I. The Debate in Intellectual Property Circles

The desire to establish an international system for the protection of intellectual property is hardly new. Differences in national protective regimes had long distorted trade in knowledge goods. Through the nineteenth century, webs of bilateral treaties were established among groups of countries. Many of these instruments conferred protection on a "material reciprocity" basis: protection was offered by country A to citizens of country B contingent on country B offering similar protection to the citizens of A. Under that system, the levels of protection varied from treaty to treaty, leading to an international regime that was, at best, haphazard.[4]

As the international market in books expanded, countries with vibrant publishing industries sought to construct a multilateral mechanism for the protection of their citizens' works abroad.[5] In 1886, these efforts culminated in the conclusion of the Berne Convention.[6] Likewise, the Paris Convention[7] finds its roots in the expansion of trade in industrial property and the reluctance of foreign inventors to exhibit their inventions at international expositions absent adequate patent, trademark, and design protection.[8]

The straightforward way to eradicate the distortions caused by divergent national schemes of protection would be to adopt a universal intellectual property law. And in the debates leading up to the establishment of the Paris and Berne Unions, many delegates argued for the adoption of universal patent and copyright codes. Thus, a stated aim of the Congress for Patent Reform that met in Vienna in 1873, and which ultimately led to the Paris Convention, was "to achieve uniform patent legislation in all the countries."[9] Even as late as 1878, delegates considered laying down "principles of uniform legislation on industrial property, which by a multipartite convention would constitute a law, to the parties to it."[10] Or as a Swiss delegate suggested, the congress should be "the prelude to a universal understanding and the formulation of the basis of the peace and welfare of the world."[11] Similarly, at the time of the intergovernmental meeting in 1883 on the proposed Berne Convention, attempts were made, particularly by the German delegation, to institute an internationally uniform system of copyright—"a codification . . . regulating in a uniform manner for the whole projected Union, . . . the totality of dispositions relating to the protection of copyright"—that would apply in each member state.[12]

Significantly, however, neither Convention was concluded on this basis. Although there was considerable sentiment in favor of universality, the delegates could not agree on whose law should be universalized. Each country considered its own law optimal and refused to consider changing it wholesale.[13] For example, at the 1878 industrial property congress in Paris, the French members, "more numerous than those of other nations, wished that the uniform universal rules be taken from the French law, while foreign delegates stood by their own laws."[14] Especially on the copyright side, the delegates also confronted the rather substantial differences between common law and civil law approaches to protection.[15]

Through the apparently frustrating debates over the merits of each of the disparate national regimes, the negotiators of both Conventions began to recognize the value of what the French termed "elasticity."[16] Both instruments abandoned efforts at universality and endorsed the principles of territoriality and national treatment.[17] Territoriality holds that each member state enjoys sovereign authority to determine the conditions under which intellectual property will exist within its borders. National treatment obliges a signatory state to offer protection to nationals of other signatory states that (at least) equals the protection it affords its own nationals. The treaties, in short, chose member state autonomy as the overarching governing principle.

In addition, both the Paris Convention and the Berne Convention imposed obligations on signatory states to provide in their domestic law certain minimum levels of intellectual property protection, so-called substantive minima. For example, the Berne Convention listed the types of works that a signatory state must protect and the minimum term of copyright protection. States could offer greater protection; they were obliged only to satisfy these minimum levels. Initially, the Paris Convention in fact contained very few substantive provisions, the more significant provisions (other than national treatment) in that first version of the treaty being the priority rules designed to facilitate acquisition of multinational rights through serial registration.[18]

This basic structure—national treatment plus substantive minima—persisted throughout the twentieth century. The substantive minima obligations of the Paris and Berne Conventions were periodically revised upward to require greater and different protection. This was more so in the case of copyright, where changing technologies drove new forms of exploitation and ensured constant revision of the text. The substantive minima in the Paris Convention evolved more slowly and less extensively. In 1900, member countries agreed to provide effective protection against unfair competition,[19] and in 1925, to provide protection for well-known marks without their having been registered.[20] The substantive provisions dealing with patents were even more minimal. In that context, the principal debates revolved (as they had done since the inception of the Convention) around what penalties, if any, could be imposed for failure to "work"—for "abusing" the patent by extracting profits from the local market, but not exploiting the invention in a manner that would also bring jobs to (and enrich) the local economy.[21]

Even by 1989, the substantive standards in the Paris Convention regarding patents, trademarks, and designs remained undeveloped compared with copyright. However, regardless of the extent of any changes made over the years, the conceptual approach of national treatment and territoriality endured as the foundation of both treaties. Countries raised the levels of protection in Paris and Berne without altering the basic character of the international intellectual property system. National autonomy—sovereignty—is, of course, a cornerstone of international law generally.[22] But it is an operating principle that has been specifically accepted and acted on for more than a century in the field of intellectual property law.

Some essential characteristics of this system are worth noting. In particular, for a number of reasons, the obligations imposed by Paris and Berne barely intruded upon the national sovereignty of signatory nations. As noted earlier, the substantive minima (even in the case of copyright) were initially quite undemanding, requiring levels of protection that were hardly exacting. The less demanding the obligations, it was thought, the more countries were likely to be drawn to the "clubs"—to become members of the Unions and enforce basic notions of intellectual property protection.[23] The Unions would thus over time be enlarged; as noted by the chairman of the 1880 congress of what became the Paris Union, Senator Bozérian of France, the Convention was "the preface of a book which is to be opened, and is not to be closed, perhaps, until after long years."[24] Moreover, the substantive minima were in most cases meant to reflect a consensus position, as codifications of commonly held national policies.[25] Thus, the Unions expected that the international regime would be informed by the experience of the member states and the solutions they found to common problems.

Even when countries of a Union recognized that there would be benefits to committing to an international principle, they would permit nations to maintain differing forms of implementation. In such cases, the principle would often be stated at a level of generality that permitted these divergent approaches to flourish (perhaps with some cognitive dissonance), with an eye to longer-term convergence as international norms evolved. For example, the obligation in the Paris Convention to provide effective protection against unfair competition allowed common law countries to restrict such claims to passing off, while civil law countries typically interpreted that provision to restrain so-called parasitic behavior (or free riding).[26] Similarly, the Berne Convention requires protection of moral rights (including the rights to claim authorship and to object to mutilation of the work), but when the United States acceded in 1989, it complied through a mélange of actions including breach of contract, defamation and trademark infringement.[27]

Indeed, even some central concepts were left open for signatory states to develop in accordance with their own national policies and values. For example, countries remained free to define the "author" of a work, and thus the initial owner of the copyright, in a fashion consistent with the philosophical grounding of their system of protection, either in individual personality or in instrumentalist financial incentives.[28] Thus, U.S. law reflects its predominantly instrumentalist orientation by recognizing employers as authors of works prepared by employees within the scope of their employment,[29] whereas the "droit d'auteur" approach of French law links ownership to the personality of the individual author and thus treats the employee as the author, even when the work is created as part of an employment relationship.[30]

Likewise, the Berne Convention—both its text and the acquis carried with it—afforded countries generous scope to create exceptions to copyright that reflected national attitudes to free speech or furthered other countervailing social policies.[31] For example, U.S. copyright law accords users broad latitude under the rubric of fair use to make unauthorized parodies of copyrighted works[32] and provides a series of specific exceptions that permit, for example, the unauthorized public performance of a musical work at a horticultural fair[33] or in face-to-face classroom instruction.[34] Civil law countries tend to favor only the latter approach (closed systems), each providing different lists of narrow exceptions tailored to its own social and economic priorities. And many countries fall somewhere between the U.S. and civilian paradigms. Although these different approaches inevitably privilege many similar acts—such as core educational or research uses, or uses implicating free speech concerns—many also reflect the exigencies of national cultural policy (or political demands and the structure of the legal system).[35]

This flexibility was ensured not only by the consensual development of Paris and Berne, but also by exclusive reliance on the quasi-legislative process of treaty revision as a means of updating the Conventions. Thus, the Paris and Berne Conventions both had established administrative arms. These were responsible for facilitating ongoing treaty revisions, but they had no independent lawmaking authority. The secretariats of the two Unions merged in 1893 into the Bureaux for the Protection of Intellectual Property (BIRPI), and in 1967 the World Intellectual Property Organization (WIPO) was established to assume its functions.[36] However, WIPO, in theory, remained a member state–driven organization; although its various committees issued reports that opine on the meaning of the Conventions, these interpretations are not binding on member states.[37] Furthermore, although later versions of the Conventions permitted the referral of disputes regarding compliance to the International Court of Justice,[38] this mechanism was never used.[39] Authoritative interpretation of the Conventions and their application to new issues thus never occurred outside the slow-moving process of multiparty treaty revision.

Initially, the principal members of the Paris and Berne Unions were the relatively homogeneous industrialized nations of Europe. The differences that existed among these countries reflected philosophical disagreements rather than vast social or economic disparities. But in time, as the initial drafters contemplated, the Unions grew to include a more diverse set of countries. In fact, developing countries were engaged with the international system far earlier than current debates about TRIPS might suggest.[40] A handful of developing countries were initial signatories to the Paris Convention, and a few others attended the initial conferences.

To be sure, for the most part, the Conventions applied to developing countries as a result of their colonial status,[41] and there was little leeway for them to adapt European norms to local modalities. Moreover, to the extent there was local debate about the demands of intellectual property law, that debate was hardly autonomous. Still, even under the yoke of colonial rule, there was substantial discussion of how complying with international intellectual property obligations meshed with local objectives.[42] For example, debates in India in the early twentieth century about how to implement the translation right mandated by the Berne Convention reveal an extremely inclusive and complex policy discussion in both Britain and India. Thus, there was a vibrant local debate about the political benefits (and dangers) of promoting the accessibility of European knowledge in India, and how different versions of the translation right affected those Indian interests.[43]

Later, as many of these countries gained their independence, they found themselves members of the international intellectual property Conventions and elected to remain so.[44] They engaged more fully with the international system, in part by initiating discussion of intellectual property in international fora other than WIPO, which developing countries saw as captured by right holders from the North.[45] Thus, in 1961, Brazil initiated a debate in the United Nations General Assembly on the relationship between patents and the economic development of developing countries, prompting a report by the United Nations Department of Economic and Social Affairs three years later.[46]

That report—*The Role of Patents and the Transfer of Technology to Developing Countries*—did not, as Brazil had hoped, suggest reform of the international regime embodied in the Paris Convention. Instead, the report emphasized that the needs of developing countries would best be served by focusing on capacity building at the national level. Perhaps more important, dissatisfaction among developing countries at the outcome of the report stimulated broader actions on a number of fronts. Thus, the early 1970s saw the staging of regional conferences in Latin America critically addressing the role of patent protection in developing countries, the inclusion of international patent reform in soft law declarations that framed the working agenda of the United Nations (UN), and the preparation of a further report on the Paris Convention by the United Nations Conference on Trade and Development (UNCTAD).[47]

These various initiatives over a period of time induced action within WIPO. In order to pre-empt intellectual property issues being taken up by other bodies in the United Nations, then director-general of WIPO, Arpad Bogsch, sought to establish WIPO as a specialized agency of the UN. WIPO, "born into the controversy of how intellectual property would impact the developing world," had to soften its right holder rhetoric to achieve this goal.[48] Thus, discussion of international patent reform gained traction in WIPO. In the Paris Union, prompted by national reforms in developing countries with patent systems to strengthen the working requirement, prevent other abuses of patent rights, and promote the transfer of technology, developing countries sought to revisit some of the limits on national autonomy that had been imposed by successive revisions of the Convention.[49] The focus, as before, was the working requirement.[50] But the ambition of the UNCTAD report that had provided impetus to the debate was far broader.[51]

The WIPO Secretariat initially proposed a new international instrument rather than attempt further revision of Paris. Eventually, however, the machinery for revising the existing Convention was put in place at WIPO.[52] While these efforts were ultimately fruitless, the process helped frame debates that were to take place more broadly for the last part of the twentieth century. The revision was initiated with meetings of the Ad-Hoc Group of Governmental Experts convened by the director-general of WIPO. In 1977, this group produced a Declaration of Objectives that still represents one of the most detailed statements of the role of patent protection in developing countries. Emphasizing "social justice" and the reduction of "economic inequalities between nations," the Declaration articulated nine objectives that should be taken into account in reorienting industrial property law and suggested that the Paris Convention "should be framed in light of [these] objectives, leaving maximum degree of liberty to each country to adopt appropriate measures on the legislative and administrative levels consistent with its needs and social, economic and development policy."[53]

When a Basic Proposal emerged from the working groups in 1981, it was what Pedro Roffe and Gine Vea described as "the most radical attempt to revise the [Paris] Convention in its entire history."[54] It tackled comprehensively measures that could be taken to check abuses of patents, including the failure to work a patent locally. And it contained (in paragraph 8) special provisions for developing countries as regards both local working and compulsory licenses. Some countries—such as Spain and Canada—suggested that the special provisions for the developing countries be of general application.[55] But for most of the industrialized world, these proposals were too radical. As Jerry Reichman and Catherine Hasenzahl put it: "The developing countries were as intent on lowering the international minimum standards of patent protection as the developed countries were resolved to elevate the same standards."[56] The result was a stalemate, with little hope for revision.[57]

With the conclusion of the Stockholm Protocol to the Berne Convention in 1967, the developing countries managed (for some time) to reverse the tide in the copyright context. The Stockholm Protocol sought to give developing countries room to moderate the full force of international copyright obligations. In particular, it allowed developing countries to adopt compulsory licenses to reproduction, translation, and performance rights.[58] The Stockholm Protocol never became effective because the developed world balked at ratification, but it did produce a related document which *was* ratified, namely, the Appendix to the Paris Act of the Berne Convention in 1971.[59] The mechanisms established by that Appendix were, however, substantially fettered. As a result, only a limited number of developing counties have invoked the Appendix to create compulsory licenses.[60]

Together, these initiatives represented one part of a pushback by developing countries. While somewhat more symbolic than immediately effective, these proposals helped frame the debate—as well as create an impasse at the multilateral level in general, and at WIPO in particular. But the demand for intellectual property laws of a more global reach did not abate. Unable to make headway in multilateral fora, the developed world resorted to the broader apparatus of trade relations. Annual reviews by the United States Trade Representative under the Special 301 provisions of the Trade Act identified countries that were failing to offer intellectual property protection that the United States regarded as sufficient to prevent trade distortions.[61] Because countries that did not heed this "warning" could eventually be sanctioned, Special 301—along with its more recent equivalent in the European Union, the Trade Barriers Regulation[62]—put significant pressure on developing countries to abandon their objections to raising the standards of protection. Reconceptualizing the intellectual property problem as a trade issue had another effect: it allowed developed countries to move multilateral discussions to a new forum—negotiations over the General Agreement on Tariffs and Trade (the GATT).

II. The TRIPS Debate

At the same time that dissatisfaction with WIPO was growing in intellectual property circles, many in the trade community were interested in revising the GATT regime. Over time, the coverage of that Agreement had become inadequate. It failed to deal comprehensively with many subjects that had become the objects of international commerce, including financial services, agriculture, textiles, and other commodities.[63] Furthermore, because the original agreement expressly treated protection for information products as a matter of national policy,[64] it did little to stop trade in counterfeit and pirated merchandise.[65] Finally, although the GATT was one of the few international agreements that included a compliance mechanism, that regime was becoming ineffective. The imposition of trade sanctions was predicated on a consensus among members. Thus, the loser in any dispute resolution could evade enforcement by simply withholding its approval of the adjudicators' report.[66]

The creative industries were able to seize the moment to induce what Larry Helfer terms a "regime shift" and move negotiations over international intellectual property standards from WIPO, where discussions were stalled, to the GATT framework.[67] A hint of that shift had surfaced earlier. Not only was the United States using its trade policy mechanisms unilaterally through the Special 301 process; in the late 1970s, toward the end of the Tokyo Round of GATT negotiations, an attempt was made to amend GATT to deal with trademark counterfeiting and copyright piracy. Although the issue arose too late to be considered at that time, subsequent activities paved the way for the inclusion of intellectual property in the next round, the Uruguay Round.[68] Thus, the United States coordinated actions with the European Union and Japan and in 1988, the three countries proposed a basic framework for discussion.[69] Further, the United States stepped up its own pressure.[70] Special 301 Reports were supplemented by threats to withhold duty-free treatment of products under its Generalized System of Preferences program from those developing states that the United States considered obstructionist.[71] And it entered into a series of bilateral treaty negotiations that linked the recognition of intellectual property rights to trade concessions. By the time the Uruguay Round was launched, the idea that intellectual property protection was "trade related" had firmly taken hold.[72] Forging an agreement was not, however, without intense controversy, as key divisions existed between the developed and developing world (North-South debates) and among developed countries (North-North debates).

A. The North-South Debate

The North-South debate was particularly sharp. Developed countries were facing significant challenges as production shifted to countries with lower labor costs. At the same time, however, global wealth was increasing and tastes were changing. Profits from creative output were becoming a potential source of foreign exchange, crucial to correcting trade imbalances in other sectors of the economy. Thus, while the rhetoric during the run-up to the Uruguay Round focused on the distortions of trade caused by counterfeit and pirated goods—that is, works identical to copyrighted products or using exact reproductions of protected trademarks in connection with the same type of goods—the real interests of the North were much broader.[73] If these countries were to more fully open their borders to Southern agricultural products and commodities such as textiles, they wanted to extend the international recognition of exclusive rights well beyond counterfeiting and piracy, to such matters as derivative uses of copyrighted works, to use of nonidentical marks on nonidentical goods, and to the effective protection of technological advances, geographical indications, industrial and layout designs, and undisclosed information. It was no longer acceptable to the North for countries of the South to refuse to recognize intellectual property rights and take a free ride on investments in creativity—to use knowledge products without contributing to right holders' development costs through the payment of royalties. Not only did the loss of Southern markets make worldwide incentives suboptimal, there was a concern that as global trade increased, unauthorized products from the South would flow back and depress prices in the North.[74]

As in the debate in WIPO, countries that were net importers of information products had multiple concerns about raising the level of protection. The inclusion of intellectual property within a trade regime inevitably implicated economic considerations. On that metric, countries in the South were concerned that they would be unable to innovate at world levels and would therefore not benefit in global markets from higher levels of protection. These countries thus saw the royalties imposed by intellectual property protection purely as a tax, raising the cost of information products to local citizens, and as a transfer of wealth to the developed world.[75] In the pharmaceutical sphere, the impact was especially worrisome: without a source of generic versions of patented medicines, local citizens would be excluded from access to modern therapies. Similarly, recognizing protection for agricultural products would increase the cost of adequate nutrition.[76]

Other concerns focused on the role that foreign capital would play in a globalized creative environment. Intellectual property rights are, in a sense, a voting mechanism. They use the market to create incentives to invest in the types of creative production that the voters—buyers—desire. But the only voters are those with money. Weaker economies therefore worried that even less attention might be paid to their needs, including drugs to treat uniquely local diseases, or to the manufacture of goods available at price points that indigenous populations could afford. Given the higher profits available elsewhere, even local production facilities might be channeled to the satisfaction of the demands of nonlocal populations.[77] Alternatively, if the cost of manufacturing creative works locally increased, there was a danger that more information products would be imported and local capacity would languish.

As important, developing countries worried that embedding negotiations in the GATT would obscure other dimensions of intellectual property policy making. Traditionally, normative inquiries into national policy are regarded as beyond the remit of a trade system.[78] As a result, the shift to GATT could foreclose consideration of philosophical objections to the commodification of knowledge. Stated less tendentiously, the trade focus could lead negotiators to ignore the noneconomic values that have traditionally informed intellectual property policy and to give short shrift to considerations of distributive justice.[79] If that occurred, commitments to such goals as ending hunger and poverty or providing equality of opportunity would take second stage. Development within the South might be frozen as the cost of educational materials increased, the opportunity to learn through imitation diminished, and the pool of skilled labor was channeled to the administration of the new intellectual property regime. In fact, domestic creative capacity within developing countries could even decline, leaving at least some of these states at a comparative *dis*advantage.

Despite these concerns, and over the objections of countries such as Brazil, Argentina, and India—which protested the shift from WIPO, where many of these arguments had been acknowledged, to GATT[80]—the Declaration of Punta del Este opening the Uruguay Round articulated the notion that creating minimum standards would reduce distortions to trade and ensure that enforcement measures would not become obstacles to trade.[81] Although the Declaration stressed that negotiations would be limited to those aspects of intellectual property protection associated with trade and would be without prejudice to developments in WIPO, the discussions quickly evolved into negotiations about all aspects of intellectual property protection. The North, in other words, won on the scope question. And on at least two versions of how the negotiations proceeded, which respectively stress exchange and coercion, many observers deduce that the North won on everything else as well, including its desire for a comprehensive code with rigid and substantial baselines and levels of protection that could only rise even higher. We see things differently.

1. The exchange narrative

One way to look at the negotiations was as a classic international exchange. Thus, one reason the GATT could succeed where WIPO had failed was because the Uruguay negotiations were not limited to intellectual property issues, as they were in WIPO, and instead were embedded in the broader context of world trade. In that environment, enhanced intellectual property protection could be "purchased" with concessions in other sectors, such as textiles and agriculture.[82] Under this view, the South could be understood to have accepted levels of intellectual property protection inappropriate to its economic condition in order to secure valuable benefits in terms of access to the rich markets of the North for raw materials and manufactured goods. The South, in other words, accepted the intellectual property "tax" as the cost of doing business in other sectors.

However, more was necessarily at stake. Global competition in commodities drives their prices to cost, whereas the goal of intellectual property rights is the production of supra-competitive returns. Because it was unlikely that the South could ever earn enough on its goods to compensate for the increased cost of knowledge-intensive products, if that were the entire "deal," it was distinctly lopsided.[83] And to the extent the North had the global power to resist compliance with its part of the bargain, this effect could even be exacerbated.[84]

2. The coercion narrative

That the deal was nonetheless consummated was, to many observers, a classic triumph of the North's global power. As Susan Sell, Peter Drahos, and others tell it, the North had the South over a barrel: developing countries absolutely needed wider markets to prosper, and they would do whatever was necessary to obtain access to them.[85] To drive home the point, the United States stepped up its use of trade sanctions during the course of the Uruguay Round. As threats of closed markets and lost preferences escalated, developing countries began to look at the emerging TRIPS Agreement as the lesser of two evils.[86] The proponents of higher protection also pursued a "divide and conquer" strategy. The United States, for example, singled out for special treatment countries—like Argentina and Brazil—that persistently advocated for less stringent intellectual property rules.[87] As Carolyn Deere put it, "[U]ltimately, developing countries were overwhelmed."[88]

As important to these commentators, the South appeared to have been out-lawyered. In almost contemporaneous negotiations with Canada and Mexico over the North American Free Trade Agreement, U.S. diplomats had acquired considerable experience with the linkage between trade and intellectual property; they had heard all the arguments and had answers at the ready. Developed countries were also familiar with their own domestic intellectual property laws as well as the Paris and Berne Conventions. In contrast, because some developing countries had never codified comprehensive intellectual property regimes, they arguably had little understanding of how these systems worked or how to structure exceptions to meet their unique needs. Much more accomplished at drafting, the North was able to frame the debate by advancing the first detailed, concrete, and comprehensive proposal.[89]

To observers writing in the wake of the heated negotiations, the political economy dimension of the story also appeared salient. Thus, Susan Sell describes a tight coalition of multinational intellectual property producers in the United States, the Intellectual Property Committee (IPC), which provided much of the impetus to include intellectual property in the Uruguay Round. The IPC, consisting of between eleven and fourteen corporations in the creative sector,[90] bypassed normal trade groups in which dissenting views might have been expressed. Furthermore, they enjoyed direct access, through the Advisory Committee for Trade Negotiations, to the United States Trade Representative's Office, which negotiated the Uruguay Round on behalf of the United States. In contrast, domestic information consumers were not organized (and may, indeed, have been largely unaware of the impact TRIPS might have). In any event, they had no mechanism for making their concerns known. Prior to the round, the IPC also mobilized actors in other developed countries, principally the European

Union and Japan, so that by the time negotiations began, proponents for strong protection had assembled a cohesive working group, ready to supply Northern diplomats with statistics, theoretical arguments, framing devices (including what Sell calls "rights talk"), as well as an agenda for proceeding.[91]

Viewing TRIPS through this prism of market advantage, power, and politics, it is plausible to understand the Agreement as a "one-size-fits-all" regime that ignores considerations of distributive justice and the needs of information users, and which delivered to the IPC and its associates exactly (or as Jacques Gorlin, an economist working for IPC, estimated it, 95 percent of) the protection sought.[92] Although denominated as an agreement imposing only minimum standards of protection, the requirements can certainly be interpreted as going well beyond the minimum necessary to prevent trade distortion, and as a basis for the assertions, quoted at the outset of Chapter 1, that TRIPS strips member states of much of their authority in the intellectual property realm and substitutes a single global level of intellectual property protection for the territoriality approach of the prior international regime. And indeed, there are panels of dispute resolution adjudicators that have taken the view that TRIPS significantly minimizes national discretion.[93] For developing countries, the coercion narrative is particularly plausible, for even standards that appear minimal to developed countries may be set too high for countries that have yet to develop strong creative industries.

3. The compromise narrative

A more nuanced examination of the proceedings and the final instrument tells a different story, one that suggests that TRIPS must be viewed as a compromise that recognizes each state's continuing role in formulating intellectual property policy within the context of an international arrangement.

Thus, a look at the literature surrounding the negotiations for the TRIPS Agreement suggests that proponents of strong protection may have been trying to advance their self-interest. But others persevered in the debate begun in WIPO and other UN agencies, on the economic effects of intellectual property protection and its role in helping developing countries become players in a world economy.[94] Under this view, the South's acceptance of TRIPS obligations could be viewed as a commitment strategy. From their earlier familiarity with intellectual property, Southern negotiators understood that intellectual property rights could produce dynamic benefits and that it would thus be in their countries' long-term interest to recognize them. By participating in crafting an instrument and agreeing to it, these countries could use their new international obligations to overcome local political opposition based on short-term static costs and distributive effects.[95]

Thus, most economists agree with the propositions, which are supported empirically, that productivity is crucial to economic growth and that productivity cannot increase significantly without innovation. To many, intellectual property rights are key to spurring investment in creative enterprises and encouraging the disclosure and dissemination of the results in the form of patents and publications.[96] Accordingly, it was argued that just as intellectual property enhanced welfare in the North, it would ultimately do so in the South as well. Indeed, with stronger protection in the South, "brain drains"—the exodus of skilled creative workers to places that value and protect inventiveness—would end and indigenous creativity would flourish.[97] And as in the North, market demand would steer invention and investment to products of local significance.

Even if a country initially lacked the human capital and the equipment needed for creative production, economists argued that TRIPS would prove beneficial in the long run. Strong intellectual property protection would attract foreigners to invest resources in turn-key operations that would provide opportunities for training local personnel. As skills improved to the point where local industry could thrive, foreign direct investment would be supplemented by technology transfer.[98] By assuring innovators that their investments could be recouped even after their creative works were disclosed, intellectual property rights would facilitate licensing and increase the publication and diffusion of information. In addition, association—such as occurs through joint-venturing and strategic alliances—with established foreign firms would stabilize local businesses and improve survival rates; it would also enhance the international reputations of domestic concerns and promote global marketing.[99]

Certainly, there were economists in the South, such as Carlos Alberto Primo Braga and Carlos Correa, who were skeptical about these claims.[100] In their view, countries lagging in creative capacity might pay a heavy price before they saw any benefits in the TRIPS Agreement. And even if emerging economies (such as the BRICS, Brazil, Russia, India, China, and South Africa) would ultimately benefit from strong intellectual property rights, these economists argued that the balance would never shift for the least developed nations. In their view, productivity and economic growth require much more than strong intellectual property protection; they are equally contingent on absorptive capacity (the ability of workers to learn and advance technologically) and on a legal structure that facilitates capital formation, ensures robust competition, and provides for the fair adjudication of disputes. Some saw the problem as involving more fundamental issues.[101] Ruth Gana (now Okediji), for example, argued that before TRIPS benefits could be realized, the South would have to trade its communitarian values for the "rugged individualism" on which intellectual property systems are based.[102]

The instrument that emerged reflects the complexity of these debates. The North was certainly successful on a number of fronts. For copyright, Article 9.1 of TRIPS incorporates pre-existing commitments under the Berne Convention. Further, the Agreement extends obligations to new subject matter: Article 10 mandates copyright protection for software. Articles 11 and 14 require recognition of rental rights and some performing rights. Additionally, the limits on permissible exceptions in Article 9 of the Berne Convention were extended to all works and all rights by Article 13 of TRIPS.

The treatment of trademark is little different. In Article 2.1, TRIPS carries over the obligations of the Paris Convention. As with copyright, the Agreement then expands upon prior commitments. Article 16 extends the protection of Article 6bis of the Paris Convention to service marks and enlarges the scope of trademark protection. Articles 20 and 21 limit the autonomy of countries to regulate marks. In particular, Article 20 prohibits a member state from requiring foreigners to link their marks to those of local producers. As the North desired, exclusive rights were expanded to include undisclosed information,[103] and the level of protection for designs was enhanced.[104]

The most significant changes involved patent protection. The Paris Convention was largely concerned with procedural issues, such as handling attempts to patent the same invention in successive countries.[105] Accordingly, the substantive patent obligations in the TRIPS Agreement are almost entirely new to international law. The Agreement requires protection for all inventions, provided they are capable of industrial application and include an "inventive step."[106] That provision also requires members to make patents "available and patent rights enjoyable without discrimination as to the place of invention, the field of technology and whether products are imported or locally produced." Every country must, under Article 28, prevent unauthorized manufacture, sales, offers to sell, use, and importation of patented products (with analogous provisions on unauthorized exploitation of patented processes). Protection, per Article 33, must endure for twenty years from the date of application. Prior to TRIPS, many countries regulated patent exploitation with compulsory licenses, but Article 31 constrains their ability to do so.

With respect to all forms of intellectual property, the Agreement mandates effective enforcement of rights, with detailed provisions on remedies, including criminal penalties.[107] Finally, the Agreement makes compliance with its obligations—and with the commitments carried over from the Paris and Berne Conventions—the subject of effective dispute resolution under Article 64.

It is significant, however, that notwithstanding the successes of the North in imposing these higher levels of protection, the South succeeded in securing within the Agreement language that was responsive to its concerns. The Preamble recognizes the "underlying public policy objectives of national systems for the protection of intellectual property, including developmental and technological objectives" and "the special needs of the least developed country Members in respect of maximum flexibility in the domestic implementation of laws ... in order to enable them to create a sound and viable technological base." Consistent with these declarations, Article 7 recites that the goal of TRIPS is to "contribute to the promotion of technological innovation and to the transfer and dissemination of technology, to the mutual advantage of producers and users of technological knowledge and in a manner conducive to social and economic welfare...." Similarly, Article 8 states that members retain the rights to protect public health and nutrition, and promote the public interest in sectors vital to their socioeconomic and technological development. Article 27.2 affirms that commitment by permitting countries to exclude from patentability inventions "necessary to protect *ordre public* or morality, including to protect human, animal or plant life or health or to avoid serious prejudice to the environment...." Article 27.3 further expands members' options by allowing them to exclude from patentability diagnostic, therapeutic, and surgical methods for the treatment of animals and people. It also permits states to protect agricultural products through a sui generis scheme, rather than by patent law.

Most important, the instrument defers in many respects to the member states and leaves them with considerable autonomy to accommodate the mandates of the Agreement in light of their particular circumstances. Thus, Article 1.1 indicates that members are "free to determine the appropriate method of implementing the provisions"; Article 41.5 stresses that no country is obliged to favor the enforcement of intellectual property laws over the enforcement of other laws. Further, the provisions on remedies, Articles 43 through 48, require legal systems to provide the "authority" to order discovery, injunctions, damages, and other relief, but these provisions do not mandate particular forms of relief in individual cases, thus leaving it to local decision makers to tailor remedies to local conditions. There are two other major sets of safeguards for national interests. Under Articles 13, 17, 26.2, and 30—which we collectively term the Exceptions provisions—countries enjoy leeway to modify the standards of protection in each of the principal intellectual property rights. Furthermore, Article 31 allows countries, within specified constraints, to engage in compulsory licensing of patents when local conditions require it. For example, that article, along with Articles 8.2 and 40, permits members to take action and award compulsory licenses when patent holders engage in anticompetitive practices ("abuse"). Finally, the concessions adopted in the Paris and Berne Conventions were carried forward into the new regime. Article 9.1 incorporates the Berne Appendix, and as a DSB panel subsequently found, TRIPS also recognizes the entire Berne acquis, including the minor exceptions doctrine, which traditionally gave states leeway to calibrate the scope of protection.[108]

The North also made concessions to the immediate needs of the South. To deal with distributive issues, the transition provisions of Articles 65 and 66 postponed obligations for a period of time (longer for least developed countries than for developing countries), with Article 70.8 creating special "pipeline" protection to mediate between the interests of proprietary pharmaceutical and agricultural chemical producers, on the one hand, and generic producers, patients, and farmers, on the other. Concerns about implementation were assuaged by Articles 67 and 69, which promise technical assistance and cooperation and mandate that developed country members "provide incentives to enterprises and institutions in their territories for the purpose of promoting and encouraging technology transfer" to least developed members. Confirming the idea that the move to TRIPS represents an ongoing process of collaboration among all member states, Article 68 establishes the Council for TRIPS to monitor compliance and provide a forum for further discussion.[109]

Clearly, the value of these measures to the South can be doubted. As compared with the safeguard clause in the GATT, which explicitly permits countries to suspend obligations to protect national interests,[110] the objectives and principles provisions articulated in Articles 7 and 8 of TRIPS can be read (and were later interpreted) as largely precatory.[111] As initially drafted, the compulsory license provision of Article 31 was also limited: although it permitted countries to supply the market when the right holder refused, the drafters had assumed that members would be self-sufficient. Thus, the provision permitted them to authorize only production necessary to "predominantly... supply... the domestic market of the Member authorizing such use."[112] But it transpired that some countries could not manufacture pharmaceuticals to meet their needs and, under the proviso, could no longer rely on importing medication from generic producers in other member states. In addition, transition times proved far too short, and early experience with the Agreement demonstrated that the promise of technology transfer was not met.[113] Finally, technical assistance appeared to be something of a misnomer, with developed countries offering the South "assistance" to enact the same laws that obtain in the North, rather than to identify TRIPS-compatible solutions that deal with local needs.[114]

But as it became evident during the AIDS pandemic of the late 1990s that exclusive reliance on market mechanisms was inadequate to address social concerns, many of these defects were addressed.[115] The Doha Round, although remarkably unsuccessful with regard to other subjects of international trade, dealt with the weakness in the compulsory licensing provision by increasing the flexibilities of Article 31.[116] The Ministerial Declaration effecting that change also took account of noneconomic values, such as distributive justice, stressing "the importance . . . attach[ed] to implementation and interpretation of the . . . TRIPS Agreement . . . in a manner supportive of public health, by promoting both access to existing medicines and research and development into new medicines."[117] Further, it put teeth into the seemingly precatory provisions by admonishing the Council for TRIPS to be guided in its deliberations "by the objectives and principles set out in Articles 7 and 8."[118]

Attention has also been paid to other deficiencies. The Council for TRIPS extended the transition period for least developed members[119] and has defined its monitoring obligations to include monitoring the North, to ensure its compliance with the obligation to promote technology transfer.[120] In addition, the expertise of WIPO and the Punta Del Este promise to engage with WIPO have been acknowledged. Shortly after the TRIPS Agreement went into effect, the WTO entered into an agreement with WIPO.[121] Among other things, WIPO is enlisted in providing members with technical assistance and cooperation. To the extent WIPO is now perceived as more hospitable to distributive issues, it should be better at helping the South identify ways in which domestic needs can be met consistent with its TRIPS obligations.[122] Furthermore, WIPO enjoys observer status at the Council for TRIPS, and WIPO materials are relied upon by adjudicators in dispute settlement.[123]

The Appellate Body (AB) and a recent dispute settlement panel have affirmed the view that TRIPS protects national autonomy interests—and thereby instantiates what can be considered a neofederalist regime. Adjudicators rejected the notion that the Agreement represents an invitation to enforce expectations beyond the specific commitments in the Agreement. Thus, in the *India-Pharmaceuticals* case, the United States argued that India had effectively agreed to determine the patentability of pharmaceuticals during the transition period. The AB understood that this was the position the North had wanted members to adopt, but it held that the parties were bound only by the Agreement as written, and that it did not include this obligation; that under Article 3.2 of the Dispute Settlement Understanding (DSU), adjudicators cannot "add to or diminish the rights and obligations provided in the covered agreements."[124] Similarly, the panel in the *China-Enforcement* case stressed that states retain a measure of autonomy and that obligations are determined by the wording of the Agreement, and not by the intent of particular negotiators.[125]

B. The North-North Debate

The culmination of the North-North debate can similarly be construed as affirming a neofederalist perspective on the TRIPS Agreement. In contrast to the North-South controversies—which were often about fundamental issues, such as whether the GATT was a suitable forum, whether privatizing intellectual products was morally justifiable, and whether the regimes favored by the North would be suitable to the South—debates among developed countries were largely about details of the protective regimes. These included the system for collecting royalties on videos, corporate ownership of copyrighted products, recognition of neighboring rights, rights over computer programs, moral rights, and the priority rules for awarding patents and recognizing trademarks.[126]

However, one area of contention was evocative of the debates with the South. It concerned geographical indications (GIs), which many Northern countries protected, if at all, through trademark law. If TRIPS mandated GI protection, these countries would—just like the South—experience the protection of these marks as a tax imposed by GI-rich nations on those lacking them. As Annette Kur and Sam Cocks have noted, creating new GIs—that is, instilling a sense of place into otherwise-generic products—was sure to be exorbitantly expensive.[127] Thus, universalizing GI protection was likely to freeze the haves and have-nots in place in the same way that copyright and patent protection could freeze creative capacity in developing countries. Further, the same free-rider dynamic was in play: farmers in the new world imported seeds and production methods from the old world (often, their own countries of origin), used the same terminology, and thus exploited the international reputation of the old world products. And as in the North-South debate, the demandeurs argued that recognizing GIs would benefit the resisting nations by encouraging artisanal work and educating the citizens of the new world about the value of place and tradition.[128]

Significantly, the proponents of strong GIs did not win this debate. Instead, the negotiators partly split the difference. Thus, Article 23 requires strong protection only for wines and spirits; Article 22 permits lesser protection for other geographical indications. In other respects, the negotiators left matters largely to national policy makers. Neither of the GI provisions requires members to enact new intellectual property regimes; rather, TRIPS gives each the right to choose, as between GI, trademark, and unfair competition law, the appropriate legal vehicle for protection. Indeed footnote 4 to Article 23.1 indicates that members may even provide for enforcement of GI obligations regarding wines and spirits by administrative action.[129] The transition rules are also quite robust. Under Article 24, trademarks and customary names that were adopted prior to the Agreement can continue to exist, even when they include geographical terminology.[130] To a certain extent, the negotiators also agreed not to agree: they left it to the states to continue to discuss the issue of GIs in the Council for TRIPS.[131]

The resolution of other North-North issues similarly demonstrates the compromise approach adopted in the North-South context when differing economic conditions and philosophical commitments prevail among member states. For example, the Agreement requires the recognition of rental rights for cinematographic works. However, Article 11 permits states to make an exception when the rental of such works has not yet led to widespread copying "that is materially impairing the exclusive right of reproduction" in that country.

Article 6bis of the Berne Convention mandates protection of moral rights. However, Article 9.1 of TRIPS, while otherwise rendering the Berne Convention subject to WTO dispute settlement, excludes Berne Article 6bis from the scope of dispute resolution.[132] Article 6 declines to choose between competing policy choices on the geographic scope of exhaustion. The Agreement takes no position on ownership of protected works and is similarly silent on the priority rule for patents. And Article 15.3 takes an agnostic view on the long-standing debate between the United States and the European Union on the respective merits of a first-to-use and first-to-file system for trademarks.

The DSB's resolution of disputes among developed countries also bears the imprint of compromise, rather than—as some have suggested—the notion that the DSB was delegated the right to finish an incomplete contract.[133] For example, the DSB accepted an almost risible interpretation by the United States of its own copyright statute—the claim that one provision was aimed only at exempting certain public performances of dramatic musical works—thus allowing the United States to prevail on one aspect of the *US-110(5)* case.[134] Significantly, the case did not lead to revision of U.S. law to comply with the aspect of the case that the United States lost (exceptions for certain performances of nondramatic musical works), but rather to arbitration, followed by a negotiated settlement, in which payments made by the United States fell well below the panel's estimate of damage.[135] Similarly, in the *EC-GI* case, the panel deferred to the European Union's claim that the scope of its GI protection is narrowly limited to the version of the mark that is registered.[136] As a result, the panel was unwilling to credit the United States' claim that this protection burdened trademark owners. And in the *Canada-Pharmaceuticals* case, the dispute resolution panel accepted at face value Canada's representation that its regulatory review exception was not limited to pharmaceutical products.[137]

III. The TRIPS Agreement as Concluded

In light of these observations, the claim that TRIPS imposes a "one-size-fits-all" regime appears substantially overstated. To be sure, there were elements of coercion, and questionable trade-offs may have been made between market access for commodities and intellectual property protection. However, the instrument as a whole reflects compromise both on the economic impact of protection and on the continued relevance of broader social values. It continues in the tradition of the Paris and Berne Conventions to reflect a minimum standards approach that affords member states substantial latitude regarding implementation in national law. This is not to say that as global trade increases, further harmonization will never be desirable. But the drafters ultimately recognized that for a set of nations of disparate economic and social conditions, there often was—in fact—no single optimum that could be imposed. TRIPS is a product of a single moment in history and reflects the national and international policies and interests pertaining to that moment.

Indeed, even by this metric, the Agreement was consciously inchoate. As the GI provisions exemplify, negotiators built in an agenda for further negotiations.[138] The institutional mechanism TRIPS created promotes dialogue on unresolved and unanticipated issues and was intended to move the formulation of future international intellectual property policy to a multilateral forum (and, arguably, away from unilateral trade reviews or bilateral trade relations).[139] TRIPS, in short, instantiates a neofederalist vision of the Agreement, in which states retain significant autonomy to innovate in the design of their intellectual property systems, while committing themselves to engage in an ongoing dialogue with other members of the WTO to foster the development of efficient and fair international markets in knowledge-intensive products.

Recognizing TRIPS as a genuine compact has other implications. First, some proponents of the coercion narrative have argued that TRIPS is void as a contract of adhesion.[140] Under a neofederalist view, developing countries cannot escape the commitments they made so easily. Second, the North must recognize that it did not achieve all that it hoped for in the Uruguay Round. Indeed, recent attempts to pursue international intellectual property lawmaking through such initiatives as Special 301 actions, free trade agreements, bilateral investment treaties, and the Anti-Counterfeiting Trade Agreement (ACTA) illustrate that even proponents of strong protection are aware that TRIPS is considerably less than a complete international code of intellectual property law.[141] Third, TRIPS demonstrates the benefits of situating negotiations over international intellectual property law in a wider context. The current propensity toward unilateral, bilateral, and plurilateral negotiation is producing fragmentation and destroying the predictability necessary in a legal regime aimed at encouraging creative production. A commitment from all sides to use the mechanisms established by the WTO to vindicate residual and emerging interests would be preferable. Finally, the continuity from Berne and Paris to TRIPS suggests that international intellectual property lawmaking is governed by a set of substantive norms, partially stated in the text of these instruments, but largely implicit in them. National autonomy is one of these norms; others include commitments to recognize the cumulative nature of knowledge production and the need for balance between proprietary and access interests. Recognizing and identifying the elements of what we term an international intellectual property acquis would help restore coherence in the face of fragmentation and provide the coordination essential to a truly neofederalist regime. Parts II and III demonstrate how the institutions created by the

TRIPS Agreement could bring more coherence to the international system of knowledge governance.

Illustration

Our view of the TRIPS Agreement and its history affects the force of the assertions, discussed in Chapter 1, that "TRIPS tells all countries—developed, developing and least developed—*what* they must do and *when* and *how* they must do it," and thus impedes their capacity to adjust to local conditions and new challenges. To take one hypothetical example, the lessons from history reflect on the allegation that TRIPS precludes member states from adopting working requirements in their patent laws—that the Agreement sub silentio reverses Article 5 of the Paris Convention, which had permitted member states to award compulsory licenses for failure to work the patent locally.[142]

A literal reading of the TRIPS Agreement, and one informed by the exchange or coercion narratives, makes it plausible to conclude that the working requirement is no longer available under TRIPS. A country that requires patent holders to work the product locally and prohibits them from treating information goods like any other commodity, to be supplied from the place where they are most efficiently manufactured, would appear to violate both Articles 27 and 28.[143] That is, the measure could be said to discriminate against products depending on whether they are imported or locally produced, to eliminate the patent holder's right to prevent others from making and selling the product, and to undermine the import right by permitting local producers to sell product and drive prices downward.[144] Furthermore, although Article 8 permits states to control abuse, it adds that these controls must be "consistent with the Agreement." That proviso suggests that countries can never intrude into the exclusive prerogatives of rights holders except as provided by Articles 30 (the patent Exceptions provision) and Article 31 (the compulsory licensing provision).[145] As a policy matter, requiring manufacture in a less felicitous location would also appear to undermine the comparative advantage rationale underlying the trade regime as a whole.

The neofederalist view of TRIPS leads to a different conclusion. History demonstrates that technology transfer was an important issue for developing countries. The South was worried that stronger protection would leave it at a permanent disadvantage in knowledge-intensive markets. The counterargument was that exclusive rights would facilitate disclosure and encourage diffusion of technical information. But as economists recognize, technological progress can demand more than a literature: it may also require "learning by doing."[146] Not all information is easily codified into patents or publications. Even when information is codified, it can be difficult to fully understand from a written description how to exploit the advance, and that is especially true for unskilled workers with low absorptive capacity.[147] Thus, the mere fact that property rights encourage disclosure is not enough to fulfill the promise to bring the South up to the technological levels of the North. For the South (and even within the North), imitation, fair following, and the opportunity to interact with trained employees are crucial.[148] If technology transfer is not effectuated directly (and experience under the TRIPS Agreement is mixed),[149] then a country that is lagging in an area of critical local importance should be permitted to take action when right holders are importing rather than exploiting the invention locally.

This interpretation is supported by the negotiations leading up to the Agreement, language in the instrument, and subsequent events. Thus, at the time of the TRIPS negotiations, the working requirement was a feature of the national laws of many countries, where it was viewed, much like the disclosure requirement, as one of the quid pro quos of patent protection.[150] The structure of the requirement had been debated in many successive rounds of Paris Convention negotiations, and the version of Article 5 that existed at the time the TRIPS Agreement was negotiated represented an important compromise between countries that wanted to invalidate patents for nonworking and those who wished to ban the working requirement entirely.[151] The issue was studied once again during the Uruguay Round, but while it was debated, the Agreement was signed without the members reaching an explicit resolution of their respective positions.[152]

Accordingly, were the DSB confronted with the task of determining whether a country had violated the Agreement by imposing a working requirement, it should deal with the apparent ambiguity in the TRIPS by deferring to the member state, so long as the state could cite a reason, grounded in TRIPS, for enacting the requirement. And, in fact, there is much in the language to suggest that countries can require local working. Parts of the Preamble, Article 7, and Article 8 were added to assuage the South's concerns about becoming an innovation backwater. The Preamble articulates a goal of providing least developed countries with a "sound and viable technological base," and both Articles 7 and 8 stress the notion that TRIPS would contribute to social and economic welfare and technological progress. Furthermore, Articles 8.2 and 40 specifically permit countries to prevent "abuse," the term that Article 5 of the Paris Convention uses as the category into which nonworking falls.[153] By the terms of the TRIPS Agreement, the Paris Convention remains in force,[154] and there is no specific derogation in TRIPS from the working requirement provision, as there was for the moral rights requirement of the Berne Convention. Indeed, the understanding of TRIPS as protecting a "right" to import reflects a trade perspective that fails to account for the long-held understanding of patent rights as negative rights—as the right to exclude others from importing. The working requirement, which is focused on *local* working, does not interfere with that prerogative. As long as the state complies with Article 8's proviso and issues its compulsory license in accordance with the requirements of Article 31, the DSB should read TRIPS to permit a state to fashion patent laws that take its own technological needs into account.

Our conclusion is reinforced by subsequent events. As the quotation opening the Chapter demonstrates, soon after the Agreement went into force, the United States brought an action against Brazil for enforcing a local working requirement. Brazil was concerned with another aspect of strong protection: the rise in prices associated with exclusive rights. Relying on Article 31 and the provision in Article 8 allowing members to take measures to protect public health, Brazil awarded a compulsory license on AIDS drugs to a local manufacturer in order to ensure an adequate affordable supply. Significantly, the complaint was withdrawn by the United States before it reached dispute resolution.[155] The decision to abandon the challenge has no precedential effect. Furthermore, the withdrawal can be viewed more as a product of public relations than as reflecting any legal conclusion. Still, the episode suggests that failure to work remains an acceptable basis for granting compulsory licenses, especially if it is coupled with another allegation, such as (in the actual case) inadequately supplying the local market with product at acceptable prices, or with the failure to furnish technological opportunities that permit the granting country to advance technologically.[156]

PART II

WHERE WE ARE

Dispute Resolution and Its Impact on a
Neofederalist Vision of TRIPS

PART II

3

The Dispute Settlement Understanding

Interpretation of the Substantive Features of the TRIPS Agreement

> Swiss drugmaker Novartis AG has challenged before the Supreme Court the patent rejection of its key cancer drug Glivec based on Section 3(d) of the Indian Patent Act.
>
> —Priyanka Golikeri, *Novartis Moves Supreme Court on Glivac Patent*, DAILY NEWS & ANALYSIS, August 28, 2009, *available* at http://www.dnaindia.com/money/report_novartis-moves-supreme-court-on-glivec-patent_1286024

> Does SACGHS realize that [a diagnostic exemption to patent law] is tantamount to a "compulsory license" but even worse, without any compensation for the patent owner? Did SACGHS bother to consider the impact of this recommendation on TRIPS?
>
> —Donald Zuhn, BIO Sends Letter on SACGHS Report to HHS Secretary Sebelius, Patent Docs (February 11, 2010), *available at* http://www.patentdocs.org/2010/02/bio-sends-letter-on-sacghs-report-to-hhs-secretary-sebelius.html

> [T]here are two open doctrinal questions regarding *eBay*'s application in patent cases—whether injunctions will always be denied for non-producing patentees and whether patentees will just be awarded reasonable royalties for future unauthorized use. How each of these questions is answered will affect how the eBay decision and its usage by United States courts are treated under TRIPS.
>
> —Christopher A. Cotropia, *Compulsory Licensing Under TRIPS and the Supreme Court of the United States' Decision in* eBay v. MercExchange *in* PATENT LAW AND THEORY: A HANDBOOK OF CONTEMPORARY RESEARCH 557, 572 (Toshiko Takenaka and Rainer Moufang eds., Edward Elgar 2009)

The structure of the TRIPS Agreement, the manner in which it allocates authority, and ultimately, the power it leaves to member states to respond to new challenges, depend not only on how the Agreement is read in light of its history and the frames of international and intellectual property law, but also on the interpretation it is given under the Dispute Settlement Understanding (DSU).[1] The previous Part emphasized the important ways in which TRIPS raised the substantive requirements of international intellectual property law. However, the addition of a compliance mechanism is perhaps its most significant contribution to international intellectual property law. And in some ways, that mechanism is equally new to the trade regime: the 1947 GATT followed a diplomacy-based approach to dispute resolution, but the WTO system is more judicial and less dependent upon political muscle.[2] Accordingly, whatever the truth of the narratives recounted in Chapter 2 on how TRIPS was negotiated, the effective impact of the Agreement is now determined in an essentially adjudicative fashion by the Dispute Settlement Body (DSB), composed of ad hoc panels, which serve as a quasi court of first instance, and the Appellate Body (AB) to which panel decisions may be appealed.

Analyzing TRIPS from the perspective of its "case law" is not without its problems. To date, members have initiated (formally, through "requests for consultation") approximately thirty TRIPS-based disputes.[3] In most cases, the consultations have sufficed to resolve the complaint: only seven disputes have proceeded to a panel report, and of these, only three have reached the AB.[4] As important, because the DSB is not a true analogue of a court, it creates a unique set of selection effects. In private litigation, injured parties decide when to initiate litigation. But the DSU confers the authority to bring complaints on the member states, not on right holders. It cautions members to "exercise . . . judgment" before filing a complaint;[5] presumably, countries do not take into account the same considerations that private parties do in deciding which problems to raise. States surely consider the strengths and weaknesses of their cases as well as their intellectual property strategy, but they might also consider such factors as the desire to promote public acceptance of the Agreement in less developed countries and broader geopolitical issues. Or countries may choose cases based on the persistence of the problem or the political leverage of the industries whose interests are at stake. Furthermore, because the DSU does not provide for declaratory judgment actions, disputes seeking to clear proposed legislation are not part of the mix.

There are other reasons for caution in drawing conclusions from these decisions. Since the majority of the complaints resulting in decisions have been brought by developed countries against other developed countries, the participants on both sides of the disputes have largely consisted of those who were the proponents of strong protection when the Agreement was negotiated. As a result, there have not been many cases where either of the parties has had an incentive to argue as vigorously as developing countries might for expansive interpretations of public-regarding provisions or for the principle that the states reserved considerable autonomy to themselves.[6] Furthermore, most of the cases have been decided by ad hoc panels, with panelists chosen as much for their trade expertise as for their understanding of the contours of intellectual property.[7] As Robert Howse has suggested, the AB appears to take a less formalistic view than the panels do and is more likely to consider competing public values in its decisions.[8] Thus conclusions reached by panels may not be indicative of how an issue will ultimately be resolved. Finally, although decision makers often consult prior reports in order to bring a measure of predictability to the WTO regime, DSU decisions are not formally entitled to precedential weight.[9] Accordingly, and perhaps reassuringly, the DSB has ample capacity to reevaluate the Agreement as understanding of its impact matures.

Still, studying the reports issued by the DSB is essential because, absent changes at the ministerial level, it has the final word on the extent to which national regimes can be adapted to deal with the three issues we see as salient: the diversity of the WTO's membership, the need for balance, and the ability to respond to the dynamics of the Knowledge Economy. To focus our inquiry on the impact of the interpretive methodology used by the DSB, we consider three initiatives: (1) raising the height of the inventive step, (2) creating new statutory defenses to liability for patent infringement, and (3) varying the right to relief by refusing to award injunctions automatically to prevailing plaintiffs.[10] The first initiative accommodates diversity values. The other two readjust the balance between producers, consumers, and follow-on innovators in light of technological and social developments. We probe the strength and weaknesses of the DSB's approach by asking whether it would regard the adoption of each as consistent with the TRIPS Agreement. We demonstrate that in some respects, the DSB—particularly in the reports of the AB and the most recent panel reports—promotes the values underlying our neofederalist view. However, our analysis also suggests that, in judging the TRIPS compatibility of challenged actions, panels often pursue an extraordinarily formalistic reading of the Agreement and one that is largely devoid of normative content. This interpretive regime may have some resonance with the code approach to TRIPS, or it may derive from trade-based traditions or from the lineup of the parties in these disputes. Whatever its cause, the approach endangers the resilience of the system.

I. Raising the Inventive Step

As Chapter 2 recounted, the TRIPS Agreement imposed obligations on all countries to install a patent system. Negotiators recognized that as a result product prices could rise and that the patent obligations in TRIPS would be particularly onerous for developing countries. The drafters therefore included transition provisions that delayed the time when patent rights had to be recognized and measures permitting countries to meet social needs with compulsory licenses issued to local producers. As it transpired, however, these safety valves proved ineffective. The transition period was too short, and the procedures put in place by Article 31 for compulsory licensing were difficult to utilize. The Doha Ministerial Declaration made an adjustment purportedly aimed at liberalizing the system.[11] But the provision that was added, Article 31bis, compounded the complexity of the process.

At the conclusion of the transition period, when developing countries were obliged to revise their patent laws, India chose to deal with these continuing problems by raising the level of invention (nonobviousness) required to secure patent protection. Section 3(d) of its act provides that the following is not eligible for protection:

> [T]he mere discovery of a new form of a known substance which does not result in the enhancement of the known efficacy of that substance or the mere discovery of any new property or new use for a known substance or of the mere use of a known process, machine or apparatus unless such process results in a new product or employs at least one new reactant.[12]

The provision was accompanied by the following Explanation:

> For the purposes of this clause, salts, esters, ethers, polymorphs, metabolites, pure form, particle size, isomers, mixtures of isomers, complexes, combinations and other derivatives of known substance shall be considered to be the same substance, unless they differ significantly in properties with regard to efficacy.[13]

This provision has many advantages, particularly in the pharmaceutical sector, where high prices have a significant impact on health care. Most obviously, the provision prevents evergreening: a patent holder cannot extend protection on a drug beyond an initial twenty-year term by simply patenting a new form of the identical substance. As important, § 3(d) provides a ground on which to reject some of the applications that were in the "pipeline," awaiting examination during the transition period. Thus, the measure gives India a way to protect patients who were already relying on the medicines that were the subjects of these applications, as well as the burgeoning generic drug industry that was producing the products.[14]

The provision has other advantages as well. Depending on how the Indian courts interpret "efficacy," it may not be possible to patent minor changes, such as those that reduce the need for refrigeration, offer easier methods of administration, or better target the genetic makeup of the patient population.[15] As David Opderbeck has suggested, since operating costs and profit expectations in India are likely modest,[16] India's pharmaceutical industry may not need patent protection to support investments in these activities. India could thus reap the benefits of what Jerry Reichman calls "fair following." With a comparative advantage over foreign pharmaceutical companies seeking "blockbuster" profits, India could supply its workforce with the opportunity to develop skills that move the country to the technological frontier.[17] And as research in India becomes more ambitious and tackles larger problems—such as finding cures for neglected diseases—there would be (beneficial) spillover effects well beyond its borders.[18]

But as the quotation at the beginning of this Chapter demonstrates, § 3(d) is under attack. When India used the provision to deny patent protection to Glivac (Gleevac), a drug that Novartis markets as a treatment for leukemia, Novartis promptly claimed that the rejection constituted a violation of the TRIPS Agreement.[19] The Indian courts refused to rule on the TRIPS issue. However, the United States lost little time putting pressure on India to change the provision: it quickly put India on its Priority Watch List (and in line for trade sanctions).[20]

Certainly, there are grounds to claim that India is violating its TRIPS obligations. Although the provision is cast in terms that could apply to any technological sector, the Explanation tells a different story. The details it provides, concerning "salts, esters, ethers, polymorphs, metabolites, pure form, particle size, isomers, mixtures of isomers, complexes, combinations and other derivatives," signal that the measure is squarely aimed at the pharmaceutical industry. The questions, then, are whether a measure so obviously concerned with chemical products violates Article 27.1, which provides that "patent rights shall be available and . . . enjoyable without discrimination as to . . . the field of technology," and whether the provision relies on a meaning of "inventive step" which violates the requirement in Article 27.1 that "patents shall be available for any inventions . . . provided that they . . . involve an inventive step."

A. The Nondiscrimination Clause of Article 27.1

On the discrimination issue, the first question is the level of granularity at which TRIPS regulates patent law. The negotiation history of the Agreement suggests that the goal of Article 27.1 was to deal with countries, particularly developing countries, which had not made patents available "for specific areas of technology, notably pharmaceuticals, agrochemicals or foodstuffs."[21] Thus, it could be argued that a country will satisfy Article 27.1 if it offers protection for pharmaceuticals generally, or recognizes product patents. Since India offers patent protection to both pharmaceutical products and processes, it could not be found to be discriminating in that way.

The *Canada–Pharmaceuticals* case suggests that such a limited view of the scope of Article 27's nondiscrimination provision is unlikely to prevail. In that dispute, the European Union challenged two provisions of Canada's patent law, both aimed at ensuring that a generic equivalent of a drug could be put on the market as soon as the patent on the drug expired. Section 55.2(1) dealt with regulatory review, and provided:

> It is not an infringement of a patent for any person to make, construct, use or sell the patented invention solely for uses reasonably related to the development and submission of information required under any law of Canada, a province or a country other than Canada that regulates the manufacture, construction, use or sale of any product.

Section 55.2(2), the so-called stockpiling provision, stated:

> It is not an infringement of a patent for any person who makes, constructs, uses or sells a patented invention in accordance with subsection (1) to make, construct or use the invention, during the applicable period provided for by the regulations, for the manufacture and storage of articles intended for sale after the date on which the term of the patent expires.[22]

Neither provision effectuated a total denial of patent protection for pharmaceuticals, yet Canada never seriously claimed that the provisions were therefore compliant with the Agreement. This may be a situation where the respondent, as a developed country generally interested in strong intellectual property rights, had insufficient motivation to argue for a narrow reading of a TRIPS obligation. But even if the argument were pressed by India in defending § 3(d), it is so at odds with the dominant understanding of the Agreement as establishing effective patent protection, it is likely unavailing. For its part, the *Canada–Pharmaceuticals* panel simply noted the issue and moved on.[23]

India could, however, claim that even on a more granular reading of the Agreement it is not discriminating against the pharmaceutical industry. In *Canada–Pharmaceuticals*, the panel took a rather pragmatic approach to the meaning of discrimination. While it agreed that the European Union had demonstrated that "the primary reason for passing the measure was its effect on promoting competition in the pharmaceutical sector,"[24] the adjudicators were unwilling to conclude that the regulatory review provision constituted discrimination against the industry. Without clear evidence showing that this provision would only apply to pharmaceuticals, the panel accepted Canada's formal declaration that the measure was neutral and addressed a general problem—to wit, the unintended period of exclusivity that would be created if a rival were required to wait until after patent expiration to fulfill its clearance duties.[25] It noted in particular:

> [P]reoccupation with the effects of a statute in one area does not necessarily mean that the provisions applicable to other areas are a sham, or of no actual or potential importance. Individual problems are frequently the driving force behind legislative actions of broader scope. The broader scope of the measure usually reflects an important legal principle that rules being applied in the area of primary interest should also be applied to other areas where the same problem occurs. Indeed, it is a common desideratum in many legal systems that legislation apply its underlying principles as broadly as possible. So long as the broader application is not a sham, the legislation cannot be considered discriminatory.[26]

In short, the panel comprehended that social change (in this case, the need to regulate the marketing of pharmaceuticals) has always affected the balance that a state instantiates into its intellectual property laws. Since the panel assumed that such rules would be generalized to all fields facing similar problems, it imposed upon the complainant (the European Union) the burden of demonstrating that this was not the way the provision would be used.

What this means for § 3(d) of the Indian Patent Act is, however, difficult to determine. The *Canada–Pharmaceuticals* panel did not elaborate on the types of proof that it would have regarded as demonstrating discrimination (an issue to which we return later). Thus, it is hard to predict how the DSB would assess the limited nature of the examples India provided in its Explanation of the provision. In the Canadian case, pharmaceuticals were the only product deemed potentially dangerous enough to require regulatory review. But incremental innovation is possible in virtually every field, and successive patent applications aimed at perpetuating the patent holder's exclusivity are hardly unknown.[27] It is therefore quite possible that a panel would deduce that India was not trying to solve a general problem that had simply surfaced first in connection with pharmaceuticals, but rather that it was acting in a discriminatory fashion to protect the interests of its domestic industry.

India might further attempt to defend its law by claiming that the discriminatory nature of § 3(d) could be justified as a health measure. Article 7 of the Agreement stresses that TRIPS is intended to contribute to "social and economic welfare"; Article 8.1 permits members to "adopt measures necessary to protect public health." However, the argument that Articles 7 and 8 override other obligations failed when Canada invoked it in the *Canada–Pharmaceuticals* case. The panel agreed that these provisions must be kept in mind, but it was wary of allowing them to effectuate a renegotiation of the overall balance the Agreement had struck.[28] Arguably, the Doha Ministerial Declaration—which was issued after the panel decision—could make a difference here, for it stressed the importance of implementing and interpreting TRIPS "in a manner supportive of public health, by promoting both access to existing medicines and research and development into new medicines."[29] Indeed, the noted commentator, Daniel Gervais, has suggested that post-Doha panels may give these provisions a "somewhat higher normative profile" and be more receptive to flexibilities when cast in terms of public health.[30] But the precise status of the Ministerial Declaration is uncertain,[31] and thus its influence is difficult to gauge.

B. The Definition of "Invention" in Article 27.1

Even if India were to prevail on the discrimination issue, it must also deal with a second problem: its definition of the term "invention." As Reichman noted in his early and prescient article on the TRIPS Agreement, the absence of definitions of key terms such as "invention" appears to give nations a high degree of latitude in what they regard as protected subject matter.[32] But, again, the question is one of degree. Surely, a country could not raise the inventive step to a point where no inventions were patentable. Thus, a benchmark is necessary.

In the *Canada–Pharmaceuticals* case, the panel faced an analogous problem; in that case, the question concerned whether right holders had legitimate interests in preventing rivals from generating regulatory review data during the patent period. To determine what the Agreement meant by "legitimate interests,"[33] it canvassed the practice of other WTO states.[34] In the absence of consensus, it deferred to Canada's decision.[35] The meaning of "inventive step" raises somewhat different issues from the problem of identifying the "legitimate interests" of right holders.[36] However, given the absence of definitions in the Agreement or in its negotiation history, a panel assessing the TRIPS compatibility of § 3(d) may have little choice but to consider how the term is defined by other member states.[37] If it did, it would find that many countries differ from India and do award patents on incremental innovation, such as secondary uses of known pharmaceuticals.[38] Even in the United States, which recently raised its inventive step,[39] issues such as the patentability of isomers are decided on a case-by-case basis; such patents are not excluded categorically.[40] At the same time, however, there are at least twelve countries—all developing—with laws that are designed to preclude incremental-innovation patents.[41] Thus, to the extent there is consensus, it is only partial; the DSB could go either way on the question whether India is meeting its obligation to offer patents on "inventions."

C. Comments

On balance, we believe that the appropriate response is to allow India to adopt § 3(d). The generic drug industry is one of the brightest spots in the Indian economy, and one of the world's major sources of inexpensive pharmaceuticals.[42] Constraining India's ability to regulate the terms on which this key industry operates would intrude deeply into its sovereign interests. Furthermore, the pragmatic aspects of the *Canada–Pharmaceuticals* decision should be kept in mind. India may have focused on the pharmaceutical industry because of its importance, but absent evidence to the contrary, there is no reason to believe the legislation was meant to deal only with that industry. As the *Canada–Pharmaceuticals* panel acknowledged, states must deal with problems as they arise in particular technologies. Their doing so is not always discrimination within the meaning of Article 27.1. Because states vary widely in the way that the scientific enterprise is conducted, a similar approach should be taken with regard to the question of India's definition of "invention."

Unlike *Canada–Pharmaceuticals*, we would also allow the public health dimension of the problem to inform the analysis. There is an ambiguity in what the negotiators of the TRIPS Agreement achieved. On the one hand, TRIPS adopted the discrimination provision in order to ensure the availability of product patents for pharmaceuticals. On the other hand, the Agreement and the subsequent Ministerial Declaration at Doha identified public health and access to medicines as prime countervailing concerns. Given the ambivalence inherent in the overall framework, the DSB ought to give substantial deference to local decision making.

The argument for local autonomy is, of course, somewhat attenuated when it is applied in a manner that permits India to supply generic pharmaceutical products outside its own market. Global distribution of low-cost medicines promotes public health values, but it also more acutely implicates international trade. However, concerns over trade distortions are likely overstated. Even with § 3(d), India could lawfully supply only countries that use the compulsory licensing mechanism that Doha made available in Article 31bis, countries where the innovator has declined to seek patent protection, and countries that follow India's lead and adopt similar legislation. The first category is small: very few countries are using the provision because it is too complex and because they have been under considerable political pressure to avoid it.[43] The second category is a function of the economic decisions of the innovator and therefore not India's doing.

That leaves the third category: countries that follow India and raise the inventive step. The concern that others will follow India and create a new norm of inventiveness may, in fact, be the reason for the strident opposition to § 3(d). However, the legitimacy of the Agreement depends on giving countries new to intellectual property protection some flexibility (which developed countries long enjoyed) to tailor the law to their own needs. Indeed, one panel decision has recognized the danger in viewing international norms as frozen by the practices of developed countries.[44] As important, we have seen that the TRIPS Agreement includes mechanisms that create a systemic bias in favor of increasing the level of protection. Allowing emerging countries like India to experiment creates momentum in the opposite direction and brings the international system into a more appropriate balance.

II. Creating New Statutory Exceptions

As Chapter 1 suggested, the scientific enterprise is changing in ways that the TRIPS negotiators may not have anticipated. At one time, science was considered distinct from technology, and intellectual property law was predicated on the existence of a doctrinal boundary between basic and applied research.[45] Increasingly, however, patent law recognizes private claims to core principles of knowledge that are of special significance to basic research. This may reflect the science-intensive nature of modern technology, which generates many products that have a dual character as both "basic" and "applied" science. Alternatively, it may be that changes in the organization of science, including the emergence of research organizations (such as universities) that look to patent rights to support fundamental research put pressure on the system to protect upstream innovations.[46]

The result may be, as Justice Breyer put it, that patent protection begins to "impede rather than 'promote the Progress of Science and useful Arts.'"[47] In most cases, second-comers can invent around patented inventions. Accordingly, patents are rarely true monopolies. Consumers have alternatives to the patented invention, and the patentee cannot control the pace of innovation in the field. However, fundamental building blocks of knowledge cannot be invented around. In such cases, the patent confers power in both product and innovation markets.[48] For example, the patent on an isolated gene can give the patent holder control over the use of, and work related to, that gene. Similarly, a patent on an operating system may constrain all opportunities to create applications that work on that system. With fewer consumer choices, prices rise. And with fewer researchers authorized to tackle problems in the field, fewer advances are made.[49]

After a comprehensive study of the impact of patents on genetic sequences, the Secretary's Advisory Committee on Genes, Health, and Society (SACGHS, a committee established by the U.S. Department of Health and Human Services) concluded that these patents were interfering with the delivery of diagnostic services to patients and with research on hereditary conditions; Congress has since instructed the director of the Patent and Trademark Office to consider the issue.[50] SACGHS made a series of proposals to ameliorate the problems. Among other recommendations were the following:

> The Secretary of Health and Human Services should support and work with the Secretary of Commerce to promote the following statutory changes:
>
> A. The creation of an exemption from liability for infringement of patent claims on genes for anyone making, using, ordering, offering for sale, or selling a test developed under the patent for patient-care purposes.[51]
> B. The creation of an exemption from patent infringement liability for those who use patent-protected genes in the pursuit of research.[52]

These recommendations tackle different, but related, aspects of the upstream patenting problem. The first, which proposes a "diagnostic defense," would permit health care workers to offer gene-based diagnostic testing without the need to obtain approval from the holder of a patent on the isolated gene upon which the test relies. The measure would thus create a market of diagnostic service providers, which would put downward pressure on price, increase the chances that a patient will be able to obtain insurance coverage for testing, and permit doctors and patients to obtain second opinions. The second, "research defense," would allow scientists to use patented genes to learn more about disease at the molecular level and develop new genetic tests and more efficient testing methodologies.

As the Zuhn quotation at the outset of this Chapter suggests, however, these proposals may run afoul of the TRIPS Agreement in that they reduce the opportunity of gene patent holders to exploit particular markets. Accordingly, there is a question whether the measures are narrowly enough tailored to comply with Article 30, the provision permitting members to make exceptions to the rights conferred. As with the way that India altered the inventive step in § 3(d), singling out a particular technology for special treatment also raises a question concerning the nondiscrimination provision of Article 27.

A. The Exceptions Test of Article 30

The DSB has considered the TRIPS Exceptions provisions in three cases, all decided by panels and not appealed to the AB. In *Canada–Pharmaceuticals*, the European Union had alleged that the Canadian regulatory review and stockpiling exceptions (set out earlier in the Chapter) violated TRIPS Articles 27 and 28; Canada defended on the ground that its measures fell within the scope of

Article 30. In *US–110(5)*, the European Union challenged provisions of U.S. copyright law—commonly called the "Irish bar" exception—that permitted certain public performances of musical works without the authorization of the copyright owner. One of these provisions, the "business" exception, granted absolute immunity to bars, restaurants, and other retail establishments under defined sizes and to larger establishments depending on the nature of the equipment used.[53] The second, the "homestyle" exception, was available to the same types of establishments, even if they did not meet the limits of the first provision, so long as the performance occurred through the use of an apparatus of a type commonly found in private homes. However, this second exception was interpreted (implausibly) as applying only to dramatic musical works.[54] The European Union argued that both exceptions intruded on the rights set out in Articles 11 and 11bis of the Berne Convention as incorporated into the TRIPS Agreement by Article 9.1. The United States defended the exceptions as permissible under Article 13 of the TRIPS Agreement, which is a close analogue to Article 30. In the third case, *EC-GI*, the United States alleged that the European Union's geographical indications regulation interfered with the rights guaranteed to trademark holders under Article 16, and the European Union relied on Article 17, the trademark Exceptions clause. As we describe later, that provision is significantly different from the other two.[55]

1. Methodology

To justify the SACGHS measure, the United States would face a multipart test. Each of the TRIPS Exceptions provisions imposes such a test. In the case of Articles 13 and 30, there are three parts; Article 17 is formulated somewhat differently. For patents, the test provides that exceptions are permissible if they (1) are limited, (2) do not unreasonably conflict with a normal exploitation of a patent, and (3) do not unreasonably prejudice the legitimate interests of the patent owner, taking account of the legitimate interests of third parties.

In the two cases involving three-part tests, the panels assumed that the subparts of the multipart tests must be read cumulatively.[56] Accordingly, a measure that fails any one of the prongs is invalid, regardless of how well it meets the concerns expressed in the other prongs. For instance, once Canada's stockpiling exception was found to be insufficiently limited, the *Canada–Pharmaceuticals* panel held it was incompatible with TRIPS. The panel did not consider whether it imposed significant economic injuries on the patent holder or whether the salutary effect on third parties (such as patients) outweighed these costs.[57] And although the *US–110(5)* panel embarked on a thorough assessment of the "business" exception even after it found that the exception failed the first hurdle, the adjudicators did not engage in the common law approach of allowing more of one factor to compensate for less of another.[58] As the following analysis of the SACGHS proposals demonstrates, the cumulative approach is particularly likely to truncate consideration of the important public interests that domestic legislation can serve.

2. Merits

a. *Scope of uses: "limited" exceptions.* If the United States chose to adopt the SACGHS proposals and defend them, it would first be required to demonstrate that the defenses are "limited." The term (and its cognate for copyright, "special") is not defined by the Agreement. The three panels interpreting the Exceptions provisions considered the number of rights set out in Articles 28 for patents, Articles 11 and 11bis of the Berne Convention for copyright, and Article 16 for trademarks, and then they counted the number that were impaired and the number of parties entitled to the benefits of each measure.[59] In *Canada–Pharmaceuticals*, the stockpiling exception was found not to be limited because, during the last six months of the statutory term, it negated all protection under three of the patentee's five guaranteed rights, with no limitations on the quantities produced or the market destination of the products. In contrast, the regulatory review exception was considered limited because the acts permitted (that is, those that were necessary to comply with the regulatory approval process) were narrowly bounded.[60] The *US–110(5)* panel similarly split the difference. The business exception was found to affect too many of the copyright holder's interests to be considered "special."[61] However, the homestyle exception was interpreted as applying only to dramatic musical works, such as opera and operetta, thus giving the exception "a quite narrow scope of application in practice."[62]

The *EC-GI* dispute was handled somewhat differently. To be sure, the panel counted rights. On finding only one right was at issue, and that it intruded only modestly on the exclusivity of trademarks, the panel was inclined to find the exception "limited."[63] Significantly, however, the text of Article 17 included an example ("limited exceptions. . ., such as fair use of descriptive terms"), and the panel used it as a benchmark.[64] Because fair use of descriptive terms can be invoked by an unlimited number of traders with respect to any types of goods or services, and can involve almost any mark, the panel extracted as the relevant measure of "limited" a standard that focused less on numbers and more on the purpose of trademark law: minimizing consumer confusion. The uses of GIs that were permissible under the panel's interpretation of the European Union's law were unlikely to cause much, if any, consumer confusion. Therefore, the restriction on the rights of a trademark owner was considered limited.

On its face, the diagnostic defense resembles the invalid stockpiling and business measures in that each of the exclusive patent rights is affected: making, using, selling, offering to sell, or importing diagnostics relying on patented genes. Thus, the provision may be doomed at the very first stage of the analysis. It is important to note, however, that the diagnostic defense does not curtail these rights across the board: it is only intended to facilitate testing, and only for patient care purposes. When the same inventions are made, used, sold, offered for sale, or imported for therapeutic purposes, or outside the health care context, the exception does not apply. Because genetic diagnosis for a particular disease is a onetime event in a patient's life, diagnostic uses are likely to be a much smaller source of income than therapeutic uses, which typically involve multiple treatments.

But this analysis is somewhat more nuanced than that found in the panel decisions. For example, the *Canada–Pharmaceuticals* panel did not go far beyond the point of counting rights to consider at any level of detail what the rights entailed. In the *US–110(5)* report, the analysis was even more circumscribed. The panel looked only at the rights encompassed by Articles 11 and 11bis—the rights of public performance, communication to the public, and broadcasting to the public.[65] The adjudicators did not consider them in the context of all of the rights the copyright holders retained, including the rights to control reproduction and derivative use, which lie at the core of copyright.

Counting rights may appear to have the objectivity that trade lawyers and the WTO often seek. However, the process takes insufficient notice of the multifaceted nature of intellectual property. Ironically, the panels recognized that creative works can have multiple applications and are enjoyed by different users in differing ways. But unlike the *EC-GI* panel, the *US–110(5)* and *Canada–Pharmaceuticals* panels did not do justice to that complexity by considering the relative economic value and social importance of each use or the question of the value of a particular form of exploitation to users relative to right holders. Because some of these considerations are more naturally encompassed by other subparts of the Exceptions tests,[66] the *Canada–Pharmaceuticals* panel's decision to isolate each of the parts of the inquiry made it even harder to consider those variables in determining whether a defense is limited. If that approach were used in connection with the SACGHS diagnostic defense, the United States would have no opportunity to demonstrate that the value of allowing patients to know their susceptibility to disease overshadows the value of the diagnostics market to right holders or that the profits from the diagnostics market are not critical to spurring innovations in genetic sequencing.

But even under this crabbed, formalistic analysis, the research defense is likely to survive the first hurdle. It is more like the regulatory review exception, which was found to be limited on the theory that it was confined to particular conduct—research.[67] And like the homestyle exception, which benefited only a narrow category of users (those interested in dramatic musical works),[68] this measure is restricted to research scientists in the field of genetics.

b. *Conflict with normal exploitation.* If the DSB were to reach the other parts of Article 30, the United States would next be required to show that the exceptions do not unreasonably conflict with normal exploitation of the patent. Only the *Canada–Pharmaceuticals* and *US–110(5)* panels considered this question because the trademark Exceptions provision at issue in the *EC–GI* dispute does not contain this language. Once again, the diagnostic defense will have a more difficult time than the research defense.

The messages from the two panels were mixed. Although they suggested that normal exploitation involved the exclusion of competition that could detract significantly from economic returns,[69] they accepted the notion that normal exploitation had to be something less than "full" exploitation.[70] However, they did not articulate a genuinely normative vision of "normal." To be sure, both panels offered a definition of "normal" that explicitly encompassed a normative assessment as well as an empirical analysis of what was "regular, usual, typical or ordinary," but neither acted on it.[71] Furthermore, the *Canada–Pharmaceuticals* panel recognized that certain conflicts with normal exploitation might still pass muster as not "unreasonable." But it did not elaborate on what the term "unreasonable" might mean or how it should apply to the dispute.[72] (Since the term is absent from the copyright Exceptions test, the *US–110(5)* panel did not consider it either.)

In *Canada–Pharmaceuticals*, these weaknesses were easy to ignore: the principal effect of the regulatory review exception was to cut short the period of de facto market exclusivity created when a rival was required to generate regulatory data after the patent expired. That period, the panel concluded, was "not a natural or normal consequence of enforcing patent rights."[73] It was the product of a combination of patent laws and the regulatory approval scheme—and therefore not cognizable under the Agreement as a protected form of exploitation. The panel therefore had no need to address normative questions or provide a theory of reasonableness. (The stockpiling exception might have forced the adjudicators to engage with both issues, but they never reached these questions because of the cumulative nature of the Article 30 analysis.)

In contrast, the *US–110(5)* dispute should have required the panel to consider the meaning of "normal" and thus engage in a normative analysis. Instead, however, the panel conducted only an empirical inquiry, counting in lengthy detail the number of restaurants, bars, and musical works that would potentially license the work but for the defense,[74] and extrapolating losses that could, with "a certain degree of likelihood and plausibility . . . acquire considerable economic or practical importance."[75] As Jane Ginsburg has commented, the analysis thus sought only to "anticipate what the empirical situation [would] be, [rather] than [provide] an explanation of what the right holder's markets *should* cover."[76]

If adjudicators were to replicate this narrow approach to analyze the effect of the proposed diagnostic defense, they would likely conclude that it would conflict with normal exploitation. As a matter of empirics, it is clear that patent holders currently extract economic advantage from the diagnostics market through exclusive licensing. Were the United States to adopt the SACGHS proposal, these fees would likely drop. However, under a truly normative reading, the result might be different because the DSB would be required to consider whether patent holders *should* have a right to control access to alternative testing services and prevent patients from securing insurance coverage or second opinions.

The research defense could also be considered to interfere with normal exploitation. As the SACGHS Report found, patent holders are asserting rights in that market as well.[77] Intriguingly, however, the *Canada–Pharmaceuticals* panel recognized that "[t]he specific forms of patent exploitation are not static . . . for to be effective exploitation must adapt to changing forms of competition due to technological development and the evolution of marketing practices."[78] The panel never explained what this meant. However, the statement could be read to permit members to begin granting patents to upstream innovation while ensuring, through a new defense, that these rights do not chill further research activity. Indeed, without the possibility of constructing new defenses, states might be reluctant to expand intellectual property rights in the first place lest that precluded them from preserving an appropriate overall balance.

c. *Unreasonable prejudice to legitimate interests.* If the adjudicators were to assess the SACGHS proposals under the third step of Article 30, both the diagnostic and the research defenses would likely be regarded as compliant. Articles 30 and 13 are similar with regard to this step of the Exceptions provision, except that Article 13 makes no explicit reference to the legitimate interests of third parties. Both the *Canada–Pharmaceuticals* and the *US–110(5)* panel acknowledged the third step involved a normative assessment.[79] However, despite recognizing that economic arguments were "incomplete and thus conservative,"[80] the *US–110(5)* panel merely reiterated its arithmetic arguments.

In contrast, the *Canada–Pharmaceuticals* panel made good on its promise to consider the challenged measure from a normative perspective. After clarifying that legitimate interests were not coextensive with legal rights,[81] it searched for a benchmark by which to assess the legitimate interests that should not suffer unreasonable prejudice. Finding no standard in the text or in the negotiation history of TRIPS, it used state practices as illustrative examples. Focusing on national laws permitting the use of patented products for scientific experimentation, it found the regulatory review exception (essentially an experimentation defense running in favor of generic drug producers) "justifiable in the sense that [it was] supported by relevant public policies or other social norms."[82] Moreover, while some countries with regulatory review exceptions lengthened the term of the patent as a trade-off to patent owners, the panel found no consensus on this practice. In the absence of agreement within the "community of governments," it was willing to accept Canada's choice to permit use for the purpose of regulatory review without extending the patent term.[83] Thus, the panel held that the patent holder's interest in stopping these practices was not "legitimate." Although the panel recognized that third party interests could also be taken into account, it did not reach the issue and thus avoided ruling on Canada's assertion that these included general societal interests, including those associated with health care.[84]

The *EC-GI* case was once again qualitatively different. First, the panel understood the clause of Article 17 referring to "legitimate interests" as a "proviso," rather than as an additional step in the analysis.[85] Formally, therefore, its analysis of legitimate interests was relevant to the question of whether the exception was limited. Second, the fair use example in Article 17 was available to inform the panel's judgment.[86] Third, it took a close look at how the tension between trademarks and GIs played out in practice.[87] Finally, the panel considered the interest of third parties, which it defined to include consumers.[88] Finding only three problematic instances of concurrent use of GIs and trademarks, and noting a provision in the European Union's law to accommodate trademark owners, the panel determined that the EU regulation took their legitimate interests into account.[89]

Given the close attention that the panels paid to normative considerations as informed by state practices, both SACGHS proposals stand a chance of satisfying the third step. As noted earlier, SACGHS advanced numerous policy reasons to justify the diagnostic defense. These reflect the interests of patent holders in preserving markets for exploitation of the patent, as well as the interests of doctors, patients, and societal interests in health. Several other nations have grappled with the same problem. The contours of their legislation typically differ from the SACGHS proposal. For example, the European Patent Convention excludes diagnostics from patentability, but the measure applies only to processes (and not to products used in those processes) and only to procedures performed directly on the patient's body (for instance, with a stethoscope).[90] However, in the absence of consensus, a panel may well defer to the policy choice of the United States.

The research defense is on even firmer ground. As the *Canada–Pharmaceuticals* panel recognized, Article 30 was intended to encompass a set of existing national exceptions, specifically including "acts done for experimental purposes."[91] Furthermore, many member states have research exceptions that cover all patents.[92] To be sure, they are somewhat more limited in scope, covering only research done on the patented invention, not research using the invention. Once again, however, in the absence of true consensus, the panel should defer to the U.S. position.

B. The Nondiscrimination Clause of Article 27.1

Somewhat surprisingly, even if the United States could justify the SACGHS proposals under Article 30, it would also face a challenge rooted in the technological neutrality principle of Article 27. In *Canada–Pharmaceuticals*, Canada argued that Article 30 alone regulated the permissibility of exceptions to patent rights under TRIPS.[93] Thus, any provision that met the criteria of Article 30 would be exempt from the requirement of technological neutrality. However, the panel disagreed:

> Article 27.1 prohibits discrimination as to enjoyment of "patent rights" without qualifying that term. Article 30 exceptions are explicitly described as "exceptions to the exclusive rights conferred by a patent" and contain no indication that any exemption from non-discrimination rules is intended.[94]

In other words, the panel read Article 27.1 as a structural provision, part of the fabric of the Agreement as a whole, which can be transposed to the analysis of other provisions.[95]

If Article 27 does apply, both SACGHS proposals are vulnerable to challenge, as both apply only to one technology: gene patents. As we saw in the case of § 3(d) of the Indian law, the DSB has acknowledged that a problem could arise in one area before it arises in others. It has therefore shifted the burden of proof on the question of discrimination, requiring the complainant to show that the challenged measure is not susceptible to general application. In this dispute, however, it would be relatively easy for a challenger to make that showing because in both measures, only genes and gene patents are mentioned. In the case of the diagnostics defense, the United States might argue that the defense includes only genes because only gene patents interfere so significantly with social welfare. Thus, it is, in fact, a rule of general applicability. It could not, however, adopt the same tactic for the research defense because patents can interfere with research in all fields of technology.

The United States could, however, use a different strategy for the research defense. It could circumvent the Article 27.1 challenge entirely by drafting the defense to cover research on all patented inventions.[96] However, were the United States to take that tack, *Article 30* would then prove a more formidable obstacle. The prior analysis, and in particular the panel's treatment of the homestyle exception in the *US–110(5)* case, suggests that a measure that implicates several rights is more likely to be considered "limited" if only a few right holders are affected.[97] Thus, the broader the United States draws the research defense to comply with Article 27.1 and the more researchers receive its benefit, the less likely it will be considered sufficiently narrow to comply with Article 30.

This result is perverse. If the technological neutrality principle applies across the board, then it requires states to enact broader measures than they regard as necessary to meet their needs. The outcome conflicts with the norm contained in Article 30 that expressly requires the availability of exceptions to be evaluated in terms of whether they are "limited." A targeted exemption that differentiated among types of invention would limit a patentee's rights only in areas where there was a perceived imbalance between public and private rights. A formalist commitment to technological neutrality is thus inconsistent with a purposive reading of the TRIPS Agreement.

C. Other Considerations: Health

Were the United States so inclined, it could also argue that because the SACGHS proposals are intended to improve health care, they deserve special treatment. First, as was argued in the *Canada–Pharmaceuticals* case, the United States could suggest that both Articles 27.1 and 30 should be interpreted with health concerns in mind. Second, for the diagnostics defense, it could rely on Article 27.3(a), which permits members to entirely exclude from patentability "diagnostic, therapeutic and surgical methods for the treatment of humans or animals."

As suggested earlier, the first strategy is difficult to evaluate because, post-Doha, the question whether health care is relevant to the interpretation of the Agreement as a whole is unresolved. It is equally impossible to predict how the Article 27.3 argument would fare as there is no dispute resolution proceeding on point. One issue is whether the defense contemplated by SACGHS fits within the exclusion. For genetic diagnostics, the physician takes a sample from the patient and sends it to a laboratory for analysis. But as noted earlier, the term "diagnostic" could be given a more limited interpretation, involving only procedures performed directly on the patient's body. Adjudicators inclined to consider how other states have proceeded may therefore reject the United States' interpretation, despite the obvious limitations on domestic legal experimentation that this approach entails.

As troublesome is the question whether Article 27.3 permits member states to take action less drastic than excluding diagnostics from the scope of patentability. A defense to infringement has much to recommend it. It is more favorable to inventors than outright exclusion. Furthermore, it preserves incentives to invest in identifying and characterizing genes because it allows patent holders to earn profits in the therapeutic sector, which may well be the more valuable market. It also means that patents can be used for other purposes, such as to attract investors and collaborators.[98] In contrast, an exclusion would eradicate all of the benefits of patenting. Recognizing the "lesser included" defense to infringement also permits states to deal selectively with only those uses that pose particular difficulties. Thus, this approach also recognizes the multifaceted nature of intellectual property and the variety of ways in which knowledge-intensive products can be enjoyed and rights over them exploited. Because this reading gives states more tools for balancing the rights of users against those of innovators, a neofederalist vision of the Agreement would favor this interpretation.

At the same time, however, all three panel decisions suggest that this reading is unlikely. The adjudicators were literalists and formalists. If the text specifies exclusion, then it is likely they will take the position that if a state is concerned enough with gene patents, it must deem genes unpatentable. A narrow reading is also consistent with a view of TRIPS as structured to protect existing levels of intellectual property protection. Because it requires states to take a very large step, with potentially severe repercussions for health care, the all-or-nothing interpretation decreases the likelihood that a state will take any action at all.

It is not unknown for international instruments to adopt a provision that offers member states circumscribed choices. But the extent to which that choice is circumscribed is inevitably informed by the nature of the overall agreement; the TRIPS Agreement, even in provisions that are not in optional language, reserves substantial choice to member states. This can be contrasted, for example, with optional provisions in EU harmonization directives. Article 5(2) of the European Trademark Directive, which allows (but does not require) member states to afford dilution protection to certain marks against use on dissimilar goods, has been interpreted by the European Court of Justice as also offering such protection against uses on similar goods.[99] Notwithstanding that an EU member state could offer *no* dilution protection, the Court later held that once a state decides to offer any dilution protection it could do so only in full compliance with the expanded reading that the Court had given to the provision. It could not opt for the lesser included option.[100] But this opinion was rendered in the context of a system where comprehensive harmonization of registered trademark law had been effected and under a default assumption of common EU rules. International law is not the same as EU law, because the international system is of a different character than the European Union. Common market-driven harmonization within a homogeneous regional grouping requires more tightly defined obligations and necessarily intrudes to a greater extent on national sovereignty.[101] Indeed, this point is driven home by the fact that EU member states have formally ceded sovereignty to a standing set of powerful governmental institutions that are quite different from the WTO in terms of the scope of their authority and their relationship to domestic institutions and lawmaking. As we have shown in Part I, the TRIPS Agreement is also quite different from EU law. It proceeds on the premise of national choice, and thus lesser included options should be available to WTO member states, provided of course that the option selected does not otherwise violate the Agreement.

D. Comments

As the opening quotation suggested, neither of the SACGHS proposals is likely to survive scrutiny if the interpretive mode utilized in *Canada–Pharmaceuticals* and *US–110(5)* is adopted. Both decisions essentially took an accountant's approach to the issues, counting rights, calculating the value of "lost" markets, and extrapolating from existing statistics the value of potential future markets. Neither panel fully appreciated the complexity of creative works. Neither panel recognized that the value to users and to producers could differ, and that a method of exploitation of real significance to a particular user group could be of minor importance to the right holder. Neither panel gave any indication it understood what scholars have traditionally called the "delicate balance" that intellectual property law must strike to motivate knowledge production without simultaneously chilling knowledge acquisition.[102]

The *EC-GI* panel was somewhat better in this respect. It did less counting and more probing into the actual harm that trademark holders would suffer as a result of concurrent use of the geographical terms in their marks. It also considered the measure as a whole, allowing the interpretation of the provision to be informed by all of the component parts the drafters thought relevant. However, the *EC-GI* panel was at a distinct advantage: the specific fair use example provided by Article 17 guided its analysis. Going forward, drafters would be well served to consider the difference examples can make. They illuminate the normative component of the analysis, which adjudicators may otherwise miss, ignore, or minimize.

As important, examples create benchmarks. In the absence of a standard, the DSB is likely to consult existing state practices. There are clearly benefits to that approach. States are likely to take into account the various interests implicated by intellectual property legislation. By incorporating their practices into the interpretation of international principles, adjudicators almost automatically bring a normative dimension into the analysis. Moreover, looking to the states is at the heart of the Brandeisian notion of the states as laboratories. And as Rochelle Dreyfuss and Andy Lowenfeld suggested, "[D]omestic practices of member states . . . are relevant not because they apply of their own force, but because they shed light on two significant issues: the understanding of the parties when the Agreement was signed, and the practicalities of requiring compliance [as requested by the complainant]."[103]

At the same time, there are dangers in relying too heavily on national practices. It is likely to result in privileging developed countries, with long histories of intellectual property protection, vis-à-vis members who must devise their laws in a post-TRIPS environment. Of course, international law could develop interpretive mechanisms to ameliorate this problem. For example, Larry Helfer has argued that any analysis of state practice should consciously look to the laws of states at every stage of development.[104] (Indeed, this was the approach we took in the previous example, where we suggested consideration of the laws of both developed and less developed countries in interpreting the term "invention.") As important, the intellectual property literature includes a rich body of intellectual property theory, and the opening for normative assessment provides a vehicle for adjudicators to use this scholarship to develop international law. Because this literature is likely to take account of technological changes sooner than a large number of states can adjust their practices, reliance on scholarship also offers the DSB a way to ensure that the Agreement is not read as frozen in time.

We are not the only commentators to note that the cumulative nature of the inquiry accentuates these problems by cutting off the analysis before reaching the final prong of the test.[105] For example, in copyright cases, if the challenged provision was not considered "limited," adjudicators would never reach the second step of the Article 13 test. Accordingly, they would never have occasion to follow the normative approach we propose for interpreting "normal exploitation."[106] Similarly, in trademark and patent disputes, decision makers would not consider the interests of "third parties," even though TRIPS drafters made it an explicit requirement of the analysis and the *EC-GI* panel interpreted the term capaciously.[107]

The panels' failure to construe the Exceptions provisions in a manner that allows for consideration of the public interest was compounded by their unwillingness to take serious account of the trade-related aspect of the TRIPS Agreement. Although the complainant won on the stockpiling measure in *Canada–Pharmaceuticals* and on the business exception in *US–110(5)*, the challenged measures were factually quite different. The United States had permitted rebroadcasts of music in small establishments *within the United States*. Since there was no possibility of re-rebroadcast abroad, the potential loss in terms of trade was extremely limited. It consisted only of the claim that without the exception local U.S. establishments would have paid licensing fees for the relevant rebroadcasts. In contrast, Canada was apparently permitting generic drug companies to stockpile drugs for sale *around the world*; accordingly, Canada's laws had a potentially serious impact on global trade in pharmaceuticals. Thus, while the two panels arguably reached the right results, they did so, in part, for the wrong reasons. Had the adjudicators paid closer attention to impact on world trade (rather than on rotely counting rights), they would have left states with more room to maneuver. In particular, emerging economies would benefit from such an approach. If complaints about activities with only local effects were regarded skeptically, developing countries would have more leeway to provide their populations with easier access to educational materials and training opportunities. Because their manufacturing capacities are modest, raising the inventive step, adopting new defenses, or taking other novel approaches would be less likely to affect world trade in a meaningful way (and this would be especially true if they also made demonstrable efforts to confine distribution to intrastate trade). While the DSB could certainly be called upon to evaluate such actions, taking international trade effects into account would correlate the degree of flexibility a country enjoys with its stage of development (as measured by its influence on trade in knowledge goods).[108]

Finally, there is the question whether it is appropriate to view the nondiscrimination provision of Article 27.1 structurally. To be sure, nondiscrimination is a cornerstone of the both the intellectual property and the trade system. But nondiscrimination based on nationality—national treatment—is not the same as nondiscrimination as to field of technology. An efficient global market requires equal treatment of all traders, but nothing so cosmic turns on treating all fields of technology alike, and the placement of these provisions within the Agreement is a clue to their disparate significance. The obligation to accord national treatment is found in Part I of the Agreement, General Provisions and Basic Principles; nondiscrimination by field of technology is in Part II, Standards Concerning the Availability, Scope and Use of Intellectual Property Rights, and applies only to patents.

But the reasons for rejecting the structural approach to Article 27.1 go well beyond textual formalism. Many of the core doctrines of patent law (inventiveness, disclosure) revolve around the knowledge of a person with ordinary skill in the art; these doctrines necessarily distinguish by fields of technology. More important, panels considering this form of discrimination would do well to think of the provision as a cross-subsidy: the favorable treatment that one field receives redounds to the benefit of others. Cross-subsidies can, however, be dangerous because they burden one arena with the problems of another. Requiring fields to be treated alike with respect to the Exception provision is particularly problematic because it negates the ability of states to provide targeted responses to local concerns. Moreover, because this approach requires states to apply the same solution to every field (whether needed or not), it creates an impediment to recalibrating the level of protection. As with the formalistic interpretation of Article 27.3, the hierarchical approach to Article 27.1 turns TRIPS into an engine for protecting producer interests at the expense of other values.

III. Varying the Right to Relief

As suggested in Chapter 1, the Knowledge Economy is characterized by fundamental changes in the organization of information production. Among other things, products have become more complex, with the result that many more patent rights must be negotiated in order to obtain freedom to operate. Transaction costs rise, double marginalization problems proliferate, and there are more potential holdouts to block product development. In some fields, patent holders have formed pools to deal with these issues.[109] But there are areas in which third parties have begun to purchase patent rights. Some of these "nonpracticing patentees"—or "nonpracticing entities" (NPEs)—may perform an aggregation function similar to pools, but other NPEs are opportunists: they buy patents of doubtful validity in the hope of finding a complex product that can be said to infringe. They then sue the producer, hoping that they will recover damages that reflect the cost the defendant would incur if required to change the product to avoid the patent.[110] In industries in which it is difficult to efficiently search the prior art, the ransom NPEs can extract becomes a tax on innovation.

In *eBay Inc. v. MercExchange*,[111] the United States Supreme Court was faced with such a ransom situation: a patent on a business method that constituted a small component of a large system (the popular internet auction site) was found to be infringed. The trial court denied a motion for a permanent injunction, but the United States Court of Appeal for the Federal Circuit reversed, taking the position that injunctive relief can be denied at the end of the case only in exceptional circumstances. Vacating the Federal Circuit's judgment, the Supreme Court stated:

> [A] plaintiff seeking a permanent injunction must satisfy a four-factor test before a court may grant [injunctive] relief. A plaintiff must demonstrate: (1) that it has suffered an irreparable injury; (2) that remedies available at law, such as monetary damages, are inadequate to compensate for that injury; (3) that, considering the balance of hardships between the plaintiff and defendant, a remedy in equity is warranted; and (4) that the public interest would not be disserved by a permanent injunction.[112]

In a separate opinion, Justice Kennedy pointed to specific areas where injunctive relief could be withheld. These included where "[a]n industry has developed in which firms use patents not as a basis for producing and selling goods but, instead, primarily for obtaining licensing fees" (the NPE situation); "[w]hen the patented invention is but a small component of the product the companies seek to produce and the threat of an injunction is employed simply for undue leverage in negotiations"; and in cases involving business method patents, where the patents are often of "suspect validity."[113]

Justice Kennedy's approach could have even broader applicability. It could, for example, provide a partial solution to the problems engendered by gene patents. Whole genome sequencing, which requires learning a patient's entire genetic endowment, would require a multiplicity of patent licenses. A holdout on one patent—"a small component of the product"—could be denied injunctive relief, thereby allowing the practice of personalized medicine to go forward. In the public interest, courts could similarly refrain from enjoining laboratories offering second opinions when the patent holder refuses to authorize such use. Commentators have offered other suggestions: courts could withhold injunctive relief against open innovators—those who serve the public by putting their advances in a domain where their developments are freely accessible,[114] or from those who fail to disclose relevant patents to standard-setting organizations.[115]

Indeed, this is not the first time that the U.S. Supreme Court has suggested that injunctive relief can be an inappropriate remedy for intellectual property infringement. In *Campbell v. Acuff Rose Music, Inc.*,[116] the Court found a parody of a copyrighted song to be fair use. However, it dropped a footnote suggesting another limit on injunctions:

> Because the fair use enquiry often requires close questions of judgment as to the extent of permissible borrowing in cases involving parodies (or other critical works), courts may also wish to bear in mind that the goals of the copyright law . . . are not always best served by automatically granting injunctive relief when parodists are found to have gone beyond the bounds of fair use. . . .
>
> [In such cases,] there may be a strong public interest in the publication of the secondary work [and] the copyright owner's interest may be adequately protected by an award of damages for whatever infringement is found.[117]

As the third quotation at the beginning of this Chapter suggests, however, there is a question whether this approach complies with the TRIPS Agreement. In particular, *eBay* could be said to violate the requirement of Article 44, which states that "judicial authorities shall have the authority to order a party to desist from an infringement." In addition, the denial of injunctive relief could be considered a type of compulsory license, requiring the United States to comply with Article 31 of the TRIPS Agreement.

A. The Applicability of the Remedies Provision of Article 44

The DSB has yet to consider a problem like the one presented by *eBay*. The closest dispute is *China–Enforcement*, which, among other things, addressed the manner in which China handled infringing and counterfeit trademarked goods. In that case, the United States complained that China was failing to fulfill the requirements of two provisions of the TRIPS Agreement, Articles 46 and 59.

Article 59 mandates that "competent authorities shall have the authority to order the destruction or disposal of infringing goods in accordance with the principles set out in Article 46." And Article 46 provides: "In order to create an effective deterrent to infringement, the judicial authorities shall have the authority to order that goods that they have found to be infringing be, without compensation of any sort, disposed of outside the channels of commerce in such a manner as to avoid any harm caused to the right holder, or ... destroyed."

The United States claimed that Chinese law violated these provisions because the basic law (and associated regulations) provided that the customs authorities should give infringing goods to social public welfare organizations or sell them to the right holder at an agreed price; if the goods could not be disposed of in those ways, the authorities were to eradicate the infringing features and auction the goods. Only when the infringing features could not be eradicated was customs to destroy the goods.[118] The United States argued that auction did not remove the goods from channels of commerce and neither did distribution because welfare organizations might sell, rather than use, the goods they received. Since these goods could be defective, they could harm the trademark holder's reputation. And forcing the right holder to buy goods it had never authorized likewise caused harm.

1. Methodology

The *eBay* case and the *China Enforcement* panel report raise a methodological problem not present in our analysis of the initiatives discussed earlier: in both situations the contested rule leaves room for discretion on the part of courts or enforcement authorities. In those contexts, it may be tempting to mount a challenge to specific exercises of discretion. However, the TRIPS Agreement does not guarantee perfect administration of national law in every instance. Furthermore, the AB has made clear that panels should not assume that member states will exercise discretion inconsistently with their TRIPS obligations.[119] Thus, it should not be possible to bring a complaint until a pattern or practice emerges that reveals the operation of the rule in practice. Moreover, the *China–Enforcement* panel put a heavy burden of proof on the United States. For example, the panel required the United States to provide examples of situations in which customs authorities donated substandard goods to welfare organizations,[120] to prove that donation could cause reputational injuries,[121] and to show that the authorities lacked the discretion to refuse to use an alternative that could harm the right holder.[122] The United States lost on that aspect of its trademark claim in part because it furnished insufficient proof.[123]

For *eBay*, this likely means that a challenger would be required to show how courts have interpreted the Supreme Court's four-part test. For example, the complainant might show that the courts of appeals had adopted rigid rules that systematically limit the discretionary authority of district courts. Thus, if courts were to decide that NPEs should never be enjoined, that might raise a compliance issue. NPEs may be performing a useful function by adding liquidity to the patent market and by shifting the cost of pooling away from patent holders to a commercial venture. Accordingly, precluding NPEs from obtaining injunctive relief in all circumstances could have a significant impact on the full enjoyment of patent rights. However, absent articulation of an absolute rule, furnishing proof could be extremely difficult. Because many disputes settle as soon as liability is determined, the number of cases that reach the remedial stage is small. These cases are also subject to selection effects. The closest are the least likely to settle, but they are also the least likely to set a clear pattern for the DSB to evaluate.

2. Merits

It may also be difficult to challenge *eBay* on the merits. In contrast to the *Canada–Pharmaceuticals* and *US–110(5)* panels, the adjudicators in *China–Enforcement* took a markedly more deferential attitude. China is one of the few developing countries that have been respondents in TRIPS disputes, and it was sued soon after it entered the WTO; perhaps it argued more vigorously for state autonomy interests than had respondents that are more developed. Or perhaps the panel responded to the politics of the situation or to the criticism of the earlier panel reports. More likely, however, the decision reflects the very different character of the remedial provisions of the Agreement. These provisions give member states considerable scope.[124] Thus, Article 44 requires that judicial authorities have "the authority to order a party to desist from an infringement"; it does not mandate that the relief be awarded. As the *China–Enforcement* panel put it: "The obligation is to 'have' authority, [it is] not an obligation to 'exercise' authority."[125]

The other enforcement measures are to similar effect. All the remedial provisions contain the formulation "the judicial authorities shall have the authority." Furthermore, Article 41, on General Obligations, clarifies that these provisions do not oblige states to devote more resources to the enforcement of intellectual property rights than to other laws.[126] And the very first provision of TRIPS emphasizes the point: Article 1.1 gives members freedom to determine the appropriate method of implementing the Agreement within their own legal systems and practice.

Nonetheless, the enforcement provisions do not give states an entirely free hand, and the procedure envisioned by *eBay* may be inadequate. Article 41.1 sets out the key general requirements: effective and expeditious action, and remedies sufficient to deter future infringement. The procedural requirements are not problematic. U.S. courts may be slow, but they are equally slow in all kinds of cases; intellectual property disputes are thus treated just like cases involving other legal regimes. The deterrence issue is more difficult. The four-factor test set out in *eBay* requires the court to consider whether the right holder could be adequately compensated with money damages. But adequate compensation may not be enough to deter infringement. After all, if a user is in no danger of being enjoined and is required to do no more than pay the ordinary licensing fee, there is little point in avoiding infringement. Taking the risk of getting caught and sued would cost no more—and could cost less—than negotiating a license and paying royalties.

The problem may, in fact, be even more fundamental. The rationale that appears to underlie *eBay*—and certainly lurks in the *Campbell* footnote—is that there are reasons, grounded in social welfare considerations, to *not* deter certain acts that technically constitute infringement. For example, Justice Kennedy's decision in *eBay* suggests that while the discretionary rule is partly designed to control abuse, it also tolerates a degree of infringement in order to mitigate the effect of possibly invalid patents. Similarly, the *Campbell* Court footnote stands for the proposition that as between denying the public certain desirable works and tolerating infringement, the Court would choose the latter.

Still, the United States could prevail. The enforcement provisions are cast in general terms; the essence of Article 1.1 is that member states control the means of implementation, and the DSB could take the view that the enforcement provisions merely regulate the *system* of relief and do not dictate particular remedies for specific cases. Thus, the argument would be that so long as a member state offers at least the palette of remedies denominated in TRIPS, and the mix deters infringement overall, it complies with both the general and the specific enforcement obligations. The United States could justify tolerating some infringement with the *eBay* rule because it effectively deters infringement in other ways, such as through the use of treble damages in certain cases of willful infringement.

Whether this argument would succeed depends (once again) on the granularity with which the DSB reads the provisions. If Article 41.1 requires deterrence in every class of cases, then the *eBay* approach is vulnerable to challenge. But if the courts are more nuanced, then the approach could survive. For example, in the NPE situation, if courts take account of the function the plaintiff-NPE plays (as aggregator or troll), whether the NPE invests in research and development, and whether it strategically delays asserting claims to maximize their ransom value, then the decision to deny relief is, essentially, a compulsory license designed to correct abuse.

C. The Application of the Compulsory Licensing Provision of Article 31

Conceptualized as a compulsory license, *eBay* is also vulnerable to a challenge based on Article 31. (If *eBay* were extended to copyright, consistent with the hints in *Campbell*, it would be analyzed under Article 13 and underlying provisions of the Berne Convention.)[127] Of course, were a panel to elevate form over substance, it may reject the notion that it must go beyond the remedial provisions in its analysis.[128] However, given the common characterization of the *eBay* rule as a compulsory license, it is likely a panel would find it necessary to expand its analysis in this way.

Article 31 allows members to permit use without the right holder's authorization in specified circumstances. Relevant here are the requirements to consider applications on their individual merits and with a right of judicial review; after efforts to obtain permission from the right holder; limited to the authorized purpose; and terminable when the circumstance leading to the authorization ends. The provision also requires the payment of "adequate remuneration in the circumstances of each case, taking into account the economic value of the authorization."[129] *eBay* clearly fulfills most of these requirements. Injunctive relief is denied only after a trial and full consideration of the question whether injunctive relief should be denied. Both the decision to deny the injunction and the award of other relief is subject to appellate review.

However, in many of the cases where *eBay* potentially applies, no efforts are made to obtain permission before the infringement begins. Indeed, in almost all of them, the core problem is that permission is all but impossible to obtain: for complex products, there are too many patents to conduct a comprehensive search; in the case of standard-setting organizations, the patent holder may have withheld relevant information during the negotiation process; and in open innovation, the activity is too decentralized to monitor effectively.[130] Significantly, however, although the other requirements of Article 31 use the term "shall," the provision on permission uses the term "may" ("such use may only be permitted if . . .").[131] The *China–Enforcement* panel paid close attention to the formulation of the provisions it interpreted. It looked at each sentence in the remedial provisions to see which were subject to limiting principles, and it carefully defined relevant terms ("authority," "infringing features," "outside").[132] Notably, it paid special attention to the use of the terms "shall" and "may."[133] Thus, the use of "may" in this provision can be read as allowing states to eliminate the need to obtain permission when it would be impractical, or, as in many of these contexts, impossible, to obtain.

The issue thus boils down to money and to the meaning of the phrase "adequate remuneration taking into account the economic value of the authorization." Arguably, the term "adequate remuneration" is meant to suggest that right holders should receive the compensation they would subjectively consider adequate.[134] However, that approach would make it unlikely that any compulsory licensing scheme could survive TRIPS scrutiny. A right holder opposed to the use could always demand a price the compulsory licensee could not afford to pay. If the underlying rationale is to permit uses that are in the public interest despite the right holder's opposition, then it is necessary to adopt an objective standard, tied to the context of the use the state is seeking to promote. For example, and as we have suggested in other writing, when compulsory licenses are used to address concerns in developing countries, the price should be determined by local economic conditions.[135] In the NPE case, where the patent is a small component of a product the plaintiff is not offering, the adequacy of remuneration should be measured by the value of the patent's inventive contribution and not by the value of the product or process as a whole.

Whether damages calculated in that way are sufficient to meet the requirements of Article 31 would also turn on how the DSB interprets the phrase "taking into account the economic value of the authorization." In keeping with the literalism of the *Canada–Pharmaceuticals* panel and the economic myopia of *US–110(5)*, "economic value" could be read to exclude consideration of the social value that the *eBay* Court was seeking to further. However, the phrase "taking into account" implies that other considerations are also relevant. Such a reading is of a piece with the *China–Enforcement* report, in which the panel recognized the distinction between the authority to consider a particular remedy and requiring its invariable application. Moreover, it is consistent with the normative understanding of intellectual property law. As Sam Ricketson suggested in connection with his analysis of exceptions and limitations, "[E]conomic considerations provide a useful starting point . . . for analysis [but it is then necessary] to add in the other values or interests of a more public kind."[136]

Other potential uses of the *eBay* rule are closer to the line of incompatibility with TRIPS. Denying injunctive relief to take account of "suspect validity" is a cheap way to solve the problem of low-quality patents. However, TRIPS guarantees a set of rights to the holders of all patents that have not been invalidated. Thus, it is arguable that the only solution available to members concerned with quality is to improve the examination system. In cases that differ from the NPE example in that the right holder is also exploiting the market, the measure of damages might need to be assessed somewhat differently from the method we propose in order to satisfy Article 31.

C. Comments

Partly because of difficulties of proof and partly because of differences in the texts of the provisions, it appears that member states can better tailor their laws to their needs by giving authorities discretion over remediation than they can by tackling problems directly, through substantive law. In one sense, the result is salutary. As Justice Kennedy stated in his conclusion to *eBay*, "The equitable discretion over injunctions, granted by the Patent Act, is well suited to allow courts to adapt to the rapid technological and legal developments in the patent system."[137] However, Justice Kennedy did not likely mean to exclude the possibility of more systematic adaptation of patent law through legislative initiative. Legislation has benefits over litigation. Although broad participation can stall change, legislative hearings give the authorities more viewpoints to ponder. Furthermore, legislators can consider the system as a whole and make complementary changes in other provisions. It would be odd to consider the TRIPS Agreement as choosing, on behalf of all WTO members, between legislative and adjudicative responses to new problems.

It is also necessary to take a realistic attitude toward the question of compensation for unauthorized use. The intellectual property industries tend to calculate losses by assuming that every infringer would buy the product at the right holder's price.[138] The argument has significant strategic value, but it often falters on reality.[139] In the cases where compulsory licensing is proposed, there are obstacles to such purchases: the user could not afford to pay or could not negotiate a license. If there is a public interest in permitting the uses, then a more realistic view of damages is in order. More important, the Doha Round recognized Article 31 as a significant part of the compromise between the interests of North and South, as well as among user groups and producers; the legitimacy of the Agreement was thus thought to depend on making that provision work. Adjudicators should approach its interpretation with the same commitment.

The *China–Enforcement* case, the most detailed panel decision thus far on enforcement, follows an approach that most closely approximates our neofederalist vision of the TRIPS Agreement. Likewise, the AB in *Havana Club* adopted a relatively narrow reading of Article 42, which generally requires that civil judicial procedures must be "made available" to enable right holders to protect against infringement. Reversing a panel determination that the U.S. Cuban Embargo regulations violated Article 42, the AB stressed that "[t]he TRIPS Agreement reserves . . . a degree of discretion to Members on this, taking into account 'differences in national legal systems,'" noting that "no Member's national system of civil judicial procedures will be identical to that of another Member."[140] More particularly, it rejected the EC argument that "a statute must not limit the discretion of the courts by directing the courts to examine certain substantive requirements before, and to the exclusion of, other substantive requirements," finding that "there is nothing in the procedural obligations of Article 42 that prevents a Member, in such a situation, from legislating whether or not its courts must examine each and every requirement of substantive law at issue before making a ruling."[141]

This result should not be surprising as enforcement is an area in which deference to national policy choices is explicit in the Agreement. More important, because enforcement enlists the machinery of the state, it acutely implicates the allocation of government resources. That concern underlies the admonition in Article 41.5 that the state need not treat enforcement of intellectual property more favorably than legal rights generally. However, that principle, although particularly significant for enforcement, has broader application. Article 41.5 is a specific application of the general principle articulated in Article 1.1, which recognizes that the legal systems and legal practices of WTO members can be very different.[142]

Observations

This Chapter studied three responses to the changing dynamics of the Knowledge Economy. Our analysis of their compatibility with TRIPS reveals a series of recurring interpretive challenges. Panels must determine the degree of granularity at which to examine compliance, establish benchmarks against which to measure deviations from TRIPS standards, and account for the diverse normative components of intellectual property law. None of these tasks is easy.

Decisions on granularity necessarily implicate sensitive questions concerning sovereignty. To determine the appropriate level of scrutiny to give national lawmaking, a panel must decide the extent to which member states agreed to an international norm over national autonomy. This cannot be achieved using a formalistic approach, such as the one adopted by the *US–110(5)* panel, which anatomized the Exceptions provision, mistook accounting for judging, and also relied heavily on dictionary definitions.[143] With a more holistic approach to the provisions of the Agreement, adjudicators would stand a better chance of identifying the space that member states agreed to reserve to themselves. For example, had the *Canada–Pharmaceuticals* panel rejected the cumulative approach to Article 30, it would have reached the countervailing considerations mentioned in the third step of the test. As a result, it would have better understood that the Exceptions provisions were included in order to give states leeway to balance proprietary interests against access considerations.

Benchmarks determine the parameters within which states can strike what the U.S. Supreme Court called the "delicate balance the law attempts to maintain between inventors, who rely on the promise of the law to bring the invention forth, and the public, which should be encouraged to pursue innovations, creations, and new ideas beyond the inventor's exclusive rights."[144] As we saw, the *EC-GI* panel had the easiest time on this issue because the Agreement provided an example of a permissible exception ("fair use of descriptive terms"). Similarly, the *China–Enforcement* panel had the curious wording of the remedies provisions ("judicial authorities shall have the authority") to guide its decision on the nature of the states' commitment to award particular forms of relief. In the absence of such clues, adjudicators have little choice but to consult state practices. Those that existed at the time TRIPS was adopted illustrate the approaches the members deemed acceptable. Thus, the *US–110(5)* panel canvassed the exceptions and limitations that states had adopted under the Berne Convention.[145] However, the DSB must be careful to consider the practices of states at all ends of the development spectrum (including outlier practices) in order to avoid construing the Agreement in ways that privilege states that had well-developed intellectual property systems before the Uruguay Round.[146] As important, the DSB must exercise a measure of deference in order to leave *all* states with the power to adapt laws to unforeseen problems. For example, just as India found it necessary to raise the inventive step to ensure access to generic drugs, the United States recently changed the analysis of the inventive step requirement to deal with the incentives patents create to discover new tax evasion strategies.[147] Thus, even if all of the states that had patent laws at the time of TRIPS interpreted "inventive step" in the same way, India's enactment of § 3(d) ought still to be given a margin of appreciation.

In some ways, the hardest questions are those raising normative considerations. While the trade regime has traditionally eschewed normative judgments, as trade brushes up against other values sidestepping these issues is increasingly difficult. That is particularly so for TRIPS, where linkage to intellectual property values is inherent in the idea of "Trade Related Intellectual Property" and explicit in terms like "*normal* exploitation" and "*legitimate* interests." Once again, state practices may provide important insights into the normative considerations that have traditionally informed intellectual property lawmaking. Encouragingly, panels have (for a variety of reasons) consulted an eclectic array of other sources, including other intellectual property agreements,[148] the 1883 Final Protocol to the Paris Convention, materials from the 1911 Paris Revision Conference, the General Report and materials of the diplomatic conferences leading to the inclusion of broadcast rights in the Berne Convention, and scholarly materials.[149] Drawing on these sources can help adjudicators flesh out the values historically thought to undergird intellectual property law. Furthermore, the regular use of these materials would promote the coherent administration of the international intellectual property regime more generally, a theme to which we return in Chapters 6 and 7. As elaborated in the next Chapter, the structural features of the Agreement should also play an interpretive role. For example, and as the Doha Declaration made clear, the Agreement should be particularly alert to the policies and objectives laid out in Articles 7 and 8 of the TRIPS Agreement.

For expository purposes, this Chapter examined the impact of adjudication thematically. That approach obscures two important observations. First, there has been significant change over time. *Canada–Pharmaceuticals* and *US–110(5)* were decided early in the life of the TRIPS Agreement. The more recent decisions—*EC–GI* and *China–Enforcement*—show a much more sophisticated understanding of the trade-offs that intellectual property law must make. Thus, they come far closer to our neofederalist vision than the earlier reports. Significantly, the number of cases reaching dispute settlement has also declined, suggesting that the member states are coming to understand that TRIPS is not the comprehensive code that some believe it to be.

Second, as noted at the outset, there are qualitative differences between the decisions of panels and those of the AB. Thus, in *India–Pharmaceuticals*, which raised the question whether India had properly implemented the pipeline provisions of Article 70.8, the AB emphasized that deference was owed to India's decisions. It was also careful to note that the express language of the Agreement cannot be modified by reference to the expectations of any one party. And in *Havana Club*, which examined the United States' recognition of Cuban trademarks, the AB refused to impute rules on ownership; as noted earlier, it was also careful to require proof that discretion had been exercised in a manner inconsistent with the Agreement. We will return to these reports in Chapter 4.

4

Interpretation Continued

The Structural Features of the TRIPS Agreement

> To the extent that "Three Track" says that the United States can delay foreign applicants effective patent protection within a reasonable period of time, this is an invitation to foreign governments in emerging nations to create their own unique procedures that make it impossible for Americans or nationals from developed countries to obtain effective patent protection. Consider, for example, the situation where [a country] set[s] forth a national patent law... whereby examination within ten years from filing would be obtained only in the event that the first filing anywhere in the world is hand delivered.... Such a procedure would be a clear violation of any reasonable understanding of the various treaty rights guaranteed to patent applicants under both Paris and TRIPS. Yet, "Three Track" differs only in degree in its discrimination against foreign applicants.
>
> —Harold C. Wegner, *"Three Track" TRIPS Treaty Violations, Testimony Before the US PTO on Three-Track Examination Proposal* (75 Fed. Reg. 31763, July 20, 2010), *available at* http://www.ip-watch.org/weblog/wp-content/uploads/2010/07/Wegner-ThreeTrack-July27.pdf

> First, the protection of U.S. databases in Europe under existing copyright and unfair competition laws is mandated by the TRIPS Agreement and by the Berne and Paris Conventions, which all require national treatment and forbid material reciprocity. Second, there is reason to believe that the E.U. [Database] Directive's material reciprocity clause violates the residual national treatment clause of the Paris Convention for the protection of Industrial Property, which is incorporated by reference into the TRIPS Agreement of 1994, and that it also violates the most favored nation clause of the TRIPS Agreement.
>
> —J. H. Reichman, *Statement Concerning H.R. 2652 Before the Subcommittee on the Judiciary, House of Representatives*, 105th Cong. 15–16 (October 23, 1997), *available at* http://judiciary.house.gov/legacy/41121.htm

In the previous Chapter, we considered three initiatives that tested the resilience of the TRIPS Agreement to changing circumstances and its adaptability to the needs of countries at differing stages of development. The TRIPS compatibility of each initiative was dependent upon the interpretation of those provisions in the Agreement that lay out substantive standards of intellectual property protection. The Dispute Settlement Body (DSB) has analyzed several of these provisions in its TRIPS reports thus far. However, it has only twice been asked to interpret provisions that are clearly structural: the national treatment provision, which was the cornerstone of both the intellectual property and the trade system prior to TRIPS, and the most favoured nation principle (MFN), which has a long tradition in trade law, but is new to the intellectual property system.[1]

In this Chapter, we explore the interpretation of these provisions. We suggest that national treatment offers an especially appealing approach to the regulation of trade in knowledge-intensive products. As we saw in Chapter 2, it offers a way to ameliorate trade distortions without imposing a universalist—code—perspective on international intellectual property law. It does not compel any particular level of protection or limit member state policy-making choices, except in so far as it precludes discrimination against foreigners. Accordingly, the DSB can protect the trade environment by intensively scrutinizing a member state's adherence to national treatment, and yet refrain from intruding substantially on the state's autonomy or its ability to structure its domestic regime to further its own priorities. MFN appears designed to serve a similar structural function. However, because of the different characteristics of trade and intellectual property regulations, this guarantee is problematic in TRIPS. We would therefore provide less intense scrutiny of MFN claims than we would of potential national treatment violations. In Chapter 3, we noted that the *Canada–Pharmaceuticals* panel interpreted Article 27, which prohibits certain forms of discrimination in the patent field, as likewise structural;[2] here, we question that analysis and go on to consider how the provision should be applied.

Once again, we examine the DSB's impact on the resilience and adaptability of the TRIPS Agreement by focusing on how it might handle recent initiatives designed to deal with social and technological change: (1) a mechanism to share the examination workload among national patent offices and (2) the European Union's 1996 Database Directive, which protects investment in data and seeks to expand protection on a global basis via a reciprocity provision.[3] In the course of the discussion, we focus mainly on national treatment, but we also explore MFN, discrimination in the patent realm, and other facets of the Agreement that may likewise have structural dimensions (including Articles 1.1, 7, 8, 31, 41, and 44 of TRIPS, as well as provisions in Paris and Berne incorporated by reference into the Agreement).

I. Improving Examination

Many observers argue that the surest way to improve the patent system is by improving the quality of the patents that issue. With fewer patents of "suspect validity" (to use Justice Kennedy's words),[4] transaction costs would decline. In some fields, such as information technology, where there are many patents per product, costs could be reduced quite dramatically. And upstream, there might be fewer patents to constrain researchers.[5] In the Knowledge Economy, however, it is difficult for patent offices to ensure quality while maintaining control over the length of patent application pendencies. In an inventive environment, the number of applications will tend to rise, and TRIPS exacerbates the problem by extending the group of potential applicants to every citizen of WTO member states.[6] Acceleration of the pace of advancement also means that the world's patent examiners continually face technologies about which they know little.

The Paris Convention facilitates multinational acquisition of rights by allowing a patent applicant to rely, in determining the priority of invention, on the filing date of an application previously filed in another Union country in the preceding twelve months.[7] However, both the Paris Convention and TRIPS envision a system whereby each member's patent office separately examines every patent application. The Patent Cooperation Treaty (PCT) ameliorates the problem of redundancy, but it centralizes only certain examination functions.[8] Accordingly, the level of repetitive examination remains extremely high. To move toward an efficient division of labor among patent offices, the United States Patent and Trademark Office (PTO), along with other leading patent offices, is considering a program entitled Strategic Handling of Applications for Rapid Examination (SHARE).[9] Under SHARE, the USPTO would give precedence to the examination of applications filed first in the United States; it would delay examination of applications previously filed in other patent offices until after the office of first filing has completed an examination. Presumably, the first examination would furnish the USPTO with information it would otherwise have to find for itself. As other countries replicate the program, work would increasingly be shared. Furthermore, industry might respond by directing applications in particular fields to specific national offices. With increasing specialization, pendency times would be further reduced and examination quality would improve.

Patent practitioners have, however, claimed that the system would violate the TRIPS Agreement.[10] Because an application filed first in a foreign country would be examined by the USPTO only after the foreign examination, while a contemporaneous application first filed in the United States would not suffer a similar delay, the SHARE program would "affect the ... acquisition" of U.S. patent rights by the applicant who filed first outside the United States, arguably in violation of the national treatment guarantee of Article 3.[11] That is, applicants who file first abroad in foreign countries would find themselves at the back of the queue, and their ability fully to enjoy U.S. patent rights would be somewhat curtailed: they would be unable to enjoin infringement in the United States or obtain monetary relief until their U.S. patents issue. As the Wegner quotation set out at the beginning of the Chapter suggests, a country could take this strategy to an extreme and essentially deprive patentees of the enjoyment of their patent rights. Furthermore, critics claim that SHARE would violate Article 4 of the Paris Convention (as incorporated into the TRIPS Agreement by Article 2.1) because it would deprive those filing first abroad of the right to "enjoy, for the purpose of filing in other countries, a right of priority" during the twelve-month term provided by Paris. SHARE's compatibility with MFN is also an issue, but we defer its examination to the discussion that follows the case studies.

A. The Application of the National Treatment Provision of Article 3 of the TRIPS Agreement

The issue of national treatment has arisen in several GATT disputes prior to and since the establishment of the WTO framework.[12] However, in GATT Article III, the bar is on discrimination based on the source of products, and in Article XX, the GATT provides a list of General Exceptions to the obligation.[13] In TRIPS, Article 3 bans discrimination based on the nationality of right holders, and there is no General Exceptions clause (although narrow exceptions under existing intellectual property instruments were preserved and, as we discuss later, there are other provisions that could be interpreted as substitutes). National treatment challenges under TRIPS have been considered in detail only twice: the first dispute reached the Appellate Body (AB); the more recent was decided only by a panel.[14]

In the first case, the *Havana Club* dispute, the United States had imposed a boycott on the registration and enforcement of Cuban-owned trademarks. However, it created a system to permit non-Cuban successors in interest to enforce these marks (at least in theory). Americans were required to obtain a license from the Office of Foreign Asset Control. A license was required of other nationals as well; in addition, they were confronted by a ban on U.S. courts recognizing their rights. Because the United States had never granted a license to anyone, the practical effect of the two procedures was identical. Nonetheless, the European Union challenged the measure, claiming it violated the national treatment provision. The panel that initially heard the case was persuaded by the identical treatment in practice and rejected the European Union's claim.[15] On appeal, however, the AB reversed. It was not satisfied with practical equality. Finding that "the significance of the national treatment obligation can hardly be overstated," and that the guarantee of national treatment had "long been a cornerstone of the Paris Convention and other international intellectual property conventions,"[16] the AB would not permit textual discrimination to be salvaged by practical realities. Because non-U.S. successors in interest faced an "extra hurdle" in obtaining protection, the provision at issue was found to violate national treatment.[17]

The *EC-GI* dispute was essentially the inverse. In that case, the United States challenged an EU regulation on geographical indications (GIs) that treated agricultural foodstuffs differently depending on where they were from. Products that originated in the European Union could be certified directly through procedures set up in EU member states. But those seeking GI protection for products from a non-EU country had to obtain an inspection from an authority based where the goods were located. Because the TRIPS Agreement permits countries to comply with their GI obligations in a variety of ways,[18] many countries did not have an inspection system. The United States therefore alleged that the regulation discriminated against foreigners. The European Union claimed that there was no discrimination because this differential was not based on the citizenship of right holders; it was based only on the location of the goods for which protection was sought. The panel rejected the European Union's argument. Instead of placing weight on the lack of differentiation in the text itself, the panel looked at who was affected, as measured by the actual impact of the regulation as it operated in practice. That is, the panel did not merely determine whether EU nationals were, as a matter of law, necessarily treated differently from foreign nationals. It also looked at who was more likely to seek protection for foodstuffs grown in the European Union and who was more likely to seek protection for foodstuffs grown outside the European Union. The panel determined that there was a clear link between the location of the goods and the nationality of the applicant seeking GI protection. It concluded that the regulation denied "effective equality of opportunities"[19] because it imposed an "extra hurdle" on foreigners' ability to enjoy GI protection.[20]

The SHARE program clearly complies with the national treatment obligation under the test enunciated in *Havana Club*. Because nothing in U.S. or international law requires an applicant to file in the country of origin prior to filing abroad, all members of WTO countries are formally eligible for whatever benefits accrue under SHARE by filing first in the United States. Thus, there is no discrimination on the face of the provision. However, it may well be that foreign inventors would be less likely to file first in the United States (albeit not with the same certainty that it would be EU citizens who secured GI protection based on European locations under the EU GI regulation). Filing first in their home country's patent office allows applicants to hire local attorneys to prosecute in their native language and to defer the added expense of filing abroad until they know more about the validity of their patents and the potential commercial success of their products.[21] Given the practicality-based inquiry in *EC-GI*, an argument can be made that if the United States were to adopt SHARE, it would be violating the national treatment provision.

But the *EC-GI* case is not dispositive of whether the SHARE program violates the national treatment obligation because the case was not framed in a way that led the panel to fully address whether, or under what circumstances, different treatment in practice might be justified. Further guidance might be found in decisions regarding national treatment under the GATT. In GATT cases, the DSB (like GATT panels before it) distinguishes between de jure and de facto discrimination. Adjudicators stringently scrutinize discrimination that is clear on the face of a challenged measure. For example, in a pre-TRIPS case touching on intellectual property, a panel found that the United States had violated the national treatment obligation of the GATT by providing one procedure for enforcing patent rights on imported products and a different procedure for enforcing patent rights on domestic products. Although the procedure for foreign products was not radically different from the procedure for domestic products—and even had offsetting benefits—the panel found a national treatment violation.[22] (*Havana Club*, which similarly involved a measure that was discriminatory on its face, is consistent with that reasoning.)

However, in cases where discrimination is not apparent on the face of the challenged law, the analysis in GATT cases is somewhat different. As Robert Hudec observed, while adjudicators have been literalist in the way they have tied the de facto analysis to the text of GATT Articles III and XX, the AB has in fact built a substantial degree of deference into its adjudication of these claims. Thus, before finding a de facto violation, it has considered the purpose of the challenged measure, whether there are less restrictive alternatives for achieving that purpose, and the effect the measure has on competition.[23] In Hudec's view the AB's method (derived from seeking to determine the circumstances in which panels might have regard to the "aims and effects" of legislation) reflects a long-standing aversion to "inquir[ing] into the purpose and motivation behind domestic . . . measures" and thus second-guessing state decision making, while acknowledging that states can have valid internal reasons for legislating in ways that happen to have a disparate impact on foreigners.[24] Thus, while the AB insists that the actual motivation behind legislation is irrelevant, it objectively analyzes the challenged measure to determine whether "it is applied in a way that affords protection to domestic products"[25] (in other words, whether the policy is protectionist). Furthermore, the AB claims that protective application can be ascertained "from the design, the architecture, and the revealing structure of the measure."[26]

Because of differences in the GATT and TRIPS national treatment guarantees and the absence in TRIPS of the General Exceptions provision on which the AB built much of its GATT analysis, it is risky to rely entirely on GATT cases in determining whether SHARE violates the national treatment obligation of TRIPS. Nonetheless, in *Havana Club*, the AB endorsed the use of GATT jurisprudence in resolving the TRIPS national treatment question.[27] And in *EC-GI*, where the TRIPS issue was embedded in a dispute that raised questions of national treatment under the GATT,[28] the panel cited GATT cases in considering the TRIPS national treatment issue.[29] The reasons to rely on these GATT cases go beyond the commonality of the term "national treatment": both Agreements have exceptions motivated by similar concerns. The General Exceptions provision in the GATT allows states to refuse to accord national treatment in order to pursue social policies that reflect their own national needs and values (including, ironically, innovation policy);[30] TRIPS has functional substitutes. Examples include Article 1.1, which the AB has labeled "an important general rule in the TRIPS Agreement,"[31] and Articles 7 and 8, which were stressed in the Doha Ministerial Declaration.[32]

Thus while SHARE, like the EU GI Regulation, can be challenged for having a disparate effect on foreigners, the outcome is likely to depend on more than a mere "head count" of whether foreigners are disproportionately affected. In *EC-GI*, the panel (not unlike the AB in adjudicating GATT cases) considered "the design, the architecture, and the revealing structure of the measure."[33] It was particularly struck by the near one-to-one mapping of the nationality of those applying for EU GI registrations and the location of the goods, observing:

> [T]he distinction made by the regulation on the basis of the location of a GI will operate in practice to discriminate between the group of nationals of other Members who wish to obtain GI protection, and the group of the European Communities' own nationals who wish to obtain GI protection, to the detriment of the nationals of other Members. *This will not occur as a random outcome in a particular case but as a feature of the design and structure of the system.*[34]

In other words, the *EC-GI* panel discerned from the structure of the EU regulation that it "affords protection to domestic products." That feature is not present in SHARE. While it is certainly true that U.S. inventors are more likely to file first in the United States,[35] there are already foreign inventors who do so as well.[36] Unlike in the GI situation, where the entire point of a GI is to derive a reputational benefit from the location in which goods are grown or made, inventions have no geographic significance. Admittedly, some countries make filing first abroad more difficult,[37] and SHARE, in a sense, puts pressure on these countries to change their rules on foreign filing (or examine applications more quickly). The issue of how far one country can effectively impose regulatory rules on other WTO members has never been entirely clear under GATT law.[38] While the *EC-GI* panel may well have been influenced by the obligations the European Union was imposing on other countries (including the establishment of a certification procedure and office), SHARE would require much less of other member states. If the Agreement were read so rigidly as to reach such a benign and attenuated impact, member states would be unable to experiment with ways of coping with the changes that TRIPS itself has wrought.[39]

An analysis of the TRIPS Agreement's functional substitutes for the General Exceptions clause also makes it likely that a challenge to SHARE would be rejected. Article 1.1 recognizes that the method of implementing TRIPS obligations implicates the autonomy interests of member states; that it would be inappropriate to expect countries to entirely change their legal cultures upon joining the WTO. Under this provision, then, the United States is entitled to deference as to how it structures its examination procedures, so long as the procedures are not applied in a manner that protects U.S. patent applicants and disadvantages foreigners.[40] In the case of SHARE, the measure is not designed to favor American applicants: the initiative is a way to grapple with high pendency rates. Assigning initial responsibility for related patent applications to a single office certainly creates efficiencies. And allocating responsibility to the office of first filing is a rational choice. If the efficiency gains are large enough, even applications first filed abroad should wind up with earlier examination under this system. Furthermore, solving the pendency problem through a mechanism that promotes work sharing furthers the goals of the TRIPS Agreement in that fast, efficient, and effective examination contributes to "the promotion of technological innovation and to the transfer and dissemination of technology" as envisioned by Article 7. To the extent that patents of "suspect validity" can be used by nonpracticing entities (or others) to extract excessive rents, improving examination can also be considered under Article 8, as an "appropriate measure . . . to prevent . . . abuse." Furthermore, it envisions a type of international cooperation that is within the spirit of the Agreement.[41]

Of course, Hal Wegner is partly right: in the quotation set out earlier in this Chapter, he suggests that if there are no limits on filing rules, a country could extend the pendency period for foreign applications by many years and require hand delivery of applications, thus effectively denying foreigners almost the entire benefit of their patents. But he is wrong to think that when it comes to interpreting TRIPS, matters of "degree" are irrelevant. Were the DSB to consider the program he posits, it probably would find a violation. The structure of his hypothetical program suggests it would apply in a way that protects locals at the expense of foreigners. Furthermore, it is an unduly burdensome way to achieve the goal of reducing pendencies. In contrast, the SHARE program does not eliminate the term; it merely delays issuance. Presumably, the applicant would be entitled to claim provisional rights during most (if not all) of the delay period. In cases of excessive delay, the measure could include an offset, such as extending the patent term.[42]

B. The Application of the Priority Provision of Article 4 of the Paris Convention

Article 2.1 of the TRIPS Agreement obliges member states to comply with Articles 1 through 12 and 19 of the Paris Convention. Article 4 of Paris gives patent applicants who file in one TRIPS country the right to enjoy "for the purpose of filing in the other countries . . . a right of priority" for a period of twelve months.[43] The question whether the SHARE program would violate this provision turns on what is meant by "right of priority" for "the purpose of filing in other countries." If it includes only the right to priority of invention (for example, the right to use the first filing date to determine novelty and nonobviousness), then SHARE would not intrude. SHARE would delay examination, but would use the Paris priority date to determine rights to a patent. If, on the other hand, priority includes the order in which the second office examines filed applications, then SHARE would violate Article 4.

This issue has never been raised in an international tribunal, so it is not possible to know for certain how it would be resolved. Ostensibly, Article 4 is a formidable obstacle. As noted in Chapter 2, apart from national treatment, the priority mechanism was arguably the most important patent provision in the Paris Convention. In a sense, it too is a cornerstone of the international system in that it permits patent applicants to obtain international rights through a series of successive national applications. Like national treatment, it does so while preserving the autonomy of each member state to develop patent policy tailored to its needs. Thus, it could be said that the level of scrutiny accorded to SHARE's compatibility with Article 4 should be equivalent to the high degree of scrutiny given to its effect on national treatment.

But a closer look at the priority provision in Paris is necessary. The crux of the provision is that it preserves priority of *invention*. That is, Article 4 is significant to the international regime because, as subsection B expressly states, it gives patent applicants the ability to delay foreign filings for twelve months by providing them with immunity from events that occur after the first application is filed. The order of *examination* is not relevant to producing that system. While rules that interfere with the validity of claims should therefore require intensive scrutiny, that level is inappropriate for an initiative, such as SHARE, which merely allocates examination resources. If the measure is examined more deferentially, a challenge based on the Paris Convention is not likely to prevail.

The AB's decision in *India–Pharmaceuticals* furnishes support for the view that the Paris Convention does not dictate deep scrutiny on this implementation issue. In that case, the question was whether India had complied with the pipeline provisions of Article 70.8 of the TRIPS Agreement, which required it to preserve the patentability of new pharmaceutical and agricultural chemical products during the transition period between joining the WTO and enacting fully compatible patent protection.[44] India had done so with an ordinance and administrative regulations, and the United States challenged both the substance of the regulation and the form of the legal instrument by which India had established the pipeline mechanism. The AB rejected the substantive challenge, which the United States based on the claim that it had a legitimate expectation of greater protection:

> The legitimate expectations of the parties to a treaty are reflected in the language of the treaty itself. The duty of a treaty interpreter is to examine

the words of the treaty to determine the intentions of the parties. This should be done in accordance with the principles of treaty interpretation set out in Article 31 of the Vienna Convention. But these principles of interpretation neither require nor condone the imputation into a treaty of words that are not there or the importation into a treaty of concepts that were not intended.[45]

Indeed, even as to the procedural issue the degree of scrutiny was minimal:

> Members shall be free to determine the appropriate method of implementing the provisions of this Agreement within their own legal system and practice. Members, therefore, are free to determine how best to meet their obligations under the TRIPS Agreement within the context of their own legal systems. And, as a Member, India is "free to determine the appropriate method of implementing" its obligations under the TRIPS Agreement within the context of its own legal system.[46]

India's discretion was not, however, unfettered. The AB reasoned that it clearly "cannot be" that "only India can assess whether Indian law is consistent with India's obligations under the WTO Agreement."[47] Because the rules it enacted did not provide sufficient legal certainty in the face of a countervailing statute, the AB, in fact, upheld the challenge of the United States.

This analysis suggests that some degree of scrutiny of the SHARE program would be warranted, but the initiative would likely survive. Since the Paris Convention requires only that "any subsequent filing in any of the other [member] countries . . . shall not be invalidated by reason of any acts accomplished in the [twelve month] interval,"[48] it is improbable that the DSB would allow the imputation into Article 4 of any requirement that second filers be accorded priority of examination. The Paris Convention and the TRIPS Agreement protect national autonomy to choose between a first-to-file and a first-to-invent system for awarding patents, and to choose between a rule of absolute or relative novelty.[49] They should likewise be read to allow states to regulate the order in which national examiners do their jobs.

II. Database Protection

As computer technology has advanced, it has facilitated the production of comprehensive databases with many user-friendly features, permitting search, extraction, and other forms of data manipulation. The economic importance of digitized compendia has increased as online access has expanded through the growth of bandwidth, server capacity, and public use of the internet. At one time, data compilations were protected by copyright in most countries, either under a sweat of the brow theory or on the basis of the selection, coordination, or arrangement of the data. However, legal changes in the early 1990s undercut the sweat of the brow theory. Indeed, in *Feist Publications, Inc. v. Rural Telephone Service Co.*, the United States Supreme Court raised doubts as to whether Congress has the constitutional authority to protect unoriginal factual compilations under copyright.[50] Furthermore, the comprehensiveness and manipulability of digitized databases make copyright protection for the selection, coordination, and arrangement less significant economically.

In 1996, after considerable debate, the European Commission proposed a directive to harmonize the protection of databases throughout the European Union. Partly to address the new technological environment and partly to bridge philosophical differences between the copyright approach of common law jurisdictions (which rewards labor) and the droit d'auteur systems more prevalent in civil law countries (which tie rights more closely to authorial creativity), the Commission proposed a two-track approach. First, the threshold of creativity necessary to support copyright protection was set at the level that prevailed in continental Europe. This effectively repealed the United Kingdom's "sweat" copyright. However, the Commission augmented the copyright approach with a sui generis right that protected the investment in the compilation and maintenance of databases. Although copyright protection was extended on a national treatment basis, as required by the Berne Convention (and the TRIPS Agreement), the Commission took the view that the sui generis database right was not covered by any international convention. As a result, the European Union considered itself free to insert a reciprocity provision and condition protection for a foreigner's databases on equivalent protection for EU producers in that foreigner's home country. At the time of the initial proposal, the United States controlled the overwhelming majority of the global database market, and the Commission also supported its proposal with the argument that enhancing protection for investment of databases in Europe would increase the market share of European database providers.[51]

The proposal was enacted;[52] the question is whether the TRIPS Agreement should be interpreted to bar the European Union from conditioning protection for foreigners on reciprocity. Since database protection addresses a type of creative work whose commercial potential was not fully appreciated at the time of the Uruguay Round, one issue is whether it is nonetheless within the scope of the Agreement. If it is, then the second issue is whether the European Union's decision to require reciprocity violates national treatment. Again, we defer MFN issues for later consideration.

A. The Scope of the TRIPS Agreement

Nominally, TRIPS would appear to take a narrow view of the scope of international protection. In Article 1.2, the Agreement denominates seven specific categories of protection (those that are the subject of Sections 1 through 7 of Part II of the TRIPS Agreement: copyrights, trademarks, geographical indications, industrial designs, patents, layout-designs (topographies) of integrated circuits, and undisclosed information). However, Section 1 is entitled "Copyright and Related Rights," and the legislative history and structure of the EU measure suggest that database protection is "related." Furthermore, in Article 2.1, the TRIPS Agreement incorporates by reference "Articles 1 through 12, and Article 19, of the Paris Convention." The form of database protection created by the European Union is arguably covered by Article 10bis of the Paris Convention, which requires "effective protection against unfair competition,"[53] a protection for commercial ethics that is defined to preclude "competition contrary to honest business practices."[54] And as will be discussed in the next section, the national treatment provision of Article 3 broadly defines "intellectual property," and thus appears to encompass "certain modalities of protection," irrespective of whether they are listed in TRIPS as a category of subject matter to be protected.[55]

The DSB has considered the scope issue only once. In the *Havana Club* dispute it was asked to determine whether protection for trade names was cognizable under the TRIPS Agreement. The panel had found it was not, on the theory that it was not one of the subjects mentioned in Sections 1 through 7 of TRIPS. The AB rejected the argument. It held:

> We interpret the terms "intellectual property" and "intellectual property right" with reference to the definition of "intellectual property" in Article 1.2 of the TRIPS Agreement. The textual reading of Article 1.2 is that it establishes an inclusive definition and this is confirmed by the words "all categories"; the word "all" indicates that this is an exhaustive list.[56]

Furthermore, the AB reasoned that to exclude trade names, which are covered in Article 8 of Paris, would be to ignore the plain meaning of Article 2.1 of TRIPS, which specifically incorporated Articles 1 through 12 of that Convention.[57] Finally, the AB found nothing in the negotiation history of the TRIPS Agreement suggesting that members were opposed to the inclusion of trade names.[58]

The question whether the scope of TRIPS extends to database protection is, of course, distinguishable from the trade name issue in *Havana Club*. Trade name protection was well known at the time that the TRIPS Agreement was negotiated, and the AB's decision was highly influenced by the trade name protection required by Paris Article 8. Although the juxtaposition of the lists in

TRIPS Articles 1.2 and 2.1 created a degree of ambiguity, it could be resolved fairly easily by consulting the negotiation history. In contrast, sui generis database protection was not well known at the time TRIPS was negotiated. The European Union was considering protection almost simultaneously with the Uruguay Round, but it did not enact the Directive until TRIPS was completed. The European Union obviously did not consider its sui generis scheme a species of "unfair competition," and, as to the United States, the *Feist* Court seemed to believe that the utilization of data is not only not unfair; it may even be a constitutional right.[59] The meaning of "related" is similarly murky. One definition derives directly from TRIPS: Article 3 specifically mentions the rights of performers, producers of phonograms, and broadcasting organizations—in other words, what civil law systems regard as "neighboring rights." The European Union clearly did not think the term included rights over databases, and the holding in *Feist* suggests that a copyright approach is not suitable for data.

It is difficult to predict how the DSB would decide this issue. Unfair competition is not self-defining; in that way, it is different from the other types of protection covered by TRIPS, such as trademark law, where the DSB has suggested that WTO member states share common understandings.[60] Unfair competition can be conceptualized as an adjunct to trademark law, as an underlying principle of trade secret law, as an impetus for consumer protection law, or as focused on dishonest commercial practices. Even within the European Union, where trademark law has been comprehensively harmonized, little agreement exists on the content or form of unfair competition protection. In the United States, there have been numerous cases about the meaning of Article 10bis of Paris and its implementation in U.S. law, and a major source of the tension is the conspicuous divergence between American notions of unfair competition and those that prevail in continental Europe.[61] "Relatedness" is likewise an opaque concept. For example, in the United States, the courts have grappled on numerous occasions with the question whether a state-protective regime should be considered so closely related to copyright (or patent) protection that it must be regarded as pre-empted by federal law.[62] In the European Union, cases involving free movement of goods similarly raise tricky classification issues.[63]

It is also somewhat difficult to decide how this matter ought to be resolved from a normative perspective. On the one hand, it can be argued that the DSB should decline to reinterpret the open language of the Agreement to impose an obligation to protect new forms of creativity (such as the production of databases). Rather, it should leave it to the states to bargain for their inclusion in TRIPS. As the AB in the *India–Pharmaceuticals* report stressed, "The duty of a treaty interpreter is to examine the words of the treaty to determine the intentions of the parties."[64] Since countries cannot easily envision future technologies, they cannot "intend" to protect them. For example, it cannot be said that there was any intention to agree on protecting databases as such during the Uruguay Round. More important, there are benefits in requiring the parties to bargain for the inclusion of new intellectual property rights. In the interim, as new knowledge-intensive products become commercially significant, states can experiment with whether incentives are needed to spur investment and tinker with the shape of the protective regime. Decisions on whether to leave the market alone, on whether to intervene, and on the appropriate contours of the right (threshold requirements, scope, and defenses) will likely vary as each state works at finding the appropriate balance between user and producer interests.[65] In time, when a measure of consensus has been reached, negotiators in future rounds could draw on the experience and internationalize protection.

There are many examples of this dynamic. Topographies (layout designs of integrated circuits) were included in TRIPS through a bargaining process. In 1984, the United States had enacted the Semiconductor Chip Protection Act.[66] The measure had a soft reciprocity provision, and several countries eventually enacted complying legislation.[67] Eventually, the United States successfully included topography protection in the Uruguay Round.[68] Significantly, states' experience with topography protection produced innovations at the multinational level. Thus, the provision that was finally adopted included an important limitation: Article 37 is one of the few provisions of the Agreement that includes an affirmative safeguard for the rights of users. Similarly, the status of trade secrecy protection was dubious under Paris.[69] Article 39 of the TRIPS Agreement made clear that the protection of undisclosed information is part of the requirement to protect against unfair competition; significantly, the provision also clarified the terms of protection. Of course, the process does not necessarily lead to a comprehensive solution: for example, Article 39.3 provides limited guidance on the obligation to protect test data submitted for government approval, leading to substantial state experimentation (and not inconsiderable tension).[70] Prior to TRIPS, states similarly experimented with the form of protection for geographical indications.[71] In the Uruguay Round, they reached consensus on the need for protection, but not on the contours. These were left to the Council for TRIPS as part of its so-called built-in agenda.[72]

On the other hand, there can be benefits to using open-ended provisions, such as Paris Article 10bis on unfair competition, to incorporate new forms of creativity into TRIPS. It is in the very nature of the Knowledge Economy that new forms of creativity will evolve. In recent years, there has been an institutional impasse within the WTO. The Council for TRIPS has been unable to make progress on the built-in agenda. And aside from recognizing the deficiencies of Article 31, the Ministerial Conference has been similarly quiescent.

Thus a mechanism for assimilating new forms of protection automatically might be desirable. In fact, a similar dynamic has been usefully employed at the national level to ensure that intellectual property protection reflects modern creative developments. For example, the United States Supreme Court read the open-ended language provisions of the Patent Act to keep patent law abreast of technological developments in the biotechnology sector.[73] There is, however, a timing question. If the DSB acts prematurely, it will curtail national experimentation. But there is a mechanism to modulate its response. As we saw in Chapter 3, when terms in the Agreement are undefined, the DSB will often consult state practices. As long as it waits until there is genuine consensus among a significant number of member states, there will be sufficient opportunity to develop the experience necessary to understand the nature of the incorporated obligation.

On balance, however, we believe it would not be advisable to interpret open-ended provisions in a way that requires the incorporation of new substantive rights into TRIPS. The incorporation mechanism used in national lawmaking works because any mistakes can be readily corrected through legislation or even judicial action.[74] But the stalemate within the WTO means that its lawmaking machinery is not currently up to that task, and the DSB hears too few cases to rely on its ability to change course.

The logic of both approaches to updating TRIPS—waiting either for renegotiation of the Agreement or for a substantial consensus to develop—also depends on states making *independent* decisions on whether and how new forms of creativity should be protected. In that context and as discussed later, the real problem with the Database Directive is its reciprocity provision. We turn to that issue in the next section.

B. The Application of the National Treatment Provisions of Article 3

Even if the substantive minima in TRIPS are not read as requiring states to protect nonoriginal databases, the European Union's decision to withhold national treatment could be considered a violation of the Agreement. If the goal of TRIPS is to create a global marketplace in the fruits of creative endeavors, then a broad application of the national treatment guarantee is needed to ensure that all such works are included in the worldwide regime. Allowing states to evade their national treatment obligations by labeling new forms of protection as something other than intellectual property would encourage the proliferation of protective regimes. In the end, the creative community would once again confront the problems caused by distorted marketplaces.

Thus, a strong argument can be made that even if database protection is considered neither related to copyright nor a species of unfair competition protection, it is subject to Article 3, which uses the term "intellectual property" and does not include a list of protected subject matter. The protection of Article 3 already extends beyond the substantive minimum standards in the Agreement. As the *EC-GI* panel recognized, when a state raises the level of protection above these substantive minima, it is still required to extend protection on a national treatment basis.[75] Furthermore, Article 6, which expressly left the issue of exhaustion open and thus permits member states to make their own rules on parallel importation, nonetheless requires the states to apply the same rule to domestic and foreign right holders. Given the fundamental nature of the commitment to national treatment, the requirement should also apply to new forms of "intellectual property," even when they are not considered mandated by the substantive provisions of TRIPS.[76]

The level of scrutiny given to such a provision is a separate issue. As noted previously, the *Havana Club* and *EC-GI* reports are the only DSB decisions that applied the national treatment provision to intellectual property, and as we saw, the panels appear to continue in the tradition of according less severe scrutiny to de facto discrimination than to de jure discrimination. In the case of the EU Database Directive, the explicit differential between foreign and EU data compilers on the face of the Directive would likely be considered de jure discrimination and thus a per se violation of national treatment.[77] And even if it could be argued that foreign compilers can obtain the benefit of EU protection by incorporating in the European Union, the "design and structure of the system" evinces a protectionist agenda. Admittedly, there is a sense in which the reciprocity provision might be thought to undercut that conclusion. After all, it expresses the view of the European Union that all compilers should enjoy similar benefits. Reciprocity can, however, be a particularly pernicious approach to international lawmaking. The EU Directive is intrusive because it requires other countries to adopt identical protection and limits the international community's opportunity to compare different ways to deal with the same commercial problem.[78]

To be sure, the SHARE program could be considered similar to the Database Directive because it too would pressure other countries to examine applications that were later filed in the United States more quickly. SHARE is, however, not discriminatory on its face. Furthermore, it represents a more benign extrusion of policy. It would not tell countries how to examine applications. Rather, it envisions international cooperation.[79] SHARE would also rely on institutional mechanisms that TRIPS requires (that is, an office and procedures for granting patents). In contrast, the database provision requires countries to enact entirely new statutory schemes. In the *EC-GI* case, that problem was particularly acute. The TRIPS Agreement expressly reserved to member states discretion as to the "legal means" by which to protect geographical indications,[80] but the EU regulation required states to create inspection systems to the specifications of the European Union.

Observations

The initiatives analyzed in this Chapter raised questions about the structural aspects of the TRIPS Agreement. We begin our observations with the three provisions on discrimination: the national treatment provision of Article 3, which was discussed earlier; Article 4's MFN clause; and the requirement in Article 27.1 (discussed in Chapter 3) that patent rights "be available... without discrimination as to the place of invention, the field of technology, and whether products are imported or locally produced." We argue that these provisions are all quite different—that the second may be ill-conceived, and the last may not even be structural—and that each must be interpreted in a manner that reflects its particular role in preserving the integrity of the international intellectual property, trade, and patent systems. The DSB has not generated a nuanced approach to discrimination, but other adjudicatory systems recognize that distinct policy concerns require the application of varying levels of scrutiny to different forms of discrimination.[81] The clear differences between the functions of Articles 3, 4, and 27 warrant an analogous approach.[82] We then consider other provisions that, like national treatment, can be interpreted in a way that protects the integrity of the global trade regime while preserving the neofederalist values we see as underlying the TRIPS Agreement.

A. Discrimination

1. *Discrimination under Article 3 (national treatment)*. As recounted in Chapter 1, TRIPS is seen by some of its proponents as a code, a view that highlights as its signature feature the promulgation of worldwide enforceable substantive standards of intellectual property protection. However, the DSB reports reviewed in this section demonstrate that the national treatment obligation may have more bite. In both *Havana Club* and *EC-GI*, the substantive claims lost. In the substantive part of *Havana Club*, the European Union relied on Article 6quinquies of the Paris Convention and Articles 15 and 16 of TRIPS to claim that the United States must register and enforce valid Cuban marks. The AB rejected the European Union's broad reading of these provisions, finding instead that the United States had considerable discretion to "determine the conditions for filing and registration of trademarks."[83] But as we saw, the United States lost on the national treatment argument: it could not treat foreign owners of Cuban marks differently from domestic owners. In *EC-GI*, the substantive

claim (discussed in Chapter 3) that the EU GI regulation interfered with trademark rights under Article 16 lost, but the regulation was nonetheless held to violate national treatment.

The difference in outcomes can be explained by the divergent character of the provisions at issue. The centrality of national treatment to the integrity of the trade regime persuaded the DSB to give intensive scrutiny to the compatibility of the challenged measures with this foundational principle. Both measures were found wanting. Significantly, however, these determinations did not substantially constrain the policy choices of either the United States in *Havana Club* or the European Union in *EC-GI*. The United States was permitted to pursue its policy of isolating Cuba, so long as the isolation equally affected Americans and foreign interests. The European Union could continue to protect its agricultural infrastructure. It was merely required to accept applications directly from producers of foodstuffs grown outside the European Union. Indeed, soon after the European Union amended the regulation in accordance with the WTO report, NAPA received EU GI status for wine from the Napa region of California.[84] National treatment, in other words, combines solicitude for undistorted trade with a continuing commitment to national autonomy. It is thus a crucial component of the neofederalist structure we propose.

At the same time, these two reports (and the GATT cases on which they rely) are far from perfect. The DSB tied its decisions tightly to text (both of the relevant WTO Agreement and of the challenged measure); its reports offer little by way of analytical elaboration or normative explanation. In the absence of such guidance, adjudicators could easily reach results that fail to track the problems national treatment is intended to solve. An elaboration of the analysis should, first, clearly affirm that the intensity of scrutiny depends on whether the challenged measure is discriminatory on its face (de jure discriminatory) or merely discriminatory in its impact (de facto discrimination). Neither *Havana Club* nor *EC-GI* made that distinction in those terms.[85] Yet the outcomes of these disputes are consistent with that approach. Furthermore, the approach itself is consistent with national and regional practices related to trade. For example, the United States and the European Union deal in that way with adjudication under the Commerce Clause and the free movement guarantee, respectively.[86] Most important, the distinction makes considerable sense. There is such a high likelihood that facially discriminatory measures are meant to prefer locals over foreigners, such discrimination should be a per se violation of the Agreement. (Or, to put it another way, if the motive for the measure is not discriminatory, it should be possible to structure it in a manner that does not differentiate on a de jure basis.) In contrast, a rule can have a discriminatory impact for a variety of reasons. The impetus for the measure may be unrelated to trade (or to economic activity more generally). As the SHARE program demonstrates, the impact may have more to do with the actions of other countries than with those of the country whose measure was challenged. Accordingly, adjudicators should be much more wary about rejecting these measures.

Second, the DSB should develop a more transparent analysis of de facto discrimination. As Hudec noted, the AB is, in fact, sensitive to intrusion into states' choices on nontrade policies. But while the AB is willing to look at the structure of a measure to infer protectionism (or the lack thereof), it has refused to directly consider the motivation behind the challenged legislation. Hudec suggested:

> It may be the sensitivity of this area, however, that explains the choices made by the Appellate Body thus far. . . . The fact that this policing activity intrudes upon domestic regulatory sovereignty leaves the new WTO legal institutions particularly exposed to damaging criticism from national governments that do not yet fully accept the WTO's authority in this area. Recognizing this very exposed position, the Appellate Body may well have concluded that the safest refuge from political criticism was to stay as close as possible to the shelter of the legal texts accepted by governments.[87]

This crabbed approach has arguably created difficulty in resolving trade disputes; it is clearly problematic in the intellectual property context. The creative industries of each member state are a product of its culture, social structure, intellectual history, education system, wealth, and industrial policy. And these industries, in turn, determine the content of each nation's intellectual property laws, as well as the allocation of resources that each state devotes to its information and legal infrastructure. Because the mix of creative industries will vary from country to country, the laws of any one will almost inevitably have a differential impact on the others. The reluctance, in the name of national autonomy, to consider the motivation behind intellectual property measures is, at the end of the day, destructive of national autonomy because it reduces the lawmaking choices of WTO member states. In fact, this problem goes beyond the analysis of national treatment. As we saw in Chapter 3, the failure to consider the justifications for a challenged action is endemic to the DSB's intellectual property jurisprudence.

Admittedly, it would be a mistake for the DSB to make value judgments on national policies. However, it should be possible to consider the reasons that led a state to act without simultaneously evaluating the wisdom of its action. For example, the legislative material surrounding the Database Directive suggests that it was enacted opportunistically, to provide for Europeans protection that the United States Supreme Court was denying to Americans.[88] In contrast, the United States has long struggled to reduce pendency periods, and the history of its efforts does not reveal any intent to privilege Americans over other applicants.[89] Allowing countries whose measures are challenged to offer a range of proof, grounded in the policies underlying the TRIPS Agreement (such as those articulated in Articles 7 and 8), would provide them with more flexibility. It would liberate them to make the complex judgments necessary to balance the interests of rights holders against interests such as health, cultural development, and expressive freedom. Of course, states may offer disingenuous rationales for their laws. To avoid that problem, the DSB should base decisions concerning justifications in contemporaneous materials explaining the rationale for the law. It should also give complainants an opportunity to demonstrate that the proffered rationale is a sham and consider whether the same policy could be pursued in ways less distortive of trade.

2. *Discrimination under Article 4 (most favoured nation)*. Article 4 of the TRIPS Agreement applies the MFN guarantee that has a long tradition in trade relations to intellectual property. In *Havana Club*, the AB characterized its incorporation as noteworthy:

> As a cornerstone of the world trading system, the most-favoured-nation obligation must be accorded the same significance with respect to intellectual property rights under the TRIPS Agreement that it has long been accorded with respect to trade in goods under the GATT. It is, in a word, fundamental.[90]

In that dispute, the challenged legislation treated foreigners from a single country—Cuba—differently from other foreign nationals. The AB noted that the provision was discriminatory on its face, and found that it violated MFN.[91]

The AB did not, however, provide an analytical framework for adjudicating other MFN claims. Clearly, MFN is a benchmarking device. While national treatment compares the treatment of domestic rights holders and foreigners, MFN compares foreigners with each other. However, *Havana Club* did not expressly say whether—or how—the MFN analysis should distinguish between de jure and de facto discrimination. Nor did the AB explain how MFN ought to be applied outside the particular context of the Cuban embargo regulations, which were essentially designed as a trade measure, to isolate Cuba from the U.S. market. The application of the provision to core intellectual property regulation is far from straightforward.

Even in the trade context, MFN appears to be problematic. The GATT and the GATS both allow exemptions from MFN treatment.[92] And as the 2004 Sutherland Report on the WTO found, there are so many derogations from the requirement that, among WTO members, "MFN is no longer the rule; it is almost the exception."[93] It is not difficult to understand why derogations from

MFN are so common: those who have studied the trade regime find the welfare effects of MFN to be indeterminate. In some cases, the obligation may even be harmful. For example, in an extensive review of the literature, Henrik Horn and Petros Mavroidis suggest that "[t]he positive view of MFN often seems based on the presumption that discrimination is inherently undesirable from an economic point of view."[94] The authors go on to show that ex ante, it is not possible to prove that a measure that differentiates among foreigners is economically unsound. They do note, however, that MFN protection strongly influences bargaining strategy, leading to outcomes that tend to liberalize trade by lowering trade barriers.[95] More simply, it amplifies the benefits that any two countries extend to one another bilaterally.

For TRIPS, the stringent application of MFN is particularly troubling. Indeed, it is noteworthy that in more than a century of negotiations over multilateral international intellectual property agreements, there has never been a suggestion that the multinational system requires an MFN guarantee. As an observer at the time of the negotiation of the Berne Convention observed, the inclusion of MFN in earlier, bilateral copyright conventions was derided as an "unhappy borrowing" from commercial treaties.[96] While bargaining strategies over intellectual property are sure to deviate from bargaining over trade concessions, the work on trade suggests that the effect of MFN in TRIPS would be to increase the level of intellectual property protection worldwide: the effect of one country raising the level of protection would be felt by every trader who sought to do business with that country. But provisions that cause increases in the level of protection are not always a "benefit" (or, as the WTO puts it, an "advantage, favour, privilege or immunity") in the sense that lower tariffs reduce trade barriers to countries that can take advantage of MFN. As we note in earlier Chapters, enhancing protection is not inherently desirable in a regime that depends on balancing the interests of producers and users. Frederick Abbott gives the example of a bilateral agreement between the United States and Morocco to provide extensive protection for premarket clearance data for pharmaceuticals. Without MFN, the two countries could confine the benefits to American and Moroccan drug companies. But MFN requires these countries to extend the same protection to all others, eliminating the ability of generic producers in India to sell in either one, as well as the ability of consumers in the United States and Morocco to acquire cheaper drugs from India (or any other WTO member).[97] This level of protection may be appropriate for the United States, but it creates more harm to consumers in Morocco than an agreement restricted to protecting the output of U.S. companies. And it hurts all countries with important generic drug industries.[98]

The differences between trade and intellectual property law suggest that even if MFN is a "cornerstone of the world trading system," it does not have "the same significance with respect to . . . the TRIPS Agreement," as suggested in the

Havana Club report. Thus, our intuition is that MFN complaints about core intellectual property provisions should receive a reduced level of scrutiny. Our view is supported by the failure of TRIPS to provide for the same types of exemptions as are available under the GATT. While most of its exceptions to the MFN obligation are designed to grandfather pre-existing international rules, the GATT takes a more permissive approach. For example, it permits countries to enter into free trade agreements without requiring them to extend the benefits of those agreements to other WTO members.[99] That provision is not repeated in TRIPS. Yet, it is difficult to understand why TRIPS would afford less room for member states to maneuver than does the GATT. Accordingly, while we interpret the national treatment provision as an absolute bar to de jure discrimination, we would permit states to tender justifications for laws that distinguish on their face between different groups of foreigners.

As to de facto discrimination, the AB in *Havana Club* did not reach the question, but we would mirror the analysis of national treatment and suggest less intensive review than for de jure cases. Further, given our skepticism about MFN, we would argue for an even lower standard of review for de facto discrimination in the MFN context than we suggested for de facto national treatment cases. Differential impact is frequently caused by the practices or laws of the foreign states in question, and grows out of disparities among national intellectual property systems and the infrastructure that supports them. Thus, almost any national measure could be challenged as a de facto violation of MFN. Accordingly, we would put a burden on the complainant in de facto MFN cases to demonstrate how the challenged measure undermines the creative environment, seriously distorts trade in knowledge goods, or interferes with the multilateral framework for developing intellectual property law.

A lower standard of review would not mean that the MFN provision lacked all bite. For example, the Database Directive treats database producers from countries that reciprocate with the European Union differently from those that do not. However, it is facially neutral because any country is equally entitled to reciprocate with the European Union. Thus, the impact on countries that do not reciprocate with the European Union should be categorized as de facto, rather than de jure, discrimination. But even though we would accord it less scrutiny, we believe a challenge to the Directive should be sustained. While it is true that the failure to enact database legislation is not the responsibility of the European Union, the Directive was intended to directly influence the lawmaking dynamic of other states. The Directive clearly contemplates differential treatment, and it uses the resulting trade distortions to induce conforming action abroad. As we saw in connection with national treatment, reciprocity provisions can undermine national experimentation and render the intellectual property system less able to find optimal solutions to technological change. Thus, they ought, as a general matter, to be condemned (at least if the level of effective intrusion in the affairs of the foreign country is as extensive as in the case of the reciprocity provision of the Database Directive).

What of the SHARE program? It is even more obviously facially neutral. However, it too could be considered to be a de facto violation of MFN because applicants from countries (such as France) that require their nationals to apply domestically first would be treated differently from applicants from countries that permit their inventors to choose the country of first application. Further, it would treat applicants who file first in countries that examine rapidly differently from applicants in countries that examine slowly. But surely the SHARE program is on firmer ground than the Database Directive. As we saw in connection with national treatment, the SHARE program would be less intrusive; it might gently influence countries to examine more quickly, but it would not expressly deploy a measure that pressures them to adopt the program. At worst, it could be viewed as encouraging other countries to experiment with procedures that would benefit the global system as a whole, rather than undermine it.

3. *Discrimination under Article 27.1 (place of invention, field of technology, and whether patented products are imported or locally produced)*. In Chapter 3, we saw that the *Canada–Pharmaceuticals* panel treated Article 27.1 as a structural provision and equivalent in operation to the guarantees in Articles 3 and 4.[100] Thus, Canada would not have been permitted to use Article 30, the patent exceptions provision, to excuse a measure that discriminated against a particular field of technology. We suggested in Chapter 3 that this was a mistake, that Article 27.1 was not a structural guarantee. We noted that its application to Article 30 was illogical in that Article 30's test requires that exceptions to patent rights be limited, but if Article 27.1 requires the exception to apply to every field of technology, it would be nearly impossible for a state to enact an exception limited enough to meet the test. Now that we have seen the operation of the national treatment and MFN provisions, it is easier to see just how anomalous the panel's interpretation actually is.

Clearly, Article 27 destroys the nice dichotomy between structural and substantive provisions. The negotiation history of the TRIPS Agreement demonstrates that the provision was intended to guarantee protection for a variety of subject matter previously unprotected by patent in a number of countries.[101] In that regard, it looks like a substantive minimum provision relating to subject matter. But because the provision is cast in terms of nondiscrimination, it can also be interpreted as structural, applying to all of the provisions of patent law. Admittedly, there are reasons to support the latter interpretation. First, as we saw in connection with MFN, the drafters of the GATT appear to have a normative preference for nondiscrimination that goes beyond any demonstrable benefits in terms of social welfare. Second, the guarantee of nondiscrimination essentially turns Article 27.1 into a precommitment strategy, binding members to trans-substantive patent law as a way to prevent industries from dissipating resources by demanding special forms of protection.

But neither of these justifications has much to recommend it. As the earlier analysis suggests, discrimination is not always bad. Indeed, the DSB (despite its reservations) has gone to considerable lengths to make sure that beneficial and benign discrimination is tolerated. Furthermore, even if TRIPS was intended to influence national polities to enact an intellectual property regime,[102] it is far from clear that the TRIPS Agreement was meant to protect the structure of domestic political economies at such a granular level. Indeed, the effect that TRIPS might have on domestic political structures is quite complex (and dealt with in more detail in Chapter 5). More important, there is a flaw in equating the relationship between Article 27.1 and the entirety of patent law to the relationship between Article 3 and TRIPS. Applying Article 27.1 to the Exceptions provision of Article 30 emasculates one of the strongest safeguards that TRIPS offers to state autonomy interests. In contrast, the crucial feature of the national treatment provision is that it permits the DSB to police free trade quite strictly, but without intruding too deeply on national interests. A heavy-handed application of the same jurisprudence to substantive provisions, and in particular to substantive provisions like Article 30 that were drafted to give states a degree of flexibility in how they implement TRIPS, would substantially undermine autonomy.

The same can be said of applying Article 27.1 to Article 31, which lays out the conditions permitting states to issue compulsory licenses. If Article 27.1 were applied to Article 31 to create an additional condition for awarding a compulsory license, states would have greater difficulty addressing the problems that compulsory licensing is thought to solve. For example, it would be impossible for a state to issue a compulsory license only on pharmaceutical products because that would discriminate against a particular field of technology. Likewise, in Chapter 2, we demonstrated the importance of interpreting the TRIPS Agreement in ways that permitted states to impose working requirements. Article 27.1 should not be read as an obstacle. To put this differently, national treatment implicates foundational aspects of the WTO system, and any derogation from it is therefore necessarily suspect. But technological differentiation will sometimes effectuate the purposes of the Agreement by making the marketplace for knowledge-intensive products work more efficiently for everyone. Article 27.1 must accordingly be read as something other than structural.

However, even if Article 27.1 is not structural, there remain questions as to its scope of application and how its prohibition of discrimination should be interpreted. The *Canada–Pharmaceuticals* panel (chaired by Robert Hudec) was enthusiastic in its use of GATT jurisprudence on this issue. Thus, it distinguished between de jure and de facto discrimination.[103] But the *Canada–Pharmaceuticals* panel also suggested that the rulings on discrimination have "necessarily been based on the precise legal text in issue, so that it is not possible to treat them as applications of a general concept of discrimination."[104] Instead, it sought to "define the concept of discrimination to the extent necessary to resolve" the issue before it.[105]

The panel's instincts were right in so far as it sought to distinguish de facto and de jure discrimination. Members should be encouraged to enact rules that are not de jure discriminatory even when the problem to which the legislation is addressed arose in only one industry. Historically, intellectual property has operated from exemplars.[106] While some changes may retain a narrow ambit of application, others may turn out to have broader significance. As the *Canada–Pharmaceuticals* panel pointed out, "[I]ndividual problems are frequently the driving force behind legislative actions of broader scope."[107] For example, while the *eBay* rule on injunctive relief discussed in Chapter 3 may have been aimed at the information technology sector, such as the auction technology at issue in the case, the rule it lays down is facially neutral. Because such a provision would protect any industry where there are many patented components of a larger system, it will benefit any industry where there are patent thickets. For example, it could become significant in the genomics sector. In order to encourage countries to enact facially neutral laws, the DSB must treat laws that constitute de jure discrimination more strictly.

Although de jure discrimination should be treated more strictly than de facto discrimination in the context of both Article 27.1 and Article 3, that does not mean that the level of scrutiny should be the same. In the Article 3 context, a measure that is facially discriminatory is rejected out of hand. But as with MFN, a less intrusive inquiry may be warranted for Article 27.1 cases. Furthering the goals underlying patent law may require differential treatment of different "fields of technology" or "place of invention," and (as we saw in Chapter 2) may require attention to "whether products are imported or locally produced." For example, if patents in the genomics sector tend to be very broad, but patents in the mechanicals sector are very narrow, then a state may wish to enact specific legislation that ensures that genomics patents do not "'wholly pre-empt' the public's access to the 'basic tools of scientific and technological work.'"[108] Adjudicators should, accordingly, consider whether a challenged provision promotes innovation, which is, after all, one of the goals of the TRIPS Agreement.

For de facto discrimination, we would require adjudicators to identify a discriminatory policy in the structure of the challenged measures. This is consistent with *EC-GI* and borrows from the approach of the AB in GATT cases. We, however, recommend (as we did in connection with national treatment and MFN) that the DSB also permit a state whose action is challenged to offer an explanation or justification, grounded in the goals of the TRIPS Agreement and, given the provision's placement, also in goals unique to patent law. The complainant would then be allowed to show that substantially less restrictive alternatives were available to achieve the stated goal. For example, a state adopting the *eBay* rule should be permitted to show that it was necessitated by a change in the creative environment (such as the rise of enforcement by nonpracticing entities and the nature of software patents); the complainant could rebut with evidence that substantially less restrictive alternatives were available or that the rationale was a sham.

4. *Summary.* The guarantees of nondiscrimination cannot all be treated alike. Some are true "cornerstones," others not. And the guarantees are foundational to different aspects of the WTO edifice. This is a phenomenon not unknown to national and international legal systems. To reflect it, courts assessing the validity of legislation use a variety of techniques, including the intensity of scrutiny, levels of deference, margins of appreciation, analysis of the fit between the purpose of the challenged law and the means by which that purpose is pursued, or by shifting burdens of proof. Given this variety, we are reluctant to adopt a particular framework. However, our analysis allows us to offer some thoughts.

First, alleged violations of national treatment should be afforded closer scrutiny than laws that are challenged under MFN or, for patents, discrimination by field, place of invention, or place of production. The AB has recognized the foundational importance of national treatment to both GATT and TRIPS. Moreover, it is a cornerstone of a neofederalist system in that it allows members to pursue policies tailored to their distinct needs, and to test solutions to new problems. At the same time, however, the commitment to national treatment preserves the integrity of trade in knowledge-intensive products. Superficially, MFN appears similar to national treatment, but it is an uneasy transplant from the trade regime to intellectual property. The ill-fitting nature of MFN to core intellectual property regulation means that the DSB should treat MFN claims more skeptically. Article 27.1 is on a different plane: it does not strike us as structural and—contrary to the approach in *Canada–Pharmaceuticals*—we would permit a country to use the exceptions provision in Article 30 to excuse discrimination. That approach would best allow national laws to reflect the diversity, complexity, and historical contingency of patent law.

Second, each guarantee has its own internal logic and function. Thus, the appropriate approach to one form of discrimination cannot be completely defined by reference to the framework adopted to analyze the others. Clearly, national treatment claims deserve more scrutiny than do the others. But beyond that observation, there are dangers to oversimplifying the analysis. For example, the justifications appropriate to defending an MFN claim will often be different from the acceptable rationales for discriminating based on whether the patented products are imported or locally produced (see Chapter 2).

Third, we believe it is valuable to distinguish between de jure and de facto discrimination. The distinction encourages members to frame laws in ways that are clearly consistent with their obligations. Furthermore, it supports the neofederalist structure of the Agreement: states function best as laboratories when they enact broad principles that can be easily adapted to other areas and used by other countries where similar problems occur.[109]

Fourth, some of the measures we considered in this Chapter were questionable because, in effect, they require other countries to take particular action. Reciprocity provisions are the clearest case because they mandate conformity with the enacting state's conditions in order to secure equal treatment in that country. But other laws may similarly require action by other states. For example, SHARE could influence other states to revise their examination procedures in order for their applicants to obtain speedy examination in the United States. We suggest adjudicators have regard to this dynamic and the effect it has on the autonomy of other member states. We would not classify every measure with such an effect as a violation: there is simply too much variation among the creative industries, laws, and practices of other states. Instead, the DSB should consider the degree of coercion involved and the extensiveness of the intrusion. For example, the EU's GI regulation outsourced the cost of certifying and investigating uses of EU geographical indications and thus would have imposed significant expenditures on other states. Furthermore, it would have curtailed the ability of other states to experiment with GI protection—something that the TRIPS Agreement expressly guarantees. The Database Directive's reciprocity provision is also coercive, but somewhat less intrusive: it would require the enactment of new statutes with identical protection and conclusion of an agreement with the European Commission. In contrast, the reciprocity provision in the U.S. Semiconductor Chip Protection Act was less coercive: it required only substantial conformity with the principles underlying the United States' approach. SHARE is not coercive and substantially less intrusive: it would require little more than changing the speed of an office function that is already mandated by TRIPS.

B. Other Structural Features

There are other features of the TRIPS Agreement that may have structural roles similar to that of national treatment. These include Articles 1.1, 7, and 8, which are easily identified as plausible candidates because they are found in Part I of the Agreement, on General Provisions and Basic Principles. But there may be others. As our discussion of Article 4 of the Paris Convention demonstrated, these include the ability to obtain protection on an international basis; they also include overarching principles of enforcement, such as those found in Article 41. Their nature can be determined by a purposive reading of the text; provisions that are crucial to preserving an open trade environment in intellectual property are more likely to be structural. Other criteria include historical pedigree—for example, national treatment has been a fundamental precept of international intellectual property law for more than a century. Another set of possibly structural provisions include those aimed at maintaining the "club" by ensuring that TRIPS nations do not defect, and that TRIPS is hospitable to new members. And to the extent that our view of TRIPS as neofederalist is right, other candidates for structural status include those that are vital to protect the autonomy of states to tailor the law to their individual circumstances and to experiment with the challenges of technological and social change.

1. *Article 7 (objectives)*. Article 7 sets out, as the objectives of TRIPS, that it "contribute to the promotion of technological innovation and to the transfer and dissemination of technology, to the mutual advantage of producers and users of technological knowledge and in a manner conducive to social and economic welfare, and to a balance of rights and obligations." As with MFN, Article 7 is the first textual appearance of this principle in a multilateral intellectual property instrument. However (unlike MFN), it expresses principles that have long been fundamental to intellectual property law.

Subsequent international negotiations affirm this commitment. The WIPO Copyright Treaty on digital copyright, which was completed soon after TRIPS, includes in its preamble the need to "maintain a balance between the rights of authors and the larger public interest, particularly education, research and access to information."[110] Five years later, during the Doha Round, the Ministerial Declaration stressed that Article 7 was an integral part of the TRIPS Agreement and that the Council for TRIPS should bear it in mind in monitoring compliance (and, in effect, determining whether countries are complying). While the Declaration was made in the context of a health crisis and precipitated an amendment to the Agreement,[111] the provision on Article 7 was (like the rest of the Declaration) not confined to that context and was viewed as explaining—not modifying—the Agreement.[112]

We have already seen several ways in which reference to Article 7 would improve decision making. The previous discussion of discrimination in this Chapter illustrated the reluctance of the DSB to avoid consideration of state justifications for differential treatment. But in the context of TRIPS, the AB would not be in the "exposed position" Hudec described. Article 7 provides it with a powerful textual hook. It is hard to see how the DSB would be vulnerable to political criticism if it accepted an explanation grounded in agreed international norms. For example, no one could criticize the DSB if it upheld, against a differential impact challenge, a provision that contributed to "the promotion of technological innovation" and was "conducive to social and economic welfare" or "the balance of rights and obligations."

Similarly, in Chapter 3, we saw that the *Canada–Pharmaceuticals* and *US–110(5)* panels were slow to inject normative content into considerations of what counted as normal exploitation of the right or legitimate interests of the right holder. As with de facto discrimination, Article 7 provides a framework that would have improved the reasoning. Furthermore, and especially in *Canada–Pharmaceuticals*, the panels structured their analyses to limit consideration of countervailing interests. Article 7's reference to the "mutual advantage of producers and users" demonstrates why an approach that precludes consideration of the reasons underlying a state's action is wrong. Of course, the *Canada–Pharmaceuticals* panel was right that Article 7 (as well as Article 8) cannot be used to interpret the Exceptions provisions in a manner that would "'renegotiate' the overall balance of the Agreement."[113] However, there is a vast difference between revising the Agreement and taking into account a textual provision to which countries are committed.

More generally, greater use of Article 7 would not become a charter for eroding intellectual property rights. Its endorsement of the goal of promoting technological innovation and achieving the "mutual advantage of producers and users" equally safeguards right holders' interests in effective protection. Thus, a member state might challenge a provision that undermines the innovative environment on the ground that it shifts the balance too far in favor of users. Article 7 is, in short, not a commitment to any particular vision of intellectual property. Rather, it is a structural commitment that helps define the parameters in which member states can make different intellectual property choices appropriate to their needs.

2. *Article 8 (principles)*. Article 8, which was also stressed in the Ministerial Declaration at Doha, provides a list of specific interests that states might consider in crafting their intellectual property laws. These include health, nutrition, economic and technological development, and competition. These interests, although found in many *national* laws, have only recently been expressly stated in international intellectual property instruments. The provision recognizes, however, that countries (especially developing countries) that are new to intellectual property will need to deal with the costs of their new commitments. To be sure, Article 8 is explicitly limited to "measures [that] are consistent with the provisions of this Agreement." That language is puzzling, but it is highly significant because, in fact, it confirms that the Agreement as a whole is flexible and furnishes states with considerable room to maneuver in order to further the varied interests set out in Article 8. Article 8 reflects the experience of states that have long had intellectual property law and elevates that experience into an international principle. For example, while the WTO does not include an agreement on antitrust law, Article 8 recognizes that abuse of intellectual property rights is possible and that protection for competition is an essential

component of the system. As with Article 7, this provision effectuates principles of neofederalism.

3. *Article 1.1 (nature and scope of obligations).* Article 1.1 encompasses three structural principles. Most prominently, it endorses national autonomy by leaving member states free to "determine the appropriate method of implementing the provisions of this Agreement within their own legal system and practice." This principle, which was recognized by the AB in *India–Pharmaceuticals* and the panel in *China–Enforcement*,[114] restates a fundamental assumption of the international intellectual property system: international norms confine national policy choices, but they do not define them. Indeed, other provisions of the Agreement reflect this principle in varying degrees of particularity. Thus, although Article 41 requires members to provide judicial procedures to enforce intellectual property rights, Article 41.5 confirms that there is no "obligation to put in place a judicial system for the enforcement of intellectual property rights distinct from that for the enforcement of law in general." Furthermore, footnote 4 to Article 23.1 permits member states to use administrative, rather than judicial, actions when implementing their obligations to protect geographical indications on wines and spirits. Once again, and as *China–Enforcement* made clear, the commitment to national autonomy does not justify derogations from basic obligations.[115] But the framework leaves enough room to take account of different legal traditions and wide differences in available resources.

A second feature of Article 1.1 is that it identifies TRIPS, like the Paris and Berne Conventions, as a minimum standards agreement and not an intellectual property code. Thus, once again, it emphasizes neofederalism values. And, once again, there are limits. Although Article 1.1 allows member states to implement more extensive protection, it prevents them from doing so if such protection would "contravene the provisions of this Agreement." Implicitly, this language thus suggests a third principle, that the Agreement imposes ceilings on member states—a species of user rights. We return to the question of recognizing and developing that concept in Chapter 7.

4. *Articles 4 of the Paris Convention and Article 5 of the Berne Convention (securing protection).* These provisions, which are applicable through Articles 2.1 and 9 of TRIPS, are fundamental to establishing an international system of intellectual property protection. They have a strong historical pedigree, with an effect similar to national treatment. For industrial property (patents, trademarks, and designs), the priority mechanism of Article 4 facilitates the acquisition of protection and, particularly in the trademark context, global trade. But even though rights in subsequent countries are awarded on the basis of a single priority date, the rights obtained in each country are independent of one another.[116] This leaves each country free to apply its own principles of law to each application without interference from others.[117] We would therefore scrutinize challenges

based on these provisions strictly; however, we would allow a state that imposed a restriction on serial application to offer a justification in order to help the DSB determine whether the imposition was truly in conflict with the contemplated purpose of the priority provision. Thus, while we do not think that Article 4 addresses the priority of *examination* underlying SHARE, a closer case would be presented by a measure that truly impinged on the ability of the patent applicant to file successive counterpart applications.

In copyright, multinational protection is achieved not through a registration mechanism, but instead by precluding registration—or any other formalities—as a precondition to protection. Thus, as with the national treatment provision, which applies even to nonguaranteed protection, a member state is not permitted to condition copyright protection on compliance with formalities, even if the protection it offers is over and above that required by the substantive provisions of Berne or TRIPS. For instance, a member that decided to protect perfumes under copyright should be required to extend protection without imposing formalities, even though protection of scents through copyright is clearly not required.[118] Similarly, a country is not permitted (absent a justification that takes its measure beyond the scope of the formalities prohibition) to impose formalities on extensions of the term of protection beyond the international minimum (life plus fifty).[119]

5. *Other provisions.* At a more granular level, there are also questions about the dominance of one provision relative to another. As we saw, *Canada–Pharmaceuticals* saw Article 27.1 as applicable to Article 30. We concluded this was wrong. But as we saw in connection with the *eBay* initiative in Chapter 3, a harder question may be presented by the relationship between Articles 44 and 31, on whether a state can deny injunctive relief without complying with the long list of conditions imposed by Article 31 on compulsory licenses.[120] On the one hand, the choice between an administrative and judicial mechanism for authorized third-party uses of patented subject matter implicates legal culture and the role countries assign to the adjudicatory function. On the other hand, a state should not be permitted to avoid a restriction in TRIPS through characterization of the legal mechanism it chooses (remedy versus compulsory license). The decision to add enforcement obligations to the international intellectual property regime constitutes recognition of the importance of sure and adequate relief to the incentive function of intellectual property rights. Thus, Article 44 might be read to supplement the options available under Article 31.

Similarly, the reach—and thus the potential structural status—of the Exceptions provisions of Articles 13, 17, 26.2, and 30 is unclear. While it made no sense for *Canada–Pharmaceuticals* to extend the scope of Article 27.1 to exceptions expressly regulated by Article 30, given the latter's requirement that exceptions be "limited," it is more plausible to extend Article 30 to other aspects of patent rights, such as duration under Article 33. The Exceptions provisions present a hard case because they are nominally designed to provide members with room to maneuver. The international intellectual property system depends on the ability to deal exceptionally with particular circumstances, reflecting the values of complexity, diversity, and historical contingency discussed in Chapter 1. The ability to create exceptions therefore vindicates national autonomy interests and is, accordingly, an important aspect of maintaining the multinational "club." Thus, one would expect that provisions permitting unauthorized uses would be a structural feature of any comprehensive intellectual property regime.[121] In fact, however, WTO panels have read the Exception provisions in TRIPS in ways that *constrain* choice rather than promote flexibility. In a sense, the texts of these Exceptions also represent "unhappy borrowings." The four provisions were transplanted from Article 9.2 of the Berne Convention. In Berne, however, the standard applied only to the reproduction right, and operated against a background rule with respect to which the states otherwise enjoyed substantial autonomy. Accordingly, it is difficult to regard these particular Exceptions provisions, both as written and as interpreted, in a structural fashion.

Exploring the scope of the provisions of TRIPS, Paris, and Berne and the relationships among them has allowed us to tease out candidates for what we have called "structural status." With the proliferation of international instruments in intellectual property, and the involvement of new institutions in intellectual property lawmaking, fragmentation will make the task of providing a structural framework for international intellectual property lawmaking harder and more significant; it will also raise new questions about the analysis of the MFN guarantee of TRIPS. We explore these issues in Chapter 6. Before that, however, we consider the question of how the interpretation of the TRIPS Agreement accommodates the operation of each member's political economy as it relates to intellectual property law.

5

TRIPS and Domestic Lawmaking

> The public increasingly recognises the need for reform. That was why Piratpartiet—the Pirate party—won 7.1 per cent of the popular vote in Sweden in the European Union elections. This gave us a seat in the European parliament for the first time. Our manifesto is to reform copyright laws and gradually abolish the patent system.... This is our entire platform.
>
> —Christian Engström (newly elected member of the Swedish Pirate Party to the European Parliament), *Copyright Laws Threaten Our Online Freedom*, FT.com, FINANCIAL TIMES, July 7, 2009

> Whereas copyright legislation typically evolves from a compromise among all the affected parties, giving rise to a consensus, the Fairness in Music Licensing Act... arrived on a decidedly different track.... Restauranteurs held the Sonny Bono Copyright Term Extension Act hostage until they secured passage of this unrelated legislation in their own interest.
>
> —MELVILLE B. NIMMER AND DAVID NIMMER, 2 NIMMER ON COPYRIGHT § 8.18[C][2][b](Matthew Bender rev. ed. 2010)

> Patent-term extensions and the Bolar exemption are self-canceling provisions which, taken together, have no net effect on the length of the exclusive marketing period of most new drugs.
>
> —Alfred B. Engelberg, *Special Patent Provisions for Pharmaceuticals: Have They Outlived Their Usefulness?*, 39 IDEA 389 (1999)

In Chapters 3 and 4, we looked at how the Dispute Settlement Body (DSB) assessed particular legislative initiatives. We expressed concern that the approaches it adopted do not give member states sufficient flexibility to tailor their laws to their social circumstances or enough leeway to adapt to change. In fact, however, the autonomy interests of states, particularly democratic states, may be even more tightly constrained. In this Chapter we probe the TRIPS Agreement to see whether it is sufficiently neofederalist to accommodate institutional and political realities at the national level. TRIPS was arguably developed in an environment of heightened interest in intellectual property, at a time when it was becoming very clear that knowledge assets would play an important role in the global economy. But as the preceding quotation from the Pirate Party illustrates, a high degree of skepticism has recently set in. Aggressive enforcement of intellectual property rights has provoked a backlash, particularly in the online context. More generally, changes in technology have brought into question many of the assumptions underlying intellectual property law. At the same time, concerns about such matters as the environment and human rights have become more prominent. In developing countries intellectual property rights are even more contentious, for they collide with issues crucial to human subsistence. Many of these countries are struggling to meet their new obligations while simultaneously dealing with the distributive consequences of enacting high levels of intellectual property protection.

As intellectual property lawmaking has become more fiercely contested, reforms occur only when lawmakers can use every device available to them within their political economies and legal systems. As the history of TRIPS itself demonstrates, packaging matters: an initiative may be more acceptable if the burdens imposed by new rights are accompanied by offsetting benefits. Furthermore, it can take time for new technologies to diffuse and for the political system to fully assimilate them, both socially and legally. States need flexibility during the period of assimilation to experiment with different levels of protection and develop an understanding of how best to regulate. Finally, capacity is of the essence: a country needs a sophisticated legal and administrative infrastructure in order to fully assess options and frame solutions that further national needs while complying with international norms. In interpreting and administering the TRIPS Agreement, the WTO must begin to reckon with the political realities presented by packaging, diffusion, and capacity.

I. Packaging

It is a feature of lawmaking in many countries that discrete issues are dealt with as part of larger legislative initiatives, with components of the legislative package addressed to divergent constituencies. Typically, WTO disputes involve only the piece of legislation that is said to violate a covered agreement. However, disaggregating individual measures from their broader legislative context ignores the political reality that intellectual property laws are not always enacted as discrete mandates. As innovation ecosystems evolve, new actors emerge, new forms of production arise, and new relationships form between users and proprietors. Accommodating these changes will often require a suite of interrelated reforms. These new measures shift the incidents of protection, creating winners and losers relative to the status quo. One example is the U.S. Copyright Revision Act of 1976, in which wholesale reforms were agreed upon through trade-offs and compromises among interested groups, and then enacted into law by Congress.[1] To put our question another way: Does the deference Article 1.1 extends to "method[s] of implementing the provisions of this Agreement within [members'] own legal system and practice" include recognition of this dynamic?

So far, the DSB has not interpreted Article 1.1 in this way. Consider, for example, the exemption of certain public performances of musical works from the scope of copyright liability, which was at issue in the US–110(5) case discussed in Chapter 3.[2] That provision—the so-called Irish bar exception—was expanded as part of a political package that included the extension of the copyright term by twenty years. The net result—the Sonny Bono Copyright Term Extension Act[3]—contained benefits (term extension) to all copyright holders, in exchange for a reduction in protection (exceptions for certain business establishments) that affected a few copyright holders (the holders of copyrights in musical works). It also produced a social benefit in that it made music more readily available in public spaces. The same lawmaking process can be observed in patent law. A good example here is the 1984 extension of the term of U.S. patent protection on pharmaceuticals subject to regulatory review.[4] In exchange for lengthening the term, Congress enacted the "Bolar exemption," which permitted generic drug manufacturers to use patented pharmaceuticals for the purpose of generating the information needed for market clearance.[5] The net result—the Drug Price Competition and Patent Term Restoration Act (commonly called the Hatch-Waxman Act)[6]—was a package that added to the protection enjoyed by patent holders in the pharmaceutical industries, while accelerating public access to low-cost medicines after patent termination.

But despite the obvious trade-offs inherent in these legislative measures, WTO adjudicators analyzed each challenged measure as a discrete reform. In the case of the Sonny Bono Act, the Irish bar provision was the subject of a complaint by the European Union, and part of the measure was invalidated. However, the US–110(5) panel's 120-page analysis never alluded to the provision's complicated etiology or to the compromise it embodied. The Hatch-Waxman Act has not been challenged, but a somewhat analogous Canadian law was. The Canadian law included the regulatory review provision that allowed generics to generate market clearance data, but it did not extend the term of pharmaceutical patents. Although the WTO panel in *Canada–Pharmaceuticals* noted this key difference between Canadian and U.S. law, it did not believe that the absence of that trade-off should in any way affect its decision.[7]

This "discrete" approach to adjudication (by which we mean that discrete parts of legislative compromises are broken out for individual assessment) can produce perverse consequences. Not only does it unravel carefully negotiated legislative deals, it does so in a systematic way. Because TRIPS principally sets minimum standards, WTO dispute resolution operates as a one-way ratchet: complaints can lead to the invalidation of measures that *reduce* the level of intellectual property protection, but typically they will not reach measures that *increase* protection. Thus, compromises will always unravel in the same direction, requiring nations to change those features of their legislation that benefit user groups while protection-enhancing provisions stay in place.

On occasion, user groups may be able to challenge a protection-enhancing measure in a domestic court, claiming that the increase in protection undermines national values and constitutive agreements that protect public access. For example, the other half of the Sonny Bono Act—the term extension benefit given to copyright holders—was challenged as going beyond congressional authority. If such a challenge invoked the same level of scrutiny that the WTO gives to reductions in protection, the systematic effect would be corrected. However, there is no reason to believe that the approach to review will be the same. In fact, the term extension in the Sonny Bono Act was subjected to an extremely deferential standard of review—ironically, a standard that not only deferred to congressional judgments, but also allowed such judgments to be based in part upon international considerations.[8] As a result, although the Irish bar provision was struck down in the WTO, the term extension was upheld by the U.S. Supreme Court.

To make matters worse, this is an iterative process. As interest groups come to understand the situation, they could exploit it. Intellectual property holders may become quick to agree to provisions that reduce the level of protection in exchange for the protection-enhancing legislation that they want, knowing that the reductions can be successfully challenged at the international level. Indeed, because interest groups transcend borders, it may even be that domestic rights holders actively promote TRIPS challenges themselves.[9] For example, the Irish Music Rights Organization, which helped convince the European Union to bring the *US–110(5)* case, works closely with performing rights organizations in the United States—that is, the organizations that represented the principal domestic losers in the deal embodied in the Sonny Bono Act. Alternatively, user groups may be less willing to consider compromise, or they may try to avoid a TRIPS challenge by burying provisions that pertain to intellectual property laws in legislation that is less obviously subject to WTO scrutiny, such as food and drug, consumer protection, telecommunications law, or other regulatory provisions. In the end, nations lose the flexibility to deal effectively and transparently with the issues that emerge at the frontiers of knowledge production.

In prior Chapters, we noted the problems of applying trade principles developed under the GATT to intellectual property. In a sense, the problem identified here is the converse: the failure to treat trade and intellectual property similarly when they exhibit the same needs. Thus, in the earliest years of multilateral trade negotiations, there were fears that national priorities and the dynamics of domestic lawmaking might undermine the emerging international order. To accommodate those concerns, the text of the 1947 GATT, as expanded in subsequent rounds and later subsumed within the WTO trade regime, includes cushioning—provisions that save the agreement as a whole even when a member cannot fulfill particular obligations. For example, the General Exceptions provision of Article XX permits members to deal with issues of overarching national importance, such as preservation of public morals, health, and cultural treasures.[10] Under Article XXVIII, a state that finds it necessary to reduce concessions in one sector is permitted to negotiate compensatory concessions in other sectors.[11]

The apparent absence of similar safeguards to protect the viability of the TRIPS Agreement, particularly in its early years, is troubling. As Warren Schwartz and Alan Sykes have argued, "[T]he parties to trade agreements ... enter the bargain under conditions of uncertainty. Economic conditions may change, the strength of interest group organizations may change."[12] Better, they say, for the bargain to be adjusted than for members to leave. We believe the same is true of TRIPS: if it is to endure, comparable strategies are necessary. The institutional and international concerns that prompted caution in the GATT trade regimes (especially in its earliest stages) need to be recognized in the intellectual property context as well. Moreover, these concerns will persist in TRIPS because national priorities will inevitably change in response to technological developments. In Chapter 3, we emphasized that there are provisions in the TRIPS Agreement that can be interpreted as functional substitutes to Article XX. We similarly believe that there should be analogues to the compensatory-concessions philosophy of Article XXVIII. Where intellectual property provisions come into law through a process of give-and-take among stakeholders in the creative industries, we suggest that these circumstances should be taken into account in the dispute settlement process. As Kyle Bagwell and his coauthors explain, the theory underlying Article XXVIII is that a state that adopts a policy impinging on its trade commitments can nonetheless be regarded as GATT-compliant if balancing concessions maintain market access overall.[13] In the intellectual property context, where compliance with TRIPS commitments can raise the price of goods, market exclusivity is a more important metric than market access. Thus, our argument is that a provision reducing the level of protection may survive scrutiny so long as it is part of a legislative deal that preserves market exclusivity overall. There are a variety of scenarios that should be considered; we focus on those that reflect actual or likely legislative compromises.

A. Contemporaneous Intraregime Trade-offs

The background to the US–110(5) dispute illustrates perhaps the most typical variation, in which a single statutory reform includes both a provision that enhances protection and one that reduces it within the same intellectual property regime. As noted earlier, the danger in such cases is that the different components of the trade-off will be subjected to different levels of scrutiny, notwithstanding that the general level of protection—both before and after the reform—is approximately constant. If one provision (the decrease in protection) is invalidated, while the other is upheld, then the bargain is undone. Thus, we argue that adjudicators should take into account the broader legislative context in which the challenged provision was enacted.

Clearly, the DSB must still review the challenged measure; the mere existence of a trade-off does not confer immunity. National legislators might be tempted to sacrifice the interests of foreigners for the benefit of domestic interests. Thus, the DSB must ensure compliance with the national treatment obligation under Article 3. Furthermore, the package overall must comply with the minimum standards provisions of TRIPS. However, the level of scrutiny the DSB applies to the trade-off issue should not be overly strict, and it should not require a one-to-one correspondence between benefits and detriments. For example, the Sonny Bono Act was overinclusive, in the sense that the benefits of the Act (term extension) accrued to all copyright owners, while the contraction (the reduced scope of public performance rights) affected only holders of rights in nondramatic musical works. But everyone who lost protection (right holders whose music was played in an establishment covered by the provision at issue in US–110(5)) also enjoyed the benefits of a longer term of protection. Since the imbalance, overall, was in the direction of increasing copyright protection, it accords with the protective slant of the Agreement.[14] To the extent that US–110(5) was viewed as a close case on the merits, consideration of the broader context might have led the DSB to decide it in favor of the United States.

Obviously, valuation of the costs and benefits will present difficult issues. In the case of Hatch-Waxman, for example, many patent holders complain that term extension does not fully compensate them for the exclusivity lost by the regulatory review exception.[15] And as the Nimmer quotation at the beginning of this Chapter suggests, not everyone was satisfied with the bargain embodied in the Sonny Bono Act. Furthermore, in cases in which the trade-off is underinclusive, in that the parties who were adversely affected did not enjoy equivalent gains, this approach may not save the legislation in question. However, our suggestion to take account of trade-offs should not be rejected simply because it will not always yield a finding of compliance; in fact, its limited ability to save challenged legislation suggests that this approach would not undermine the basic gains of the TRIPS Agreement.

B. Contemporaneous Interregime Trade-offs

There could be situations where a legislature reduces the level of one form of intellectual property protection while increasing protection in another intellectual property regime. For example, the U.S. Congress could decide to eliminate design patents and liberalize trade dress protection for product designs. Similarly, it could limit copyright protection of software to wholesale piracy of the literal aspects of programs, while explicitly endorsing the case law holding that software and computer processing are patentable.[16] In both cases the reduction in protection is arguably challengeable—the design reform under Article 25 and the software provision under Article 10.1.

The fidelity of the Appellate Body (AB) to text may make such interregime trade-offs unlikely to be considered by adjudicators, but we believe that a broader perspective of the overall reform should again (though in fewer circumstances than with intraregime trade-offs) save particular provisions from invalidation. This argument will be hardest to make where the TRIPS Agreement explicitly provides for protection of stated subject matter within specific regimes, as might be the case, for example, with respect to the protection of software under copyright law. It might also be difficult where the duration of protection is precise and differs between regimes, or where other incidents of protection (such as what amounts to infringement) are clearly stated in the TRIPS Agreement and are radically different from one intellectual property regime to another.[17]

But intellectual property regimes are converging such that there are instances in which particular subject matter could rationally be protected under more than one rubric. Moreover, regulatory liberalization of the information industries has facilitated active cross-sectoral consolidation, particularly in the media.[18] The result is that players in these sectors are less invested in specific strategies, or in particular intellectual property rights, for appropriating gains and recapturing investments. At the same time, the technological changes that are leading to convergence may require nations to experiment with different legal approaches in order to decide which works best. Because TRIPS permits members to expand protection above the stated minimum standards, in the interim, protection may become excessive. Thus, it is important that the TRIPS Agreement not be read to prevent member states from later switching legal regimes or rolling back excessive protection to the international minimum.

For example, were the United States to abolish its design patent system,[19] the action could provoke a complaint based on Article 25 of the TRIPS Agreement, which requires "the protection of independently created industrial designs that are new or original." But trade dress protection for product design under § 43(a) of the Lanham Act arguably provides a scope of protection that, while not identical, is comparable (and probably in practice more effective) than that available through the current design patent system.[20] If the abolition of patents on design prompted a challenge under Article 25, could the United States claim that the expansion of trade dress protection satisfied its TRIPS obligations? The thresholds for protection and the subject matter of industrial design protection under Article 25 are amenable to the application of widely different rules in national law. In such a case, the ability of producers to capture the return guaranteed by the design provisions of the TRIPS Agreement should be accorded greater weight than the form that the protection takes.

Again, the existence of a trade-off should not be considered dispositive of compliance. Further examination is needed. As noted previously, compliance with minimum standards requires rough equality between the trade-offs. Adjudicators should also make sure that the change does not violate other TRIPS guarantees (such as national treatment). Further, when the intellectual property regime is changed, a finding of compliance should depend on whether the affected parties must make fresh investments in order to take advantage of the substitute form of protection.[21]

C. Contemporaneous External Trade-offs

The hardest case for taking account of legislative trade-offs is presented by the situation where the benefits are accorded outside the forms of protection encompassed by the TRIPS Agreement. For example, although the principal offsets in the Hatch-Waxman Act are found in the Patent Act, the deal was partially executed through provisions in the Food, Drug, and Cosmetics Act (FDCA).[22] Presumably, other packages could be created in this way as well, and there could be situations where the public benefits are in intellectual property legislation while the protection-enhancing provisions are in other laws (or vice versa). Should this legislative strategy affect the weight given to the trade-off?

When a measure is challenged in the WTO, the DSB has not been deterred from reviewing compatibility with TRIPS just because the legislation is not labeled as an intellectual property instrument. For example, in *Havana Club*, the AB reviewed a measure that was contained in the Omnibus Appropriations Act of 1998; the provision at issue was part of a regime implementing the U.S. policy of isolating Cuba.[23] But the DSB tends to be formalistic. Because the TRIPS Agreement expressly permits substitution of nonintellectual property regimes in certain clearly identified cases,[24] it could invoke an expressio unius est exclusio alterius argument to refuse to apply the same reasoning when a country claims that it has satisfied TRIPS obligations with a measure that is not labeled as intellectual property.

Admittedly, even if the AB were to take a less formalistic view and consider such packages as a whole, there would be problems. Relying on compensating protections that are outside the intellectual property system (as defined by TRIPS) has many of the same problems as other trade-off analyses. But valuation problems are exacerbated because the forms of protection are likely to differ sharply from those of standard intellectual property regimes. In addition, shifting the regime of protection may radically undermine investment-based expectations (reliance interests) that are at the heart of the TRIPS bargain. Consider again the design example. Because design producers were surely aware of trade dress protection when they made their initial investments, their expectations would not be dashed by abolishing design patent protection. Similarly, players in the pharmaceutical business are well informed about the regulatory regime imposed by the FDCA. In other situations, the change in regimes may be less foreseeable and more disruptive. For instance, switching from a patent system to a bounty system or to a tax subsidy regime would present problems. The returns, and the rate at which they are provided, are highly dissimilar.[25] There would be transition problems for those who made their investments in reliance on patent protection because they may not be in a position to fully utilize their tax benefits to offset costs. Further, an assessment of equivalence should arguably take into account the indirect, nonmonetary benefits of the regime relinquished. For example, patents are used for signaling and to facilitate cross-licensing and pooling; similar benefits may not be available through a tax-based approach.[26]

But there may be circumstances when such external trade-offs should be taken into account. As the FDCA and design examples demonstrate, the impact of change on a rights holder's expectations will not always be dramatic. In such cases, adjudicators should accord deference to national political choices. This is especially true when the TRIPS obligation is expressed in language that is more in the nature of a standard rather than a specific rule, where the provision implicates the allocation of national resources, and, of course, where the Agreement specifically recognizes national autonomy.[27] It is also worth noting that the places where TRIPS currently envisions nonintellectual property regime enforcement are instances where international protections are in flux (the protection of plants and geographic indications);[28] similar flexibility would be useful in other situations that involve emergent norms (such as trade secrets and rental rights).

D. Countervailing Considerations

The regard for trade-offs that we propose is analytically similar to the importance we previously placed on requiring the DSB to go beneath the surface of legislation to consider its normative basis. Just as we saw in Chapter 4 that the AB's reluctance to become enmeshed in state justifications in the context of de facto discrimination paradoxically limits national autonomy, so too does the failure to recognize trade-offs that are the product of legal, cultural, political, and commercial realities. Nonetheless, we recognize that requiring panels to expand the scope of their inquiry could be problematic. This approach requires more fact-finding about the content and nature of the challenged law. In large part, the DSB relies on information provided by the parties to the dispute and intervenors, but there are cases in which the analysis has proceeded on an apparently mistaken understanding of the relevant national law. For example, as discussed in Chapter 2, in the US–110(5) dispute, the panel relied on an implausible reading of the statute. For trade-offs, where more than one measure must be assessed, these problems multiply. And the process introduces other complications. Decision making will be more complex and the approach could undermine WTO norms. Allowing states to use packaging as a defense could also interfere with democratic values.

1. Decision making

One problem has been alluded to throughout: measuring trade-offs will certainly add to the work required to resolve TRIPS disputes. While we acknowledge that this is true, we do not believe it to be dispositive. Our proposal adds to the workload in two ways. First, it requires adjudicators to define the terms of the package. Just as the panel in US–110(5) misunderstood the legislation, so too could a panel misunderstand a package. For example, in *Canada–Pharmaceuticals*, the panel proceeded as if there was no link between the regulatory review exception and the extension of patent term in the United States.[29] As demonstrated by the Engelberg quotation at the outset of this Chapter, this approach was contrary to available evidence. However, the DSB could take action to minimize the danger of misconstruing the nature of packages. For example, it could put a burden on states that wish to take advantage of a claimed trade-off to establish its terms through contemporaneous documentation. Once that requirement is articulated, members will surely develop legislative techniques that make the trade-offs they enact into law explicit. Such techniques can only be advantageous, both to the efficiency of WTO dispute resolution and to the transparency of domestic legislation.

Second, the DSB will be required to evaluate the trade-off to determine the overall effect of the package. The evaluation is likely to be difficult, especially in the case of interregime or external trade-offs. Such evaluations are, however, likewise a problem with the WTO agreements as a whole: each round of negotiations requires members to determine whether the benefits they receive in one area are worth the costs suffered in other sectors. Members have not pulled out of the WTO because of the difficulty of this task, even after the Uruguay Round made valuations even more complex by requiring trade-offs between intellectual property and trade protection. Admittedly, accurate valuation is more critical in the rule-bound context of adjudication than it is in the diplomatic environment of negotiation, where members retain the sovereign authority to broker deals. However, these kinds of calculations are also inherent in the Dispute Settlement Understanding (DSU). When a country fails to implement a ruling within a reasonable time, the other party is permitted to seek compensation or, if need be, suspend obligations under other covered agreements.[30] Both compensation and cross-sectoral retaliatory sanctions require difficult computations and, in the latter case, an assessment of both losses and the equivalence of proposed compensatory measures.

2. WTO norms

It could also be claimed that our proposed approach is incompatible with evolving norms within the WTO. Thus, there are two decisions touching on intellectual property where a measure was rejected notwithstanding claims of offsets. In *US–337*, importers of intellectual property were required to litigate claims of infringement in one court, whereas domestic producers could use a different forum, with different procedures and joinder possibilities.[31] The United States argued that the procedure for imports created offsetting benefits and, in any event, did not produce different outcomes. But the panel rejected the claim and invalidated the measure. To the extent it accepted the possibility of offsets, it held that "elements of less and more favourable treatment could thus only be offset against each other to the extent that they always would arise in the same cases and necessarily would have an offsetting influence on the other."[32] In the end, it reasoned that "such an interpretation would lead to great uncertainty about the conditions of competition between imported and domestic products and thus defeat the purposes of Article III [of the GATT]."[33] In *Havana Club*, the panel had accepted an argument of substantive equality, which was based on offsetting disadvantages for each class of trademark holder. Although the AB did not explicitly reject the approach, it required a standard of proof regarding the impact of the offsetting harms that the United States could not meet.[34]

But these cases can be distinguished. Both concerned denials of national treatment. As we argued in Chapter 4, national treatment is significantly different from the substantive provisions of the TRIPS Agreement. It ensures the integrity of the trade and intellectual property systems. But it does so without substantially limiting the policy choices open to member states in regulating their creative environments. Thus, the right to discriminate against trading partners is the one element of sovereignty that a nation clearly cedes when it joins the WTO and the international intellectual property system; the same cannot be said of all the substantive provisions. While the centrality of national treatment to the trade and intellectual property regimes demands a high standard of proof on compliance with GATT III (or TRIPS Article 3), the substantive provisions are minimum standards. As such, they must be interpreted to give member states leeway.

More important is an objection that relates to the analogy we draw to GATT XXVIII. The GATT contemplates consultation among trading partners before action is taken, while we do not. We agree that a practice of consultation is far preferable. It would avoid surprises and create an opportunity for member states to discuss approaches to new problems. An avenue that provides for dialogue on a forward-going basis would be a worthwhile addition to the Agreement. But the inability to impute a specific consultation requirement should not doom our approach. If some sort of consultation with trade partners is regarded as important, it could be fostered by having panels entertaining complaints consider whether the state made voluntary attempts to address the issue in the Council for TRIPS before changing its law. There is also some flexibility to achieve a similar result through the remedial provisions of the WTO. Thus, one way to avoid unraveling domestic deals would be by requiring compensation in lieu of compliance—which, in fact, is precisely the approach the United States took in the *US–110(5)* case.[35] Although this approach has problems of its own,[36] arbitration over the payment obligation could be considered to substitute for a consultation requirement.

We also recognize another normative objection to our proposal as regards external trade-offs, which is that there will be too much "linkage" among legal regimes; that as linkages spread from one area to another, the WTO Agreement could become a global constitution. Specifically for intellectual property, there is a danger if nonintellectual property laws (that is, laws outside the scope of the TRIPS Agreement) can be proffered as evidence of compliance with the Agreement, then symmetry might be said to demand that these laws should also be subject to challenge under TRIPS. We reject the inevitability of that argument. In the cases envisioned here, the packaging of nonintellectual property with intellectual property measures provides a nexus between the enactment and the TRIPS Agreement. In such cases, the intent to effectuate an intellectual property result can be presumed (the Hatch-Waxman Act's provisions are examples). But when a nonintellectual property law is enacted as a freestanding measure, it should not automatically invoke TRIPS obligations. Without the intellectual property packaging, no motivation should be imputed.

3. Democratic values

It has been forcefully argued that the constraints imposed by the WTO system enhance democratic values because they operate as a precommitment strategy that reduces rent seeking by certain powerful interest groups. An approach that relaxes those constraints is, arguably, a move in the wrong direction. More prosaically, it could be said that any system that promotes logrolling is bad by definition.

In considering this issue, it is important to keep the differences between trade and intellectual property in mind. Given the theoretical premises underlying the GATT, it is easy to understand the argument that the GATT is democracy-enhancing. Under that view, free trade is regarded as an unambiguous good because reaping comparative advantages increases social wealth. Interest groups that seek to undermine free trade ("protectionists" in trade parlance) are thinking irrationally or in too short a term. Unfortunately, they include labor and other highly organized entities, while those who stand to benefit from free trade are largely unorganized consumers. Without a powerful side constraint, in the form of an enforceable international agreement, the concentrated group will win domestically, thereby undermining the good of the majority.

Whatever one might think of this argument in the trade context, it is substantially less applicable to intellectual property. In the intellectual property story, the "protectionists" (in intellectual property parlance) are still the more highly organized group, but the TRIPS Agreement barely constrains them. Instead it favors them by ensuring that they will enjoy certain minimum levels of protection. It is user groups—the groups that are less organized domestically—who are most constrained by TRIPS. In effect, the Agreement reduces their domestic leverage by exposing their legislative wins to the scrutiny of dispute resolution while leaving their legislative losses alone. And yet it is not clear that they are the ones who are thinking irrationally or in the short term. While it could be argued that TRIPS is meant to impose an optimal level of protection, that optimal is difficult to determine. Intellectual property protection has significant distributive consequences. And because knowledge is cumulative—one person's output is another's input—intellectual property law needs a domain in which access to information is assured. TRIPS largely leaves it to states to determine the appropriate balance between producer and user interests, and an overly narrow or formalistic application of TRIPS could destroy their ability to do so. Accordingly, the law must strive for a balance between producer and user interests.

A system that takes trade-offs into account can, of course, be condemned as logrolling—as facilitating the raw power of particular interest groups and other rent seekers. However, it is logrolling of a peculiar sort. Because it is effective as a defense to a TRIPS challenge only when there are compensatory benefits on all sides, it creates, in essence, leverage for the benefit of those less able to help themselves (usually, user groups) and, in the final analysis, promotes the enactment of balanced legislation. The nature of the logrolling induced by this proposal is also circumscribed. The trade-offs must be internal to the system of promoting intellectual progress and knowledge dissemination; initiatives that include a close nexus between expanded and contracted protection (such as trade-offs within a particular intellectual property regime) are more likely to survive scrutiny than those that do not have such a nexus. This system has other advantages as well. It renders lawmaking more transparent because it rewards clear articulation of the trade-offs in the legislative package.

II. Diffusion

To critics of the Uruguay Round, one of the disturbing features of the TRIPS Agreement was the rapidity with which WTO members were expected to adopt compliant intellectual property regimes. Article 65 gave developing countries five years to implement the Agreement (ten for technologies not previously protected by patents), and under Article 66, least developed countries had ten years to fulfill all intellectual property obligations. However, these periods were far too brief: developing countries could not assimilate their new obligations as quickly as TRIPS required. Indeed, as the *India–Pharmaceuticals* dispute illustrates, the political percolation required in a democracy can slow intellectual property lawmaking. Thus, India could not implement the "pipeline" provision required by Article 70.8 through its normal political process and had to resort to a municipal ordinance and administrative regulations.[37] Despite some extension of implementation deadlines, for the most part and for most countries, the transition period is now over, and most member states are expected to have laws compliant with TRIPS. Nonetheless, the lesson from the initial period should not be lost. While the AB in *India–Pharmaceuticals* gave modest weight to the political realities India confronted, we would argue that more latitude is necessary. That is especially true for developing countries, but it is so even for industrialized nations. The "gale of creative destruction" presented by new technologies, like the disruption caused by new intellectual property obligations, requires a period of assimilation and experimentation.[38]

Once again, the GATT offers an analogy. Article XIX and its associated Agreement on Safeguards provide circumstances in which a nation is allowed to suspend obligations and withdraw concessions on a temporary basis, to give the country the time it needs to mount effective competition against sudden increases in imports that result from unforeseen developments and cause, or threaten to cause, serious injury.[39] Under this provision, compliance is, essentially, measured over time. We adapt that philosophy to suggest ways in which a similar approach could be used to allow states to respond to changes in the level of exclusivity resulting from social and technological developments. Admittedly, a calculation based on increasing imports is not directly transferrable to the TRIPS Agreement because TRIPS commitments have a more complex effect on imports: they can lead to a decrease in imports (by raising prices to supracompetitive levels) or to an increase (by increasing incentives to exploit new markets). Instead, the problem for intellectual property is the changing forms of knowledge production and distribution. Technologies are developed, institutions change, and rights are created, triggering competitive concerns and threatening progress. Just as members may need transitional periods where they learn to deal with rising imports, they need flexibility to deal with these sorts of challenges. Analogizing to Article XIX of GATT thus provides another avenue for accommodating neofederalist values.

Indeed, an argument can be made that members need even more flexibility to deal with new technologies than with new trade problems. In the trade regime, new commodities trigger fresh negotiations. As Andrew Guzman has pointed out, these negotiations are exercises in sovereignty: an agreement to a new round of concessions represents a contract among states to cede authority under specified circumstances.[40] With TRIPS, however, new technologies may, in some cases, be automatically amalgamated into each member's obligations.[41] Since there is no room to exercise sovereign authority at the time a technology is subsumed in the international regime, greater autonomy may be needed during the diffusion period in which its ramifications become evident.

A. Supporting Emerging Industries

Closest in spirit to Article XIX (as we conceptualize it) would be measures that relax intellectual property protections to support emerging information industries. Consider, for example, the cable retransmission rules of the U.S. Copyright Act.[42] Because these provisions essentially reduce the scope of copyright protection by permitting certain free and unauthorized transmissions, they are not easily understood as a matter of copyright policy.[43] Rather, they are intended to pursue telecommunications policy—they helped to establish and stabilize cable technology when it was under development and were, in actuality, enacted through a compromise brokered by the Federal Communications Commission rather than the Copyright Office.[44] These measures were enacted before TRIPS went into effect and have not been challenged. However, if they became the subject of a complaint, they would presumably be evaluated under the Exceptions test of Article 13. Perhaps they would survive this analysis on their own. However, we would argue that their survival should not be made to depend on the happenstance of the formalistic way in which that test is administered. The retransmission rules were enacted to stimulate the economy at a crucial time in the development of a technological infrastructure important to the creative industries. If these industries are to flourish, and new industries are to emerge, then adjudicators must take a nation's decision to support these developments into account when determining compliance with TRIPS.

To be sure, there is a significant difference between the cable rules and the measures contemplated by Article XIX: under the GATT, the industrial support initiative must be temporary. At the end of the day, the United States could not have used this approach to justify an enduring cable retransmission law. However, were this form of analysis to become part of TRIPS jurisprudence, the availability of such a defense might lead Congress to put sunset provisions into future legislation that is intended to support new industries. In this connection, it is not insignificant that many argue that a sunset provision should have been included in the cable rules, and that, in fact, the retransmission right should now be changed because the exigencies that warranted it no longer exist, and—more important—because the cable industry now has so much power, it can use these rules to thwart the vitality of older technologies (such as broadcast), and to impede the development of new technologies that are not covered by the provision (such as the internet).[45]

B. Reacting to Emerging Technologies

Just as legal change can be a catalyst for developing new technologies, new technologies may be the catalyst for legal change. In assessing whether the overall level of intellectual property protection complies with TRIPS, we believe that adjudicators should take into account how changing social practices and new technological opportunities alter the balance of protection accorded to innovative works.

An example is the levy system that most European countries impose on the sale of recording equipment. Arguably, this effectuates a right of the copyright owner in that it provides compensation to authors in return for use of their work in private copying, where it would be difficult to collect royalties. However, Article 5 of the European Copyright Directive now contemplates the reduction (arguably to zero) of some of these levy payments.[46] Although the Europeans claim that the levy system falls outside the scope of the TRIPS Agreement, if the system is covered (as some contend),[47] then abolishing the levies arguably "conflict[s] with the normal exploitation of the work," in violation of Article 13.

How should such a claim be analyzed? If one looks simply at the levy reform, the abolition would appear vulnerable to challenge because private copying "could detract significantly from the economic returns anticipated from a ... grant of market exclusivity."[48] Yet, the Directive will reduce levies only when the application of digital rights management systems (DRMs) would facilitate a return by copyright owners at least equivalent to what would have been obtained under levies. To us, the technical capacity of DRMs to secure equivalent returns over time should be relevant in assessing compliance.

More generally, we believe that adjudicators should focus on the technological context in which legal rules operate. Without that perspective, replications of the one-way ratchet phenomenon described earlier in connection with the Sonny Bono Act will likely proliferate. Thus, enhanced technological capacity to infringe copyright has been cited as a justification for national measures enhancing the rights of copyright owners. For instance, anticircumvention provisions of the type enacted in the U.S. Digital Millennium Copyright Act are often defended on the grounds that widespread copying has undermined incentives for the production of digitized works.[49] Because of the deferential review under national law, these provisions tend to survive challenge.[50] If protection-contracting provisions are subjected to more intrusive scrutiny, a nation's ability to consider law and technology as a package that in combination strikes an appropriate balance of protection will be distorted: legislators will be able to take into account technology's capacity to undermine rights, but not to enhance them. Thus, if technological trade-offs can justify the enhancement of protection at the national level, they should also be available at the international level to justify contractions.

Social and legal change must also be considered in connection with initiatives that respond to the inherent nature of scientific advances. For example, as the Illustration in Chapter 1 demonstrated, many recent fundamental discoveries have a dual character; they are both principles of nature and end-use applications. As such, they are considered patentable subject matter. But as these "upstream" inventions become subject to exclusive rights, the conduct of fundamental research may be impeded and progress stifled. If this proves to be the case, it may become necessary to reduce the scope of protection, for example, by creating new and broader defenses. But any reduction in scope, if considered separate and apart from the science that drives it, could result in a successful challenge in the WTO. To avoid chilling progress, contextual examination is thus required, and the reactive nature of the contraction measure should be taken into account in resolving the challenge. If the combination of the change in science and the legal contraction maintains similar levels of protection, the legal change should not be regarded as violating minimum standards. In a sense, those who made fundamental discoveries are no worse off with a patent of narrow scope than they were if their work were considered unpatentable.

C. Countervailing Considerations

Once again, the analogy we make to Article XIX of GATT and the Safeguards Agreement can be questioned. Thus, it has been claimed that this provision is an artifact of the original GATT and has no place in the system of binding and predicable rules that has evolved over the last half century.[51] Indeed, the

United States' loss in the *Steel Safeguards Case*[52] may be an indication that no safeguard measure will ever be approved by the AB.[53] We do not believe that this observation diminishes the force of our argument. That fifty years' experience has apparently produced a clear understanding of the trade rules is heartening, but it would be a mistake to think that the knowledge that has been acquired is a function of the dispute resolution mechanism in place, or that it extends to intellectual property, which presents issues quite distinct from those arising in trade. Furthermore, we are reluctant to conclude that the absence of winning cases based on these provisions means they are ineffective. To the contrary, it is quite likely that complaints are not brought when it is clear that one of these provisions would provide a full defense. By the same token, the actions members take may well be guided by their perceptions of what actions are permissible. These provisions are, in short, background rules, and our argument is that they are as necessary in the intellectual property context as they are in trade, at least in the early years of the intellectual property agreement. A similar dynamic is evident in connection with the GATS Agreement. It envisioned short-term exemptions from the most favoured nation (MFN) provision in order to give member states an opportunity to deal with transitory problems. However, the exemptions that have been notified have not, as a rule, been withdrawn. Indeed, most are listed as of "indefinite" duration.[54]

Additionally, we should acknowledge that Article XIX has been interpreted to require a sudden increase in imports.[55] Our proposal does not require *sudden* change. However, it is not clear where the suddenness requirement comes from—it is not found in Article XIX or in the Safeguards Agreement. Nor does this requirement fit well in the context of knowledge production. To the extent that suddenness was introduced to encourage states to follow trends, extrapolate from them, and take prophylactic action to help domestic producers mitigate the effect of imports, it is not realistic for TRIPS. The Agreement covers a vast array of fields. It applies to activity that occurs in garrets and garages, in labs and lobes. Changes are not immediately apparent or public. Indeed, one of the innovations of TRIPS is the protection of confidential information and trade secrets. As a result, governments cannot be expected to follow developments in science and culture in the way that a trade ministry can monitor the effect of imports on domestic industries.

III. Capacity

So far, our examples of domestic lawmaking have largely been drawn from the problems developed countries face in responding to technological and social changes. These derive, in part, from the difficulty in anticipating or gauging the impact of change and, in part, from political factors. There is rent seeking on all sides of the debate, and new institutional actors (universities, online intermediaries, rights aggregators) further complicate the picture. The obligation to comply with TRIPS makes the political economy issues even more complex. As many of the quotations set out at the beginning of our Chapters show, those who prefer the status quo—or understand TRIPS as a comprehensive code, or as a mechanism for imposing the optimal level of worldwide protection—skew the debate by asserting that proposed modifications will violate the Agreement. As our discussion of the SHARE program demonstrated, the paucity of DSB cases can make their arguments hard to refute.

Analogous factors also affect the developing world. The politics there may appear to be less complicated, for the effect of high price on the availability of essential products makes the distributive consequences of strong protection quite salient. However, many of these countries have powerful elites who benefit from alliances with interests in developed countries. And as Ruth Okediji has suggested, less developed countries, new to democracy, may lack an organized opposition or a tradition of robust political culture.[56] The result is that many have adopted stronger intellectual property regimes than are appropriate to their needs. Some enacted intellectual property laws before the end of the transition period and thus started to bear the costs of protection before they were required to do so. Many have failed to use all of the flexibilities incorporated into the TRIPS regime.[57] For example, the Berne Appendix, incorporated into TRIPS via Article 9.1, and the revision to Article 31 made in the Doha Round were intended to allow developing countries to ensure that important works would be translated into local languages (Berne) and that there would be an adequate supply of pharmaceuticals to meet local needs (Articles 31 and 31bis). Both provisions are, however, significantly underutilized.[58]

The explanation for this phenomenon likely goes beyond a simple political economy story. A close look at the lawmaking in emerging economies, such as Brazil and India, demonstrates that as countries "lawyer up," they become more proficient at finding accommodations between their national interests and their international duties.[59] Accordingly, an important part of the explanation for inappropriately high levels of protection in these countries is that they (or those opposed to strong protection within these countries) lack the legal expertise to react to TRIPS effectively. Nor do they always enjoy the administrative infrastructure necessary to implement the Agreement in a manner that is calibrated to local conditions.

The challenges these countries face are formidable. It takes considerable ingenuity to tailor law to local realities.[60] Consider the matter of technology transfer. One way of creating educational and training opportunities is to institute a working requirement. Another is to lower the inventive step to encourage local innovators to engage in incremental innovation. Alternatively, the inventive step could be raised in order to release more information into a domain where the public can access it and build upon it. Which method will work best is far from evident; good legal (and economic) skills are needed to figure out how to promote learning while simultaneously encouraging innovation. And as Amy Kapczynski has demonstrated, even when a country identifies a regime that fits its needs, it may lack the capacity to implement it effectively. Her work, which examines implementation of § 3(d) of the Indian Patent Act discussed in Chapter 3, suggests that while India had the legal acuity to further local goals by raising the inventive step in a novel way, the Indian Patent Office is overwhelmed with applications. Accordingly, it tends to follow the decisions of foreign patent offices, even when the foreign examiners are applying a different (lower) standard of inventiveness.[61] The terms of the Agreement's flexibilities can also make astute lawyering a necessity. To return to the Berne Appendix and Article 31bis examples, both provisions interpose significant hoops, including the need to issue precise declarations, notifications, and regulations, along with a commitment to continued monitoring. Without a legal team to oversee implementation, these restrictions can quickly turn into insurmountable obstacles.

Developing countries are hampered by other significant infrastructure issues. A country that takes a novel approach to TRIPS flexibilities must risk a challenge under the DSU. As we saw, this is also a problem in the North. However, in developed countries, there are batteries of lawyers who can offer the legislature well-grounded opinions on TRIPS compatibility and—if need be—defend enactments in the Council for TRIPS, bargain for a waiver, mediate, or respond effectively in dispute resolution (and even if developed countries lose, it appears from the United States' response to *US–110(5)* that they can pay compensation rather than change their laws). And as we saw, the DSB likes to see evidence (even in cases, like *China–Enforcement*, where the challenge is to the measure on its face);[62] in developed countries, assembling such evidence may be simply a matter of hiring the right expert. In developing countries, however, the risk of facing a DSB challenge could be a deal breaker. To be sure, Article 24 of the DSU provides some relief, but it does so only for least developed countries. Furthermore, the help provided may be less than meets the eye. Article 24 admonishes members to "exercise due restraint" in challenging least developed countries and allows a least developed country that finds itself in a dispute to ask the director-general and the chair of the DSB to help mediate it. But the result of restraining disputes and mediating them is that the full scope of developing states' flexibilities has not been clarified in an authoritative way. Accordingly, a country considering a novel approach may have insufficient information to properly assess whether it is TRIPS compliant.[63]

The absence of a legal and administrative infrastructure—and the concomitant absence of guidance—also influences ongoing negotiations. Thus, another reason developing countries may be enacting laws that set inappropriately high levels of protection is that they are pressured to so do through threats of trade sanctions, such as under the Special 301 provisions of U.S. trade law,[64] and through bilateral free trade agreements (FTAs), European Partnership Agreements (EPAs), and bilateral investment treaties (BITs), each of which may include obligations that go well beyond TRIPS. In the absence of good lawyers, it may be that developing countries sign on to these agreements because they have a difficult time evaluating the demands being made, understanding the extent to which they exceed TRIPS requirements, or marshaling the will to reject them.[65]

The DSB has been somewhat sensitive to the special problems developing countries face. For example, in the *China–Enforcement* dispute, the panel accepted China's unfettered right to impose its censorship policy, even though it interfered with full dissemination of works subject to the TRIPS Agreement.[66] That finding was easily made—Article 17 of the Berne Convention, which was incorporated into TRIPS via Article 9.1, leaves states free to engage in censorship. Significantly, however, the panel also gave China a great deal of discretion regarding the actions it was required to institute to prevent copyright piracy. The United States had complained that China set thresholds for enforcement that permitted extensive copying, but in evaluating China's performance, the DSB took into consideration details of China's political and economic situation. These included the culture of China's retail sector, the capacity of its judicial system, and its traditions of law enforcement.[67] Furthermore, the panel stressed Articles 1.1 and 41.5, autonomy-protective features of the TRIPS Agreement.[68] China's discretion was not, however, unlimited. While China was allowed to engage in censorship, the panel required it to provide copyright protection.[69] And, presumably, the calculus on appropriate thresholds will change over time, as China's creative industries develop, its private sector grows, and its businesses are restructured.

The AB's handling of the *India–Pharmaceuticals* dispute is similar. In that case, the adjudicators were careful to acknowledge that India chose an administrative route to deal with its pipeline obligations because of the political obstacles it faced in enacting a statute.[70] Furthermore, the AB emphasized the admonition in Article 1.1 that implementation choices are left to member states.[71] And it rejected the notion (adopted in the panel decision) that India must "eliminate any reasonable doubts" on protection.[72] But there were, once again, limits to the DSB's willingness to accommodate capacity or political problems. Because there were contradictions in Indian law that failed to create a sound legal basis for the protection of pharmaceuticals, the AB held that India had failed to meet its obligations.[73] The AB, in other words, provided India with flexibility to deal with its politics, but in the early years of TRIPS, India needed better lawyering to take advantage of that leeway successfully.

The DSB could do even more to protect developing countries. As we saw, adjudicators are often influenced by state practices. For example, in the *US–110(5)* dispute, the DSB began its evaluation of the United States' Article 13 Exceptions defense by considering practices under the Berne acquis. Although the panel was careful to say that exceptions were not "frozen" in time,[74] the practices it consulted were necessarily those of the countries that formed the acquis—those that belonged to the Berne Union and had sufficient experience with copyright to develop exceptions. That methodology may help developed countries evaluate their compliance with TRIPS, but it will not be as useful to those countries that are searching for novel approaches. Indeed, such countries may become even more wary of adopting measures suited to their own society and politics if they think that the metric of compliance is limited to the laws of developed countries. As Larry Helfer has suggested, when using state practices to construe the TRIPS Agreement, the DSB should instead consider approaches taken by countries currently at the same level of development as the respondent, or by developed countries when they were at earlier stages of development.[75]

Nations struggling with capacity problems would also benefit from more frequent opportunities to obtain authoritative interpretations of the TRIPS Agreement. The DSU does not permit countries to bring declaratory judgment actions. However, the addition of such a procedure would permit members to clear novel measures prior to enactment. Advance knowledge of TRIPS compatibility might simplify the politics of enacting new legislation and reduce the costs associated with it. For example, the litigation and debate over § 3(d) of the Indian Patent Act might have abated had it been possible for India to clear the provision in advance through the DSB.[76]

There may also be a role for nonviolation complaints. In the GATT, a member can bring such a complaint when an objective of that Agreement is impeded as the result of any measure applied by another member state, whether or not it conflicts with the text of the Agreement.[77] In the Uruguay Round, however, negotiators were unsure whether these actions were appropriate to the TRIPS Agreement.[78] Accordingly, they imposed a moratorium, subject to reconsideration by the Council for TRIPS.[79] The moratorium remains in effect in part because there is considerable fear that lifting it would hurt developing countries. After all, one of the complaints that the United States had lodged in the *India–Pharmaceuticals* case concerned its legitimate expectations regarding pipeline protection. India won on the issue because the AB construed that allegation as an effort to establish a nonviolation complaint, and therefore within the scope of the moratorium;[80] had the moratorium been lifted, India might have lost. It is also not insignificant that those who view TRIPS as an international intellectual property code trumpet the adoption of a nonviolation complaint procedure because they see it as a mechanism for more completely commodifying knowledge-intensive products.[81]

Nonetheless, Susy Frankel has suggested that developing countries might benefit from the opportunity to bring nonviolation complaints.[82] She argues that developing countries had expected that TRIPS would mark the limit of their international intellectual property obligations and that the use of unilateral and bilateral actions to raise protection to TRIPS-plus levels frustrates that expectation. Such a complaint could not be structured as a violation of the Agreement: Article 1.1 clearly permits members to grant more extensive protection than TRIPS requires. However, a nonviolation complaint along these lines might be successful. In a GATT case, *US–301*,[83] the European Union had claimed that a U.S. law that mandated unilateral actions when U.S. trade rights had been abrogated violated the undertaking to resolve trade disputes in the DSB. The panel decided in favor of the United States, but only because the United States agreed to base § 301 actions on determinations of violations made by a panel or the AB and adopted by the DSB.[84] Although a TRIPS-plus case would be substantially different—it would, by definition, not be raising claims consigned to the DSB—it would, like *US–301*, use a WTO agreement as a shield, to protect states from unilateral pressure.

Adding the possibilities of declaratory judgment and nonviolation complaints would not, however, be sufficient. Because both types of actions would be new (one to the WTO, the other to TRIPS), they would be harder to win than ordinary complaints. Thus, access to good lawyers and expert evidence would be even more critical. As important, then, is to find ways to help developing countries present their cases. One idea would be to make it easier for amicus curiae to file briefs. While the DSB has set out the circumstances in which it would accept amicus briefs, it has subsequently displayed a marked reluctance to accept them (let alone take them into account).[85] Liberalizing that practice—or creating some other avenue for involving nongovernmental organizations (NGOs) in dispute resolution[86]—would be of considerable value, especially to countries that are too advanced to be entitled to special consideration under Article 24 of the DSU and to least developed countries that wish to clarify their obligations through full-fledged dispute settlement. As José Alvarez notes, because the WTO legal staff tends to take up the slack when the DSB needs information that the parties fail to provide, it can have significant impact on decisions.[87] However, the WTO staff has substantially less experience with intellectual property than with trade regulation. In contrast, the NGOs that are likely to participate—organizations such as Doctors Without Borders, Oxfam, Third World Network, or Knowledge Ecology International—are immersed in these issues. The perspectives these organizations provide to adjudicators will likely be richer than that provided by the WTO staff; they would also usefully supplement the arguments propounded by developing countries.

In addition, it would be beneficial to develop a less formal and costly avenue for testing TRIPS claims. The obvious place to develop such a mechanism would be in the Council for TRIPS. Although the Council is not a part of the formal dispute resolution system, it monitors compliance with the Agreement. Its implementation reviews provide members with the opportunity to discuss compatibility questions.[88] More transparent deliberations would provide information to developing countries on the standards the Council is using to determine compliance, and the arguments it finds convincing. In addition, deliberations within the Council might give content to the language in Articles 7 and 8, which, as we saw in the previous Chapters, are crucial to protecting autonomy values, particularly for developing countries. To be sure, the states best situated to utilize this procedure will, once again, be developed countries and emerging economies with significant capacity. But transparency would leverage the capabilities that exist. Emerging countries successful in convincing the Council to accept novel measures would serve as models to others; the legal innovations they adopt would furnish templates to the countries that are still struggling.

The WTO also has significant authority to address capacity problems outside the DSU system. Article 67 of the TRIPS Agreement requires developed countries to provide technical assistance to less developed member states. With a better understanding of the flexibilities incorporated into TRIPS, countries would be able to craft laws more responsive to their needs. Unfortunately, however, anecdotal evidence suggests that this type of guidance may not be forthcoming: at least some of the technical advisers appear to be Trojan horses, furnishing technical advice that favors the needs of their own countries rather than the interests of the state they are advising.[89] But that could easily change. Much of the advice is currently provided under an agreement between the WTO and the World Intellectual Property Organization (WIPO).[90] While past experience suggests that WIPO's commitment is to increasing intellectual property protection, it has now begun to pursue an ambitious "Development Agenda."[91] As a result, its technical assistance may become more development-oriented. Once again, the Council for TRIPS could also play a proactive role. It has already expanded its mandate beyond policing the minimum standards, to include compliance with the obligation to provide technology transfer.[92] It could presumably take the further step of monitoring technical assistance to make sure it is appropriate to the country to which it is given.

The politics of capacity can also be addressed by other intergovernmental agencies. As organizations such as the World Health Organization, the Food and Agriculture Organization, the Secretariat for the Convention on Biological Diversity, and the United Nations Sub-Commission on the Promotion and Protection of Human Rights begin to understand how the TRIPS regime can affect matters within their purview, they are developing their own approach to intellectual property norms.[93] In Chapter 6, we suggest ways in which these organizations could help to improve both TRIPS implementation and dispute resolution. In Chapter 7, we consider the recognition of norms that transcend TRIPS and constitute what we call an international intellectual property acquis. Such an acquis, including user rights and substantive maxima, would help turn TRIPS—and the international intellectual property regime—into a more balanced system for the creative community worldwide.

PART III

WHERE WE ARE HEADED

Intellectual Property Lawmaking for
the Twenty-First Century

6

The WTO, WIPO, ACTA, and More

Fragmentation and Integration

An ACTA [Anti-Counterfeiting Trade Agreement] should have high level enforcement standards, not those that simply reiterate TRIPS, but rather clarify existing TRIPS obligations and go beyond TRIPS, along the lines of the IPR Chapters the U.S. government has negotiated in its Free Trade Agreements.

—Eric Smith, Response to Request for Public Comments on the Anti-Counterfeiting Trade Agreement, 73 Fed. Reg. 8910 (February 10, 2008), *available at* http://www.iipa.com/pdf/IIPAACTAletter-toUSTRfinal03212008.pdf (including data on the effect of copyright piracy on the U.S. economy)

The full text of the treaty remains secret, but a document leaked to the public shows that ACTA could include criminal measures, increased border search powers, and encouragement for Internet service providers to cooperate with copyright holders.

—Electronic Frontier Foundation, FOIA: Anti-Counterfeiting Trade Agreement, *available at* http://www.eff.org/cases/eff-and-public-knowledge-v-ustr

In recent years, the protection of TK [traditional knowledge] has received increased attention in various international forums, including the Convention on Biological Diversity (CBD), the World Intellectual Property Organization (WIPO), the International Labour Organization (ILO), the Food and Agriculture Organization (FAO), the World Health Organization (WHO), the UN Educational, Scientific and Cultural Organization (UNESCO) and the UN Commission on Human Rights.

—Sophia Twarog and Promila Kapoor, *Introduction and Overview in* Protecting and Promoting Traditional Knowledge: Systems, National Experiences and International Dimensions, xii, UNCTAD/DITC/TED/10 (Sophia Twarog and Promila Kapoor eds., United Nations, Geneva 2004)

The first Part of this volume argued that TRIPS must be viewed through a neo-federalist lens. We noted that both the history of the TRIPS Agreement and its structure suggest that the negotiators of the Uruguay Round did not create a code—a one-size-fits-all regime that imposes rigid obligations on all member states. Rather, the Agreement gives states substantial latitude to tailor their law to the circumstances of their creative sectors, to deal with local distributive concerns, and to further policy preferences orthogonal to the intellectual property system. This view enhances the long-term legitimacy of the international intellectual property system. Moreover, it makes TRIPS a more resilient instrument, for it leaves member states free to find ways to cope with technological change and the organizational alterations these induce.

But many economists and traders do not agree with that analysis; they prefer to see TRIPS as a code; as setting (or setting in motion a move toward) a globally harmonized level of intellectual property protection, one that imposes a globally optimal incentive to produce knowledge-intensive goods. The examination of dispute resolution in Part II demonstrated that at least some developed countries—and a few Dispute Settlement Body (DSB) adjudicators—share that position. And as the quotations preceding our earlier Chapters suggest, to some in the intellectual property community, optimum protection is not enough. They argue that the Agreement should be read as comprehensively commodifying intellectual products, eliminating spillovers so that the public pays for every benefit derived from knowledge-intensive goods.

While the Doha Declaration[1] and the most recent DSB reports—particularly *China–Enforcement*[2] and *EC–GI*[3]—would seem to have reoriented the debate over the character of TRIPS in favor of a strong dose of national autonomy, that is not the end of the story for international intellectual property lawmaking. Although there is stasis within the WTO, the quotations at the outset of this Chapter demonstrate that there are moves afoot internationally to alter the level of protection. Most are aimed at making the intellectual property regime more code-like, but some address distributive concerns or bolster autonomy arguments. Thus, the creative community and member states, as well as international institutions and nongovernmental organizations (NGOs) with an interest in intellectual property, all appear to have drawn one or more lessons from the Uruguay Round, and from the shift in negotiations over international intellectual property lawmaking from the World Intellectual Property Organization (WIPO) to the WTO.

First and foremost, they learned that regime shifting can work.[4] As Chapter 2 recounted, while matters were stalled in WIPO, the Uruguay Round established a dramatically new intellectual property order, complete with new institutions (the Ministerial Conference, the General Council, and the Council for TRIPS) and a mechanism to ensure compliance (the DSB). Second, these groups found that their interests could be furthered by embedding intellectual property issues in a broader context. The shift to the WTO brought a new sensibility—a trade focus—to the table; as important, negotiating intellectual property issues in a trade regime created an international opportunity for cross-sectoral bargaining. Nations (mostly in the North) that would benefit from higher intellectual property standards could couple their demands with the promise of greater access to their markets, and thus pay off the nations (mostly in the South) that would be harmed by these higher standards. Third, the success of TRIPS made clear the strategic implications of the capacity problem we saw in the last Chapter: for countries lacking an adequate legal and economic infrastructure, the social welfare effects of increasing protection are difficult to compute and easily overshadowed by the immediate benefits of increased trade. Fourth, the creative industries found that it helps to give the problem a moral twist by calling it "piracy" and "counterfeiting"; negotiations can always be extended later to cover other matters. Thus, the Tokyo Round introduced intellectual property into the negotiation of the General Agreement on Tariffs and Trade (GATT)[5] with talk of the trade-distorting effects of copyright piracy and trademark counterfeiting, but when the TRIPS Agreement matured, it included seven forms of exclusivity and deemed many kinds of uses to be within the control of right holders.[6]

International lawmaking since the Uruguay Round has taken a wide variety forms; it has been used by many different actors; it has taken place in many different fora and under a variety of conditions. Some instruments are developed with substantial input from the public and interested NGOs (for example, those emanating from WIPO and the World Health Organization [WHO]);[7] some are (as the second quotation at the beginning of this Chapter notes) negotiated almost entirely in secret. Some actors resort to older regimes, such as human rights conventions[8] or the Convention on Biological Diversity (CBD).[9] Others create new instruments: free trade agreements (FTAs) and bilateral investment treaties (BITs);[10] regional arrangements, such as the Central American Free Trade Agreement (CAFTA) and European Union directives;[11] plurilateral initiatives, including the recently promulgated Anti-Counterfeiting Trade Agreement (ACTA) and the Transpacific-Partnership (TPP) Agreement;[12] or new multilateral instruments, such as the WIPO Copyright Treaty (WCT), the WIPO Performances and Phonogram Treaty (WPPT), and the pending WIPO Treaty for the Visually Impaired.[13] Some moves produce "hard law" in the form of new treaties, but the outputs from others are softer. For example, WHO has issued a global strategic plan on public health innovation and intellectual property,[14] as well as guidelines on TRIPS;[15] WIPO has a full-blown Development Agenda working on several capacity-building projects,[16] and its standing committees have produced nonbinding instruments on a variety of matters.[17] In addition, some conventions establish their own (rival) governance structures (ACTA, CBD)[18] or include their own systems for dispute resolution (bilaterals, CAFTA, the European Court of Human Rights [ECHR]).[19]

The impulses behind these initiatives and their relationship to TRIPS are also varied. In some cases (many of the bilaterals and ACTA), the intent is to strengthen perceived inadequacies by raising the standards of protection; others deal with issues that were not fully contemplated when TRIPS was negotiated, such as internet distribution (WCT) and genetic discoveries (EU Biotech Directive). But as the Twarog and Kapoor quotation indicates, some of the instruments add TRIPS-plus requirements in order to rectify the distributive consequences of TRIPS. They create rights over traditional knowledge, folklore, or in the case of the CBD, genetic information and, in effect, provide the South with a return on its own knowledge-intensive endowments.[20] Alternatively, they attempt to alleviate the negative impact of TRIPS through principles that enhance state and personal autonomy (WIPO Development Agenda, human rights initiatives).

The fragmentation of international lawmaking is not a new phenomenon or unique to intellectual property, and the challenges it raises have been widely noted.[21] However, it takes on a special dimension in the intellectual property context. TRIPS promotes the creation of private rights in order to induce changes in behavior: the investment of time, money, and labor in creative production and, in the case of patent law, increased disclosure of technological information. Often, the payoffs from these investments lie far in the future; indeed, some intellectual property systems are predicated on long periods of protection. As a result, the possibility of a regime shift that will change the creative environment, or the risk that the rules of one institution will conflict with those of another, can thwart the core objectives of the law. Uncertainty may lead potential innovators to discount the rewards they expect. Thickets of new rights (such as those produced by layering rights under the CBD over those guaranteed by TRIPS) can be difficult and costly to negotiate. In some cases, disputes may cycle among tribunals. For example, facets of the *EC–GI* dispute have been heard over the years in national courts, regional courts, and the ECHR.[22] The possibilities of conflicting decisions and inadequate (or excessive) relief can make creative activity (or follow-on innovation) less desirable ventures.[23]

At the same time, however, there are benefits in fragmentation—or, as some might more optimistically say, "pluralism" or "regulatory competition."[24] We have seen that the trade mentality of the WTO can obscure key issues in intellectual property, particularly the need for a balanced regime that prevents the innovators of one generation from imposing insurmountable obstacles on those who would follow on their work. The expertise of an organization such as WIPO, with strong intellectual property traditions, is therefore invaluable. Similarly, providing the WTO with information from institutions such as WHO, which deal directly with the distributive consequences of intellectual property protection, could help WTO staff, DSB adjudicators, and future negotiators better understand the impact TRIPS can have on social welfare. Regulatory competition can also lead to more rapid consideration of new issues. The WCT, for example, addressed problems raised by internet distribution of copyrighted materials before any national legislature did so.[25] In addition, the distribution of intellectual property authority over institutions with various competencies can compensate for restrictions that TRIPS is perceived as imposing on the latitude of states to experiment. The development of counternorms may create more room to maneuver, and the institutions themselves serve as laboratories for generating alternative approaches. Perhaps most important, organizations with expertise in areas touching on intellectual property can help states with weak capacity to fully utilize the flexibilities found in TRIPS, to analyze proposed bilaterals, and to withstand unilateral pressure.

While the efforts of the many international organizations with an interest in intellectual property—and the many more nongovernmental actors working in this space—are too numerous to describe in this volume, this Chapter provides a flavor of the problem with a few examples of initiatives that have led to fragmentation. It then considers ways to integrate these developments into the WTO framework and to gain the benefits of regulatory competition while minimizing its costs. The next Chapter builds on our examination of the existing system. We consider the successive repetition of similar norms in a range of disparate institutions as establishing the contours of an international intellectual property acquis. The acquis could serve as a framework for structuring future debates at both the international and the national level and thus minimize fragmentation and bring a measure of coherence to the knowledge governance system.

I. Fragmentation

A full taxonomy of recent initiatives would differentiate between provisions that raise the standards of protection set out in TRIPS, those that add wholly new requirements, those that seek to clarify ambiguous terms in TRIPS in ways that enhance right holder prerogatives,[26] as well as those that protect the public domain and advance norms supporting the use of TRIPS flexibilities. Together, these measures contribute to the fragmentation problem: the proliferation of rules, standards, and norms within the international intellectual property system. For simplicity, we classify one group of initiatives as commodification efforts; the others as attempts to insulate states and information-intensive products from such moves through the promulgation of counternorms, measures that clarify the space where TRIPS does not require commodification (and where it may be impermissible, either doctrinally or normatively).

A. Commodification Initiatives

Much of the discussion of so-called TRIPS-plus initiatives has focused on the recent spate of bilaterals and, to a somewhat lesser extent, regional agreements.[27] Although there are many of these arrangements, including agreements among the countries of the South,[28] the United States and the European Union in particular appear to have acted on at least two of the lessons of TRIPS: standards can be raised if negotiations over intellectual property are embedded in a trade context and involve so many economic sectors that countries with capacity and leverage deficits will have difficulty evaluating the instrument or adequately protecting their intellectual property interests.

Many in the current crop of agreements add new forms of protection. For example (and among many other intellectual property provisions), the U.S.-Morocco FTA requires the parties to refrain from recognizing the principle of international exhaustion of patent rights, an issue expressly left open by Article 6 of TRIPS.[29] The FTA between the United States and Chile requires trademark protection for sounds, even though Article 15 of TRIPS permits states to require that marks be "visually perceptible"[30] (and the question whether, and in what circumstances, sounds can serve as trademarks has been on the recent agenda of the WIPO Standing Committee on Trademarks).[31] Many of the agreements also require signatories to give effect to instruments that are not incorporated into TRIPS and which impose obligations not otherwise required by the WTO. For example, the EU–Central America FTA requires the parties to comply with the WCT and the WPPT, to "make all reasonable efforts" to comply with the Trademark Law Treaty, and to ratify the Protocol Relating to the Madrid Agreement Concerning International Registration of Marks.[32] Other FTAs use somewhat different language, requiring actual ratification of assorted treaties or "recognition" of their importance.[33] Some even specify particular methods of recognition. For example, the U.S.-Singapore FTA requires implementation of the WCT in terms almost identical to the U.S. Digital Millennium Copyright Act.[34]

In addition to injecting new requirements, the FTAs deal with matters that are already covered in TRIPS: in these cases, they either reiterate TRIPS norms or raise the standards of protection above that level. For instance, the U.S.-Morocco FTA requires patent protection for plants,[35] even though Article 27.3(b) of the TRIPS Agreement permits countries to protect agriculture through sui generis schemes. Several agreements, including the U.S.-Jordan and U.S.-Chile FTAs, require recognition of WIPO's Joint Recommendation Concerning Provisions on the Protection of Well-Known Marks, which provides a definition of "well known" for purposes of Article 16 of TRIPS and extends trademark protection beyond consumer confusion so that it also covers several forms of dilution (including blurring, tarnishment, and free riding).[36]

ACTA (when it comes into force) will depart even more dramatically from TRIPS. As its name suggests, the parties negotiating ACTA (the United States, Canada, the European Union, Switzerland, Japan, Korea, Singapore, Australia, New Zealand, Mexico, Jordan, Morocco, and the United Arab Emirates) clearly learned the first and fourth lesson of TRIPS: shift regimes, and then claim it is out of a concern for counterfeiting and piracy. TRIPS arguably does not fully address piracy concerns, for it can be interpreted as creating a great deal of latitude regarding enforcement: Article 1.1 leaves implementation decisions to the states; Article 41.5 does not require states to enforce intellectual property differently from other laws; and Articles 44 through 46, 50, 53, and 56 use the convoluted expression "authorities shall have the authority" over injunctions, damages, and other remediation devices. The developed countries raised concerns about these limits on enforcement obligations in the Council for TRIPS, but they were largely unsuccessful in provoking a sustained discussion.[37] Eventually, the United States attempted to resolve the matter by bringing the *China–Enforcement* complaint. But as we saw in Chapter 4, the panel largely deferred to China, leaving it with considerable discretion to decide what constitutes copyright counterfeiting and which remedies are most appropriately awarded. Moreover, the panel interpreted the requirement for triggering criminal obligations—the phrase "on a commercial scale"—as including a quantitative dimension, to give China substantial leeway to decide when these measures were applicable.[38]

But shifting to a new regime and reframing the problem has apparently produced a different result. Thus, some of the provisions in ACTA appear quite similar to TRIPS, but merely transplanting them could be enough to effectuate a change in meaning. For example, ACTA's provisions on relief use the phrase "judicial authorities have the authority."[39] While ACTA does not create a binding mechanism to ensure compliance, its more stringent approach to enforcement will surely shade the interpretation of the phrase by any forum having regard to the context of the agreement, so that it comes to mean something quite different from the way it was construed by the *China–Enforcement* panel.[40] In addition, the new regime will generate its own set of norms and standards. For example, ACTA's criminal provisions define "on a commercial scale" as "carried out ... for direct or indirect economic or commercial advantage."[41] As a result, countries must act on even low-volume counterfeiting. ACTA also creates a series of presumptions regarding damages that are unknown to TRIPS.[42] Its remedial measures at the border are considerably stricter. Among other things, right holders can require authorities to stop goods that are in transit, including (apparently) in transit between countries where the goods are not subject to the control of a right holder.[43] Furthermore, ACTA includes provisions on digital distribution of knowledge-intensive products. It imposes requirements concerning technological protection measures and addresses the liability of third parties such as service providers for the infringement activities of end users.[44]

Despite the name, ACTA appears to cover activities that go well beyond trademark counterfeiting and copyright piracy. Although some sections expressly exclude patents and protection of undisclosed information, the rest do not. Presumably, these measures cover patents and secrets, even though use of neither is traditionally considered to constitute counterfeiting or piracy.[45] And in many places, ACTA uses the term "infringement,"[46] which includes acts that are clearly not piracy or counterfeiting. Similar measures may soon work their way into other instruments, including regional and plurilateral agreements such as the TPP Agreement (which now includes Australia, Brunei, Chile, Malaysia, New Zealand, Peru, Singapore, the United States, and Vietnam).[47]

WIPO has also been actively engaged in formulating new intellectual property standards. The WCT and WPPT—the "WIPO Internet Treaties"—create protective regimes for digital distribution of copyrighted materials. In addition, WIPO has a set of standing committees that routinely monitor the creative environment, identify emerging issues, and make concrete proposals. For instance, soon after the internet went into widespread commercial use, WIPO made a recommendation on how to localize trademark infringements and proposed criteria helpful in deciding jurisdictional and choice of law issues in the digital environment.[48] WIPO also crafted the aforementioned Joint Recommendation Concerning Provisions on the Protection of Well-Known Marks.

It could be argued that these sorts of instruments do not pose fragmentation concerns precisely because they are TRIPS-*plus*. That is, since Article 1.1 of TRIPS provides that "[m]embers may ... implement in their law more extensive protection than is required by this Agreement," additions cannot be considered inconsistent with it. The WCT and WPPT, for example, were negotiated against the backdrop of TRIPS; they were intended to deal with the digital environment, which TRIPS negotiations did not reach, and they were expressly infused with the same concepts of flexibility and balance that appear in TRIPS.[49] Similarly, new technological opportunities appear to have motivated a flurry of activity regarding genomic advances.[50] Furthermore, many of these new agreements specifically mention TRIPS. ACTA, for example, states in its preamble that the intent is to complement TRIPS; it also recognizes "the principles set forth in the Doha Declaration on Public Health" and specifically invokes the public-regarding principles of Articles 7 and 8 of TRIPS.[51]

At the same time, however, TRIPS Article 1.1 includes a proviso: more protection is permissible "provided that such protection does not contravene the provisions of this Agreement." A close look at the new international intellectual property instruments suggests that these initiatives can be in real tension with TRIPS. Consider, for example, the impact of the new instruments on health. The TRIPS Agreement gave states substantial leeway to protect health, and the Doha Declaration further emphasized that commitment. Yet several of the new instruments put the authority of states to deal with access to essential products in jeopardy. Most obvious is access to food. Article 27.3(b) of TRIPS permits countries to use sui generis systems to protect plants, and the Convention for the Protection of New Varieties of Plants permits farmers to save seed for their own use.[52] Under the patent scheme required by many of the FTAs, farmers will be required to make new purchases every year, thus raising their costs.

Access to pharmaceuticals is similarly threatened. The FTA provisions on exhaustion give right holders control over the importation of lawfully acquired products. Thus, they deny the citizens in states where pharmaceuticals are expensive the opportunity to buy medicines on the open market in places where they are cheap, and import them.[53] The premarket clearance provisions of the FTAs further complicate drug availability for impoverished countries. Article 39.3 of TRIPS requires protection of undisclosed information only against "unfair commercial use." While TRIPS leaves the question of what is "unfair" largely to the states, some of the new provisions define it, thereby reducing member states' flexibility to determine the terms of exclusivity. As Carlos Correa observed, such provisions create the legal fiction that information disclosed to one country nonetheless remains a trade secret in another.[54] Thus, the provisions could be used to bar one country from simply relying on another country's perception that a drug is safe. According to Fred Abbott, the result is that patentees can both prevent local manufacture of generic drugs and also block importation from elsewhere.[55] In short, the provisions undermine the compulsory licensing provisions of TRIPS, including the approach specifically introduced by Article 31bis during the Doha Round.

ACTA would further exacerbate the fragmentation problem in the pharmaceutical arena. Generic medicines in transit between two countries where they are not patented (or are subject to compulsory licenses) have been stopped under current law. Indeed, India brought a complaint against the European Union claiming these seizures violate TRIPS and the GATT.[56] The complaint was withdrawn, and it is not clear how it would have been resolved.[57] Under ACTA, however, it is clear that signatories would be required to seize such goods. While some of the provisions of ACTA will not apply to patents or undisclosed information, pharmaceutical products are shipped with labels that include names under various nomenclature systems and detailed information on use and contraindications; right holders could base their claims on the unauthorized use of the copyright or trademarks associated with these materials.[58] (Indeed, they are likely to do so because patent law will be ineffective if the contention is that the merchandise is fake and lacks the patented ingredient.) Yet any country that did follow ACTA and seized such goods would become the subject of a complaint in the DSB and might well lose. The problems created by contradictory obligations are further complicated in that the international arena is simultaneously spawning norms that take matters in a contrary direction.

B. Counternorms

The lessons of TRIPS have not been lost on the developing world. Calling unauthorized uses of information products "piracy" works for these countries as well: under the heading of "biopiracy," they have shifted rights over genetic information to the CBD, where they have obtained considerable leverage over the exploitation and patenting of local genetic resources, and are working to obtain even more.[59] Similar efforts are underway in WIPO and in the International Labour Organization (ILO) to obtain control over use—to stop the pirating—of traditional knowledge and folklore.[60] These measures could be conceptualized as commodification initiatives. Looking forward, however, some of them might instead be regarded as allocating ownership to collectives, and thus as placing information in an accessible domain where it is somewhat protected from full commodification.

For the most part, however, developing countries (and related norm entrepreneurs) have drawn from the first lesson of TRIPS, on regime shifting, and have moved intellectual property discussions to specialized international organizations that share their interest in preserving flexibilities and state autonomy.[61] Many of these organizations are specifically involved in development issues; their interest in intellectual property springs from the perception that the requirements of TRIPS can be adapted to promote development goals. Thus, for example, the UN Conference on Trade and Development (UNCTAD) has issued reports on intellectual property, technology transfer, and direct investment.[62] With the International Center for Trade and Sustainable Development, it has a project aimed at "capacity building," which in their terminology refers to improving residents' technological and creative capabilities. Among other things, UNCTAD issued a Resource Book on TRIPS and Development.[63] Such materials included can, to some extent, also compensate for the problems that we have categorized as questions of capacity—the economic and legal capacity of these countries to craft domestic laws that are both compliant with TRIPS and responsive to local needs. For example, the Resource Book sets out the obligations imposed by TRIPS, the negotiation history, as well as sections on "Possible Interpretations." It includes detailed advice on such matters as the flexibilities in the patentability requirements of Article 27 and meeting the obligations for awarding compulsory licenses under Articles 31 and 31bis. An analysis of relevant WTO jurisprudence is also included (although, as noted in previous Chapters, the existing case law may be too sparse to provide significant guidance).[64]

Other regime shifts have brought intellectual property discussions to venues where the distributive consequences of TRIPS obligations are particularly clear. The involvement of WHO is a good example. This organization's main work lies in coordinating health issues within the United Nations (UN) system, where it issues scientific reports on health policy, assesses health risks, and furnishes technical information relevant to health care delivery.[65] TRIPS, however, has made WHO sensitive to the impact of patent and data exclusivity rights on the price of pharmaceuticals. As a result, it has devoted considerable effort to fostering new intellectual property norms for both the South and the North. Focusing on the South, it has (like UNCTAD) issued guidelines to help countries deal with their intellectual property obligations, including descriptions of the flexibilities within TRIPS and other international instruments that commodify knowledge goods. It has even provided guidance on the benefits of regime shifting.[66] And it has adopted a global strategic plan on public health innovation and intellectual property, which focuses attention on neglected diseases (that is, diseases that afflict the residents of countries too poor to offer sufficient incentives through the patent system), building the innovation capacity of developing countries, and—most especially—improving access to medicines.[67] In its work regarding the North, WHO uses its position as the premier global coordinator of health care to admonish developed countries to consider the impact of pharmaceutical patents on the price of medicines, and to recognize the flexibilities that TRIPS gives members to adjust their laws to their medical needs.[68] In addition, WHO funds the activities of various other international organizations and NGOs involved in drug development and delivery.[69]

Norm development is also occurring in the human rights arena. The changes here are, however, highly complex. Some human rights regimes, such as the Universal Declaration of Human Rights, protect the rights of authors.[70] Analogously, both the UN Educational, Scientific and Cultural Organization (UNESCO), in the Universal Declaration on the Human Genome and Human Rights,[71] and the Council of Europe, in its Convention for the Protection of Human Rights and Dignity,[72] have conceptualized individual control over the genome as a human right.[73] As such, these provisions add normative heft to commodification arguments in TRIPS and elsewhere. Still, most of the work in this arena is focused on the rights to health, education, and free expression; it is aimed at building human capacity and promoting access to knowledge products. Accordingly, the norms generated provide strong support for state efforts to fully utilize TRIPS flexibilities and resist further moves to protect knowledge-intensive goods. For example, UNESCO considered the impact of copyright protection on education and completed a project on intellectual property and human rights.[74]

As Larry Helfer and Graeme Austin detail, other human rights organizations, such as the United Nations Human Rights Council, the Committee on Economic, Social and Cultural Rights, and the Food and Agriculture Organization (FAO), have become heavily involved in mediating the juncture between the rights of the creative industries and the interests of others in access to the innovations produced.[75]

Developing countries have also put a new twist on regime shifting: they have discovered that it can pay to shift negotiations back to WIPO. At first blush, WIPO may appear an odd venue to consider TRIPS flexibilities. WIPO's stated mission is to "promote intellectual property throughout the world." Furthermore, it administers almost all the major intellectual property conventions, and it runs an Arbitration and Mediation Center that, among other things, offers trademark holders an opportunity to contest ownership of internet domain names under the Uniform Domain Name Dispute Resolution Policy adopted by the Internet Corporation for Assigned Names and Numbers (ICANN).[76] But despite its strong identification with intellectual property protection, WIPO is in many ways ideally positioned to deal with the effect of TRIPS on development and with the impact of changes in the technological environment on TRIPS. Its many activities in the intellectual property field provide it with considerable expertise in tailoring intellectual property protection to new demands. As important, when negotiations moved to the WTO and WIPO lost its near-exclusive control over international intellectual property law, the two organizations entered into an agreement "to establish a mutually supportive relationship."[77] Because WIPO's main role in that relationship is to furnish technical assistance to developing economies, it has a unique window on their needs. Most significantly, because WIPO focuses solely on intellectual property, there is no possibility of paying off enhanced protection with benefits in other areas. Thus, when countries interested in strengthening the intellectual property system are forced to negotiate under the auspices of WIPO, they must account for the distributive consequences within the intellectual property system. For example, and as Graeme Dinwoodie has noted, when the negotiators of the WIPO Internet Treaties considered new provisions to deal with the internet, they were forced to specifically consider the issue of balance.[78]

For these reasons, many observers have high expectations for WIPO's Development Agenda.[79] As originally conceived in 2004 at the behest of Brazil and Argentina,[80] the plan was to consider the relationship between intellectual property protection and the UN Millennium Development Goals and to implement the development-oriented provisions of the TRIPS Agreement, including operationalizing Articles 7 and 8 of the TRIPS Agreement (on objectives and principles) and the Doha Declaration. To these ends, WIPO created the Provisional Committee on Proposals Related to a WIPO Development Agenda. In successive sessions, various proposals were taken up and a permanent committee was created, open to participation by WIPO member states as well as interested intergovernmental organizations. It has proved hospitable to participation by such NGOs—which, in recent years, WIPO has defined capaciously.[81]

As of the committee's most recent progress report, the proposals were grouped into nineteen projects, with substantial headway noted on several of them.[82] In addition to projects aimed at marshaling resources and matching them to the needs of individual states, activities focus on improving the legal, economic, and data infrastructure of developing countries, fostering regional cooperation in administering intellectual property law, and helping countries manage their own intellectual property systems. Most important for these purposes, one goal of the Development Agenda is to provide expertise in developing legal strategies for accommodating the challenges developing countries face.[83] Thus, one project is designed to "promote norm setting activities related to IP that support a robust public domain in WIPO's Member States," and includes studies of various national laws that exploit TRIPS flexibilities.[84] Another coordinates the activities of other international organizations interested in promoting access to knowledge and technology.[85] The Agenda also extends beyond intellectual property law. Thus, one task is to develop ways of fully utilizing the flexibilities of TRIPS Articles 8, 31, and 40 to fashion antitrust regimes (competition laws) that cabin the reach of right holders.

WIPO has also engaged in norm-setting activities related to exceptions and limitations from intellectual property protection.[86] The proposed Treaty for the Visually Impaired would permit unauthorized reproduction of copyrighted works in formats suitable to the blind, including through the circumvention of technological protection measures. The Treaty would also facilitate exportation and importation of these works.[87] The WIPO Standing Committee on Copyright and Related Rights has issued a series of reports on copyright limitations and exceptions which provide both a normative framework and a survey of existing national rules.[88] The Standing Committee on Patents has similarly been engaged in mapping the landscape on exclusions, exceptions, and limitations on patent rights, with special attention to public health, education, and research.[89]

NGOs have also involved themselves in post-TRIPS norm development.[90] Some, like Doctors Without Borders, have come to these issues through their interests in matters—such as health care—that are affected by the strength of intellectual property rights.[91] Others are directly interested in knowledge-based issues. The open innovation community, for example, has questioned the empirical claims for strong protection, and the Creative Commons has sought to develop a contractual alternative to intellectual property protection, one better attuned to follow-on innovation.[92] A group of law professors has published a comprehensive review of TRIPS, with a special focus on the effects of the DSB's narrow reading of the Exceptions provisions of Articles 13, 17, 26.2, and 30. The group has also promulgated a formal proposal for amending the Agreement to clarify its flexibilities and to transform it into a more balanced instrument.[93] And separate coalitions of NGOs and scholars have looked beyond TRIPS and issued declarations demanding a moratorium on proposals to expand international intellectual property rights, calling for the reconfiguration of existing rights to better promote development objectives, and advocating reforms designed to further the public interest dimension to intellectual property law.[94]

II. Integration

The fragmentation described earlier is, like much of the fragmentation in international law, of several types. Some of the recent initiatives are supportive of TRIPS. For example, the recognition of authorship interests in the Universal Declaration of Human Rights is aligned with the protection accorded by the Berne Convention and the TRIPS Agreement. There are also cases where a new rule alters an existing standard, but states can comply with both regimes. For example, a state can fulfill both an FTA requirement to provide strong protection for plants and TRIPS Article 27.3(b), by simply recognizing plants as patentable subject matter. In these situations, the proliferation of norms is not problematic from the point of view of compliance, although it restricts the policy choices left to the parties.

But because regime shifting occurs mainly out of a desire to bring about changes in direction or perspective, incoherence is often a major risk. For example, although both ACTA and TRIPS are concerned with the distribution of inauthentic goods, when ACTA comes into force, its signatories could find themselves bound by inconsistent obligations. As we saw, ACTA may require the seizure of goods in transit; but a dispute of the type that arose between India and the European Union could easily end with a WTO decision that such seizures violate the free trade regime of the GATT or undermine the flexibilities of TRIPS.[95] In some cases, it is the underlying norms that clash. The CBD and some of the human rights work, for example, recognize an individual's right to control his or her genome. At the same time, under TRIPS and the Biotech Directive, the owners of genes are those who isolate and purify them. A country that refuses to grant a patent on an isolated gene may thus violate TRIPS, but a country that grants such a patent without the consent of the gene's source could find itself the subject of arbitration and conciliation under the CBD.[96] Even when the norms in two instruments appear to be similar, burdens of proof may be allocated differently and produce inconsistent results in close cases.[97]

Arguably, TRIPS contains a built-in mechanism for partially integrating subsequent intellectual property agreements through the most favoured nation (MFN) provision of Article 4. Many of the obligations with which we are concerned arise in agreements forming free trade areas, which are exempt from MFN treatment under Article XXIV:5 of the GATT. However, it is not clear that the intellectual property portions of these agreements are included in the exemption. Article 4 of TRIPS sets out several exceptions to MFN, but it does not mention free trade areas. And as we have seen, GATT provisions are not automatically assimilated into TRIPS.[98] Furthermore, freestanding intellectual property agreements, such as ACTA, are certainly not exempt. Given the lack of exemption, some writers appear to assume that MFN is fully integrative—that once two or more WTO countries agree to an intellectual property measure among themselves, the new obligation is immediately applicable in all members.[99] In fact, however, when countries A and B agree to raise levels of protection (for example, to enact dilution protection), MFN only requires them to extend that enhanced protection to nationals of all WTO members; it does not require other WTO members to adopt equivalent measures in their own domestic laws. Thus, nationals from C and D will obtain enhanced protection (for example, dilution protection) in A and B, but C is not required to provide that (dilution) protection to citizens of A or B or D.

Still, MFN could have real consequences in third countries, albeit indirectly. For example, nationals of C may have a difficult time trading in an environment in which there are different levels of protection in C, on the one hand, and A and B, on the other, in that a national of C who wishes to sell goods under the same mark in A, B, and C cannot adopt a mark that would violate A's or B's dilution protection. Depending on the size of the A and B market and the patterns of commercial exchange, the commercial effect for an international trader is similar to C enacting the protection to which A and B have agreed. Thus, there is certainly some integration that derives from MFN, but it is not perfect integration. And as we have repeatedly suggested, there is reason to be wary of this form of integration. MFN ratchets up protection without offsetting benefits to states that, as a practical matter, must endure the consequences of enhanced protection. Moreover, it does so in the context of knowledge production, where more protection is not necessarily optimal protection. Because we would analyze MFN violations with substantial deference, MFN alone will not integrate the international intellectual property regime.[100]

For both innovation and the WTO, fragmentation is an especial concern. Because intellectual property law is complex and the facts are technologically complicated, it is attractive to rely on the varying expertise of all the institutions involved in norm development. But since the law is aimed at shaping the future behavior of private actors, its goals can easily be undermined by uncertainty.

This is a problem for every institution involved in generating intellectual property norms, and the approaches to integration that we suggest in this section may apply more generally. But we focus on the WTO. As the institution with the most effective compliance mechanism, it is on the front line. The DSB has the opportunity—some might say obligation—to bring a measure of coherence to the current intellectual property regime through its decisions on which norms to take into account when interpreting the TRIPS Agreement.[101] Moreover, through both its adjudication and lawmaking activities, the WTO can develop new ways to promote integration.

A. Adjudication: The DSB

Problems akin to fragmentation can also exist in national laws. In wholly domestic cases, however, inconsistency and cycling can usually be avoided through the plenary authority of courts over the parties; devices such as consolidation, forum non conveniens, lis pendens, and choice of law rules; and resort to a supreme court.[102] In the international arena, many of these doctrines are unknown, and there is no hierarchy among tribunals. Moreover, the jurisdiction of dispute resolution bodies tends to be limited. The DSB, for example, has authority only over disputes that arise under the WTO agreements.[103] Thus, it cannot directly resolve disputes under ACTA, the CBD, or an FTA. Nonetheless, in his Report of the Study Group of the International Law Commission, Martti Koskenniemi suggested that through the rules of customary international law—the Vienna Convention on the Law of Treaties[104] and doctrines such as lex specialis, lex prior, lex posterior, and jus cogens—and with judicious use of their competence to determine competence, international tribunals could bring about a significant degree of integration.[105]

Consider, for example, a WTO dispute between two countries, both signatories to a version of the CBD that requires an applicant for a patent on a genomic invention to obtain informed consent from the possessor of the material from which the genetic information was extracted. The complaint alleges that the respondent violated its TRIPS obligations by denying patent protection when consent had not been obtained. A panel following an aggressive version of the Koskenniemi approach might deem the dispute to be within TRIPS, and therefore subject to its judicial authority, but to regard the CBD as applicable under a doctrine of lex specialis, as a "relevant rule of international law applicable to the relations between the parties" under Article 31.3(c) of the Vienna Convention. In such a case, the panel might avoid a second complaint (and an inconsistent result) by finding that the CBD requires signatories to deny patents when informed consent is lacking, and that such denials do not violate TRIPS.

There are, however, costs to this aggressive approach. Allowing the DSB to opine on measures from other sources would effectively turn the WTO agreements into a world constitution and the DSB into a global supreme court. Weaknesses in the DSB's decision making would then be generalized to other areas. Moreover, the rules announced might create one-size-fits-all regimes, even in fields where global harmonization is clearly unwarranted.[106] Legitimacy would also be an issue. After all, the members of the WTO agreed to have their GATT, GATS, and TRIPS disputes adjudicated in the DSB, not disputes arising under other instruments, such as the CBD. Finally, if every international tribunal followed a similar approach, the overlaps in jurisdiction could give rise to rampant forum shopping. The risks of uncertainty would be aggravated rather than ameliorated.[107] Better, it is argued, to consider the WTO a "self-contained" regime, closed to considerations of other rules and standards.[108]

So far, the WTO appears to have steered a middle course. On the one hand, the Appellate Body (AB) has rejected the most extreme version of the "self-containment" argument: in its very first case, it stated that WTO agreements cannot be read "in clinical isolation from public international law."[109] On the other hand, the DSB has also refused to engage in the type of aggressive integration suggested by the International Law Commission. Thus, in *Mexico–Soft Drinks*, which raised a conflict between Mexico's obligations under the GATT and the North American Free Trade Agreement (NAFTA), Mexico argued the DSB should decline jurisdiction in favor of NAFTA dispute resolution, or read the General Exceptions provision of GATT Article XX to permit Mexico to take the action required under NAFTA. The AB refused to take either step. Under the DSU, the DSB cannot "diminish the rights and obligations provided in the covered agreements,"[110] and the AB interpreted that to mean that it cannot decline to hear a case properly brought before it. Furthermore, the AB confined the use of Article XX to national, as opposed to international, obligations.[111] A DSB panel put yet another nail in the coffin of the fully integrative approach. In *EC–Biotech*, the panel interpreted the reference in Article 31.3(c) of the Vienna Convention to "the relations between the parties" as meaning the parties of the WTO, not merely the parties to the dispute.[112]

The middle course, and especially the *EC–Biotech* decision, was heavily criticized by the Koskenniemi Report as thwarting integration and perpetuating inconsistency.[113] As Robert Howse has pointed out, the panel's approach misapprehended Article 31.3(c), which does not require *application* of other law, but only that it "be taken into account." Article 34 of the Vienna Convention further cabins the application of that other law by barring interpretations that impose obligations on third-countries without their consent.[114] For intellectual property, these limits are particularly important (whether derived through Howse's interpretation or that of the *EC–Biotech* panel). As we saw in connection with

MFN, the laws of one country can have an indirect impact on all others. Accordingly, a rule that would require the WTO to apply international agreements that involve fewer than all the WTO members could have untoward consequences. For example, Jordan's FTA with the United States requires recognition of the Joint Recommendation on Well Known Marks and therefore mandates extremely broad protection against trademark dilution. If, in a dispute between Jordan and the United States, the DSB relied on that measure to require dilution protection, it would be essentially forcing *all* traders interested in doing business in Jordan or the United States to avoid dilutive marks, even when they are not likely to be confusing. As FTAs with this provision proliferate and become enforceable through the DSB, increasing numbers of traders will be affected, creating the functional equivalent of a new world standard. That would produce a high measure of integration, but at the cost of forgoing all semblance of international agreement.

At the same time, however, self-containment is equally unattractive. Once the Uruguay Round linked trade and intellectual property, linkage to a broader array of norms is inevitable. TRIPS deals with a small sphere of intellectual property issues (mainly minimum standards); however, the history, experience, and scholarship on the interaction between intellectual property, creativity, knowledge production, technological change, education, training, and consumption are deep and complex. Detaching TRIPS adjudication from the rich fabric of other international initiatives would distort the creative environment and ignore important values, such as commitments to free speech and distributive justice. Furthermore, whatever the merits of *EC–Biotech*, it must be read in conjunction with the AB's stated willingness to consider public international law. Thus, even if other instruments are not regarded as binding under Article 31.3(c) of the Vienna Convention, the DSB could use them interpretively, to determine "the ordinary meaning to be given the terms of the treaty in their context and in light of its objective and purpose" per Article 31.1 of the Convention.[115] In fact (and as Koskenniemi and Howse also note), under a variety of rubrics, the DSB has sought guidance in general principles of international law and has relied on other specialized instruments to keep the WTO Agreements current with international developments.[116] Since this view is not reliant on the binding nature of the principles in question, it admits to consideration of both TRIPS-plus initiatives in the form of bilaterals, regionals, and plurilaterals, but also the softer law produced by international organizations and NGOs.

TRIPS disputes offer ample opportunities for norm integration through interpretation. As we saw in Part II, there are many open-ended provisions in TRIPS. These include the objectives and principles of Articles 7 and 8, which were stressed in Doha; the meaning of "ideas, procedures, methods of operation or mathematical concepts" in Article 9.2 of the copyright provisions; "confusion" in Article 16.1 of the trademark provisions; or "invention" and "making, using, offering for sale, selling, or importing" a patented product in Articles 27.1 and 28.1. There are also many issues in TRIPS that demand specialized knowledge. Some involve questions about the nature of intellectual property, such as understanding the normative underpinnings of the Exceptions provisions of the TRIPS Agreement or the history of the Berne and Paris Conventions. Some issues are highly technical, such as identifying the actions required to protect health or avoid serious prejudice to the environment under Article 27.2. Still others require empirical information, such as when "widespread copying of [cinematographic works] is materially impairing the exclusive right of reproduction" under Article 11, or what constitutes a national emergency justifying compulsory licensing under Article 31(b), or the kinds of activities that could restrain competition under Article 40.

As we have seen, the DSB has been floundering on such issues. For example, in *Canada–Pharmaceuticals* and *US–110(5)*, the panels recognized that normative considerations have a role to play in the Exceptions provisions, but the adjudicators failed to expound on what the norms were.[117] Similarly, although the DSB admits that certain forms of discrimination are not actionable, it has eschewed evaluation of state motivation, and thus has adopted tests that are both over- and underinclusive.[118] We argued in earlier Chapters that part of the problem was the absence of examples, benchmarks, and guidance. Panels took what they could from the existing Agreement—for example, the *EC–GI* panel relied heavily on the specific example (fair use) provided by the trademark Exceptions provision (Article 17). Panels also sought guidance in state practices. But as we noted, state practices are often deficient. Because the best defined practices are those of countries with long-standing experience in intellectual property, with the capacity to tailor law to their circumstances, and with the power to withstand pressure, relying solely on state practices privileges the North over the South. As important, states—even in the North—often do not have well-considered practices for dealing with the changes wrought by recent technologies or with the institutional and industrial reorganizations technological changes can cause. The norms developed by other international organizations and through bilateral, regional, and plurilateral agreements could ameliorate these problems by supplying the DSB with a larger set of practices, as well as the considered opinions of the international community. At the same time, relying on this work interpretively would avoid some cycling (admittedly, not all of it), and it would bring a measure of coherence to the international intellectual property regime as a whole.

The DSB must, however, develop a theory as to the weight to be given to materials drawn from outside the WTO. One approach, suggested by the International Law Commission, is to rely on interpretive canons, such as lex specialis, lex prior, lex posterior, and jus cogens. However, these solve very few of the problems in the intellectual property arena. To the extent intellectual property has any jus cogens, the principles are likely to be identical to the open-ended provisions of Articles 7 and 8. Indeed, one of the challenges of intellectual property moving forward is to identify principles of that character; we address that question in Chapter 7. The other canons may contribute to the analysis, but their formalism might tend to accentuate the mechanical nature of DSB adjudication that we critiqued in prior Chapters. The canons are also incomplete as a method of integrating simultaneous developments in a wide range of institutions responding to disparate concerns. Accordingly, we would analyze questions of integration by addressing four variables: the source of the instrument (principally, the expertise of the organization promulgating the instrument, which is certainly a part of the theory underlying lex specialis), the timing of the provision (the premise underlying lex prior and lex posterior), governance issues (including the status of the provision as hard or soft law, opportunities for participation, transparency, and consensus), and the relationship between the measure's coverage and the coverage and principles of TRIPS.[119]

1. WIPO initiatives

Developments at WIPO offer the strongest case for norm integration through TRIPS interpretation. TRIPS is, after all, built on WIPO conventions, the Agreement contemplates the continued involvement of WIPO, and there is a formal agreement between the WTO and WIPO.[120] Indeed, even under the restrictive *EC–Biotech* test, some WIPO instruments may qualify as binding on the entire WTO and therefore amenable to consideration under Article 31.3(c) of the Vienna Convention. While the memberships of WIPO and the WTO are not coextensive, there are very few countries that do not belong to both, and for the most part, the states that are in WIPO but not the WTO are absent for purely geopolitical reasons.[121] WIPO is not a "single undertaking," so there will be instruments that are not joined by all members, but other measures enjoy wide participation. As the panel in *US–110(5)* noted when it decided "to seek contextual guidance . . . in the WCT," that instrument was unanimously concluded at a diplomatic conference attended by 127 countries, most of which also participated in TRIPS negotiations.[122]

In addition to the legitimating benefits that derive from WIPO's unique relationship with the WTO, many WIPO initiatives evince the characteristics that we suggest favor integration. They are the product of WIPO's considerable expertise in understanding intellectual property law and its effect on innovation. As the administrator of almost every principal intellectual property convention prior to TRIPS, its resources are unparalleled: it has an extraordinary library of historical documents, and well-trained personnel from around the world with long-standing experience in protecting knowledge products. Although, as noted, WIPO's stated mission is to "promote intellectual property throughout the world," it was also "born into the controversy of how intellectual property would impact the developing world."[123] Its technical assistance efforts on behalf of the WTO, as well as its dispute resolution arm, give it an opportunity to directly experience the impact of intellectual property on development and on user groups.

In fact, several DSB decisions have relied on WIPO materials. For example, the adjudicators in *Havana Club* and the *US–110(5)* cases consulted the 1883 Final Protocol to the Paris Convention, materials from the 1911 Paris Revision Conference, and the General Report and materials of the diplomatic conferences leading to the inclusion of broadcast rights in the Berne Convention.[124] Furthermore, the *US–110(5)* panel relied directly on the WCT to interpret the scope of Article 13's Exceptions provision, noting that "the wording of the WCT, and in particular of the Agreed Statement thereto . . . supports, as far as the Berne Convention is concerned, that the Berne Union members are permitted to provide minor exceptions to the rights provided under Articles 11 and 11bis."[125]

WIPO initiatives must, however, be considered on an individual basis. First, there is the temporal question. The wording of Article 31.1 of the Vienna Convention—that terms should be interpreted "in their context and in light of [the treaty's] objective and purpose"—might suggest that the DSB should limit itself to materials that existed at the time of the negotiations of TRIPS and not take into consideration initiatives that significantly postdate TRIPS. For example, the *US–110(5)* panel was careful to note that the WCT was concluded only a year after TRIPS.[126] Nonetheless, a strong case can be made for consulting later initiatives. Intellectual property laws are intended to promote change; freezing the law could undermine that function. As Neil Netanel argued in connection with the interpretation of the copyright provisions of TRIPS:

> TRIPS drafters must have been well aware [that] the Berne Convention is a dynamic instrument . . . and [that] the rapid development of copyright-related technology require[s] an ongoing process of interpretation and reinterpretation within the framework that Berne sets forth.[127]

Although Netanel was concerned only with developments that occurred soon after TRIPS, the argument is even more pertinent to changes that take place during periods when WTO lawmaking is quiescent, but technological change proceeds unabated. Indeed, the more distant from TRIPS, the more likely the measure will reflect members' efforts to cope with new developments in TRIPS-consistent ways. If the overarching interpretive project is to keep TRIPS nimble—responsive to change—then the argument is even stronger.

The DSB should, however, consider a second timing question. Because rapid technological change has facilitated the cross-border flow of knowledge goods, it has provoked a rush to regulate at the international level without any period of domestic experimentation with the law or a deep understanding of the impact of the new technology. The DSB should be wary of incorporating these premature solutions into the TRIPS system. For example, among other things, the WCT requires "adequate legal protection and effective legal remedies against the circumvention of effective technological measures,"[128] but at the time the WCT was adopted, there were no national laws on "hacking" (breaking through) technological measures in place.[129] Should the adequacy of legal protection in the digital environment arise in a TRIPS dispute, the DSB could integrate the WCT into TRIPS by adopting its approach to encryption technologies, just as it looked to the WCT on the scope of permissible exceptions in the *US–110(5)* case. But the DSB should hesitate before going so far. The WCT's exceptions provision emanated from a long-standing international commitment to balance. However, the WCT's effort to protect copyright owners against hacking occurred before the intellectual property community understood how digital rights management systems would be applied to copyrighted works, or how consumers would respond to encryption.[130]

Another variable goes to governance. Reference by the *US–110(5)* panel to the exceptions provision in the WCT was, in a way, surprising because the WCT was not in force at the time the DSB cited it.[131] However, the status of a measure as "hard law" should not be dispositive as to whether it should be integrated into TRIPS jurisprudence.[132] The WCT was produced through an open process, with broad participation from the member states and civil society; the result was consensus on most issues (in particular, on the provision on which the DSB relied). Consistent with that approach, we would endorse the use of more informal actions, such as the Reports of Standing Committees, Model Laws, or the advice given by WIPO technical advisers to WTO members. Whether they are incorporated, and the weight to be given to them, should depend, among other things, on whether they were negotiated transparently, with broad opportunities for participation (by countries as well as civil society), and whether they were the products of genuine consensus.[133] When these conditions are present, then the DSB should be entitled to use the measure as indicative of the judgment of the international community. Adjudicators could glean further evidence from how states and jurists reacted to the instrument and from how many WIPO members formally adopted the conclusions.

Thus, for example, while the *US–110(5)* panel took account of the WCT, the *China–Enforcement* panel rejected the use of a report by the WIPO Committee of Experts on Measures Against Counterfeiting and Piracy and the Draft Model Provisions for National Laws set out in a memorandum by the International

Bureau of WIPO.[134] There had been no agreement on these materials, and the panel held they should not be "elevate[d] to the status of the proper interpretation of a treaty text that was negotiated in another forum and that *was* finally agreed."[135] In contrast, we would advocate use of the Joint Recommendation on Well Known Marks to determine the meaning of "well known" because that part of the Joint Recommendation was adopted by consensus. However, we would not use the Joint Recommendation to decide whether TRIPS should be interpreted to require protection against dilution.[136] In fact, the drafters' foray into dilution protection was met with opposition from Argentina and other developing countries. They refused to join that part of the Joint Recommendation on the theory that it increased the level of trademark protection well beyond the likelihood-of-confusion standard set out in the Paris Convention and the TRIPS Agreement.[137]

The DSB must also take into account a constellation of factors dealing with the relationship between TRIPS and the instrument in question. Integrating instruments dealing with the same intellectual property subject matter as TRIPS should be relatively straightforward. Most of the WCT, for example, deals with core copyright (albeit as applied in the digital context). Accordingly, the DSB was right to consider its approach to exceptions when interpreting TRIPS. However, the provisions on hacking created a new species of right—sometimes called paracopyright. Similarly, WIPO is considering new forms of protection for folklore and traditional knowledge. It is difficult to see how the DSB could easily integrate these developments into the TRIPS Agreement. The legitimacy of the WTO and its dispute resolution system strongly depends on the requirement that adjudicators not "*add* or diminish the rights and obligations provided in the covered agreements."[138]

Declining to integrate new rights comes at a price, however, for these measures could give rise to cycling. While direct attempts to enforce protection for folklore would be outside the covered agreements, and therefore not within the DSB's jurisdiction, the proposals will (as with intellectual property in general) affect third parties. For example, WIPO's proposed Provisions for the Protection of Traditional Cultural Expressions/Expressions of Folklore would provide indigenous peoples with the legal right to "preclude the grant, exercise and enforcement of intellectual property rights acquired by unauthorized parties over traditional cultural expressions/expressions of folklore and derivatives thereof."[139] Should the Provisions become an international obligation and require states to deny copyright protection in unauthorized cultural expression, WTO members would be in a difficult position. A state that denied copyright protection could become the subject of a TRIPS dispute, while the denial of folklore protection could become the subject of whatever enforcement mechanism WIPO adopts. Thus, while our integrative approach could improve TRIPS adjudication and bring a measure of coherence, it could not deal with all inconsistencies. (Of course, as WIPO develops this proposal, it would ideally consider ways to minimize the conflict by tackling the definition of ownership and building a bridge between TRIPS and the Provisions.)

For those who view TRIPS as a code, the question of integration might also turn on whether the WIPO instrument raises or lowers protection, or insulates works from further commodification. TRIPS permits states to increase protection (except in so far as it would "contravene the provisions of the Agreement"),[140] but it does not expressly address lowering standards or the effects of counter-norms. As a result, instruments that commodify information are arguably different from the ones that decommodify knowledge or protect against commodification. But this critique misses the point of the integration through interpretation approach, which takes non-WTO law into account not because it represents the "relations between the parties" under Article 31.3(c) of the Vienna Convention, but because it reflects the actual meaning of the Agreement. In fact the *US–110(5)* panel used the WCT in exactly this way: it bolstered the determination that TRIPS encompasses the minor exceptions doctrine of the Berne acquis. Accordingly, the panel upheld certain unauthorized (decommodified) uses. Integrating the WIPO's Development Agenda, or a standing committee's work on exceptions and limitations would not *necessarily* constitute a derogation from the Agreement.

2. Bilateral and regional trade agreements

While we concluded that many WIPO instruments were good candidates for integration in TRIPS dispute settlement, the status of bilateral and regional trade agreements presents a closer question. Even if they cannot be deployed under the reading of Article 31.3(c) of the Vienna Convention in *EC–Biotech*, they might be used interpretively under Article 31.1. The comprehensive bilateral and regional agreements, such as the FTAs concluded by the United States and the European Union, were essentially trade agreements and thus do not carry the imprimatur of special intellectual property expertise. But because the FTAs were adopted after TRIPS, some provisions may represent attempts to clarify open-ended or unclear terms, especially those causing problems in state law reform efforts. Furthermore, they are hard law, and many of the provisions in these agreements appear in near-identical form in many FTAs, spanning a broad array of countries at many different stages of technological development. Thus the provisions of FTAs (particularly those common to several instruments) could be considered akin to state practices; we have previously argued the DSB should take these into account in clarifying undefined terms and considering normative issues.

At the same time, however, the process by which these agreements were concluded does not represent the type of governance that we believe fully supports integration. They are largely negotiated in secret with little participation by civil society.[141] In many cases, the partners are a developed and a developing country. While fifteen years' experience with TRIPS and the capacity-building projects noted earlier may have enhanced the sophistication of the developing world,[142] there is an enduring question about the asymmetric capacities and leverage of the parties. For instance, the U.S.-Korea FTA required 169 changes in Korean law and none in the law of the United States, suggesting that the United States had the upper hand in the negotiations (and Korea is hardly a developing country).[143] Furthermore, because the FTAs are comprehensive agreements, the provisions on intellectual property in any particular agreement may have involved compensatory benefits in other sectors covered by that instrument. If the DSB is to integrate FTA norms into TRIPS and apply them to the entire WTO, it should look for broader participation and deliberation and compensatory benefits that extend to the entire WTO membership.

For example, were the DSB faced with the problem of interpreting Article 39.3 of the TRIPS Agreement on undisclosed pharmaceutical data, it would be confronted with an extremely open-ended provision: the measure protects data originating through "considerable effort" against "unfair commercial use." Several regionals and bilaterals have, in effect, interpreted these standards by providing precise minimum terms for the protection of premarket clearance data.[144] It would be convenient for the DSB to use the common features of these instruments to shed light on the meaning of the terms in TRIPS—and thereby bring some coherence and certainty to the international law of trade secrecy. At the same time, however, the countries that agreed to the detailed provisions likely received a compensatory benefit for agreeing to measures that raise the cost of pharmaceuticals. Were the DSB to import a meaning from these agreements into TRIPS, countries that did not receive that benefit will still have to pay the higher prices. For this particular provision (others may be different), the integrative benefit may not even be quite as large as it may seem. Since countries bound by both a bilateral and TRIPS could comply with both agreements by simply adopting the higher standard, no country will face inconsistent obligations.

As we saw, bilateral and regional agreements not only include freestanding provisions (such as the one on data exclusivity), but also require recognition of other international instruments. These "incorporated obligations" might be analyzed somewhat differently. Again, even if they are not binding under Article 31.3(c) of the Vienna Convention, there is a strong case for their incorporation as reflective of the ordinary meaning of the TRIPS Agreement. Many of the instruments preceded the TRIPS Agreement and were certainly a part of the context in which the drafters of the WTO operated. Most were also negotiated within WIPO. Thus, they enjoy legitimating factors (such as expertise) wholly apart from the legitimation that comes from being part of a formally binding instrument. And their inclusion in bilaterals and regionals supplies significant new information. For example, and as we saw, although parts of the Joint Recommendation on Well Known Marks received broad support, there were dissenting views expressed regarding the measure on dilution. Thus, we suggested that the DSB should be hesitant about relying on that part of the Recommendation in interpreting the scope of trademark rights and rejected the notion of the DSB enforcing the dilution provision simply because it appeared in a bilateral agreement between the parties to a dispute. However, as the number of agreements incorporating the Recommendation increases, and most especially if some states enact dilution laws on their own initiative, the argument for interpreting TRIPS as covering dilution grows. As we noted earlier, traders would have a great deal of difficulty in a global environment in which some countries took inconsistent attitudes toward dilution protection. Thus, integration would be particularly valuable.

3. ACTA and other instruments specific to intellectual property

Like the bilateral and regional agreements, ACTA will be a formally binding instrument. But unlike bilaterals and regionals, it deals exclusively with intellectual property. Accordingly, there is no danger that it was adopted as a result of exogenous trade-offs unavailable to nonsignatories. To the contrary, since it covers only intellectual property issues, its interpretive status is similar to that of WIPO instruments: its use could be justified as lex specialis, as crafted by experts focused on intellectual property matters.[145] Indeed, the final version of ACTA can be viewed as incorporating the reaction to *China–Enforcement* throughout much of the developed world. As we saw, the panel interpreted the Agreement as giving states substantial flexibility regarding enforcement decisions; arguably, it left so much room to the states that counterfeiting and piracy remain a problem, despite the enduring interest of the trade regime in that issue, dating from at least the time of the Tokyo Round. The definitions of such terms as "commercial scale" and authorities shall "have the authority" in ACTA arguably provide a more accurate read on what TRIPS sought to accomplish than does the panel decision.[146] Since the DSU does not recognize stare decisis and the AB has yet to speak on the issue, the next WTO complaint on these issues could offer an opportunity for the DSB to revise the definitions of these terms, and both improve the law and make it more coherent.

But there is a significant impediment. ACTA's potential status as a binding instrument under national law has been questioned in both the European Union and the United States.[147] More important for our purposes, it was negotiated entirely in secret and solely by the potential signatories—indeed, with a level of secrecy so stringent that even the European Parliament was left uninformed, in possible violation of EU law.[148] Civil society was not permitted to participate. And since, as drafted, ACTA appears to go well beyond counterfeiting and piracy, it cannot be viewed as a document written to reflect the way in which WTO members interpret TRIPS to deal with those issues. Even if the DSB were to confine its use of ACTA to those provisions that are about piracy and counterfeiting, there would be a problem. As we saw, the provisions on in-transit seizure arguably undermine TRIPS flexibilities regarding compulsory licensing. Relying on them would thus produce a more integrated trade environment, but at the cost of running roughshod over the compromises that lie at the core of the TRIPS Agreement.

4. Other initiatives

The bulk of the counternorm agenda stands on a different footing from the TRIPS-plus initiatives. Few measures were adopted in the context of a binding international instrument. Instead, they draw their legitimating authority from the prestige of the organizations that promulgate them: WHO, from its preeminent role in coordinating global health care; UNCTAD, from its expertise in development issues; UNESCO, from its familiarity with cultural and educational issues. In a sense, these initiatives should be perceived as more legitimate subjects of integration than commodification moves. As Christopher May has observed, there are limits to the ability of the proponents of strong protection to continually shift regimes. At some point, the shift to a new regime signals that the participants in the prior regime consistently rejected the objectives sought. But there are good reasons to address health concerns in WHO, or nutritional concerns in FAO, or development concerns in UNCTAD. The issues involved are often profoundly technical and empirical—which medicines are essential; which foods are safe; what actions best promote technology transfer? Others are normative—how should rights be balanced; which of a right holder's expectations are legitimate; what roles should the expectations of third parties play? None of these questions can be answered solely from the perspective of trade law or practice. Accordingly, the views of organizations acting within the sphere of their special expertise should be considered particularly pertinent to clarifying elements in the TRIPS Agreement. Indeed, the Doha Declaration has elevated the significance of the distributive and development goals that inform many of these initiatives. The DSB has yet to operationalize Articles 7 and 8, which were emphasized in the Declaration provisions; the views of expert organizations, with substantial experience thinking about "the transfer and dissemination of technology," "social and economic welfare," "public health and nutrition," and "abuse," would furnish particularly valuable guidance.

Of course, governance issues must also be taken into account. On the one hand, the work of these organizations tends to be transparent and participatory. Moreover, several of these institutions support civil society and rely heavily on its input. On the other hand, such institutions may appear to be heavily weighted in the decommodification direction. But that is not necessarily the case. Organizations like WHO and FAO recognize that intellectual property protection is needed to spur the next generation of pharmaceuticals and the production of plants and animals that are more nutritious and better adapted to environmental conditions. The human rights institutions are equally diverse. In fact, the intellectual property cases that have been litigated under a human rights rubric tend to be those that protect the interests of proprietors, not the public.[149] Furthermore, because these organizations are open, they provide the opportunity for those with contrary views to participate.

Were the WTO to consider the factors we have enumerated in determining how much deference to accord this material, there would be interesting side benefits. Negotiators of other initiatives would have an incentive to make their deliberations more open and participatory. By the same token, more states would be motivated to involve themselves fully in the work of all the entities with intellectual property interests. For example, deliberations over ACTA might have been more open had the negotiators thought that transparency would enhance the likelihood that ACTA would be used to interpret TRIPS.[150] And more states might have been willing to participate in the negotiations under those circumstances. Interpretive approaches thus not only allow for updating of international norms, they can also improve the political and institutional economy in more systemic ways.

B. Lawmaking: The Council for TRIPS, the WTO, and Beyond

Despite the explosion of intellectual property initiatives analyzed in this Chapter, changes in the creative environment will ultimately necessitate formal revisions of TRIPS. While some scholars have elevated the role of the DSB in completing the process of commodification that began with the TRIPS Agreement,[151] the legitimacy of international law ultimately requires party agreement; it cannot be sustained over the long term through an adjudicatory mechanism alone.[152] The WTO dispute settlement process is far removed and insulated from appropriate democratic pressures (both by inherent institutional place and by current rules on transparency of process). There is also a selection bias in that the disputes that come to resolution are a product of geopolitical calculation and legal capacity. And many of the staff and participants in the DSB are not especially attuned to the nuances of intellectual property law.

However, through its lawmaking activities, including most notably deliberations in the Council for TRIPS, the WTO can reduce fragmentation in ways that are more legitimate and effective. Unlike efforts to incorporate non-WTO norms in the DSB, integration in a multilateral legislative setting is less likely to provoke suspicion. So far, the Council has contributed little to the ongoing challenge of the Knowledge Economy; involving other organizations in its deliberations might overcome its apparent inertia. Drawing other institutions into the WTO framework not only would enhance the output of the Council, but also would improve the work of these other institutions. Opportunities to participate in Council deliberations would sensitize these organizations to the costs of fragmentation, alert them to situations where cycling is likely to occur, and lead them to consider ways to reconcile their agendas with TRIPS. Treating other institutions as partners in the international intellectual system might thus usher in an era of regulatory cooperation rather than regulatory competition.[153]

The Council for TRIPS is already charged with addressing many of the issues on which other organizations are working and where integration is thus most sorely needed. At the conclusion of the Uruguay Round, several important issues were left open, and the Council was given the responsibility of overseeing their continued consideration. These include added protection for geographical indications for wines and spirits,[154] questions concerning protection for living plants and animals,[155] the applicability of nonviolation complaints to the TRIPS Agreement,[156] and extra assistance for least developed countries.[157] In 1998, the Council was asked to consider electronic commerce in information products,[158] and in the Doha Round, it was assigned several additional tasks, including some of the issues discussed earlier, such as reconciling TRIPS with development goals, and considering the relationship between the TRIPS Agreement, the CBD, and the protection of traditional knowledge and folklore.[159] In a separate statement on public health, the Council was also instructed to examine questions on access to medicines.[160]

The crucial step is to develop procedural mechanisms to take advantage of the vast array of expertise operating in the intellectual property arena. In theory, the Council is already constituted in a manner conducive to regulatory cooperation. It meets regularly, and its deliberations have some degree of both transparency and outside participation. It has the power to grant observer status on a regular or ad hoc basis. Furthermore, it issues annual reports that, along with meeting minutes, working documents, and decisions, are available on the WTO website.[161] These materials alert NGOs and other interested parties to the issues on which it is deliberating. In practice, however, the Council has not taken full advantage of the opportunities to link its work to that of other organizations. While it has granted regular status to WIPO (which is not surprising given that TRIPS contemplates an ongoing relationship between the WTO and WIPO), other intergovernmental organizations are invited to attend deliberations only on an ad hoc basis. Purportedly, observer status is granted whenever the expertise of an institution is relevant to the issues on the agenda,[162] but that does not appear to be a uniform practice. For example, even though there are developments in the CBD that are directly relevant to TRIPS, the effort to give observer status to the Secretariat of the CBD has met an "ideological or possibly a political stone wall."[163]

A more permanent and deeper relationship with these institutions would be highly desirable. The presence of outside organizations with experience in particular aspects of the Knowledge Economy would not only bring the access interests of developing countries to the fore, it would identify to the Council areas where strengthening protection is necessary. For example, counterfeiting and piracy remain important concerns. At the behest of a group of developed countries, the Council has taken the issue up repeatedly, but the discussions have not progressed, and ACTA may, in part, be a result of that stalemate. Had the World Customs Union,[164] which works on border matters, been given a seat at the Council, it might have made the continuing problems with TRIPS clearer to those opposed to considering the issue.[165]

In addition, a clear understanding of emerging problems is likely to produce more integrated solutions. For example, WHO might be useful in finding an approach to data exclusivity that mediates between Article 39.3 and the obligations imposed by FTAs and regional agreements. Similarly, when faced with another regime with a compliance mechanism, the Council might find approaches to TRIPS that minimize the risk of cycling. In some cases, the problem may be solved through interpretation of TRIPS (or, more accurately, by persuading member states to defer to the Council's judgment at least temporarily). In situations where resolution would require a revision of the Agreement, the Council could use existing mechanisms within the institutional structure of the WTO to bring potential solutions to the attention of the Ministerial Council.[166]

As important, providing other organizations with a seat at the Council would make it easier for them to identify areas where fragmentation is particularly problematic and encourage them to structure their initiatives in a manner that avoids inconsistency and cycling.[167] For example, as previously noted, WIPO's Provisions for the Protection of Traditional Cultural Expressions/Expressions of Folklore, which would currently preclude the enforcement of copyrights acquired by unauthorized parties over traditional cultural expression, could instead be formulated to protect folklore in ways that reduce conflict with the copyright provisions of TRIPS. Similarly, the Secretariat of the CBD could use a liability rule to protect the interests of individuals in their genomes without necessarily affecting patentability requirements.

Inclusion in Council deliberations might also encourage these organizations to develop techniques for minimizing the consequences of unavoidable fragmentation. For example, Joost Pauwelyn and Luiz Eduardo Salles have suggested that the drafters of international instruments could put choice of forum provisions in their agreements and thereby avoid problems like the one that arose in *Mexico–Soft Drinks*.[168] It may be that action by the General Council of the WTO will be required to formalize relationships with other organizations and to regularize their status as observers.[169] The General Council should do so selectively. Just as we suggested that the DSB use governance as a criterion for deciding on the incorporation of non-WTO law, so too should governance be factored into decisions on which organizations are entitled to participate on a regular basis.

When TRIPS is revised, the WTO should also consider textual linkages between TRIPS and the work of other institutions. Other WTO agreements explicitly reference principles set out by expert international bodies such as the Codex Alimentarius Commission or the International Organization for Standardization.[170] These measures provide member states with safe harbors or otherwise signal (to both states and the DSB) the range of flexibility available under the agreement in question. Some linkages are more dynamic. For example, GATT Article XV requires consultation with the International Monetary Fund on certain issues within their joint interest. The WTO could create similar collaborative mechanisms with WIPO, WHO, FAO, and other organizations that gather and analyze technical information that bears on TRIPS issues. Admittedly, technical issues can have normative and political components, and full deference to technocratic decision makers will not always be appropriate.[171] But as we saw, there are many places in TRIPS where a knowledge base that extends beyond intellectual property and trade is necessary. So long as deference is confined to institutions that practice good governance and are aware of the full implications of their actions, their technical input would be invaluable.

To be sure, these efforts would not solve all fragmentation problems. More attention must be paid in international law generally to techniques for mediating among international organizations. These would include agreeing on techniques for allocating authority among international organizations; concepts of primary jurisdiction to recognize a hierarchy of relationships among international actors; devising tools analogous to doctrines of lis pendens and forum non conveniens, which allow a tribunal seized with power over a dispute to defer to another tribunal with a closer connection to the parties or the claims; and applying doctrines such as res judicata to prevent cycling. In addition, the international community might follow the move in national adjudication from canonical choice of law rules, such as lex loci delicti and lex loci contractus, to a less formalistic analysis, one that depends more on the nature of the dispute, the goals of the law, and the strengths and interests of the international institutions that promulgated the relevant norms.

In the meantime, individuals and states may also have a role to play in ameliorating fragmentation. To some extent, individuals can mediate among international organizations in that there are experts and NGOs that make regular appearances in every institution considering an issue within their areas of interest. These participants could alert the institutions to inconsistencies and risks of cycling and help them find approaches that bring more coherence to the system as a whole. In some countries, international obligations are enforced in local courts through private intellectual property disputes. Decisions in these cases may also identify techniques for avoiding fragmentation.[172] States can also sidestep problems by exercising restraint in the cases they choose to pursue. The remedy phase of a GATT dispute between the European Union and Ecuador over bananas provides an example. In that case, the European Union refused to comply with a judgment it lost, and in the initial arbitration, Ecuador was authorized to suspend TRIPS obligations regarding EU intellectual property. Although it found a way to do so without imposing costs on local authors or causing consumer confusion within Ecuador, retaliation could have led to cycling. Ecuador was, after all, obliged to protect EU intellectual property rights not only under TRIPS, but also under the Paris, Berne, and Rome Conventions—an issue the arbitrators refused to consider.[173] Fortunately, the parties settled, and a clash between TRIPS and the other agreements was avoided.[174] But this will not always happen: the case could equally have resulted in retaliation, followed by a claim by the European Union against Ecuador based on the Berne, Paris, or Rome Convention.[175] In short, while the actions of states and private actors can minimize the cost of fragmentation, they cannot by themselves effect integration.

The procedural and institutional devices examined in this Chapter likewise will not fully integrate the international intellectual regime. In Chapter 7, we turn to another approach. We develop the contours of an international acquis, the recognition of a series of enduring commitments that might constrain some forms of fragmented lawmaking and achieve greater coherence within the international framework. To some extent, fragmentation is an outcome of a skewed political economy. Thus, Chapter 7 also addresses the development of substantive maxima—user rights—that would, through international regulation, ensure balance in national intellectual property law.

7

An International Acquis

Integrating Regimes and Restoring Balance

> A closer look at the existing international IP *acquis*, in particular the TRIPS Agreement, reveals a basic principle on which the notion of ceilings to IP protection can be based: Both the Paris Convention as well as TRIPS subject additional protection to the condition that it does not *contravene* the provisions of the respective Agreement. TRIPS therefore does not only create a "floor" of minimum protection, but opens the door to ceilings which place a binding maximum level to the protection of IP.
>
> —Annette Kur and Henning Grosse Ruse-Khan, *Enough Is Enough—The Notion of Binding Ceilings in International Intellectual Property Protection,* in INTELLECTUAL PROPERTY IN A FAIR WORLD TRADE SYSTEM: PROPOSALS FOR REFORMING THE TRIPS AGREEMENT 359, 401 (Annette Kur ed., Edward Elgar 2011)

> "Public interest" . . . is a shifting concept that requires a careful balancing of competing claims. . . . This balancing process occurs in all national copyright systems, even in those which proclaim the rights of authors most absolutely, and . . . the same has been true of the Berne Convention.
>
> —SAM RICKETSON AND JANE C. GINSBURG, 1 INTERNATIONAL COPYRIGHT AND NEIGHBOURING RIGHTS: THE BERNE CONVENTION AND BEYOND § 13.02, at 756 (2d ed. Oxford University Press 2005)

The ferment in norm formation that we saw in Chapter 6 is unlikely to abate. Nations in the North with an interest in commodifying their knowledge-based output will continue to shop for (or create new) institutions that will endorse or develop higher standards of intellectual property protection, while those countries at the opposite end of the development spectrum will not abandon the search for fora more solicitous to user interests, distributive justice, health, and development. While the previous Chapter offered suggestions on procedural and institutional mechanisms for integrating all of these activities into the TRIPS Agreement, new interpretive approaches can go only so far. They are essentially backward-looking solutions; they do not preclude fragmentation and thus can only resolve the problems fragmentation produces. Yet coherence is essential to robust innovation: creativity cannot flourish without a greater degree of certainty than the current regime permits. Of course, in a neofederalist system of the type we propose, absolute certainty is not realistic and, moreover, is less than ideal if national experimentation and cross-border trade are both valued. We believe, however, that it is possible to do better.

In this Chapter, we suggest that the time has come to crystallize the learning accumulated in the century and a half since the multinational system was born. We tease out and make explicit the elements of what we term an international intellectual property "acquis"—a set of basic principles that form the background norms animating the intellectual property system. The concept of an acquis is relatively new to international law. The WTO borrowed it from EU law, where the phrase "acquis communautaire" has in recent years been used to describe the body of existing legal principles and commitments to which new members of the European Union must ascribe.[1] In this sense, it is easy to see why it made sense for the Dispute Settlement Body (DSB) to adopt the term; like the European Union, the WTO involves a "single undertaking," and new members must sign up to the entire range of principles that govern the membership. However, the term also has a functional dimension. The Appellate Body (AB) referred to the concept of an acquis in *Japan–Taxes on Alcoholic Beverages* to explain that panel reports should be relevant in adjudicating future disputes because this practice would protect legitimate expectations.[2] And later scholarly treatment of the concept suggests that it reflects efforts not only to protect legitimate expectations, but also to fill gaps, and to create certainty and predictability.[3] Moreover, the *US–110(5)* panel, which issued the first TRIPS report to refer to an acquis (the Berne acquis), appeared to add another dimension to the concept, regarding the acquis as a body of principles reflected in a treaty regime even if not always expressed.[4]

The concept of an acquis is therefore fluid. We adopt it here as much for its functional characteristics as for its (relatively new) international application. While an acquis is typically associated with a particular instrument or institution, the goals of an acquis are equally relevant to the international intellectual property system as a whole. Recognizing elements as cross-cutting features underlying all instruments constituting the system would facilitate the resolution of international disputes and rectify the problems in decision making that we saw in Chapters 3 and 4. In TRIPS, it would clarify the normative underpinnings of intellectual property law, flesh out the principles and objectives found in Articles 7 and 8 of the TRIPS Agreement, and enable the DSB to situate particular challenges in the broader context of knowledge governance.

Moreover, the acquis would complement the devices of integration discussed in Chapter 6 as a means of bringing coherence to the international intellectual property system.

Prospectively, the acquis would create a legal framework to structure future international lawmaking and thus reduce the incidence of fragmentation. It would furnish a useful guide to international negotiators, especially those who are unfamiliar with intellectual property law and lore. As it develops in response to new challenges, the acquis would harness the expertise of the diverse array of institutions now operating in this arena. By establishing the norms to which all participants in the intellectual property system can be regarded as having subscribed, the acquis would focus debate and reduce the transaction costs of mediating among multiple conflicting initiatives. For developing countries, broad acceptance of the principles in the acquis would provide bargaining leverage, help address the challenges of political economy, and ameliorate the problems of capacity that we have discussed in earlier Chapters.

We draw the content of the acquis from national and international intellectual property law along with associated jurisprudence and scholarship. An examination of these sources reveals that certain principles have a historical pedigree that elevates them to the status of an agreed norm. The minor exceptions doctrine, which was recognized as part of the Berne acquis in the *US–110(5)* report, furnishes an example. Other fundamental norms can be gleaned from the frequency with which they appear across a variety of instruments. Some elements derive from the factors we discussed in Chapter 1: diversity, balance, and historical contingency. Other components emanate from the purposes that first instigated the move to international law, namely, the interdependence of nations in the production of knowledge and trade in knowledge-intensive goods. Experience with TRIPS shows that intellectual property cannot be isolated from broader public policy concerns, such as a commitment to expressive values or access to essential medicines. Thus, in establishing the acquis, we do not confine our examination to purely intellectual property instruments.

We begin this Chapter with an explanation of why we believe the time to be ripe for articulating these transcendent principles. We next initiate the process of identifying the elements of the acquis, including principles we regard as emerging. We start with those that protect access because many of these are latent in international intellectual property instruments, and one important goal of constructing an acquis is to make them explicit. We then proceed to principles that protect proprietary interests and national autonomy, and reflect the interdependence of nations. We conclude with a discussion of the ways in which the acquis might shape the future progress of the international intellectual property system, including how it might be used to supplement Articles 7 and 8 of TRIPS, and applied and enforced in a variety of settings.

I. The Need for an Acquis

Chapter 6 traced developments in international intellectual property law and noted the fragmentation that these developments produced. However, the history recounted suggests a broader point: the pressures on the international intellectual property system are mounting. International instruments follow one another in rapid succession, promulgating rules, standards, and norms on an array of overlapping issues. Thoughtful interpretation can lessen some of the pressures but it cannot deal with all of them as the rules, standards and norms often cut in opposite directions and are of differing legal stature. While instruments raising the level of protection are often hard law, those that further access and other public-regarding interests tend to be softer.[5] In this climate, a new paradigm is necessary.

TRIPS can be viewed as the catalyst: its adoption produced a fundamental change in the political landscape of intellectual property law. The Paris and Berne Conventions essentially protected foreign nationals against blatant copying. This required relatively basic rights for authors, traders, and inventors. Although the standards were raised over time, they remained relatively unintrusive. Enforcement (almost exclusively through political pressure) was lax; nations retained a great deal of latitude to pursue policies tailored to their own political objectives and consistent with their own culture and priorities. The TRIPS Agreement imposed higher standards of international protection, particularly for technological innovations. It also introduced a compliance mechanism backed up by trade sanctions. Thus, it constrained states' flexibility.

As previous Chapters demonstrated, more recent events introduced further constraints. The unrelenting advocacy of a "code view" of TRIPS has led developed nations to expand protection for right holders far beyond the requirements of TRIPS. For developing countries, the dynamic is different, but the results are often similar. Many of these nations considered their acceptance of TRIPS as capping their international intellectual property obligations. However, they soon found themselves subject to further unilateral and bilateral trade pressures, which exacerbated rather than ameliorated political and capacity asymmetries and led to TRIPS-plus standards and fragmentation.[6] In addition, TRIPS was adopted on the cusp of important changes in science and technology without expressly addressing the legal reforms that these advances would require. Although many of these emergent issues were put on the agenda of the Council for TRIPS, negotiations in the WTO stalled, prompting further fragmentation rather than consolidation of intellectual property lawmaking in a single institution. For example, the World Intellectual Property Organization (WIPO) adopted treaties on copyright and performers' rights in the digital environment; a group consisting largely of developed countries successfully advanced the Anti-Counterfeiting Trade Agreement (ACTA) to raise enforcement standards beyond TRIPS; and higher levels of intellectual property protection are a part of the Trans-Pacific Partnership (TPP) Agreement currently being negotiated by the nations of the Asia-Pacific region.[7]

A backlash soon followed. Many perceived TRIPS and its progeny as lacking sufficient protection for users and as leaving little room for states to further their own cultural policies, tailor the law to local economic needs and capacities, and adapt to new technological challenges. Thwarted in their efforts to ensure access to essential medicines in the midst of an epidemic, developing countries resisted TRIPS, ultimately achieving an amendment of the Agreement at Doha.[8] Emboldened by that success, user groups and developing countries brought other multilateral efforts to commodify knowledge to a halt: the proposal for a database treaty was suspended and then shelved;[9] the 2000 Diplomatic Conference on an audiovisual performers' treaty collapsed without agreement;[10] and the discussion of a broadcasting treaty disintegrated amid acrimonious debate.[11] Simultaneously, developing countries initiated the production of counternorms by introducing the Development Agenda within WIPO (while also seeking protection for their own intellectual resources, such as folklore).[12] And international organizations, such as the UN Conference on Trade and Development (UNCTAD) and the World Health Organization (WHO), began to pay attention to intellectual property matters and to act as magnets for the increasing numbers of interested NGOs.[13]

This crescendo of activity has worried scholars, leading to several suggestions for reform. Keith Maskus and Jerry Reichman proposed a moratorium. Until more is known about the impact of high standards of protection, they suggest "a time out" on international lawmaking.[14] Others analyzed the TRIPS Agreement as a contract of adhesion and argued that it might be open to rescission.[15] More proactively, Bernt Hugenholtz and Ruth Okediji proposed a soft law instrument delineating exceptions and limitations on the rights of copyright owners.[16] And a conference of scholars in Washington recently issued a declaration spelling out the public interest components of intellectual property policy.[17] Working within the WTO framework, Annette Kur and her collaborators developed a formal proposal for amending the TRIPS Agreement and transforming it into a more balanced instrument.[18] We do not disavow those efforts; indeed, their goals are largely at one with our arguments.[19] And they could achieve important ends. However, we think proposals to abrogate or modify TRIPS are unrealistic in the present climate and that it would be dangerous to take multilateral negotiations off the international table when so much commodification is occurring under the table, through secret negotiations over new plurilateral and bilateral agreements.[20] Furthermore, new initiatives to create freestanding instruments would exacerbate fragmentation even if they redress some of the substantive concerns about excessive protection.

In our view, any comprehensive solution to the turmoil in international intellectual property lawmaking must tackle three essential issues. First, it must grapple with the inevitability of regime shifting. Since the WTO is not institutionally suited to assume exclusive responsibility for responding to the dynamism of the creative environment, there will always be other institutions involved in intellectual property lawmaking. Their efforts will, however, be interrelated: any change made by one instrument or institution will necessarily affect others. Accordingly, the solution must apply across the entire intellectual property system—to all international intellectual property lawmaking and in all institutional settings. Otherwise, it will not fully address fragmentation or reduce uncertainty.

Admittedly, a set of meta-norms, such as we contemplate for the acquis, is rare in international law. But it is not unknown. For example, Benedict Kingsbury, Nico Krisch, and Richard Stewart have proposed the development of global administrative law—procedural principles that would similarly cut across institutions.[21] We believe, however, that meta-norms will not operate effectively if they are limited to the procedural realm. One reason for the ferment in intellectual property is that the stripped-down approach of conventions such as Paris and Berne, which mainly articulate minimum rights for authors and producers, is inappropriate to instruments that impose more stringent constraints on member state autonomy. Thus, the second goal of a comprehensive solution is to ensure that new international intellectual property instruments are substantively balanced. The rights of users, which were largely implicit in the older instruments and were primarily effectuated through the exercise of national flexibilities, must now be articulated in equivalent detail to those of authors and producers.

Third, experience suggests that the political economy of intellectual property tends to narrow policy options for many states. As we saw in Chapters 3 through 5, the DSB has decided so few TRIPS disputes, there are many aspects of the Agreement that have yet to receive an authoritative interpretation. As a result, advocates for strong protection can use the Agreement rhetorically, to block domestic legislation even when it is TRIPS-compliant. In developing countries, this problem is particularly severe: there are even fewer DSB reports dealing with the flexibilities of unique interest to these countries. Moreover, many of these states are still suffering from capacity deficits. To compound matters, they must also grapple with the linkage of intellectual property and trade, which gives developed countries with large markets exceptional leverage to impose TRIPS-plus standards. An international acquis would validate the range of policy choices that are available to national lawmakers. By legitimating these options as a part of the background rules animating effective intellectual property law, the acquis would reduce the political leverage of powerful states and impede their efforts to compel the adoption of high standards that ignore local interests.

To achieve these goals, we offer principles that we see as at the core of the acquis. We do not, however, intend to exhaustively articulate the acquis; our hope is that other scholars and policy makers will take up the challenge and augment our efforts. Moreover, we expect that the acquis will grow as new lawmaking occurs and new technological challenges are confronted. The capacity of the acquis to evolve dynamically is essential if it is to retain an ongoing legitimacy, without which countries might be tempted to withdraw from the international system.

II. The Content of the Acquis

We draw the content of the acquis from national and international sources along with associated jurisprudence and scholarship. International intellectual property treaties (including the WIPO instruments and TRIPS) represent a clear starting point, but they are not the end point of analysis. If the acquis is to realize the goal of bringing coherence to international lawmaking, it must reflect the work of certain nonintellectual property institutions as well. For example, human rights principles are increasingly part of intellectual property lawmaking and adjudication at national,[22] regional,[23] and international[24] levels. They comport in many instances with fundamental constitutional values at the national level. Their integration within intellectual property has become the subject of substantial scholarly attention.[25] And even WTO adjudicators have not been wholly resistant to referring to such external (even soft) sources of law, as in the *Shrimp-Turtle* dispute.[26]

In identifying the international acquis, we would also have regard to national principles. Historically, treaties merely established the boundaries within which national political processes created the substantive balances that are appropriate to the circumstances of each different domestic order. Because so much of the balance in intellectual property law has been achieved in the spaces left open by international law, looking simply at the bare text of international agreements would skew the acquis toward overcommodification. The acquis must therefore take account of principles well established at the national level in both developed and developing countries. Reference to state practices to inform international law is commonplace and was approved by the panel in the *US–110(5)* case to determine the content of the Berne acquis.[27] The panel's decision in that case also illustrates that the principles of the acquis do not require verbatim replication in numerous national instruments to suggest an international consensus. Instead, we are searching for normative equivalence.

Having established the sources of the acquis, we would identify the content of the acquis by focusing primarily on three constellations of factors.

First, we consider the pedigree of the principle, especially its iteration in multiple instruments, across a variety of institutions. Tomer Broude and Yuval Shany describe these as multisourced equivalent norms.[28] Repetition suggests a consensus about the validity of the principle, a consensus that should not require renegotiation each time that international lawmakers get to work. Second, we look at the issues we have considered throughout this volume: the cumulative nature of intellectual property, which demands balance among the interests of generations of producers and concern for those who build upon and use their work; the contingent nature of technology, which requires opportunities for experimentation and an openness to new creative paradigms; and a commitment to diversity. Third, we include in the acquis principles that are directed at solving problems of interdependence, that is, dealing with phenomena so global in effect that no state has the regulatory power to resolve them on its own. We consider the acquis as it applies to the interests of users, producers, nations, and the international regime as a whole.

A. Access-Regarding Principles

We begin with the portion of the acquis that deals with access interests because these have received short shrift in most international intellectual property lawmaking. As noted earlier, this omission is understandable in that the early instruments were genuinely minimum standards regimes—as Reichman describes it, islands of protection in a sea of public accessibility.[29] But as we have recounted, the political economy of intellectual property tends to favor the enlargement of the islands, with the result that the important contributions made by the sea—the domain of accessible knowledge—needs to be more explicitly established and protected.[30] These principles have a number of functions. They protect the wellsprings of creativity (ideas, fundamental principles of nature, generic expressions), ensure that the frontiers of knowledge can be continually moved forward, invigorate a competitive marketplace for ideas and products, and guarantee that individuals and nations enjoy the capacity to grow, learn, and interact.[31] Because they circumscribe the control of authors, traders, and inventors, the access-regarding provisions create the balance that is essential to intellectual property lawmaking.

Such provisions can take a number of forms, consisting of subject-matter exclusions, including minimum thresholds for protection; limits on scope, such as exceptions and limitations that guarantee the rights of users, competitors and follow-on innovators; and provisions that curb abuse of intellectual property rights. These concepts have a solid pedigree and widespread recognition at both the national and international level.

1. Subject matter exclusions

All areas of intellectual property laws contain thresholds and other exclusions from protection. These are reflected in both international and national law. In copyright law, the Berne Convention mandates that "the protection of this Convention shall not apply to news of the day or to miscellaneous facts having the character of mere items of press information."[32] In addition to incorporating the quotation right, TRIPS provides that "[c]opyright protection shall extend to expressions and not to ideas, procedures, methods of operation or mathematical concepts as such," a bar which is reiterated in the WIPO Copyright Treaty (WCT).[33] And both TRIPS and the WCT preclude the grant of copyright in data, notwithstanding any compilation copyright that might exist.[34]

The Paris Convention and the TRIPS Agreement take a similar approach to trademark law. The Paris Convention precludes the grant of registrations for marks consisting of flags or state emblems,[35] and gives states flexibility to reject marks whose registration would be contrary to public order.[36] TRIPS requires states to accord trademark protection to signs "capable of distinguishing the goods or services of one undertaking from those of other undertakings." This language suggests that words and symbols used generically should be in the public domain.[37] Furthermore, TRIPS permits states to condition registrability on use of the mark, thereby preserving unexploited signals for public use.[38]

International patent law is somewhat less explicit. The Paris Convention did not take any position on the subject matter of patents. TRIPS, however, defines patentable inventions that are "new, involve an inventive step and are capable of industrial application," implying that laws and principles of nature are excluded from protection.[39] In addition, TRIPS permits states to exclude diagnostic, surgical, and therapeutic methods; plants (so long as they are subject to sui generis protection); animals; and any invention necessary to protect public order, life, health, or prevent serious prejudice to the environment.[40]

While these exclusions may appear sparse, an examination of national legislation, judicial opinions, and commentary provides considerably more information on their breadth and content. Although none have been the subject of international dispute resolution, there are a few cases where these international provisions have been expressly interpreted by national courts. For example, a UK court has affirmed that the prohibition of protection for ideas in TRIPS imposes a ceiling on permissible protection.[41] Indeed, Mr. Justice Arnold went further in that case and held that Article 2 of the WCT excludes protection for programming languages because they are methods of operation.[42] Likewise, the Canadian Supreme Court has suggested that Berne imposes an originality prerequisite for copyright protection; the Court was essentially deriving an implicit threshold from the text of the international instruments it was interpreting.[43] As

Daniel Gervais explained, the notion of "work" in the Berne Convention may support a requirement of originality, in the sense of intellectual creation, to the exclusion of other criteria.[44]

In addition, national laws demonstrate the fundamental character of these exclusions and thresholds. Virtually all copyright systems exclude ideas and facts from protection. Almost without exception, national trademark laws preclude protection for functional product features and generic terms.[45] Patent laws exclude protection for laws and principles of nature and require that inventions be new and inventive. As the U.S. Supreme Court put it in *Bilski v. Kappos*, "The concepts covered by these exceptions are 'part of the storehouse of knowledge of all men ... free to all men and reserved exclusively to none.'"[46]

In addition to these ubiquitous exclusions from protection, there are a series of other exclusions that are pervasive enough to establish their pedigree. In copyright, many countries deny protection to methods of operation and functional works.[47] Most countries limit trademark protection to marks that remain in use.[48] Patent statutes typically exclude mathematical methods, aesthetic creations, inventions related to plants and animals, diagnostic methods, and inventions necessary to safeguard the public order.[49] Some developing countries have raised the inventive step to exclude protection for second uses of previously patented materials.[50]

Finally, regard to national law shows that as these principles evolve, they become more deeply embedded into the background norms of the intellectual property regime. For example, although EU legislation has thus far resisted adopting a general standard for the originality of all works throughout Europe, the requirement that a work be "the author's own intellectual creation" in order to be protected has now been repeated in harmonization instruments pertaining to such diverse works as software, databases, and photographs.[51] Over time, this standard may arguably become a general test of originality, precluding the grant of copyright protection to sweat-of-the-brow-based works that fail to meet it.[52]

At a minimum, then, our survey of international and national sources expands on the point made in the first quotation at the outset of this Chapter: the international acquis includes a set of access-regarding principles that can act as ceilings on protection. The building blocks of creativity and the basic components of expression must be in the public domain. Accordingly, laws of nature cannot be patented, ideas and facts cannot be the subject of copyright protection, and generic terms and functional features cannot be registered as trademarks. Nor, if these principles are to be respected, can they be commodified by other legal regimes. Furthermore, the acquis recognizes a consensus that nations can enact other exclusions to maintain competition, reduce transaction costs, protect the social order, and ensure that authors and inventors need "to deposit more than a penny in the box" in order to make the intellectual property "turnstile revolve."[53]

2. Scope of protection

Each intellectual property regime also includes a series of scope limitations. Some are highly specific. At the international level, the Berne Convention includes a mandatory quotation right.[54] It also contains measures permitting states to enact a series of specific exceptions aimed at validating uses of copyrighted materials for teaching and reporting, as well as compulsory licenses for various broadcasting purposes.[55] For developing nations, these provisions are supplemented by the flexibilities available in the Berne Appendix.[56] Furthermore, Berne permits states to set a temporal limit on protection (so long as it exceeds a set period, for most works, fifty years after the author's death).[57] For trademark law, the TRIPS Agreement permits states to revoke trademarks after three years of nonuse or if the mark has lost distinctiveness, such as through uncontrolled licensing.[58] The geographical indications, industrial design, and topography provisions include a set of targeted limitations.[59] In patents, TRIPS gives states the right, under defined conditions, to issue compulsory licenses to meet local needs.[60] Furthermore, it permits states to limit patents to twenty years after filing.[61] For all intellectual property rights, TRIPS leaves states with substantial discretion on the remedies available when third parties are found to infringe protected works, and gives broad scope for national provisions authorizing government use without the permission of the right holder.[62]

In addition to these specific exceptions and limits on scope, international instruments include provisions setting out general tests for other exceptions that states may wish to create. The origin of all these tests is Article 9.2 of the Berne Convention, which applied only to exceptions to the reproduction right. However, TRIPS negotiators adapted that provision to create Exceptions tests that apply to all uses of copyrighted works and, with some modifications, to the use of patents, trademarks, and designs.[63] Later, the WCT adopted a test similar to the copyright formulation found in the TRIPS Agreement.[64]

Once again, national laws enrich our perspective and help us understand the underlying norms. Virtually all legal systems impose temporal limits on protection for copyright and patent; such limits are mandated by the U.S. Constitution.[65] All have first sale or local exhaustion doctrines.[66] In addition, states have enacted a diverse range of exceptions. For example, the EU Copyright Directive lists twenty specific limitations that EU states may impose on the rights of copyright holders, including copying for private use; using material for the purpose of caricature, parody, or pastiche; or using a work for teaching or scientific research.[67] In addition, EU directives mandate the availability of certain exceptions in all member states. Thus, the Copyright Directive requires an exception for ephemeral copies;[68] the Software Directive ensures that users can reverse engineer computer programs to obtain interoperability information; that Directive also permits users to make backup copies, a right that cannot be overridden by contract.[69] By the same token, trademark laws permit descriptive fair uses of protected marks as well as uses in news reporting and parody.[70] Patent laws similarly contain various exceptions: for experimental purposes,[71] engaging in testing for premarket clearance purposes,[72] reseeding crops,[73] and noncommercial use.[74] Finally, states have begun to realize that modulating remedies can ensure that intellectual property rights are not used to hold innovation ransom.[75]

Some countries also use the strategy of an open-ended, general exceptions provision to permit use of protected works by third parties. An increasing number have transposed versions of the Exceptions tests as they are laid out in the TRIPS Agreement.[76] Two panels of the DSB have interpreted these provisions narrowly. However, these decisions were heavily criticized by scholars,[77] and at least one national court has read the transposed version of the TRIPS copyright provision in ways far more respectful of access interests.[78] The fair use provision of U.S. copyright law illustrates how extensive this latitude for diverse third-party uses can be.[79] Unlike the interpretation of the TRIPS provisions, it articulates a nonexhaustive and noncumulative list of factors, whose collective weight determines when the social use of a copyrighted work trumps the benefits of authorial control. In the words of Justice Brennan, limiting the copyright holder's control

> is not some unforeseen byproduct of a statutory scheme intended primarily to ensure a return for works of the imagination. . . . This distinction is at the essence of copyright. The copyright laws serve as the "engine of free expression," only when the statutory monopoly does not choke off multifarious indirect uses and consequent broad dissemination of information and ideas. To ensure the progress of arts and sciences and the integrity of First Amendment values, ideas and information must not be freighted with claims of proprietary right.[80]

The UK Copyright Act likewise permits fair dealing with copyrighted works, albeit for the particular purposes of research, private study, criticism, review, and news reporting.[81]

As the Brennan quotation suggests, when states implement the flexibilities provided by the international agreements, they also pay attention to access interests safeguarded by commitments outside intellectual property. Some of these are based in other international agreements. Thus, Lionel Bently and Brad Sherman have noted that "the European Convention on Human Rights, and the jurisprudence of the Strasbourg Court, appears to offer an important backdrop for the interpretation for a number of the [statutory copyright] defences."[82] Indeed, the UK Court of Appeals has recognized that human rights commitments should not only inform the interpretation of existing exceptions in the UK statute, but would also, if necessary, provide the basis to develop a public interest defense that would validate uses even beyond those permitted by the fair dealing defense.[83]

While these measures are diverse, an analysis of their collective underpinnings reveals broader principles. Even when works are protected, there are important social uses (both commercial and noncommercial) that should not be within the control of the right holder. Many of these measures are designed to grow the knowledge base (for example, measures that permit teaching and experimenting); others recognize the cumulative nature of knowledge production and free material for current development and for the enjoyment of future generations (quotation and reverse engineering defenses). Other defenses permit each user to adapt works, tinker with them, and individuate them in ways that satisfy the user's own creative inclinations (exhaustion, parody, descriptive and personal use defenses). These provisions also further free speech values and facilitate robust competition. And they promote the interest in diversity because they allow states to pursue local objectives, including public health, nutrition, and morality. An examination of the methodology of these provisions reveals another important objective: while some are specific, states also employ open exceptions to enable intellectual property law to respond effectively to changing social conditions.

3. Curbing abuse

The international system has long understood that intellectual property rights can be abused despite the limits discussed previously. Historically, this concern was at its zenith in connection with patent rights, which provide the strongest level of control. Thus, the Paris Convention allows states to issue compulsory patent licenses to check abuse (including failure to work).[84] TRIPS similarly permits compulsory patent licenses.[85] In addition, it recognizes that other intellectual property rights can be misused, and it permits states to regulate anticompetitive practices in all forms of intellectual property through cognate bodies of law.[86]

States have similarly acted to protect the competitive environment. They treat intellectual property law and competition law as two sides of a coin and achieve balance through exceptions to intellectual property, through competition law, or through a combination of the two.[87] For example, when the European Commission was drafting the Database Directive, it recognized the dangers of granting exclusive rights to data that were available from a single source. During the deliberative process, the European Court handed down its *Magill* decision,[88] indicating a willingness to use competition law to intervene and constrain excessive assertions of intellectual property rights. As a result, the Commission decided that competition law might serve as a functional substitute for the sole source compulsory license, and the Directive was adopted on that basis.[89] Competition law mechanisms are thus part of the intellectual property toolbox.[90] Indeed, a combination of both strategies is vital to protect the creative environment. The public-regarding aspects of intellectual property law are typically asserted defensively and therefore primarily benefit individual defendants, while competition violations can be policed by the state and provide systemic protection of the creative environment. Intellectual property law defenses are easily established without substantial factual development; competition law cases are resource- and expertise-intensive, but may provide generous damage awards to encourage private attorneys general. Intellectual property law focuses on the allegedly infringing use, while competition law analysis looks at the conduct of the right holder and takes into account its market power in determining the impact of its actions.

4. Emerging elements

As we have previously discussed, the Knowledge Economy is not static. Accordingly, intellectual property law must constantly adapt to new technological settings. Indeed, this principle was explicitly affirmed at the WCT Diplomatic Conference in 1996.[91] Likewise, the *US–110(5)* panel rejected the argument that permissible exceptions had been "frozen in time" and was receptive to the notion that evolving markets and consumer preferences would change the interpretation of the copyright Exceptions provision.[92]

National and regional legislatures have been equally responsive to this concern. For example, while the WCT requires states to guarantee the integrity of technological protection measures used to safeguard intellectual property rights in the digital environment, the implementing EU Copyright Directive requires member states to ensure that these measures do not override certain public-regarding exceptions.[93] And numerous national laws have created exceptions specific for particular technologies, such as the right to back up computer software, to make ephemeral copies while browsing the internet, and to limit the liability of internet intermediaries for using trademarks to trigger keyword advertising.[94] Similarly, the Biotechnology Directive, along with national implementing legislation and associated case law, have adapted patent principles to the challenges posed by genomic science.[95]

In light of the importance of adaptation, we see value in articulating a fuller range of exceptions (or the freedom to create exceptions) that should be regarded as part of the acquis. For reasons discussed in previous Chapters, we would not want the international community to adopt a measure prematurely. However, we would expressly include optional principles in the acquis in order to ensure that states can experiment and tailor law to their needs with the confidence that they will not be subject to a WTO complaint or trade pressure. We take the point that optional lists of exceptions can be interpreted as exhaustive.[96] However, the very purpose of including options in the acquis is to encourage the development of new access provisions, and to provide a mechanism for those with expertise in emerging areas to contribute to global policy development. To the extent these measures transcend borders and implicate common challenges, the incorporation of specialized knowledge could help alleviate capacity problems. Examples of such commitments to future law development might include provisions to deal with private ordering,[97] open innovation (peer production), and private copying.[98] As discussed further later, the acquis should also include a commitment to deal with the mounting cost of defending the identical activity in sequential litigation in a series of national courts.[99] We illustrate how the adaptation issue should be approached in the next section.

B. Rights of Authors, Traders, and Inventors

Historically, international intellectual property law has been driven by the agendas of authors, traders, and inventors. For example, the Berne Convention originated in meetings presided over by the author Victor Hugo, who was the president of what became the Association Littéraire et Artistique Internationale.[100] Similarly, inventors, desiring to exhibit their inventions at the Vienna Exposition of 1873 wanted assurance that the works would not be copied. The Paris Convention was the result of their efforts.[101] This etiology is reflected in the content of these instruments, which largely articulate the rights of authors and producers. Thus, by reason of pedigree, iteration, relationship to the creative process, and global interdependence, the acquis clearly includes the right to control reproduction of copyrighted works; the right to prevent confusing uses of a mark; the right to exclude others from (among other things) making, selling, or using patented products; and mechanisms to facilitate multinational acquisition of rights. For all regimes, the acquis also includes a commitment to provide effective enforcement. There is no need for us to retread this ground.

The challenge of the Knowledge Economy is therefore not in identifying the basic rights; it lies instead in addressing the emerging elements of the acquis, the adaptation of the core rights to reflect the impact of new technologies and the vast expansion of global trade. Consider, for example, the problem of widespread infringement through digital distribution of protected works. Right holders have experienced difficulties in effectively enforcing their interests because defendants are dispersed across the globe and can be difficult to find. Furthermore, much of the activity spans multiple jurisdictions, yet the regulatory power of each state is confined to its own territory and judicial system.

To overcome these hurdles, right holders look for a choke point. In several recent cases, they have pursued intermediaries on a variety of legal theories, often revolving around the concept of secondary liability. Examples include cases that attempt to impose liability on manufacturers of copying technologies for infringements caused by those who use their equipment; on purveyors of peer-to-peer file-sharing software for the activities of those who download material without right holders' permission; on internet service providers for subscribers' infringing postings; and on other intermediaries, such as auction sites on which counterfeit products are allegedly sold.[102] But despite much litigation, the problems of global distribution have yet to be resolved.[103] Case law is inconsistent across jurisdictions.[104] The resulting uncertainty for right holders, intermediaries, and the public could interfere with the development of global business models and full exploitation of the potential of the internet.

The development of e-commerce thus highlights the increasing interdependence of nations and the need for a global solution to new technological challenges. Given the leverage that right holders continue to enjoy, they have been actively pursuing an international approach—principally ACTA—to deal with this issue. But ACTA negotiations on this point largely failed.[105] The failure demonstrates that there is a corollary to the principle of balance that we have repeatedly endorsed: what might be called a "preservation of balance" principle which requires that the balance within the intellectual property regime must be comparable before and after technological change.[106] ACTA was negotiated in secret. However, leaked documents suggest both that early drafts were unbalanced and that the drafters sought to use accommodation to the internet as an opportunity to shift the line between permissible and impermissible uses in favor of right holders. The early version sought to impose an obligation on countries to install a system of graduated response, which would require service providers to disable the internet connections of their customers after receiving repeated notices of *claimed* infringement—without any judicial finding that the allegations of infringement were valid.[107] Moreover, it failed to provide safeguards for the interests of users that mirrored those found in the bricks and mortar world.[108] According to the French Conseil D'Etat, procedures of this type violate the fundamental human rights of internet users.[109]

The pedigree and iterative nature of this problem of delocalized infringement suggest that the acquis must be understood to include a commitment to effective enforcement in the digital environment. However, any instrument that effectuates this goal must also include provisions that safeguard legitimate uses. Thus, while we would endorse a secondary liability regime, we would incorporate limits that permit the development of platform technologies and accompanying business models. In an article with Annette Kur, we drew on the adjacent body of tort law to construct a balanced rule.[110] We suggested a right of action for inducing counterfeiting or for failure to expeditiously respond to manifest infringement. In our view, this formulation is sufficiently robust to catch egregious infringements. However, it would leave room for the development of new distribution technologies and businesses. Others have also proposed solutions to the digital distribution dilemma, and we are confident that further experimentation will refine these proposals.[111] Ultimately, we would hope that a rule delineating the scope of secondary liability would be adopted as an international mandatory standard. The acquis should recognize the need to develop such a solution.

The in-transit seizure cases discussed in the previous Chapter are likewise a symptom of the problem of easy distribution across borders in a time of freer trade. As the WTO complaint filed by India against the European Union to protest the seizure of generic medicines suggested, however, these actions may interfere with rights guaranteed by the GATT and TRIPS Article 31bis.[112] Furthermore, they are effective partly because they are abusive in that they require shippers to engage in costly litigation far from their bases of operations. While the acquis clearly requires measures to facilitate right holders' ability to protect their markets, it should also include a commitment to prevent sharp practice. Once again, considerable experimentation may be required to identify solutions appropriate to local conditions. For example, it may well be better to mandate export controls at the point where the allegedly infringing goods are put into the stream of commerce (that is, at a location convenient to the shipper). TRIPS already permits states to control export;[113] ACTA makes it a requirement.[114] However, these measures do not fully grapple with the ramifications of such actions: jurisdiction, choice of law, and logistical concerns regarding proof of infringement—that is, doctrines that protect due process, competition, and national autonomy and that assure prompt access to lawfully shipped products. The acquis should be understood to include a commitment to find solutions to both sides of the export problem.

Of course, in a free trade environment characterized by widespread online and off-line distribution, choke points will not always be available or fully effective. Attempts at developing regional and multinational agreements on a transborder litigation system for all intellectual property disputes are under way, but none has reached fruition.[115] However, a more focused response has been available for some time. Thus, the Internet Corporation for Assigned Names and Numbers has adopted the Uniform Domain Name Dispute Resolution Policy (UDRP) to resolve a certain class of trademark-domain name disputes without the need to locate and assert personal jurisdiction over the infringing registrants.[116] Formally, the UDRP is soft law, but it is made effective by a mix of contract and technology, and policed through "appeals" to national courts.[117] Experience with the UDRP suggests that the acquis should include a commitment to develop procedural innovations to ensure efficient adjudication of transnational disputes to protect the interests of producers (and users as well).[118]

C. National Autonomy

As should be apparent from the discussions of both access-regarding principles and proprietary rights, states retain considerable flexibility to fulfill the objectives of intellectual property law in ways that are tailored to their individual conditions. The emphasis on flexibility suggests the acquis also includes a norm of national autonomy, a principle with an unimpeachable pedigree. As we recounted in Chapter 2, an early attempt to establish a multinational intellectual property regime advanced a model based on universality. But that model was firmly rejected. Instead, the premise of the Paris and Berne Conventions was respect for sovereignty. Subject to narrow exceptions, nations were free to determine their own innovation policies as long as they did not discriminate against foreigners.

As international law began to impose more requirements on national law, it began to explicitly endorse the national autonomy principle. Thus the Preamble to TRIPS recognizes "the underlying public policy objectives of national systems for the protection of intellectual property, including developmental and technological objectives." Moreover, Article 1.1 includes two more specific guarantees. First, states may "determine the appropriate method of implementing the provisions of this Agreement within their own legal system and practice." Second, Article 1.1 allows states to enact more extensive protection than TRIPS requires (so long as it does not contravene the provisions of the Agreement). In addition, TRIPS gives states considerable flexibilities regarding enforcement. Article 41.5 of TRIPS confirms that there is no "obligation to put in place a judicial system for the enforcement of intellectual property rights distinct from that for the enforcement of law in general." And as we saw in Chapter 4, *China–Enforcement* interpreted the remedies provisions to give China a large margin of appreciation on how it structures relief. Even ACTA, which attempts to reduce the states' room to maneuver, nonetheless acknowledges that its enforcement requirements must take into account "differences in [states'] respective legal systems and practices."[119]

These provisions, which instantiate the principle of national autonomy, respect differences in legal culture (hence, the flexibilities on enforcement), as well as differences in local creative environments (hence, the rights retained to enact more extensive protection). Thus, they bear an intimate relationship to the nature of knowledge production and they facilitate adaptation and experimentation. National autonomy is, in short, a pillar of the international acquis.

The commitment accommodates the diverse demands of countries across a wide economic and social spectrum and recognizes that countries must have room to respond to the distributive consequences of intellectual property rights.

We recognize that there are tensions between autonomy interests and both the floors (minimum standards) and ceilings (access-regarding provisions) imposed by the acquis. For example, the proposal we advanced for an international standard delineating the circumstances in which an intermediary might be secondarily liable for infringing acts of others limits state autonomy at both ends. But the interdependence of nations in the distribution of knowledge sometimes requires that autonomy be effectuated in paradoxical ways. In this example, a uniform rule would actually further state autonomy. It would prevent a state with excessively broad protection from shutting down internet services legitimately operating in other countries. By the same token, it would bar information havens from undermining appropriate protection for intellectual property rights by failing to provide right holders with an effective and convenient mechanism for protecting their property.

D. Interdependence: National Treatment

Unlike national autonomy and the obligation to balance the interests of producers against access interests, national treatment has been expressly articulated in virtually every international instrument for a century and half. It is the paradigmatic recognition of interdependence. As we saw in connection with the Paris Convention, the inability of foreign nationals to secure protection abroad impeded the flow of knowledge through exhibition at international expositions. Likewise, Berne arose from frustration with the ease with which cheap editions of English books could be imported into England from Ireland or with which French works could be taken from Belgium to France.[120]

Because of its provenance in producer-centric agreements such as the Paris and Berne Conventions, national treatment is traditionally considered a benefit for authors, traders, and inventors. And the details of many international agreements reflect that linkage. For example, Berne ties its coverage to the nationality of the author or the place of first publication.[121] Similarly, the Paris Convention specifically mentions "remedies against infringement" in its articulation of national treatment.[122] But as public-regarding interests have come to the fore in recent years, the national treatment commitment must be viewed as applying more generally, to all the elements of the acquis, including the interests of the public. In fact, TRIPS suggests this evolution. Its national treatment provides that members shall accord "no less favorable" treatment to foreign nationals with respect to "protection" of intellectual property, which it defines for these purposes as including "matters affecting the availability, acquisition, *scope*, maintenance and enforcement of intellectual property rights as *well as those matters affecting the use of intellectual property rights* specifically addressed in this Agreement."[123] The references to scope and use recognize that foreign users have as strong an interest in enjoyment of the provisions cabining intellectual property rights as foreign authors, traders, and inventors have in securing *their* rights.

Digitization and internet distribution illustrate the need to enlarge the beneficiaries of the national treatment guarantee. Just as right holders require new protection in this environment, so do follow-on innovators, users, competitors, and intermediaries.[124] For example, news aggregators take full advantage of the internet. They incorporate works from around the globe and distribute them worldwide. The quotation right of Berne Article 10.1 is meaningless if it permits states to limit the enjoyment of that right to local users. Similarly, software is distributed internationally; Article 6.1 of the Software Directive, which permits reverse engineering to achieve interoperability, would distort trade if it permitted only EU nationals to distribute programs produced through reverse engineering. If secondary liability became the norm in line with our proposal, national treatment would require both that the cause of action be made available to all right holders and that the limits be equally extended to intermediaries, irrespective of nationality. National treatment must thus be considered both part of the acquis and equally protective of user and producer interests.

III. Applying the Acquis

In conceptualizing an international acquis, we identified principles that constitute the backdrop to all international and national intellectual property lawmaking. The international intellectual property system has been 150 years in the making; comprehensively fleshing out its underlying principles will also take time and will require the efforts of numerous scholars and policy makers. However, the benefits are potentially vast. As the acquis grows, so too will its significance. Retrospectively, it can be used interpretively, to bring coherence to the international system, and to fill gaps. Prospectively, it would create a template for crafting new intellectual property instruments, and serve as a counterweight to political pressures that induce TRIPS-plus agreements. More ambitiously, the acquis could promote a reconceptualization of international intellectual property law as explicitly recognizing the interests of users as on a par with the interests of producers.

A. Treaty Interpretation

The most obvious application of the acquis is in connection with interpreting the TRIPS Agreement. Chapters 3 and 4 demonstrated several difficulties with the DSB's approach to TRIPS. For instance, the DSB is unwilling to make normative judgments on such issues as what counts as a "legitimate interest" or "normal exploitation" in the Exceptions tests for copyright and patent, and it refuses to give substantial weight to Articles 7 and 8, which set out the objectives and principles of the Agreement. Furthermore, the DSB will not, in effect, pass judgment on the rationale underlying national legislation. The Berne acquis was somewhat helpful in shedding light on the copyright Exceptions provision in the US–110(5) case. However, the Berne acquis relates only to copyright. The principles it encompasses are all explicit provisions of the laws of developed countries. An international acquis would go much further. It would reach across disciplines and identify the commonalities among the silos of "copyright," "patent," "trademark," and related bodies of law. While we focused mainly on the laws we know (those of the United States and the European Union), an examination of the laws of other—more diverse—states is sure to reveal other background norms, statutory provisions, and practices that will further enrich and deepen our understanding of how the system should work. As we have illustrated in this initial attempt, there *are* such overarching principles, and the acquis would enable the DSB to take them into account.

Consider, for example, the illustrations with which we began the book. How can states deal with the access problems posed by gene patents? The acquis demonstrates that in a large range of existing instruments, the international community is committed to releasing the building blocks of knowledge into the public domain. With that insight, the DSB would be better placed to determine which types of regulation are compatible with TRIPS. Similarly, recognition of the relationship between competition and intellectual property law, and the importance of state autonomy in tailoring the law to local needs, would deepen the DSB's appreciation for the justifications states might assert for imposing a local working requirement under TRIPS.

An acquis would also shed light on methodological issues. The DSB has been heavily criticized for treating the three steps of the Exceptions tests in copyright and patents as cumulative. That analysis, which can stop as soon as a panel finds that a particular exception is not "limited" (the first factor in all of the Exceptions tests),[125] means that societal interests may never be taken into account. Under that approach, even the exception for laws of nature might be rejected as not "limited." The acquis exposes the fallacy in the cumulative approach. It demonstrates the strong commitment to balance inherent in all intellectual property regimes. In some cases, this is expressed explicitly. But it is often implicit—by what the system decides not to commodify. An examination of the acquis demonstrates how critical these considerations, which are accounted for in the latter two steps of the Exceptions tests, are to any analysis of a state exception. When there are broad public interests at stake, the concept of "limited" must give way to the broader exceptions that the other steps justify.

Constructing the acquis would also emphasize the structural significance of Articles 7 and 8. Although explicit reference to the broader objectives and principles underlying intellectual property law was new to international law, the ideas expressed in these provisions are fully consistent with the ethos of intellectual property law since Berne and Paris. Moreover, they have always been central to national laws, as the second quotation at the beginning of this Chapter acknowledges. And their recognition as fundamental principles of the acquis is reinforced by developments since TRIPS. Balance (reflected in Article 7) has become a dominant framing device in international lawmaking, including in the WIPO Development Agenda,[126] as well as in the WCT, where it shaped the entire negotiation process and was ultimately included in the Preamble.[127] Article 8 highlights policy values that have been endorsed by the Ministerial Council Declarations at Doha[128]—and even by the countries involved in ACTA.[129] Relying on these norms would not, as the *Canada–Pharmaceuticals* panel feared, constitute a renegotiation of the Agreement. Rather, according greater significance to Articles 7 and 8 would effectuate long-standing intellectual property commitments.

As the acquis crystallizes the principles that animate intellectual property, it should become easier to integrate the many strands of norm making we observed in Chapter 6. While we focus here on sketching only the basic contours of the acquis, the multiple institutions developing these norms could use their particular expertise to fill in the details. By recognizing that the contributions of these institutions are part of the fabric of intellectual property, the DSB, the Council for TRIPS, and other actors could more easily draw on these efforts. For example, a properly negotiated agreement on secondary liability might become part of the acquis. If the DSB were called upon to entertain a case on peer-to-peer file sharing, it could then use the acquis to determine whether the respondent was properly implementing its obligation to protect against unlawful reproduction. Thus, while in Chapter 6, we were skeptical about a full-throated endorsement of the integration approach proposed by the Study Group of the International Law Commission,[130] the development of an international acquis would accomplish many of the same goals. The acquis would be guided by substance rather than by the formal canons on which the International Law Commission relied. Thus, it would bring coherence to an increasingly fragmented system by revealing consensus rather than by resolving conflict.

Finally, a fully realized acquis would facilitate gap filling, both in TRIPS and in other instruments. As we saw, some scholars have conceptualized TRIPS as an incomplete contract, with missing terms to be supplied by the DSB.[131] We consider that approach inconsistent with the Dispute Settlement Understanding, which appears to prohibit bare judicial activism.[132] More fundamentally, we believe that the dispute settlement process is, in terms of representational legitimacy, far removed and insulated from appropriate democratic pressures. As a state-initiated and intentionally trade-centered process, it is likely to produce skewed results. In contrast, if the DSB were to draw upon the acquis as we envision it, its deliberations would be inclusive of varied national and international experience and informed by the normative underpinnings of the laws at issue. The results reached would be based on something of a consensus among nations.

Outside TRIPS, the power of the acquis to fill gaps would be even more valuable. For example, many of the recent bilaterals focus on providing additional detail to existing producer rights. They often lack provisions dealing with limits on these rights, which might prompt the conclusion that measures safeguarding user and broader societal interests are inapplicable. But viewed against the background rules of the acquis, it should be clear that these limits have not been jettisoned by silence. For example, in many bilateral investment treaties (BITs), each party agrees that it will not expropriate or nationalize the investments made by investors of the other party.[133] Because these agreements define investments to include intellectual property,[134] taken literally, the expropriation provisions would suggest that these agreements override the right to issue compulsory licenses for government use under Articles 31 and 44.2 of TRIPS.[135] Recognizing the importance of compulsory licensing options would clarify to BITs arbitrators that the investment treaties are silent only because they were negotiated against a backdrop that includes these commitments.

B. Lawmaking Templates

Treaty interpretation could be improved in many different ways; what sets the acquis apart is its capacity to operate prospectively. Negotiators of new instruments would start with a framework within which to deliberate. ACTA, for example, might look substantially different if the acquis had been in place to serve as a checklist during negotiations. Had the acquis been available to the drafters, they might have realized the importance of including provisions protective of all the interests implicated by their enforcement agenda. This might not of itself have ensured that the debate was any more transparent. However, the acquis would have compensated for the absence of advocates of these broader interests. The result might have been somewhat less one-sided; at the very least, the decision to ignore these interests would have been exposed as a conscious choice with possible political ramifications.

The acquis would also reduce asymmetries in capacity. Armed with the acquis, all participants would share a basic command of the components of an effective intellectual property system. For those developing countries that are still struggling to come up to speed with the issues involved in international intellectual property lawmaking, an acquis would be particularly helpful. And as we saw in Chapter 2, the developed countries wrote the first draft of TRIPS, thus framing the entire debate on their terms. Developing countries therefore started at a substantial disadvantage and were unable to secure specific textual commitments that reflected their interests. The acquis would have reset the default to a position more appropriate both historically and substantively; with it, the final Agreement might have encapsulated a more complete understanding of the parties' commitments. While it is too late to fully revise TRIPS, there are many ongoing negotiations where an acquis might diminish the political leverage of the demandeurs. It would be harder to pressure a weaker party to sacrifice interests that the acquis recognizes as legitimate. For example, it might be more difficult to require a country to relinquish the right of farmers to save seeds if the acquis clarified the strength of the international commitment to nutrition.

At the national level, an acquis would also be of substantial use. As we saw in the last Chapter, developing countries are now bombarded with advice—some well-intentioned, some strategic—on how best to implement their obligations. Sifting through the "guidance" provided by technical assistants sent by developed countries, WIPO, WHO, UNCTAD, and assorted NGOs is time-consuming and costly. The acquis essentially curates this input.[136] Developed countries could also benefit from the broader perspective on intellectual property that the acquis would provide. For example, negotiators of the EU Database Directive extended the database right on a reciprocity basis rather than national treatment because they saw protection for investment in databases as unrelated to existing forms of intellectual property law. The acquis would have illuminated the depth of the international community's commitment to addressing interdependence problems by affording national treatment. Furthermore, the acquis would have alerted the negotiators to the character of the Directive as a regulation of unfair competition, and therefore subject to the national treatment obligations of the Paris Convention (as we argued in Chapter 4).

C. Reorienting the Intellectual Property System: User Rights

It is often asserted that international intellectual property law (most notably, Berne, Paris, and TRIPS) constitutes only a minimum standards regime setting baseline levels of protection for authors, traders, and inventors. History suggests that this view is too simplistic. Our examination of the principal international instruments identified a number of provisions that establish maximum levels of protection. For example, under the Berne Convention, states are prohibited from interfering with the right of the public to quote from copyrighted works. Our analysis of the broader implications of these instruments, along with national laws, demonstrates that other nonproprietary interests are similarly guaranteed. In fact, a close reading of Article 1.1 of TRIPS supports this notion. While the measure permits member states to "implement in their law more extensive protection than is required by this Agreement," it also contains an important proviso. States may not do so in ways that "contravene the provisions of the Agreement,"[137] suggesting that the Agreement must also be read to include some maxima—what might be called "user rights" or, as Jessica Litman terms them, "liberties."[138]

Indeed, immediately after the TRIPS Agreement was concluded, states began to advance proposals built around the idea of user rights. At the WCT Diplomatic Conference, a variety of countries, including Australia, South Africa and Tanzania, suggested that the Conference consider adopting "mandatory exceptions" to the rights of copyright owners. Those proposals were not pursued at that time, but the discussion has intensified in recent years. In 2009, a consortium of South American countries introduced a proposed treaty to recognize access rights for the visually impaired based on recommendations from the World Blind Union.[139] Scholars and NGOs have also promoted this agenda. The soft law instrument on exceptions and limitations in copyright law proposed by Hugenholtz and Okediji includes rights to private study, teaching, and research; reverse engineering; and time, space, and format shifting.[140] Annette Kur and Henning Grosse Ruse-Khan have similarly advanced the view that certain access-regarding principles require mandatory recognition.[141] Among other things, the Kur group's amendment to TRIPS would add rights to reverse engineer and parody copyrighted works; to make strictly noncommercial use of trademarks and to use them in comparative advertising; and to make noncommercial use, educational use, and experimental use of patented inventions.[142] Most comprehensive is the draft Treaty on Access to Knowledge, which was promulgated by a group of NGOs led by the Consumer Project on Technology (now Knowledge Ecology International).[143]

In some quarters, the question whether these maximum levels of protection create "rights" for users is contentious.[144] However, once the intellectual property regime is conceived holistically, it is clear that the rights view is correct; as per Justice Brennan, limits on intellectual property protection are "not some unforeseen byproduct" of the international scheme. To fully operationalize those limits that are fundamental to the system, "exclusions" and "exceptions" must be conceived affirmatively, as the rights of consumers, competitors, intermediaries, and follow-on innovators. The acquis would buttress this reorientation of intellectual property law by identifying principles that repeat across international regimes regulating all forms of intellectual property, that are considered mandatory at the international or regional level (requiring implementation in all member states), that are duplicated in virtually all national laws, and that are aligned with other instruments where the same interests are denominated as rights.

Classifying public-regarding provisions as grants of rights is a philosophically fraught task; fully articulating the entire scope of these user rights is an ongoing project. However, our work on the acquis clarifies a few propositions. First, national treatment is best understood as applying to user rights as well as to the rights of authors, inventors, and traders. Second, access-regarding measures that are less explicit in international law can, when corroborated by iteration in national law, be regarded as so essential to the system that they amount to guaranteed rights. These would include a right of access to the fundamental principles of nature and to material that has become a part of the public domain. Third, free speech protections in national constitutions and international human rights instruments confirm that access interests in ideas, facts, and generic expressions must be carried over to intellectual property law as user rights.

Reorienting the system to recognize user rights raises a number of questions. First, if user rights are added to the acquis, then the scope of national autonomy, which we have emphasized throughout this volume, shrinks, for states will be squeezed between floors (minimum standards) and ceilings (created by user rights). However, theoretical autonomy is one thing; real autonomy requires the political ability to resist pressure. The growth of user rights provides countries interested in safeguarding access with new tools and with the international affirmation necessary to insist that their interests are recognized.

Second is the question whether characterizing certain interests as rights would make a real difference in lawmaking. We think it would. Rights talk is important rhetorically. It would counter the view of TRIPS as a code of proprietary guarantees and stimulate efforts to put proprietary and user rights on a par with one another. Thus, David Vaver would impose a "reverse three-step test," akin to the Exceptions provisions in TRIPS, which would permit the recognition of new proprietary rights under national law only if the nation in question could show a demonstrated need for them.[145] But even without imposing yet another multipart filter, reorienting the intellectual property system to recognize the equivalence of user and proprietary interests would have significant impacts both nationally and internationally. It would reaffirm the commitment to balance and bring user-centric provisions into focus as essential elements.[146] Furthermore, within some national systems, exceptions are narrowly construed; the use of rights terminology will tend to broaden the reach of these provisions and expand the scope of access interests.

Some have also questioned whether user rights would be enforceable as a matter of international law (in particular, within TRIPS). Among other things, critics argue that no state will have an incentive to challenge a failure by another country to protect users because the users whose interests are most directly jeopardized will likely be locals of that country. We believe that the agency problem is overstated. The interdependence of the global intellectual property economy means that the beneficiaries of access-regarding measures operate across borders and therefore have an interest in the enforcement of user rights in foreign markets. For example, a company as formidable as Google, faced with a French law that did not permit it to utilize the Berne quotation right, could presumably persuade the United States to bring a complaint against France to vindicate its interests. In fact, India's challenge to in-transit seizures under EU law is an example of the enforcement of user interests. The complaint was an attempt to protect the ability of generic competitors to produce pharmaceuticals under the compulsory license plan approved by the Doha Declaration and to safeguard patients' access to these medicines. Had the case been resolved in India's favor, these user interests would have been vindicated.

Conclusion

The Paris and Berne Conventions were vital steps in encouraging knowledge production. These instruments, built on principles of national autonomy and national treatment, established a global market for information goods and dramatically increased the incentive to invest in innovation. As cross-border trade blossomed, it produced a vibrant creative environment, for the ingenuity and inventiveness of each nation could flourish, and nations could both teach and learn from each other. Opportunities for international exchange have increased since Paris and Berne. Free trade regimes have matured, and digital communication technologies facilitate collaboration across borders, improve information flows, and enhance access to knowledge-intensive products from distant markets.

The TRIPS Agreement updated the historical commitments in Paris and Berne, recognized the importance of intellectual property as the subject of trade, and provided an effective means for states to resolve disputes. We are only now beginning to appreciate the impact of that development. There are those who see TRIPS in quite radical terms, whether as a supranational code or as an incomplete contract, inviting an unelected DSB to optimize global incentives to innovate. We regard the code view of TRIPS as descriptively incorrect, normatively flawed, and pragmatically misguided. It is inconsistent with the historical development of international intellectual property law and blind to the impact of strong protection on distributive and cultural interests, and it leaves the international intellectual property system unable to respond nimbly to change. More specifically, these accounts fail to appreciate the benefits of allowing states to structure their innovation policies to reflect the nature of their local creative communities, to pursue their own social and political priorities, and to experiment with responses to new social or technological challenges. Hence our neofederalist vision, which would elevate the values of balance, diversity, and historical contingency.

Our concerns are heightened by post-TRIPS developments within the WTO. Decisions in the DSB reveal a reluctance to consider the conceptual structure of intellectual property law or its links to human rights and other societal interests. In part, this is a function of the text of the Agreement; its failure to include benchmarks and examples to guide decision makers, as well as its ill-considered transpositions from trade law. But whatever the cause, TRIPS has had unfortunate consequences at both the national and the international level. Proprietary rights continually expand, both legally and rhetorically, skewing the political process in developed countries and confounding the capacities of developing nations.

Our analysis of this dynamic suggests several lessons. National treatment remains at the heart of international intellectual property law, as it was in Paris and Berne. It should be strictly interpreted to protect the integrity of the global marketplace without unduly interfering with national autonomy. In contrast, the most favoured nation obligation, imported into TRIPS from the trade regime, is ill-fitting and should be reconsidered, as should interpretive approaches tightly tethered to GATT decision making. Intellectual property law is not trade law. It cannot be reduced to an accounting exercise, objective though that may seem to trade hands. Instead, underlying norms, values, and motivations must be considered in assessing TRIPS compatibility. This is not to say that trade law has no application to intellectual property. In some ways, TRIPS took too little from the GATT. It failed to include general exceptions, safeguards, escape clauses, or a provision on modifying concessions. Functional substitutes must be recognized in TRIPS to ensure that states have the flexibilities they need to adapt to national exigencies (such as health crises) or inevitable changes in the technological environment.

Of course, the international intellectual property system transcends TRIPS. TRIPS represented a departure from the concentration of international policy making in WIPO. Now that WIPO's exclusive domain has been breached, regime shifting has become endemic. Those dissatisfied with the view of TRIPS as imposing high levels of protection seek to establish counternorms in other institutions; those who wish to see TRIPS standards augmented have flexed their power in new lawmaking venues, including through bilateral and regional agreements. The resulting cacophony has fragmented international law, increased uncertainty, undermined incentives to invest in innovation, and exacerbated political economy problems.

We therefore believe ourselves to be in what might be called an "international constitutional moment," when the time is ripe for a new paradigm.[147] Integrating diverse regimes through interpretation helps reduce the costs of fragmentation, but it cannot solve all the problems. Thus, as a complementary device, we turn to the notion of an international acquis, which would crystallize the international commitment to intellectual property protection. It would include both express and latent components of the international regime, put access-regarding guarantees on a par with proprietary interests, and enshrine the fundamental importance of national autonomy and national treatment. Although it is unlikely that the intellectual property system will ever be centrally administered in the manner of a true federal system, the acquis would facilitate a neofederalist vision because it would coordinate international lawmaking while giving due regard to the role of nation-states in that process. We hope that in this moment of fluidity, our proposal for an acquis, and indeed, this volume, will begin a conversation about the shape of the future of international intellectual property law.

NOTES

Chapter 1

1. *See, e.g.,* David C. Mowrey, *Plus Ça Change: Industrial R&D in the "Third Industrial Revolution,"* 18(1) INDUS. & CORP. CHANGE 1 (2009); Philip Ball, *Introduction, in* J. E. GORDON, THE NEW SCIENCE OF STRONG MATERIALS: OR WHY YOU DON'T FALL THROUGH THE FLOOR (Penguin Science 2006); Michael Pidwirny, *Remote Sensing, in* THE ENCYCLOPEDIA OF EARTH (August 5, 2010), *available at* http://www.eoearth.org/article/Remote_sensing; JANET ABBATE, INVENTING THE INTERNET (MIT Press 1999).
2. *See* Graeme W. Austin, *Valuing "Domestic Self-Determination" in International Intellectual Property Jurisprudence,* 77 CHI.-KENT L. REV. 1155 (2002).
3. Berne Convention for the Protection of Literary and Artistic Works, September 9, 1886, as last revised at Paris, July 24, 1971, 1161 U.N.T.S. 3 [hereinafter Berne Convention].
4. Paris Convention for the Protection of Industrial Property, March 20, 1883, as last revised at Stockholm, July 14, 1967, 21 U.S.T. 1583, 828 U.N.T.S. 305 [hereinafter Paris Convention]. The Paris Convention also addressed the protection of other forms of industrial property, such as designs, utility models, and geographical indications. *See* Paris Convention, art. 1.2.
5. Berne Convention, art. 5; Paris Convention, art. 2. In deliberations leading up to both conventions, there were debates about whether to adopt a principle of universality or territoriality; national treatment is a vote for the latter. *See* 1 SAM RICKETSON & JANE C. GINSBURG, INTERNATIONAL COPYRIGHT AND NEIGHBOURING RIGHTS: THE BERNE CONVENTION AND BEYOND ¶ 2.24 (2d ed. Oxford University Press 2005); STEPHEN P. LADAS, PATENTS, TRADEMARKS, AND RELATED RIGHTS: NATIONAL AND INTERNATIONAL PROTECTION 60–61 (Harvard University Press 1975).
6. Paris Convention, art. 4.
7. *See* 1 RICKETSON & GINSBURG, *supra* note 5, ¶ 3.12.
8. Convention Establishing the World Intellectual Property Organization, July 14, 1967, 21 U.S.T. 1749, 828 U.N.T.S. 3 [hereinafter WIPO Convention]. *See generally* Rochelle Cooper Dreyfuss, *Fostering Dynamic Innovation, Development and Trade: Intellectual Property as a Case Study in Global Administrative Law,* 2009 ACTA JURIDICA 237, 260–261 (2009).
9. Agreement on Trade-Related Aspects of Intellectual Property Rights, April 15, 1994, Marrakesh Agreement Establishing the World Trade Organization, Annex 1C, LEGAL INSTRUMENTS—RESULTS OF THE URUGUAY ROUND, vol. 31, 33 I.L.M. 1197 (1994) [hereinafter TRIPS or TRIPS Agreement].
10. TRIPS, arts. 9–21, 27–34.
11. *Id.* arts. 22–24.

12. *Id.* art. 39.
13. *Id.* arts. 25–26.
14. *Id.* arts. 35–38.
15. *Id.* art. 3.
16. *Id.* art. 4. *See, e.g.,* Appellate Body Report, United States—Section 211 Omnibus Appropriations Act of 1998, WT/DS176/AB/R (August 6, 2001) [hereinafter *Havana Club*].
17. TRIPS, art. 27.1.
18. *Id.* arts. 41–61.
19. Marrakesh Agreement Establishing the World Trade Organization, April 15, 1994, art. IX, Legal Instruments—Results of the Uruguay Round, vol. 1, 1867 U.N.T.S. 154, 33 I.L.M. 1144 (1994) [hereinafter WTO Agreement].
20. TRIPS, art. 68; WTO Agreement, art. IV.5.
21. TRIPS, art. 64; Understanding on Rules and Procedures Governing the Settlement of Disputes, April 15, 1994, Marrakesh Agreement Establishing the World Trade Organization, Annex 2, Legal Instruments—Results of the Uruguay Round, vol. 31, 1869 U.N.T.S. 401, 33 I.L.M. 1226 (1994) [hereinafter DSU]. In theory, a member that failed to comply with its obligations under Paris or Berne could be sued in the International Court of Justice. *See* Berne Convention, art. 33; Paris Convention, art. 28. However, no such cases have ever been brought.
22. *See, e.g.,* Decision by the Arbitrator, United States—Measures Affecting the Cross-Border Supply of Gambling and Betting Services—Recourse to Arbitration by the United States Under Article 22.6 of the DSU, WT/DS285/ARB (December 21, 2007); Decision by the Arbitrators, European Communities—Regime for the Importation, Sale and Distribution of Bananas—Recourse to Arbitration by the European Communities Under Article 22.6 of the DSU, WT/DS27/ARB/ECU (March 24, 2000).
23. *See, e.g.,* Susan K. Sell, Private Power, Public Law: The Globalization of Intellectual Property Rights (Cambridge University Press 2003).
24. Statement from James E. Rogan, Director, U.S. PTO at the WIPO Conference on the International Patent System (March 26, 2002) (quoting the 1966 U.S. President's Commission on the Patent System), *available at* http://www.uspto.gov/news/speeches/2002/wipo26mar2002.jsp.
25. *See, e.g.,* Kamal Saggi & Joel P. Trachtman, *Incomplete Harmonization Contracts in International Economic Law: Report of the Panel,* China—Measures Affecting the Protection and Enforcement of Intellectual Property Rights, *WT/DS362/R, adopted March 20, 2009,* 10 World Trade Rev. 1–2, 23–24 (2010).
26. Thomas L. Friedman, The Lexus and the Olive Tree: Understanding Globalization 195 (Farrar, Straus & Giroux 1999).
27. These are: Appellate Body Report, India—Patent Protection for Pharmaceutical and Agricultural Chemical Products, WT/DS50/AB/R (December 19, 1997) [hereinafter *India–Pharmaceuticals*]; Appellate Body Report, Canada—Term of Patent Protection, WT/DS170/AB/R (September 18, 2000); Panel Report, Canada—Patent Protection of Pharmaceutical Products, WT/DS114/R (March 17, 2000) [hereinafter *Canada–Pharmaceuticals*]; Panel Report, United States—Section 110(5) of the US Copyright Act, WT/DS/160/R (June 15, 2000) [hereinafter *US–110(5)*]; *Havana Club*; Panel Report, European Communities—Protection of Trademarks and Geographical Indications for Agricultural Products and Foodstuffs, WT/DS174/R (March 15, 2005) [hereinafter *EC–GI*]; and Panel Report, China—Measures Affecting the Protection and Enforcement of Intellectual Property Rights, WT/DS362/R (January 26, 2009) [hereinafter *China–Enforcement*]. Technically, there have been nine disputes as both the United States and the European Communities brought an *India–Pharmaceuticals* challenge and the Australians also filed a challenge to the EU geographical indication regulation. The cases mentioned in note 22 involved intellectual property, but only because that sector was used to retaliate against failure to comply with other provisions of WTO agreements. And one case raised a

national treatment claim under TRIPS, but it was somewhat peripheral to the principal dispute and barely addressed by the DSB. *See* Panel Report, Indonesia—Certain Measures Affecting the Automobile Industry, WT/DS54/R, WT/DS55/R, WT/DS59/R, WT DS64R (July 2, 1998).

28. *See* Jayashree Watal, *The WTO Appellate Body: The First Four Years*, 2 J. WORLD INTELL. PROP. 425, 432 (1999).
29. World Trade Organization, Ministerial Declaration of 20 November 2001, ¶ 17, WT/MIN (01)/DEC/1, 41 I.L.M. 746 (2002).
30. *See Canada–Pharmaceuticals; see also* Chapter 5.
31. *See* Robert Howse, *Comment*—China—Measures Affecting the Protection and Enforcement of Intellectual Property Rights, 10 WORLD TRADE REV. 87, 91 (2011).
32. William M. Landes & Richard A. Posner, *An Economic Analysis of Copyright Law*, 18 J. LEGAL STUD. 325, 332–333, 360–361 (1989).
33. For copyright, *see* Zechariah Chaffee, *Reflections on the Law of Copyright*, 45 COLUM. L. REV. 503, 513 (1945). For trademarks, *see* Rochelle Cooper Dreyfuss, *Expressive Genericity: Trademarks as Language in the Pepsi Generation*, 65 NOTRE DAME L. REV. 397 (1990). *See, e.g.,* Walt Disney v. Air Pirates, 581 F.2d 751 (9th Cir. 1978).
34. Letter from Isaac Newton to Robert Hooke (February 5, 1675), in THE COLUMBIA WORLD OF QUOTATIONS NO. 41418 (Robert Andrews et al. eds., New York Columbia University Press 1996). *See* WILLIAM POOLE, JOHN AUBREY AND THE ADVANCEMENT OF LEARNING (Bodleian Library, Oxford University 2010) (noting the priority fights between Hooke and Newton). For another interesting example, *see* PETER GALISON, EINSTEIN'S CLOCKS, POINCARÉ'S MAPS: EMPIRES OF TIME (Norton 2003) (providing new insights into the relationship between Einstein's theories of relativity and his work in the Swiss patent office examining applications on inventions related to the synchronization of railway clocks).
35. *See* Robert K. Merton, *The Normative Structure of Science,* in THE SOCIOLOGY OF SCIENCE: THEORETICAL AND EMPIRICAL INVESTIGATIONS 267, 273 (Norman W. Storer ed., University of Chicago Press 1973).
36. *See* Rochelle Cooper Dreyfuss, *Does IP Need IP? Accommodating Intellectual Production Outside the Intellectual Property Paradigm*, 31 CARDOZO L. REV. 1437 (2010).
37. *See, e.g.,* John P. Walsh, Ashish Arora & Wesley M. Cohen, *Effects of Research Tool Patents and Licensing on Biomedical Innovation,* in PATENTS IN THE KNOWLEDGE BASED ECONOMY 285 (Wesley M. Cohen & Stephen A. Merrill eds., National Academies Press 2003).
38. *See, e.g.,* Heidi L. Williams, *Intellectual Property Rights and Innovation: Evidence from the Human Genome*, NBER WORKING PAPER 16213 (July 2010), *available at* http://www.nber.org/papers/w16213; Kenneth G. Huang & Fiona E. Murray, *Does Patent Strategy Shape the Long-Run Supply of Public Knowledge? Evidence from Human Genetics*, 52(6) ACAD. MGMT. J. 1193–1221 (2009) (showing that more lines of research are undertaken when research tools become freely available); Fiona E. Murray & Scott Stern, *Do Formal Intellectual Property Rights Hinder the Free Flow of Scientific Knowledge: An Empirical Test of the Anti-Commons Hypothesis*, 63 J. ECON. BEHAV. & ORG. 648–687 (2007) (demonstrating that citations of research decline when the research becomes subject to patent rights); Rebecca S. Eisenberg, *Bargaining over the Transfer of Proprietary Research Tools: Is This Market Failing or Emerging?,* in EXPANDING THE BOUNDARIES OF INTELLECTUAL PROPERTY: INNOVATION POLICY FOR THE KNOWLEDGE SOCIETY (Rochelle C. Dreyfuss, Diane L. Zimmerman & Harry First eds., Oxford University Press 2001); Carlos M. Correa, *Internationalization of the Patent System and New Technologies*, 20 WIS. INT'L L.J. 523, 528 (2002). Even Walsh et al., *supra* note 37, find other forms of exclusivity that impede progress.
39. *See, e.g.,* Universal Declaration of Human Rights, December 8, 1948, art. 27, G.A. Res. 217A (III), U.N. Doc. A/810, at 71 [hereinafter Universal Declaration]; International Covenant on Economic, Social and Cultural Rights, December 16, 1966, art. 15, 993 U.N.T.S. 3, 5; LAURENCE R. HELFER & GRAEME W. AUSTIN, HUMAN RIGHTS AND INTELLECTUAL PROPERTY: MAPPING THE GLOBAL INTERFACE (Cambridge University Press 2011).

40. Universal Declaration, art. 27.1.
41. *Id.* art. 27.2.
42. *Id.* arts. 17, 19, 25, and 26.
43. Copyright Act, 17 U.S.C. §§ 107–122 (2006).
44. *Id.* §§ 110 (1) & (2).
45. *Id.* § 107; Campbell v. Acuff-Rose Music, Inc., 510 U.S. 569 (1994) (facilitating parody); Sega v. Accolade, 977 F.2d 1510 (9th Cir. 1992) (vindicating an interest in interoperability). *Cf.* Directive 2009/24/EC of the European Parliament and of the Council of April 23, 2009, on the Legal Protection of Computer Programs, art. 6.1, 2009 O.J. (L 111) 16.
46. For example, the United Kingdom and Germany. *See, e.g.,* Patents Act 1977, § 60(5)(b) (UK); Patentgesetz [Patents Act], December 16, 1980, BGBl. I, § 11.2 (F.R.G.) (last amended by laws of July 16 and August 6, 1998).
47. *See, e.g.,* Patents Act, 1970, § 3(d) (India); *see also* Leahy-Smith America Invents Act, Pub. L. No. 112-29, Sec. 14, 125 Stat. 284, 327 (2011) (altering the outcome of obviousness analyses for tax strategies).
48. *See, e.g.,* Laugh It Off Promotions CC v South African Breweries International (Finance) BV t/a Sabmark International 2005 (2) SA 46 (SCA) (S. Afr); Lila Postkarte, Bundesgerichtshof [BGH] [Federal Court of Justice], February 3, 2005, Az.: I ZR 159/02, GRUR 2005, 583. (F.R.G.) (recognizing that artistic freedom could justify limits on trademark rights); Joined Cases C-236/08-C238/08, Google France v. Louis Vuitton Malletier, Centre National de Recherché en Relations Humaines, and Viaticum [2011] All E.R. (EC) 411 (CJEU) (excluding possible liability of search engines for trademark infringement resulting from sale of sponsored advertising). *See generally* Christophe Geiger, *Trade Marks and Freedom of Expression—The Proportionality of Criticism*, 38 IIC 317 (2007).
49. *See, e.g.,* Joined Cases C-241/91P & C-242/91P, Radio Telefis Eireann and Independent Television Publications Ltd v. Commission of the European Communities (*Magill*), 1995 ECR I-743, 53, 54 (ECJ).
50. Gene M. Grossman & Edwin L. C. Lai, *International Protection of Intellectual Property*, 94 AM. ECON. REV. 1635 (2004).
51. *See, e.g.,* Amy Kapczynski, Samantha Chaifetz, Zachary Katz & Yochai Benkler, *Addressing Global Health Inequities: An Open Licensing Approach for University Innovations*, 20 BERKELEY TECH. L.J. 1031 (2005); Brian D. Wright, *Comment: Agricultural Biotechnology: The Quest to Restore Freedom to Operate in the Public Interest*, in WORKING WITHIN THE BOUNDARIES OF INTELLECTUAL PROPERTY 359 (Rochelle C. Dreyfuss, Harry First & Diane L. Zimmerman eds., Oxford University Press 2010).
52. *See, e.g.,* Pedro Roffe & Gina Vea, *The WIPO Development Agenda in a Historical and Political Context*, in THE DEVELOPMENT AGENDA: GLOBAL INTELLECTUAL PROPERTY AND DEVELOPING COUNTRIES 93 (Neil Weinstock Netanel ed., Oxford University Press 2009).
53. For an example of this type of law, see the Industrial Property Law No. 9,279, May 14, 1996 (Brazil), which was the target of a complaint by the United States before the WTO.
54. *See, e.g.,* JAMES BESSEN & MICHAEL J. MEURER, PATENT FAILURE: HOW JUDGES, BUREAUCRATS, AND LAWYERS PUT INNOVATORS AT RISK (Princeton University Press 2008); ERIC VON HIPPEL, DEMOCRATIZING INNOVATION (MIT Press 2005); LAWRENCE LESSIG, REMIX MAKING ART AND COMMERCE THRIVE IN THE HYBRID ECONOMY (Bloomsbury Academic 2008).
55. For an economic model demonstrating that the North will tend to have strong protection, see Grossman & Lai, *supra* note 50, at 1645–1647.
56. *See, e.g.,* 17 U.S.C. § 302 (2010); 15 U.S.C. § 1125(c) (2010); Council Regulation No. 1768/92 Concerning the Creation of a Supplementary Protection Certificate for Medicinal Products, art. 2.7, 1992 O.J. (L 182), *now codified as* Regulation 469/2009 of the European Parliament and of the Council of 6 May 2009 Concerning the Supplementary Protection Certificate for Medicinal Products, 2009 O.J.(L 152) 1.
57. *See generally* Daniel Benoliel & Bruno Salama, *Towards an Intellectual Property Bargaining Theory: The Post-WTO Era*, 32 U. PA. J. INT'L L. 265 (discussing the "East Asian tigers");

Gregory Shaffer, Michelle R. Sanchez & Barbara Rosenberg, *The Trials of Winning at the WTO: What Lies Behind Brazil's Success*, 41 CORNELL INT'L L.J. 383 (2008); Peter K. Yu, *Access to Medicines, BRICS Alliances, and Collective Action*, 34 AM. J.L. & MED. 345 (2008).

58. *See* ALEXANDER STACK, INTERNATIONAL PATENT LAW: COOPERATION, HARMONIZATION AND INSTITUTIONAL ANALYSIS OF WIPO AND THE WTO (Edward Elgar 2011) (describing differences driven by market size and other factors).

59. *See* Margaret Chon, *New Wine Bursting from Old Bottles: Collaborative Internet Art, Joint Works, and Entrepreneurship*, 75 OR. L. REV. 257, 266–272 (1996); Michiko Kakutani, *Culture Zone; Never-Ending Saga*, N.Y. TIMES, September 28, 1997, § 6 (Magazine), at 40 (discussing a chain novel instigated by John Updike and others); Rebecca Tushnet, *Legal Fictions, Copyright, Fan Fiction, and a New Common Law*, 17 LOY. L.A. ENT. L.J. 651 (1997). *See generally* Rochelle C. Dreyfuss, *Collaborative Research: Conflicts on Authorship, Ownership, and Accountability*, 53 VAND. L. REV. 1162 (2000).

60. *See* Digital Millennium Copyright Act, Pub. L. No. 105-304, 112 Stat. 2860 (1998) (anti-circumvention rules codified at 17 U.S.C. § 1201 (2010)); Council Directive 2001/29/EC on the Harmonisation of Certain Aspects of Copyright and Related Rights in the Information Society, art. 6, 2001 O.J. (L 167) 10 [hereinafter Copyright Directive]; WIPO Copyright Treaty, December 20, 1996, art. 11, 2186 U.N.T.S. 121, 36 I.L.M. 65 (1997) [hereinafter WIPO Copyright Treaty]. Sometimes change also requires ratcheting up the level of protection: for example, copyright owners have sought to generalize the rights tied to old technologies (such as communication by wired means) with a generalized right to make available. *Compare* Berne Convention, arts. 11 & 11ter *with* WIPO Copyright Treaty, art. 8.

61. Copyright Directive, art. 5.2(b).

62. 17 U.S.C. § 512 (2010); *also* Council Directive 2000/31/EC on Certain Legal Aspects of Information Society Services, in Particular Electronic Commerce in the Internal Market, arts. 12–15, 2000 O.J. (L 178) 1 [hereinafter E-Commerce Directive] (applying to liability of internet service providers generally, without limit to copyright).

63. *See, e.g.,* Copyright Act, R.S.C., ch. C-42, § 77 (1985) (Can.) (permitting the Copyright Board of Canada to issue a license to a user whose reasonable efforts to locate a copyright owner have been unsuccessful). *See generally* Jeremy de Beer & Mario Bouchard, *Canada's "Orphan Works" Regime: Unlocatable Copyright Owners and the Copyright Board* (December 1, 2009), *available at* http://www.cb-cda.gc.ca/about-apropos/2010-11-19-newstudy.pdf.

64. *See, e.g.,* Tiffany (NJ) Inc. v. eBay, Inc., 600 F.3d 93 (2d Cir. 2010); L'Oréal S.A.v. eBay Int'l A.G. [2009] EWHC (Ch) 1094 (UK); Case C-324/09, L'Oréal SA v. eBay Int'l, [2011] E.T.M.R. 52 (CJEU); eBay Int'l A.G., eBay Europe Sarl and eBay Belgium v. The Polo/Lauren Company LP, [2010] E.T.M.R. 1 (Bel.); Internet Auction II, Case I ZR 35/04 (BGH April 19, 2007) [2007] E.T.M.R. 70 (F.R.G.).

65. *See* Internet Corporation for Assigned Names and Numbers (ICANN), Uniform Domain Name Dispute Resolution Policy (October 24, 1999), *available at* http://www.icann.org/dndr/udrp/policy.htm (limiting arbitration to bad-faith registration of domain names); Barcelona.com, Inc. v. Excelentisimo Ayuntamiento de Barcelona, 330 F.3d 617, 628 (4th Cir. 2003).

66. *See* Graeme B. Dinwoodie & Mark D. Janis, *Lessons from the Trademark Use Debate*, 92 IOWA L. REV. 1703 (2007); Graeme B. Dinwoodie & Mark D. Janis, *Confusion Over Use: Contextualism in Trademark Law*, 92 IOWA L. REV. 1597 (2007). Some scholars would wholly immunize search engines from primary infringement liability. *See* Stacey L. Dogan & Mark A. Lemley, *Grounding Trademark Law Through Trademark Use*, 92 IOWA L. REV. 1669, 1670 (2007); Stacey L. Dogan & Mark A. Lemley, *Trademarks and Consumer Search Costs on the Internet*, 41 HOUS. L. REV. 777 (2004).

67. *See, e.g.,* Laboratory Corp. of America Holdings v. Metabolite Laboratories, Inc., 548 U.S. 124, 126 (2006) ("sometimes *too much* patent protection can impede rather than 'promote the Progress of Science and useful Arts.'") (Breyer, J., dissenting from denial of certiorari).

68. See Jonathan M. Barnett, *Property as Process: How Innovation Markets Select Innovation Regimes*, 119 YALE L.J. 384 (2009); Clarisa Long, *Patent Signals*, 69 U. CHI. L. REV. 625 (2002); Jonathan M. Barnett, *Cultivating the Genetic Commons: Imperfect Patent Protection and the Network Model of Innovation*, 37 SAN DIEGO L. REV. 987 (2000).
69. Michael J. Meurer, *Patent Examination Priorities*, 51 WM. & MARY L. REV. 675 (2009); United States Patent and Trademark Office, Three-Track Examination Proposal, 75 Fed. Reg. 31,763 (July 20, 2010).
70. *See* eBay Inc. v. MercExchange, L.L.C., 547 U.S. 388 (2006); *see also* Leahy-Smith America Invents Act, *supra* note 47, Sec. 18, 125 Stat. 329 (2011) (creating a new review mechanism for patents covering data processing methods used in the financial sector, where the problem of trolling is particularly acute).
71. *See, e.g.*, Nuffield Council on Bioethics, *Patenting DNA: The Ethics of Patenting DNA: A Discussion Paper*, ¶ 2.5 (July 23, 2002), *available at* http://www.nuffieldbioethics.org/patenting-dna [hereinafter Nuffield Council Discussion Paper]. *See also* Pamela Samuelson & Suzanne Scotchmer, *The Law and Economics of Reverse Engineering*, 111 YALE L.J. 1575, 1612–1637 (2002).
72. *See* Ted M. Sichelman, *Commercializing Patents*, 62 STAN. L. REV. 341 (2010).
73. *See, e.g.*, Report of the Secretary's Advisory Committee on Genetics, Health, and Society (SACGHS), *Gene Patents and Licensing Practices and Their Impact on Patient Access to Genetic Tests* (April 2010), *available at* http://oba.od.nih.gov/oba/sacghs/reports/SACGHS_patents_report_2010.pdf [hereinafter SACGHS Report on Gene Patents] (concluding that diagnostic tests are so easily produced from genetic information, patent rights are unnecessary to spur their development or commercialization).
74. NTP, Inc. v. Research in Motion, Ltd., 418 F.3d 1282, 1313 (Fed. Cir. 2005).
75. DAN L. BURK & MARK A. LEMLEY, THE PATENT CRISIS AND HOW THE COURTS CAN SOLVE IT (University of Chicago Press 2009).
76. BESSEN & MEURER, *supra* note 54.
77. Jerome H. Reichman, *Intellectual Property in the Twenty-First Century: Will the Developing Countries Lead or Follow?*, 46 HOUS. L. REV. 1115 (2009).
78. *See generally* THE DEVELOPMENT AGENDA: GLOBAL INTELLECTUAL PROPERTY AND DEVELOPING COUNTRIES, *supra* note 52; Susan K. Sell, *TRIPS Was Never Enough: Vertical Forum Shifting, FTAs, ACTA, and TPP*, 18 J. INTELL. PROP. L. 447 (2011).
79. *See, e.g.*, TRIPS, art. 51 (permitting, but not requiring, countries to control exports); *China–Enforcement*, at ¶ 7.224.
80. *See* Michael J. Meurer, *Patent Examination Priorities*, *supra* note 69.
81. *See, e.g.*, AMERICAN LAW INSTITUTE, INTELLECTUAL PROPERTY: PRINCIPLES GOVERNING JURISDICTION, CHOICE OF LAW, AND JUDGMENTS IN TRANSNATIONAL DISPUTES (2008); EUROPEAN MAX-PLANCK-GROUP ON CONFLICT OF LAWS IN INTELLECTUAL PROPERTY (CLIP), PRINCIPLES ON CONFLICT OF LAWS IN INTELLECTUAL PROPERTY LAW, December 1, 2011, *available at* http://www.ip.mpg.de/ww/de/pub/mikroseiten/cl_ip_eu/en/pub/home.cfm; *see also* Anne-Marie Slaughter, *Judicial Globalization*, 40 VA. J. INT'L L. 1103 (2000).
82. *See, e.g.*, Warren F. Schwartz & Alan O. Sykes, *The Economic Structure of Renegotiation and Dispute Resolution in the World Trade Organization*, 31 J. LEGAL STUD. 179 (2002).
83. *See, e.g.*, U.S. Patent 5,747,282 (filed June 7, 1995).
84. *See, e.g.*, U.S. Patent 7,655,403 (filed December 2, 2006).
85. Bryn Williams-Jones, *History of a Gene Patent: Tracing the Development and Application of Commercial BRCA Testing*, 10 HEALTH L.J. 123, 125 (2002) (noting that patents on genetic material were issued first in the United States in the wake of the Supreme Court's decision in *Diamond v. Chakrabarty*, 447 U.S. 303 (1980), holding that man-made microorganisms are patentable subject matter). The EU's Biotechnology Directive similarly recognizes the possibility of gene patents. *See* Directive 98/44 of the European Parliament and of the Council of July 6, 1998, on the Legal Protection of Biotechnological Inventions, art. 3.2, 1998 O.J. (L 213) 13.

86. *See supra* notes 71 & 73; The Senate, Community Affairs References Committee, *Gene Patents* (November 26, 2010) (Australia), *available at* http://www.aph.gov.au/Senate/committee/clac_ctte/gene_patents_43/report/report.pdf. *See also* Australian Government, Advisory Council on Intellectual Property, *Patentable Subject Matter: Final Report* (December 2010) (Australia).
87. *See* Julia Carbone et al., *DNA Patents and Diagnostics: Not a Pretty Picture*, 28(8) NATURE BIOTECHNOLOGY 784 (2010).
88. *See, e.g.,* Zhen Lei, Rakhi Juneja & Brian D. Wright, *Patents Versus Patenting: Implications of Intellectual Property Protection for Biological Research*, 27(1) NATURE BIOTECHNOLOGY 36, 37 (2009).
89. *See, e.g.,* Lori B. Andrews & Laura A. Shackelton, *Influenza Genetic Sequence Patents: Where Intellectual Property Clashes with Public Health Needs*, 3(3) FUTURE VIROLOGY 235 (2008).
90. Kyle L. Jensen & Fiona E. Murray, *Intellectual Property Landscape of the Human Genome*, 310 SCIENCE 239 (2005).
91. *See, e.g.,* Margaret A. Hamburg & Francis S. Collins, *The Path to Personalized Medicine*, 363(4) NEW ENG. J. MED. 301 (June 22, 2010).
92. *See also Patently Complicated: Case Studies on the Impact of Patenting and Licensing on Clinical Access to Genetic Testing in the United States*, 12(4) GENETICS IN MED. S1 (2010); Robert Cook-Deegan & Christopher Heaney, *Gene Patents and Licensing: Case Studies Prepared for the Secretary's Advisory Committee on Genetics, Health, and Society*, 12(4) GENETICS IN MED. S1–S2 (Supp. 2010).
93. *See* SACGHS Report on Gene Patents, *supra* note 73.
94. *See, e.g.,* Association for Molecular Pathology (AMP) v. U.S. PTO, 702 F. Supp.2d 181 (S.D.N.Y. 2010) (Sweet J.) (holding that claims to isolated DNA molecules were patent-eligible subject matter, since "the molecules as claimed do not exist in nature"), *rev'd in part*, 653 F.3d 1329 (Fed. Cir. 2011); *id.* (Bryson, J., concurring in part) (expressing the view that certain of the DNA claims at issue are overbroad); Intervet Inc. v. Merial Ltd, 617 F.3d 1282, 1294 (Fed. Cir. 2010) (Dyk, J., concurring in part); Nuffield Council Discussion Paper, *supra* note 71.
95. *See* Leahy-Smith America Invents Act, *supra* note 47, Sec. 27, 125 Stat. 338 (2011).
96. Gesetz zur Umsetzung der Richtlinie über den rechtlichen Schutz biotechnologischer Erfindungen [Statute Implementing the European Council's Biotechnology Directive], January 21, 2005, BGBl. I at 146, §1a(4) (F.R.G.). France has adopted a similar approach. *See* Code de la Propriété Intellectuelle [Intellectual Property Code], art. L613-2-1 (Fr.).
97. Case C-428/08, Monsanto Technology LLC v. Cefetra BV [2011] F.S.R. 6 (Grand Chamber CJEU) (holding that the patent on a gene in a soy plant is not infringed when the soybeans are made into meal).
98. Saggi & Trachtman, *supra* note 25, at 16.
99. TRIPS, art. 30; *see also Monsanto, supra* note 97, at ¶ 76.
100. *See* Chapter 3.
101. TRIPS, art. 27.1. In *Monsanto*, Advocate General Mengozzi suggested that it is necessary to limit gene patents to their function in order to distinguish between "discoveries" and "inventions." *See Monsanto, supra* note 97, at ¶ AG31.
102. *Cf.* New State Ice Co. v. Liebmann, 285 U.S. 262, 311 (1932) (Brandeis J., dissenting).

Chapter 2

1. Daniel J. Gervais, *TRIPS and Development, in* INTELLECTUAL PROPERTY, TRADE AND DEVELOPMENT: STRATEGIES TO OPTIMIZE ECONOMIC DEVELOPMENT IN A TRIPS-PLUS ERA 3, 5–17 (Daniel J. Gervais ed., Oxford University Press 2007); Peter K. Yu, *TRIPS and Its Discontents*, 10 MARQ. INTELL. PROP. L. REV 369, 371–379 (2006).
2. *See infra* text accompanying note 132 (giving examples of Article 6, which takes no position on international exhaustion; Article 11, which predicates protection for rental rights

on cinematographic works on the existence of widespread copying; and Article 9.1, which requires members to observe their Berne obligations to protect moral rights, but does not make that commitment enforceable through WTO dispute settlement).

3. *See* DANIEL GERVAIS, THE TRIPS AGREEMENT: DRAFTING HISTORY AND ANALYSIS (3d ed. Sweet and Maxwell 2008); STEPHEN P. LADAS, PATENTS, TRADEMARKS, AND RELATED RIGHTS: NATIONAL AND INTERNATIONAL PROTECTION (Harvard University Press 1975); SAM RICKETSON & JANE C. GINSBURG, INTERNATIONAL COPYRIGHT AND NEIGHBOURING RIGHTS: THE BERNE CONVENTION AND BEYOND (2d ed. Oxford University Press 2005).
4. 1 RICKETSON & GINSBURG, *supra* note 3, at 27.
5. *Id.* at 20.
6. *See* Berne Convention for the Protection of Literary and Artistic Works, September 9, 1886, as last revised at Paris, July 24, 1971, 1161 U.N.T.S. 3 [hereinafter Berne Convention].
7. Paris Convention for the Protection of Industrial Property, March 20, 1883, as last revised at Stockholm, July 14, 1967, art. 28, 21 U.S.T. 1583, 828 U.N.T.S. 305 [hereinafter Paris Convention].
8. *See* 1 LADAS, *supra* note 3, at 60; Pedro Roffe & Gina Vea, *The WIPO Development Agenda in an Historical and Political Context, in* THE DEVELOPMENT AGENDA: GLOBAL INTELLECTUAL PROPERTY AND DEVELOPING COUNTRIES 79, 81 (Neil Weinstock Netanel ed., Oxford University Press 2009); Petra Moser, *Determinants of Innovation—Evidence from 19th Century World Fairs*, 64 J. ECON. HIST. 548 (2004).
9. 1 LADAS, *supra* note 3, at 60.
10. *See id.* at 61.
11. *Id.* at 62.
12. *See* 1 RICKETSON & GINSBURG, *supra* note 3, at 62.
13. *See* Jane C. Ginsburg, *The Role of National Copyright in an Era of International Copyright Norms, in* THE ROLE OF NATIONAL LEGISLATION IN COPYRIGHT LAW 211, 213 (Adolf Deitz ed., ALAI 2000) (suggesting that "[a]lthough most participating countries viewed the proposition as a desirable one, they voted against it because it would have required great modifications of their domestic laws, which many countries could not implement all at once").
14. 1 LADAS, *supra* note 3, at 62.
15. *See* Gillian Davies, *The Convergence of Copyright and Authors' Rights—Reality or Chimera?*, 26 INT'L REV. INDUS. PROP. & COPYRIGHT L. 964 (1995).
16. *See* LADAS, *supra* note 3, at 63.
17. *See* Paris Convention, art. 2; Berne Convention, art. 5.
18. *See* Paris Convention, art. 4.
19. *See id.* art 10bis; G. H. C. BODENHAUSEN, A GUIDE TO THE APPLICATION OF THE PARIS CONVENTION FOR THE PROTECTION OF INDUSTRIAL PROPERTY 142 (BIRPI 1968).
20. *See* Paris Convention, art. 6bis; BODENHAUSEN, *supra* note 19, at 89.
21. *See* ULF ANDERFELT, INTERNATIONAL PATENT: LEGISLATION AND DEVELOPING COUNTRIES 72–92 (Kluwer 1971); Roffe & Vea, *supra* note 8, at 84 (citing Casimir Akerman, *L'Obligation d'exploiter et la licence obligatoire en matiere de brevets d'invention*).
22. *See* IAN BROWNLIE, PRINCIPLES OF PUBLIC INTERNATIONAL LAW 105–106, 289–290 (7th ed. Oxford University Press 2008).
23. *See* 1 RICKETSON & GINSBURG, *supra* note 3, at 76 (explaining the choices that were before the countries negotiating the original text).
24. *See* 1 LADAS, *supra* note 3, at 64 (quoting Conference Internationale pour la Protection de la Propriété Industrielle [Paris 1880], pp. 13, 16, 17, 20).
25. *See* STEPHEN M. STEWART & HAMISH SANDISON, INTERNATIONAL COPYRIGHT AND NEIGHBOURING RIGHTS § 1.16, at 9–10 (2d ed. Lexis Law Pub. 1989). The core copyright treaty, the Berne Convention, certainly could be characterized as a "consolidating treaty."

However, WIPO had on rare occasions pursued "pioneering" treaties, such as the Rome Convention for the Protection of Performers, Producers of Phonograms and Broadcasting Organizations, where the international convention moved beyond national models. *See* MIHÁLY FICSOR, THE LAW OF COPYRIGHT AND THE INTERNET: THE 1996 WIPO TREATIES, THEIR INTERPRETATION AND IMPLEMENTATION 4 (Oxford University Press 2002).

26. *See* Gerhard Schricker, *Twenty-Five Years of Protection Against Unfair Competition*, 26 IIC 782 (1995).
27. *See* H. R. REP. NO. 100-609, at 34 (1988).
28. *Cf.* STEWART & SANDISON, *supra* note 25, § 4.46 (noting latitude under the Berne Convention for national laws to determine the *owner* of the copyright).
29. *See* 17 U.S.C. § 201(b) (1994) (providing that the employer or commissioning party is the author of a work made for hire); 17 U.S.C. § 101 (1994) (defining "work made for hire" as a work prepared by an employee within the scope of his employment or certain categories of specially commissioned works where the parties agree in writing that the work is made for hire); *see also* Copyright, Designs and Patents Act 1988, § 11(2) (UK) (granting employers rights in works prepared by an employee within the scope of the employee's employment).
30. *See* Law No. 92-597 of July 1, 1992, on the Intellectual Property Code, art. L-113 (amended March 27, 1997) (Fr.) (providing for copyright ownership by employers only with respect to software).
31. *See* Sam Ricketson, *The Boundaries of Copyright: Its Proper Limitations and Exceptions: International Conventions and Treaties*, 1999 INTELL. PROP. Q. 56 (1999); Panel Report, United States—Section 110(5) of the U.S. Copyright Act, WT/DS/160/R (June 15, 2000) [hereinafter *US-110(5)*].
32. *See* Campbell v. Acuff-Rose Music, Inc., 510 U.S. 569, 594 (1994).
33. *See* 17 U.S.C. § 110(6).
34. *See id.* § 110(1).
35. For a discussion of the different exceptions found in national copyright laws, *see* Jaap H. Spoor, *General Aspects of Exceptions and Limitations to Copyright: General Report*, *in* THE BOUNDARIES OF COPYRIGHT 27 (Libby Baulch et al. eds., Australian Copyright Council 1999).
36. World Intellectual Property Organization, *WIPO Treaties—General Information*, available at http://www.wipo.int/treaties/en/general/.
37. *See* William R. Cornish, *Genevan Bootstraps*, 19 EUR. INTELL. PROP. REV. 336 (1997) (criticizing WIPO for issuing reports and comments on model laws that purport to offer interpretations of international conventions).
38. *See* Berne Convention, art. 33; Paris Convention, art. 28.
39. Moreover, no "state invoked the doctrine of retaliation and retorsion theoretically available under international law for violation of international minimum standards of intellectual property protection." J. H. Reichman, *Enforcing the Enforcement Procedures of the TRIPS Agreement*, 37 VA. J. INT'L L. 335, 339 n.17 (1997).
40. *See* Roffe & Vea, *supra* note 8.
41. 2 RICKETSON & GINSBURG, *supra* note 3, at 883–884; Roffe & Vea, *supra* note 8, at 83–84.
42. *See* Lionel Bently, *The "Extraordinary Multiplicity" of Intellectual Property Laws in the British Colonies in the Nineteenth Century*, 12 THEORETICAL INQUIRIES L. 161 (2011).
43. *See* Lionel Bently, *Copyright, Translations, and Relations Between Britain and India in the Nineteenth and Early Twentieth Centuries*, 82 CHI.-KENT L. REV. 1181 (2007).
44. *See* Ruth L. Okediji, *The International Relations of Intellectual Property: Narratives of Developing Country Participation in the Global Intellectual Property System*, 7 SING. J. INT'L & COMP. L. 315 (2003).
45. *See* Andrea Koury Menescal, *Changing WIPO's Ways? The 2004 Development Agenda in Historical Perspective*, 8 J. WORLD INTELL. PROP. 761 (2005).

46. See Roffe & Vea, *supra* note 8, at 95; Menescal, *supra* note 45, at 764.
47. See Roffe & Vea, *supra* note 8, at 94–96.
48. Deborah J. Halbert, *The World Intellectual Property Organization: Past, Present and Future*, 54 J. COPYRIGHT SOC'Y 253, 262 (2007).
49. *See* Roffe & Vea, *supra* note 8, at 91.
50. *See id.* at 96.
51. *See id.* at 97.
52. *See id.* at 97–104.
53. Basic Proposal for the Diplomatic Conference for the Revision of the Paris Convention (June 25, 1979), WIPO Doc. PR/DC/3, Objective 7.
54. *See* Roffe & Vea, *supra* note 8, at 100.
55. *See id.* at 101.
56. See Jerome H. Reichman & Catherine Hasenzahl, *Non-voluntary Licensing of Patented Inventions: Historical Perspective, Legal Framework Under TRIPS and an Overview of the Practice in Canada and the United States*, ICTSD-UNCTAD Issue Paper No. 5, at 13 (ICTSD-UNCTAD 2002).
57. *See* Roffe & Vea, *supra* note 8, at 101–103.
58. *See* 2 RICKETSON & GINSBURG, *supra* note 3, ch. 14.
59. *See* Ruth L. Okediji, *The International Copyright System: Limitations, Exceptions and Public Interest Considerations for Developing Countries*, ICSTD Issue Paper No. March 15, 2006, at 15, *available at* http://www.unctad.org/en/docs/iteipc200610_en.pdf.
60. *See* 2 RICKETSON & GINSBURG, *supra* note 3, at 957.
61. Omnibus Trade and Competitiveness Act of 1989, Pub. L. No. 100-418, 102 Stat. 1176–1179; 19 U.S.C. § 2242. For examples, see OFFICE OF THE UNITED STATES TRADE REPRESENTATIVE, SPECIAL 301 REPORTS, *available at* http://search.usa.gov/search?sc=0&query=special+301+reports&affiliate=ustrgov&locale=en&;m=. *See generally* Kim Newby, *The Effectiveness of Special 301 in Creating Long Term Copyright Protection for U.S. Companies Overseas*, 21 SYRACUSE J. INT'L L. & COM. 29 (1995).
62. *See* Council Regulation (EC) of December 22, 1994, No. 3286/94 Laying Down Community Procedures in the Field of the Common Commercial Policy in Order to Ensure the Exercise of the Community's Rights Under International Trade Rules, in Particular Those Established Under the Auspices of the World Trade Organization, 1994 O.J. (L 349) 71, as amended by Council Regulation (EC) No. 356/95 of February 20, 1995, 1995 O.J. (L 41) 3; *see generally* David Rose, *The E.U. Trade Barrier Regulation: An Effective Instrument for Promoting Global Harmonisation of Intellectual Property Rights?*, 21 EUR. INTELL. PROP. REV. 313 (1999).
63. *See, e.g.,* Peter Drahos, *Global Rights in Information: The Story of TRIPS at the GATT*, 13 PROMETHEUS 1 (1995).
64. *See* General Agreement on Tariffs and Trade, October 30, 1947, art. XX (d), 61 Stat. A-11, T.I.A.S. 1700, 55 U.N.T.S. 194 [hereinafter GATT] (providing "nothing in this Agreement shall be construed to prevent the adoption or enforcement by any contracting party of measures . . . (d) necessary to secure compliance with laws or regulations which are not inconsistent with the provisions of this Agreement, including those relating to . . . the protection of patents, trademarks and copyrights, and the prevention of deceptive practices").
65. DUNCAN MATTHEWS, GLOBALISING PROPERTY RIGHTS: THE TRIPS AGREEMENT (Routledge 2002).
66. Andreas F. Lowenfeld, *Remedies Along with Rights: Institutional Reform in the New GATT*, 88 AM. J. INT'L L. 477 (1994); Norio Komuro, *The WTO Dispute Settlement Mechanism*, 12 J. INT'L ARB. 81 (September 1995); ROBERT E. HUDEC, THE GATT LEGAL SYSTEM AND WORLD TRADE DIPLOMACY (2d ed. Lexis Law Pub. 1990).
67. *See* Laurence R. Helfer, *Regime Shifting: The TRIPS Agreement and New Dynamics of International Intellectual Property Lawmaking*, 29 YALE J. INT'L L. 1 (2004).
68. *See* MATTHEWS, *supra* note 65, at 9–15.

69. SUSAN K. SELL, PRIVATE POWER, PUBLIC LAW: THE GLOBALIZATION OF INTELLECTUAL PROPERTY RIGHTS 2 (Cambridge University Press 2003).
70. Michael L. Doane, *TRIPS and International Intellectual Property Protection in an Age of Advancing Technology*, 9 AM. U. J. INT'L L. & POL'Y 465 (1994).
71. Drahos, *supra* note 63 at 9–10.
72. CAROLYN DEERE, THE IMPLEMENTATION GAME: THE TRIPS AGREEMENT AND THE GLOBAL POLITICS OF INTELLECTUAL PROPERTY REFORM IN DEVELOPING COUNTRIES 48–49 (Oxford University Press 2009).
73. GERVAIS, *supra* note 3, at § 1.13–1.14.
74. Kamal Saggi and Joel P. Trachtman, *Incomplete Harmonization Contracts in International Economic Law: Report of the Panel*, China—Measures Affecting Protection and Enforcement of Intellectual Property Rights, *WT/DS362/R, adopted March 20, 2009*, 10 WORLD TRADE REV. 1–2 (2010).
75. *See, e.g.,* MEIR PEREZ PUGATCH, THE INTERNATIONAL POLITICAL ECONOMY OF INTELLECTUAL PROPERTY RIGHTS 51–56 (Edward Elgar 2004).
76. *See, e.g.,* Carlos Alberto Primo Braga, *The Economics of Intellectual Property Rights and the GATT: A View from the South*, 22 VAND. J. TRANSNAT'L L. 243 (1989).
77. Giuseppe Di Vita, *The TRIPS Agreement and Technological Innovation* (July 9, 2010), available at http://ssrn.com/abstract=1636962. *See also* Gene M. Grossman & Edwin L.-C. Lai, *International Protection of Intellectual Property*, 94 AM. ECON. REV. 1635 (2004).
78. *See, e.g.,* Donald McRae, *The Contribution of International Trade Law to the Development of International Law*, 260 RECUEIL DE COURS 111, 116–117 (1996); Robert Howse, *From Politics to Technocracy—and Back Again: The Fate of the Multilateral Trading Regime*, 96 AM. J. INT'L L. 94, 98 (2002); Robert Howse, *The Appellate Body Rulings in the Shrimp/Turtle Case: A New Legal Baseline for the Trade and Environment Debate*, 27 COLUM. J. ENVTL. L. 491 (2002) (noting that at one time, many "saw the GATT as a regime dedicated to the triumph of free trade over all other human concerns.").
79. *See* Primo Braga, *supra* note 76.
80. See, e.g., *GATT Negotiating Group Sets Talks This Week on U.S. Proposal, WIPO Will Join Discussion*, 4 INT'L TRADE REP. (BNA) 1358 (November 4, 1987).
81. Denominated a provision on "[t]rade-related aspects of intellectual property rights, including trade in counterfeit goods," the Declaration provided:

> In order to reduce the distortions and impediments to international trade, and taking into account the need to promote effective and adequate protection of intellectual property rights, and to ensure that measures and procedures to enforce intellectual property rights do not themselves become barriers to legitimate trade, the negotiations shall aim to clarify GATT provisions and elaborate as appropriate new rules and disciplines. Negotiations shall aim to develop a multilateral framework of principles, rules and disciplines dealing with international trade in counterfeit goods, taking into account work already undertaken in the GATT. These negotiations shall be without prejudice to other complementary initiatives that may be taken in the World Intellectual Property Organization and elsewhere to deal with these matters.

General Agreement on Tariffs and Trade (GATT), Punta Del Este Declaration, Ministerial Declaration of September 20, 1986, 25 I.L.M. 1623 (1986); *see also* GERVAIS, *supra* note 3, §1.12.
82. Alan O. Sykes, *TRIPS, Pharmaceuticals, Developing Countries and the Doha "Solution,"* 3 CHI. J. INT'L L. 47, 59 (2002); MATTHEWS, *supra* note 65, at 42.
83. PETER DRAHOS & JOHN BRAITHWAITE, INFORMATION FEUDALISM 11 (Earthscan Publications 2002).
84. *See, e.g.,* Brian Manning & Srividhya Ragavan, *The Dispute Settlement Process of the WTO: A Normative Structure to Achieve Utilitarian Objectives*, 79 U.M.K.C. L. REV. 1, 17–21, 27–29 (2010) (examining the dispute in *United States—Subsidies on Upland Cotton*, WT/DS267/

AB/R (March 3, 2005), in which the United States resisted compliance). For another example of skewed levels of compliance, see text at note 135 on the ability of the United States to pay damages rather than alter its intellectual property law.
85. See SELL, *supra* note 69; Drahos, *supra* note 63.
86. Doane, *supra* note 70, at 475, citing Mitsod Matsushita, *A Japanese Perspective on Intellectual Property Rights and the GATT*, 1992 COLUM. BUS. L. REV. 81, 89–91 (1992); MATTHEWS, *supra* note 65, at 44–45.
87. Drahos, *supra* note 63, at 15; MATTHEWS, *supra* note 65, at 33.
88. DEERE, *supra* note 72.
89. See GERVAIS, *supra* note 3, ¶¶ 1.18–19 (noting that the "common structure" found in the first comprehensive counterpart EU and US proposals "was eventually adopted and, subject to a few changes, would serve as the basis for the emerging Agreement"); *see also* MATTHEWS, *supra* note 65, at 43–44.
90. These included at various times: CBS, Du Pont, General Electric, Hewlett-Packard, IBM, Merck, Monsanto, Pfizer, General Motors, Digital Equipment Corporation, FMC, Procter & Gamble, Rockwell International, and Time Warner. *See* SELL, *supra* note 69, at 2 n.1 (1986 membership), 96 n.1 (1994 membership).
91. *See* SELL, *supra* note 69, at 51.
92. *See id.* at 55; *see also* Hanns Ullrich, *TRIPS: Adequate Protection, Inadequate Trade, Adequate Competition Policy*, 4 PAC. RIM. L. & POL'Y J. 154, 154 (describing TRIPS as a "harmonizing" document).
93. *See* Chapter 3.
94. J. H. Reichman, *From Free Riders to Fair Followers: Global Competition under the TRIPS Agreement*, 29 N.Y.U. J. INT'L L. & POL. 11 (1996–1997).
95. *See, e.g.,* John McGinnis & Mark Movesian, *The World Trade Constitution*, 114 HARV. L. REV. 511 (2000).
96. *See, e.g.,* CHRISTINE GREENHALGH & MARK ROGERS, INNOVATION, INTELLECTUAL PROPERTY AND ECONOMIC GROWTH (Princeton University Press 2010).
97. Richard T. Rapp & Richard P. Rozek, *Benefits and Costs of Intellectual Property in Developing Countries*, 24(5) J. WORLD TRADE 75 (1990).
98. *See, e.g.,* PUGATCH, *supra* note 75, at 60–64; Carlos Correa, *Trends in Technology Transfer: Implications for Developing Countries*, 21(6) SCI. & PUB. POL'Y 369, 369–374 (1994) (describing the experience in Latin American countries).
99. Rapp & Rozek, *supra* note 97, at 81, 97–99.
100. *See, e.g.,* Primo Braga, *supra* note 76; Correa, *supra* note 98, at 375–378. *See also* Carlos M. Correa, *Harmonization of Intellectual Property Rights in Latin America: Is There Still Room for Differentiation*, 39 N.Y.U. J. INT'L L. & POL. 109 (1996–1997) (noting that Latin American countries have conformed to TRIPS and questioning the degree of flexibility that they enjoy).
101. CARLOS M. CORREA, INTELLECTUAL PROPERTY RIGHTS, THE WTO AND DEVELOPING COUNTRIES 23–48 (Zed Books 2000) (summarizing the empirical evidence and concluding that the effects of TRIPS for any individual country and economic sector are difficult to foresee).
102. Ruth L. Gana, *Has Creativity Died in the Third World? Some Implications of the Internationalization of Intellectual Property*, 24 DENV. J. INT'L L. & POL.Y 109, 112–116 (1995).
103. TRIPS, art. 39.
104. *Id.* arts. 25–26 & 35–37.
105. Paris Convention, art. 4.
106. TRIPS, art. 27.1.
107. *Id.* arts. 41–61.
108. *US–110(5)*, at ¶ 6.62–6.66.
109. Kal Raustiala, *Compliance and Effectiveness in International Regulatory Cooperation*, 32 CASE W. RES. J. INT'L L. 387 (2000); J. H. Reichman, *The TRIPS Agreement Comes of Age: Conflict or Cooperation with the Developing Countries*, 32 CASE W. RES. J. INT'L L. 441 (2000).

110. GATT, art. XIX. A similar approach is planned in Article X of the GATS, General Agreement on Trade in Services, April 15, 1994, Marrakesh Agreement Establishing the World Trade Organization, Annex 1B, 1869 U.N.T.S. 183, 33 I.L.M. 1167 (1994).
111. Panel Report, Canada—Patent Protection of Pharmaceutical Products, ¶¶ 7.25–7.26, WT/DS114/R (March 17, 2000) [hereinafter *Canada–Pharmaceuticals*].
112. TRIPS, art. 31(f).
113. PUGATCH, *supra* note 75, at 138–140. *See also Report of the UK Commission on Intellectual Property Rights*, 28–30 (2002) [hereinafter CIPR Report], *available at* http://www.iprcommission.org/graphic/documents/final_report.htm (noting lack of technology transfer); Frederick M. Abbott, *Intellectual Property Rights in a Global Trade Framework: IP Trends in Developing Countries*, 98 AM. SOC'Y INT'L L. PROC. 95 (2004); Gregory C. Shaffer, *The Public and the Private in International Trade Litigation*, 50–54 (2002), *available at* http://ssrn.com/abstract=531183.
114. Amy Kapczynski, *Harmonization and Its Discontents: A Case Study of TRIPS Implementation in India's Pharmaceutical Sector*, 97 CAL. L. REV. 1571, 1636 (2009); Anselm Kamperman Sanders, *Intellectual Property, Free Trade Agreements and Economic Development*, 23 GA. ST. U. L. REV. 893, 900 (2007).
115. *See, e.g.,* John S. Odell & Susan K. Sell, *Reframing the Issue: The WTO Coalition on Intellectual Property and Public Health, in* NEGOTIATING TRADE: DEVELOPING COUNTRIES IN THE WTO AND NAFTA 1, 20–21 (John S. Odell ed., Cambridge University Press 2006) (suggesting that the AIDS crisis helped reframe the debate).
116. World Trade Organization, Ministerial Declaration of November 20, 2001, ¶ 17, WT/MIN(01)/DEC/1, 41 I.L.M. 746 (2002) [hereinafter Ministerial Declaration]. *See also* World Trade Organization, Declaration on the TRIPS Agreement and Public Health, WT/MIN(01)/DEC/2, November 20, 2001, 41 I.L.M. 755 (2002).
117. Ministerial Declaration, ¶ 17.
118. *Id.* ¶ 19.
119. World Trade Organization, Council for TRIPS, Decision of the Council for TRIPS of 29 November 2005, Doc. No. IP/C/40 (extension of the transition period under Article 66.1 for least developed country members); World Trade Organization, Decision of the Council for TRIPS of July 1, 2002, Doc. No. IP/C/25 (extension of the transition period under Article 66.1 for least developed country members for certain obligations with respect to pharmaceutical products).
120. World Trade Organization, Decision of the Council for TRIPS of February 19, 2003, Doc. No. IP/C/28.
121. Agreement Between the World Intellectual Property Organization and the World Trade Organization, December 22, 1995, art. 4, 35 I.L.M. 754 (1996).
122. *See, e.g.,* Provisional Committee on Proposals Related to a WIPO Development Agenda (PCDA), Fourth Session (June 11–15, 2007), *available at* http://www.wipo.int/ip-development/en/agenda/pcda07_session4.html (resolving that "[w]ithin the framework of the agreement between WIPO and the WTO, WIPO shall make available advice to developing countries and LDCs, on the implementation and operation of the rights and obligations and the understanding and use of flexibilities contained in the TRIPS Agreement."). *See also* Ruth L. Okediji, *The International Relations of Intellectual Property: Narratives of Developing Country Participation in the Global Intellectual Property System*, 7 SING. J. INT'L & COMP. L. 315, 327 (2003).
123. *See, e.g.,* World Trade Organization, *International Intergovernmental Organizations Granted Observer Status to WTO Bodies, available at* http://www.wto.org/english/theWTO_e/igo_obs_e.htm; Appellate Body Report, United States—Section 211 of the Omnibus Appropriations Act of 1998, WT/DS176/AB/R (January 2, 2002) [hereinafter *Havana Club*]. Use of WIPO materials in dispute settlement is discussed more fully in Chapter 6.
124. Appellate Body Report, India—Patent Protection for Pharmaceutical and Agricultural Chemical Products, ¶¶ 45 & 47, WT/DS50/AB/R (December 19, 1997) (stating that

the "imputation into a treaty of words that were not there" would not be condoned and that the DSB cannot add new requirements to the Agreement) [hereinafter *India–Pharmaceuticals*].

125. Panel Report, China—Measures Affecting the Protection and Enforcement of Intellectual Property Rights, ¶ 7.323, WT/DS362/R (January 26, 2009) (citing Article 1.1); *id.* at ¶¶ 7.552–7.553.

126. MATTHEWS, *supra* note 65, at 39–43; GERVAIS, *supra* note 3, § 1.20–1.21 & 1.25–1.27; *see also* ALEXANDER STACK, INTERNATIONAL PATENT LAW: COOPERATION, HARMONIZATION AND INSTITUTIONAL ANALYSIS OF WIPO AND THE WTO (Edward Elgar 2010) (detailing differences in approach dictated by the size of a country's market rather than its stage of development).

127. *See* Annette Kur & Sam Cocks, *Nothing But a GI Thing: Geographical Indications under EU Law*, 17 FORDHAM INTELL. PROP. MEDIA & ENT. L.J. 999, 1011–1012 (2006–2007).

128. *See* Justin Hughes, *Champagne, Feta, and Bourbon: The Spirited Debate about Geographical Indications*, 58 HASTINGS L.J. 299, 302–305 (2006).

129. *Cf. India–Pharmaceuticals* (holding that India was required to enact a statute to protect future patent rights during the transition period).

130. TRIPS, arts. 24.4–24.9.

131. *Id.* arts. 24.1–24.2, 23.4.

132. Article 3.1 of TRIPS preserves the exceptions for reciprocity found in existing intellectual property agreements, which have been central to ongoing debates about the duration of copyright in Europe and the United States. *See* Council Directive 93/98/EEC of October 29, 1993, Harmonizing the Term of Protection of Copyright and Certain Related Rights, art. 7.1, 1993 O.J. (L 290) 9 (conditioning full protection of foreign works for complete terms on reciprocal protection), codified at Directive 2006/116/EC of the European Parliament and of the Council of 12 December 2006 on the Term of Protection of Copyright and Certain Related Rights (codified version), 2006 O.J. (L 372) 12; Berne Convention, art. 7.8 (permitting signatory nations to apply the rule of the shorter term, that is, to limit foreign works to the term of protection offered in their country of origin).

133. *See, e.g.,* Saggi & Trachtman, *supra* note 74. For criticism of the suggestion that the failure of the parties to detail obligations in a more comprehensive fashion represented a delegation of authority to the DSB to fill gaps and build upon the agreement reached, see Graeme B. Dinwoodie, *A New Copyright Order: Why National Courts Should Create Global Norms*, 149 U. PA. L. REV 469 (2000); Rochelle C. Dreyfuss & Andreas F. Lowenfeld, *Two Achievements of the Uruguay Round: Putting TRIPs and Dispute Settlement Together*, 37 VA. J. INT'L L. 275 (1997).

134. *See US–110(5)*. For a longer discussion, see Chapter 3.

135. Report of Arbitrators, United States—Section 110(5) of the U.S. Copyright Act—Recourse to Arbitration under Article 25 of the DSU, WT/DS160/ARB25/1 (November 9, 2001).

136. Panel Report, European Communities—Protection of Trademarks and Geographical Indications for Agricultural Products and Foodstuffs, WT/DS174/R (March 15, 2005) [hereinafter *EC–GI*].

137. *See Canada–Pharmaceuticals*, at ¶ 7.99.

138. The "built-in agenda" includes other matters as well, such as the patentability of plants and animals and the applicability of non-violation complaints. *See* Paul Vandoren, *The Implementation of the TRIPS Agreement*, 2 J. WORLD INTELL. PROP. 25 (1999).

139. *See generally* J. H. Reichman & David Lange, *Bargaining Around the TRIPS Agreement: The Case for Ongoing Public-Private Initiatives to Facilitate Worldwide Intellectual Property Transactions*, 9 DUKE J. COMP. & INT'L L. 11 (1998).

140. *See* Donald P. Harris, *Carrying a Good Joke Too Far: TRIPS and Treaties of Adhesion*, 27 U. PA. J. INT'L ECON. L. 681 (2006); Donald P. Harris, *TRIPS and Treaties of Adhesion Part II: Back to the Past or a Small Step Forward*, 2007 MICH. ST. L. REV. 185.

141. Thus, for example, soon after the TRIPS Agreement was completed, Michael Doane suggested that "[t]he industrialized world ... must be prepared to use the GATT along with other avenues including WIPO, regional and bilateral negotiations, and mechanisms such as Special 301, to pursue the spread and evolution of international intellectual property protection." Doane, *supra* note 70, at 493–494. These avenues turned out to include the Anti-Counterfeiting Trade Agreement, March 31, 2011 Text, *available at* http://trade.ec.europa.eu/doclib/docs/2011/may/tradoc_147937.pdf [hereinafter ACTA], and other initiatives discussed in Chapter 6. *See also* Susan K. Sell, *TRIPS Was Never Enough: Vertical Forum Shifting, FTAs, ACTA, and TPP*, 18 J. INTELL. PROP. L. 447 (2011) (arguing that these instruments are intended to garner the missing 5 per cent of what the developed countries wanted in TRIPS).

142. Article 5A of the Paris Convention provides in part that:

(1) Importation by the patentee into the country where the patent has been granted of articles manufactured in any of the countries of the Union shall not entail forfeiture of the patent.
(2) Each country of the Union shall have the right to take legislative measures providing for the grant of compulsory licenses to prevent the abuses which might result from the exercise of the exclusive rights conferred by the patent, for example, failure to work.
(3) Forfeiture of the patent shall not be provided for except in cases where the grant of compulsory licenses would not have been sufficient to prevent the said abuses. No proceedings for the forfeiture or revocation of a patent may be instituted before the expiration of two years from the grant of the first compulsory license.
(4) A compulsory license may not be applied for on the ground of failure to work or insufficient working before the expiration of a period of four years from the date of filing of the patent application or three years from the date of the grant of the patent, whichever period expires last; it shall be refused if the patentee justifies his inaction by legitimate reasons. Such a compulsory license shall be non-exclusive and shall not be transferable, even in the form of the grant of a sub-license, except with that part of the enterprise or goodwill which exploits such license.

143. GERVAIS, *supra* note 3, § 2.284.
144. *See, e.g.,* J. H. Reichman, *The TRIPS Component of the GATT's Uruguay Round: Competitive Prospects for Intellectual Property Owners in an Integrated World Market*, 4 FORDHAM INTELL. PROP. MEDIA & ENT. L.J. 171, 206 (1993).
145. *See, e.g.,* Hanns Ullrich, *Expansionist Intellectual Property Protection and Reductionist Competition Rules: A TRIPS Perspective*, EUI Working Paper Law No. 2004/3, *available at* http://escholarship.org/uc/item/0hz9g1d5;jsessionid=B9AF4305046EE561AE5C7ADA7BE81A4E#page-1.
146. *See, e.g.,* INTELLECTUAL PROPERTY RIGHTS, DEVELOPMENT, AND CATCH UP: AN INTERNATIONAL COMPARATIVE STUDY (Hiroyuki Odagiri, Akira Goto, Atsushi Sunami & Richard R. Nelson eds., Oxford University Press 2010); Kenneth J. Arrow, *The Economic Implications of Learning by Doing*, 29 (3) REV. OF ECON. STUD. 155–173 (1962).
147. *See, e.g.,* PUGATCH, *supra* note 75, at 58–59.
148. *See, e.g.,* Reichman, *supra* note 94; Ronald J. Gilson, *The Legal Infrastructure of High Technology Industrial Districts: Silicon Valley, Route 128, and Covenants Not to Compete*, 74 N.Y.U. L. REV. 575, 590 (1999).
149. See Bernard M. Hoekman, Keith E. Maskus & Kamal Saggi, *Transfer of Technology to Developing Countries: Unilateral and Multilateral Policy Options*, 33 WORLD DEVELOPMENT 1587 (2005).
150. Paul Champ & Amir Attaran, *Patent Rights and Local Working under the WTO TRIPS Agreement: An Analysis of the U.S.-Brazil Patent Dispute*, 27 YALE J. INT'L L. 365–393, 369 (2002).

151. *Id.* at 371–372. For an account of the negotiations over the regulation of the working requirement by the Paris Convention, *see* GRAEME B. DINWOODIE ET AL., INTERNATIONAL INTELLECTUAL PROPERTY LAW AND POLICY 436–445 (2d ed. Lexis Nexis 2008); *see also* Reichman & Hasenzahl, *supra* note 56.
152. *See* DINWOODIE ET AL, *supra* note 151, at 373–379.
153. *See* Paris Convention, art. 5A(2) (*quoted in* note 142). To be sure, in order to comply with the consistency proviso of Article 8, the state would presumably be required to follow the many steps set out in Article 31. The determination to award a license would have to be made on the individual merits of the case, after consultation with the right holder, and the license would need to be limited to the specific needs that induced its award and provide the right holder with adequate remuneration (including not only the value of the product produced, but also, perhaps, the value of the training furnished). Furthermore, this understanding of Article 31 assumes that it is not trumped by Article 27's antidiscrimination provision. In the next Chapter, we take up that question. But aside from that hurdle, there should be no problem under TRIPS.
154. Article 2.1 of TRIPS provides: "Nothing in Parts I to IV of this Agreement shall derogate from existing obligations that Members may have to each other under the Paris Convention."
155. *See* Request for Consultation by the United States, Brazil—Measures Affecting Patent Protection, WT/DS199/1G/L/385/IP/D/23 (June 8, 2000).
156. *See also* Bryan Mercurio & Mitali Tyagi, *Treaty Interpretation in WTO Dispute Settlement: The Outstanding Question of the Legality of Local Working Requirements*, 19 MINN. J. INT'L L. 275 (2010) (agreeing that the provision in the Paris Convention regulating working requirements survives TRIPS).

Chapter 3

1. Understanding on Rules and Procedures Governing the Settlement of Disputes, April 15, 1994, Marrakesh Agreement Establishing the World Trade Organization, Annex 2, LEGAL INSTRUMENTS—RESULTS OF THE URUGUAY ROUND, vol. 31, 1869 U.N.T.S. 401, 33 I.L.M. 1226 (1994) [hereinafter DSU].
2. David Palmeter, *National Sovereignty and the World Trade Organization*, 2 J. WORLD INTELL. PROP. 77, 79 (1999); *see also* Rochelle Cooper Dreyfuss & Andreas F. Lowenfeld, *Two Achievements of the Uruguay Round: Putting TRIPS and Dispute Settlement Together*, 37 VA. J. INT'L L. 275 (1997).
3. *See* World Trade Organization, Disputes by Agreement, *available at* http://www.wto.org/english/tratop_e/dispu_e/dispu_agreements_index_e.htm?id=A26#selected_agreement.
4. These are Appellate Body Report, India—Patent Protection for Pharmaceutical and Agricultural Chemical Products, WT/DS50/AB/R (September 5, 1997) [hereinafter *India-Pharmaceuticals*]; Appellate Body Report, Canada—Term of Patent Protection, WT/DS170/AB/R (September 18, 2000); Panel Report, Canada—Patent Protection of Pharmaceutical Products, WT/DS114/R (March 17, 2000) [hereinafter *Canada-Pharmaceuticals*]; Panel Report, United States—Section 110(5) of the U.S. Copyright Act, WT/DS/160/R (June 15, 2000) [hereinafter *US-110(5)*]; Appellate Body Report, United States—Section 211 Omnibus Appropriations Act of 1998, WT/DS176/AB/R (August 6, 2001) [hereinafter *Havana Club*]; Panel Report, European Communities—Protection of Trademarks and Geographical Indications for Agricultural Products and Foodstuffs, WT/DS174/R (March 15, 2005) [hereinafter *EC-GI*]; and Panel Report, China—Measures Affecting the Protection and Enforcement of Intellectual Property Rights, WT/DS362/R (January 26, 2009) [hereinafter *China-Enforcement*]. Technically, there have been nine disputes as both the United States and the European Union brought an *India-Pharmaceuticals* challenge and the Australians also filed a challenge to the EU geographical

indication regulations. In addition, as mentioned in Chapter 1, there have been two disputes in which measures affecting the intellectual property sector have been used in retaliation for failure to comply with other provisions of WTO agreements, and one case where a somewhat peripheral national treatment claim was barely addressed by the DSB. *See* Panel Report, Indonesia—Certain Measures Affecting the Automobile Industry, WT/DS54/R, WT/DS55/R, WT/DS59/R, WT DS64R (July 2, 1998).
5. DSU, art. 3.7.
6. To be sure, third parties may submit statements, but they too must have a trade interest in the dispute. *See* DSU, art. 4.11.
7. Indeed, under DSU, art. 8.1, the qualifications to serve on a panel include having "taught or published on international trade law or policy, or served as a senior trade policy official of a Member"; equivalent knowledge of intellectual property is not mentioned. Indeed, those cases where an intellectual property expert has been a member of the panel (such as *China–Enforcement* and *EC–GI*) are ones in which adjudicators have proven more sensitive to the types of inquiries we advocate. *Cf. Canada–Pharmaceuticals* (patent dispute decided by a panel that included a copyright expert).
8. ROBERT HOWSE & MAKAU MATUA, PROTECTING HUMAN RIGHTS IN A GLOBAL ECONOMY: CHALLENGES FOR THE WORLD TRADE ORGANIZATION (Montreal: ICHRDD 2000); *see also* Robert Howse & Efraim Chalamish, *The Use and Abuse of WTO Law in Investor-State Arbitration: A Reply to Jürgen Kurtz*, 20 EUR. J. INT'L L. 1087, 1094 (2010). However, few adjudicators specially versed in intellectual property law have served on the AB.
9. DSU, art. 3.2; Marrakesh Agreement Establishing the World Trade Organization, April 15, 1994, art. IX, sec 2, LEGAL INSTRUMENTS—RESULTS OF THE URUGUAY ROUND, vol. 1, 1867 U.N.T.S. 154, 33 I.L.M. 1144 (1994) [hereinafter WTO Agreement] (noting that DSU cannot change obligations of the parties and only the Ministerial Conference and General Council can render authoritative interpretations of the agreements). *But see* Felix David, *The Role of Precedent in the WTO—New Horizons?* (2009), *available at* ssrn.com/abstract=1666169. *See also* World Trade Organization, *Legal Effect of Panel and Appellate Body Reports and DSB Recommendations and Rulings* (2003), *available at* http://www.wto.org/english/tratop_e/dispu_e/disp_settlement_cbt_e/c7s2p1_e.htm (noting that a key objective of dispute settlement is to enhance predictability).
10. There are other approaches to ensuring the availability of upstream inventions, such as exempting fundamental building blocks of knowledge (such as genes) from patent protection or reducing their scope. *See* the illustration in Chapter 1. For similar proposals limited to the context of health care in developing countries, *see* CARLOS CORREA, INTEGRATING PUBLIC HEALTH CONCERNS INTO PATENT LEGISLATION IN DEVELOPING COUNTRIES (South Centre 2000), *available at* http://apps.who.int/medicinedocs/en/d/Jh2963e/1.html.
11. World Trade Organization, Ministerial Declaration of November 20, 2001, WT/MIN(01)/DEC/1, 41 I.L.M. 746 (2002) [hereinafter Ministerial Declaration]. *See also* World Trade Organization, Declaration on the TRIPS Agreement and Public Health, WT/MIN(01)/DEC/2, November 20, 2001, 41 I.L.M. 755 (2002).
12. Patents Act, 1970, § 3(d), amended by Patents (Amendment) Act, 2005 (India).
13. *Id.*
14. *See* TRIPS, art.70.8, described in Chapter 2.
15. *See* Shamnad Basheer & Prashant Reddy, *The "Efficacy" of Indian Patent Law: Ironing Out the Creases in Section 3(d)*, 5(3) *Script-Ed* 232 (August 2008), *available at* http://www.law.ed.ac.uk/ahrc/script-ed/vol5-2/basheer.asp.
16. *See* David W. Opderbeck, *Patents, Essential Medicines, and the Innovation Game*, 58 VAND. L. REV. 501 (2005) (noting that Indian drug companies have not institutionalized the "blockbuster model" of working on drugs only if there is a potential for considerable return).

17. See generally J. H. Reichman, *From Free Riders to Fair Followers: Global Competition under the TRIPS Agreement*, 29 N.Y.U. J. INT'L L. & POL. 11 (1997).
18. A robust generic drug industry would, in general, have an important impact both within India and outwith. *See* Robert C. Bird & Daniel R. Cahoy, *The Emerging BRIC Economies: Lessons from Intellectual Property Negotiation and Enforcement*, 5 Nw. J. TECH. & INTELL. PROP. 400 (2007) (suggesting that countries like India could make substantial profit from the export of pharmaceuticals, particularly under the compulsory license provisions of Articles 31 and 31bis).
19. Novartis AG & Anr. v. Union of India & Others (2007) 4 MLJ 1153; Mike Palmedo, *India Supreme Court to Hear Arguments In Case Over Section 3(d)*, InfoJustice.org (November 28, 2011), *available at* http://infojustice.org/archives/6264.
20. OFFICE OF THE UNITED STATES TRADE REPRESENTATIVE, 2010 SPECIAL 301 REPORT 26 (April 30, 2010) ("One concern in this regard is a provision in India's Patent Law that prohibits patents on certain chemical forms absent a showing of increased efficacy. While the full import of this provision remains unclear, it appears to limit the patentability of potentially beneficial innovations, such as temperature-stable forms of a drug or new means of drug delivery.").
21. *See Canada–Pharmaceuticals*, at ¶ 4.6 n.27 (noting the EC's submission on the negotiating history of the Agreement) & ¶ 7.90.
22. *See id.* at ¶ 2.1.
23. *See supra* note 21.
24. *Canada–Pharmaceuticals*, at ¶ 7.104. *See also id.* at ¶ 7.94 ("pharmaceuticals were the only products mentioned in Canada's 1991 legislative debates on the enactment of Sections 55.2(1)").
25. *Id.* at ¶ 7.99 ("With regard to the issue of de jure discrimination, the Panel concluded that the European Communities had not presented sufficient evidence to raise the issue in the face of Canada's formal declaration that the exception of Section 55.2(1) was not limited to pharmaceutical products.").
26. *Id.* at ¶ 7.104.
27. For example, the problem of continuation applications intended to snare later developments is hotly debated in the United States. *See, e.g.,* Mark A. Lemley & Kimberly A. Moore, *Ending Abuse of Patent Continuations*, 84 B.U. L. REV. 63 (2004). *See also* KSR v. Teleflex, 550 U.S. 398 (2007) (raising the standard of inventiveness for all fields of technology).
28. *Canada–Pharmaceuticals*, at ¶¶ 7.25–7.26
29. Ministerial Declaration, ¶ 17.
30. DANIEL J. GERVAIS, THE TRIPS AGREEMENT: DRAFTING HISTORY AND ANALYSIS ¶ 2.87 (3d ed. Sweet and Maxwell 2008); Daniel J. Gervais, *TRIPS and Development, in* INTELLECTUAL PROPERTY, TRADE AND DEVELOPMENT: STRATEGIES TO OPTIMIZE ECONOMIC DEVELOPMENT IN A TRIPS-PLUS ERA 3, 19 (Daniel J. Gervais ed., Oxford University Press 2007).
31. *See, e.g.,* Duncan Matthews, *WTO Decision on Implementation of Paragraph 6 of the Doha Declaration on the TRIPS Agreement and Public Health: A Solution to the Access to Essential Medicines Problem?*, 7 J. INT'L ECON. L. 73, 82–83 (2004) (canvassing views).
32. Reichman, *supra* note 17, at 31.
33. TRIPS, art. 30.
34. *Canada–Pharmaceuticals*, at ¶ 7.69.
35. *Id.* at ¶ 7.82. Similarly, the *US–110(5)* panel investigated the exceptions other countries had adopted to determine the meaning of the parallel copyright Exceptions provision, Article 13. *See US–110(5)*, at ¶¶ 6.67–6.70 (discussing minor exceptions doctrine).
36. *Canada–Pharmaceuticals*, at ¶ 7.69.
37. *Cf.* Dreyfuss & Lowenfeld, *supra* note 2, at 290.

38. *See, e.g.,* Susy Frankel, *A Patentable Invention: Will Current Proposed Law Reform Clarify Patentable Subject Matter?*, NEW ZEALAND BUS. L. Q. 350 (2005) (discussing recognition of so-called Swiss claims); Richard A Castellano, *Patent Law for New Medical Uses of Known Compounds and Pfizer's Viagra Patent*, 46 IDEA 283 (2006).
39. KSR v. Teleflex, 550 U.S. 398 (2007); *see also* Leahy-Smith America Invents Act, Pub. L. No. 112-29, Sec. 14, 125 Stat. 284, 327 (2011) (altering the outcome of obviousness analyses for tax strategies).
40. Mark Metzke, *Targeting Enantiomer Product Hopping With a New "Obviousness" Standard*, 14 U.C.L.A. J.L. & TECH. 1 (2010).
41. *See* CAROLYN DEERE, THE IMPLEMENTATION GAME: THE TRIPS AGREEMENT AND THE GLOBAL POLITICS OF INTELLECTUAL PROPERTY REFORM IN DEVELOPING COUNTRIES 79 (Oxford University Press 2009) (listing the Andean Community, Argentina, China, India, Malaysia, Dominican Republic, Chile, and Uruguay).
42. Janice Mueller, *The Tiger Awakens: The Tumultuous Transformation of India's Patent System and the Rise of Indian Pharmaceutical Innovation*, 68 U. PITT. L. REV. 491 (2007).
43. *See, e.g.,* Samuel Mintzer Fuchs, *Intellectual Propriety: Compulsory Licenses through the TRIPS Agreement and the Doha Declaration on Public Health*, ISP Collection Paper 854, 6 (2010), *available at* http://digitalcollections.sit.edu/isp_collection/854 (noting that it took Canada six years to use the interim system to get approval to sell Apotex in Rwanda); Gail E. Evans, *Strategic Patent Licensing for Public Research Organizations: Deploying Restriction and Reservation Clauses to Promote Medical R&D in Developing Countries*, 34 AM. J. L. & MED. 175, 185–186 (2008).
44. *US-110(5)*, at ¶ 6.59.
45. *See* Funk Bros. Seed Co. v. Kalo Inoculant Co., 333 U.S. 127, 131 (1948) (holding that packets containing mixtures of bacteria were "no more than the discovery of some of the handiwork of nature" and hence unpatentable); Brenner v. Manson, 383 U.S. 519 (1966) (defining the utility required for patent protection as end-use rather than research-use utility). *See also* O'Reilly v. Morse, 56 U.S. (15 How.) 62 (1853) (holding that abstract principles are not statutory subject matter).
46. *See, e.g.,* Diamond v. Chakrabarty, 447 U.S. 303 (1980); State Street Bank & Trust Co. v. Signature Financial Group, Inc., 149 F.3d 1368 (Fed. Cir. 1998), *cert. denied*, 119 S.Ct. 851 (1999).
47. Lab Corps. v. Metabolite Laboratories, 548 U.S. 124, 126 (2006) (Breyer, J., dissenting from the dismissal of certiorari).
48. In this context, product market means the market for products, processes, and the products of processes.
49. *See, e.g.,* Fiona Murray et al., *Of Mice and Academics: Examining the Effect of Openness on Innovation*, Nat'l Bureau of Econ. Research Working Paper No. 14819 (2009), *available at* http://www.nber.org/papers/w14819; Kenneth G. Huang & Fiona E. Murray, *Does Patent Strategy Shape the Long-Run Supply of Public Knowledge? Evidence From Human Genetics*, 52 ACAD. MGMT. J. 1193–1221 (2009); Rebecca S. Eisenberg, *Bargaining Over the Transfer of Proprietary Research Tools: Is This Market Failing or Emerging?*, *in* EXPANDING THE BOUNDARIES OF INTELLECTUAL PROPERTY: INNOVATION POLICY FOR THE KNOWLEDGE SOCIETY (Rochelle Dreyfuss, Diane L. Zimmerman & Harry First eds., Oxford University Press 2001); Carlos M. Correa, *Internationalization of the Patent System and New Technologies*, 20 WIS. INT'L L.J. 523, 528 (2002).
50. Sec'y's Advisory Comm. on Genetics, Health, and Soc'y, Report on Gene Patents and Licensing Practices and Their Impact on Patient Access to Genetic Tests (2010), *available at* http://oba.od.nih.gov/oba/sacghs/reports/SACGHS_patents_report_2010.pdf [hereinafter SACGHS Report on Gene Patents]; Leahy-Smith America Invents Act, *supra* note 39, Sec. 27, 125 Stat. 338 (2011).
51. The SACGHS Report on Gene Patents considered the impact of product patents on isolated genes as well as the impact of process patents on associations between genes and

disease. For purposes of exposition, we limit our discussion to the effect of these proposals on product patents.
52. SACGHS Report on Gene Patents, *supra* note 50, at 97.
53. For a fuller summary of the provisions of the business exception regarding establishments that did not meet the space limits but might still be immune from liability, see Graeme B. Dinwoodie, *The Development and Incorporation of International Norms in the Formation of Copyright Law*, 62 OHIO STATE L.J. 733, 749–750 nn.65–66 (2001).
54. As we noted in Chapter 2, this interpretation was not likely a correct reflection of U.S. law. However, the panel decided the case on that basis.
55. Article 17 uses neither "normal exploitation of the work" nor "unreasonable prejudice" as reference points. It also includes an example of permissible use—absent in the other two provisions—which guided the panel's decision in *EC–GI*. *See EC–GI*, at ¶¶ 7.650 & 7.654. Furthermore, when asked to interpret the provision, the panel adopted a holistic interpretation of the provision, recognizing that the "second step" was in reality a qualification of the first. *Id.* at ¶ 7.649.
56. *Canada–Pharmaceuticals*, at ¶ 7.20; *US–110(5)*, at ¶ 6.74.
57. *Canada–Pharmaceuticals*, at ¶¶ 7.36 & 7.38.
58. *See, e.g.,* Barton Beebe, *An Empirical Study of U.S. Fair Use Opinions, 1978–2005*, 156 U. PA. L. REV. 549 (2008).
59. *Canada–Pharmaceuticals*, at ¶¶ 7.32–34, 7.44, 7.49; *US–110(5)*, at ¶¶ 6.131–133; *EC–GI*, at ¶ 7.651. The *Canada–Pharmaceuticals* panel did not, however, accept "that the curtailment of legal rights can be measured by *simply* counting the number of legal rights impaired by an exception." *Canada–Pharmaceuticals*, at ¶ 7.32 (emphasis added).
60. *Canada–Pharmaceuticals*, at ¶ 7.45.
61. *US–110(5)*, at ¶¶ 6.131–6.133.
62. *Id.* at ¶ 6.148.
63. *EC–GI*, at ¶¶ 7.651 & 7.657.
64. *Id.* at ¶ 7.648.
65. *US–110(5)*, at ¶¶ 6.131–6.133.
66. The *Canada–Pharmaceuticals* panel concluded that the first step in the three-step test did not require consideration of the economic impact of the defense because that concern was taken up by the second and third steps of the test. *Canada–Pharmaceuticals*, at ¶ 7.49; *see also US–110(5)*, at ¶¶ 6.113 & 6.131.
67. *Canada–Pharmaceuticals*, at ¶ 7.45.
68. *US–110(5)*, at ¶¶ 6.149 & 6.159.
69. *Canada–Pharmaceuticals*, at ¶ 7.55.
70. *US–110(5)*, at ¶¶ 6.167 & 6.196; *Canada–Pharmaceuticals*, at ¶ 7.54. The patent standard in Article 30 (but not the copyright equivalent in Article 13) allows such conflicts provided they are reasonable. It would thus appear to afford member states greater latitude on the second leg of the patent Exceptions test. But in both provisions, the permissible conflict is measured against the same norm, that is, "normal exploitation."
71. *US–110(5)*, at ¶ 6.166; *Canada–Pharmaceuticals*, at ¶ 7.54 ("The term ['normal'] can be understood to refer either to an empirical conclusion about what is common within a relevant community, or to a normative standard of entitlement. The Panel concluded that the word 'normal' was being used in Article 30 in a sense that combined the two meanings.").
72. *Canada–Pharmaceuticals*, at ¶ 7.59.
73. *Id.* at ¶ 7.57.
74. *See, e.g., US–110(5)*, at ¶ 6.208.
75. *Id.* at ¶¶ 6.180 & 6.187.
76. Jane C. Ginsburg, *Toward Supranational Copyright Law? The WTO Panel Decision and the "Three Step Test" for Copyright Exemptions*, 187 REVUE INTERNATIONALE DU DROIT D'AUTEUR 3, 17 (2001).
77. SACGHS Report on Gene Patents, *supra* note 50.

78. *Canada–Pharmaceuticals*, at ¶ 7.55.
79. *Id.* at ¶ 7.73; *US–110(5)*, at ¶¶ 6.224–6.227.
80. *US–110(5)*, at ¶ 6.227.
81. *Canada–Pharmaceuticals*, at ¶ 7.68.
82. *Id.* at ¶ 7.69.
83. *Id.* at ¶ 6.82.
84. *Id.* at ¶ 7.67.
85. *EC–GI*, at ¶ 7.648.
86. *Id.* at ¶ 7.662.
87. *Id.* at ¶ 7.648.
88. *Id.* at ¶ 7.676.
89. *Id.* at ¶ 7.674.
90. Convention on the Grant of European Patents, October 5, 1973, as revised by the Act of November 29, 2000, art. 53(c); Japanese Patent Act, art. 29-1; Patents Act 1977, § 4A(1)(b) (UK).
91. *Canada–Pharmaceuticals*, at ¶ 7.70 (citing MTN.GNG/NG11/W/76 of July 23, 1990, Status of Work in the Negotiating Group: Chairman's Report to the Group of Negotiations on Goods, Part III, Section 5, paragraph 2.2).
92. *See, e.g.*, Patents Act 1977, § 60(5)(b) (UK); Patent Act, § 11.2 (1998) (F.R.G.).
93. *Canada–Pharmaceuticals*, at ¶ 7.87.
94. *Id.* at ¶ 7.91.
95. *See* Chapter 4 (discussing the nature of structural provisions).
96. SACGHS was charged only with the task of making recommendations on gene patenting; thus it could not recommend a broader defense. However, it suggested that TRIPS compliance would require it. *See* SACGHS Report on Gene Patents, *supra* note 50, at 95.
97. *US–110(5)*, at ¶ 6.148. In *EC–GI*, the panel acknowledged that the number of right holders may not matter, *EC–GI*, ¶ at 7.650, but in that case, only a single right was affected; here, as in *US–110(5)*, several rights are implicated.
98. *See, e.g.*, Clarisa Long, *Patent Signals*, 69 U. CHI. L. REV. 625 (2002).
99. *See* Davidoff v. Gofkid, [2003] E.T.M.R. 42 (ECJ 2003).
100. Adidas-Salomon v. Fitnessworld Trading Ltd, 2003 E.C.R. I-12537 (ECJ 2003).
101. For a comparative discussion of harmonization efforts in the European Union and the United States, see HARMONIZATION OF LEGISLATION IN FEDERAL SYSTEMS: CONSTITUTIONAL, FEDERAL AND SUBSIDIARITY ASPECTS—THE EUROPEAN UNION AND THE UNITED STATES OF AMERIKA [sic] COMPARED (Ingolf Pernice ed., Juris Publishing 1996).
102. *See, e.g.*, Katherine J. Strandburg, *The Research Exemption to Patent Infringement: The Delicate Balance Between Current and Future Technical Progress*, in INTELLECTUAL PROPERTY AND INFORMATION WEALTH: ISSUES AND PRACTICES IN THE DIGITAL AGE 107 (Peter K. Yu ed., Praeger 2007); Daniel S. Hurwitz, *A Proposal in Hindsight: Restoring Copyright's Delicate Balance by Reworking 17 U.S.C. § 1201*, 2005 UCLA J. L. & TECH. 1; Maureen A. O'Rourke, *Striking a Delicate Balance: Intellectual Property, Antitrust, Contract, and Standardization in the Computer Industry*, 12 HARV. J.L. & TECH. 1 (1998).
103. Dreyfuss & Lowenfeld, *supra* note 2.
104. Laurence R. Helfer, *Adjudicating Copyright Claims Under the TRIPS Agreement: A Case for a European Human Rights Analogy*, 39 HARV. INT'L L.J. 357, 431 (1998).
105. *See, e.g.*, Martin Senftleben, *Towards a Horizontal Standard for Limiting Intellectual Property Rights? WTO Panel Reports Shed Light on the Three-Step Test in Copyright Law and Related Tests in Patent and Trademark Law*, 4 IIC 407 (2006); Ruth Okediji, *Toward an International Fair Use Doctrine*, 39 COLUM. J. TRANSNAT'L L. 75, 111 (2000).
106. *See* Max Planck Institute for Intellectual Property, Competition and Tax Law, *Declaration: A Balanced Interpretation of the "Three-Step Test" in Copyright Law* (April 2010), *available at* http://www.ip.mpg.de/ww/en/pub/news/declaration_on_the_three_step_/declaration.cfm.

107. *EC–GI*, at ¶ 7.654.
108. Of course, the reformulation of trade theory as grounded in comparative advantage (as opposed to the mere free flow of goods) has allowed international regulation a more ready justification for intruding upon purely local conditions. *See* Graeme B. Dinwoodie, *The International Intellectual Property System: Treaties, Norms, National Courts, and Private Ordering*, in Gervais, INTELLECTUAL PROPERTY, TRADE AND DEVELOPMENT, *supra* note 30, at 61, 78–80.
109. *Cf.* Mark A. Lemley & Carl Shapiro, *Patent Holdup and Royalty Stacking*, 85 TEX. L. REV. 1991 (2007); Carl Shapiro, *Navigating the Patent Thicket: Cross Licenses, Patent Pools, and Standard Setting*, in 1 INNOVATION POLICY AND THE ECONOMY 119, 120 (Adam B. Jaffe et al. eds., MIT Press 2001).
110. *See, e.g., NTP, Inc. v. Research in Motion, Ltd.*, 418 F.3d 1282 (Fed. Cir. 2005); Sannu K. Shrestha, *Trolls or Market-Makers: An Empirical Analysis of Nonpracticing Entities*, 110 COLUM. L. REV. 114 (2010).
111. 547 U.S. 388 (2006).
112. *Id.* at 391.
113. *Id.* at 396 (Kennedy, J., concurring).
114. *See, e.g.,* Greg R. Vetter, *Commercial Free and Open Source Software: Knowledge Production, Hybrid Appropriability, and Patents*, 77 FORDHAM L. REV. 2087 (2009). Open innovation works are not always placed in the public domain: to keep them freely available, they may be copyrighted and licensed under a contract that requires the user to maintain their accessibility.
115. Anselm Kamperman Sanders, *Standards Setting in the ICT Industry? IP or Competition Law? A Comparative Perspective*, in OS 10 ANOS DE INVESTIGAÇÃO DO CIJE—ESTUDOS JURÍDICO-ECONÓMICOS 105 (Glória Teixeira & Ana Sofia Carvalho eds., Almedina, Coimbra 2010).
116. 510 U.S. 569 (1994).
117. *Id.* at 578 n.10 (1994) (citations omitted). The TRIPS Agreement prohibits compulsory licensing of trademarks, *see* TRIPS, art. 21, even though competition authorities have over the years occasionally tried to impose such remedies. *See In re Borden*, 92 F.T.C. 669 (1976), *rev'd*, 92 F.T.C. 807 (1978). This prohibition reflects the sentiment that valid licensing of marks requires control of the licensee by the licensor, hardly the paradigm of a strong competition law remedy. However, some courts have been willing to consider extending *eBay*'s remedial standard as regards injunctive relief into the trademark context. *See, e.g., North American Medical Corp. v. Axiom Worldwide, Inc.*, 522 F.3d 1211 (11th Cir. 2008).
118. *China–Enforcement*, at ¶ 7.193.
119. *See Havana Club*, at ¶ 259 (citing Appellate Body Report, Chile-Taxes on Alcoholic Beverages, ¶ 74, WT/DS87/AB/R, WT/DS110/AB/R (2000)).
120. *China–Enforcement*, at ¶¶ 7.289–7.291.
121. *Id.* at ¶ 7.297.
122. *Id.* at ¶¶ 7.313 & 7.343.
123. *Id.* at ¶ 7.395(b).
124. This observation is supported by *Havana Club*. *See Havana Club*, at ¶¶ 215–216.
125. *China–Enforcement*, at ¶ 7.236; *see also Havana Club*, at ¶ 215 ("Making [civil judicial enforcement] available means making it 'obtainable', putting it 'within one's reach' and 'at one's disposal' in a way that has sufficient force or efficacy").
126. TRIPS, art. 41.5.
127. *See Salinger v. Colting*, 607 F.3d 68 (2d Cir. 2010); Sam Ricketson, *International Conventions and Treaties*, in THE BOUNDARIES OF COPYRIGHT 3, 14 (Libby Baulch, Michael Green & Mary Wyburn eds., Australian Copyright Council 1999). The analogous approach in trademark law would be analyzed under Article 21. But unlike Article 31, which conditions the grant of compulsory licenses, Article 21 prohibits compulsory licensing of trademarks. *See supra* note 117.

128. *See, e.g.,* Knowledge Ecology International, General Statement to the 15th Standing Committee on the Law of Patents (SCP) (October 12, 2010), *available at* http://keionline.org/node/975 ("Finally, KEI notes that the experts failed to distinguish between compulsory licenses that are granted under the procedures of Part II of the TRIPS, concerning patent rights, and those granted under Part III of the TRIPS, concerning the remedies for infringement of those rights.").
129. TRIPS, art. 31(h).
130. Ronald J. Mann, *Commercializing Open Source Software: Do Property Rights Still Matter?*, 20 HARV. J.L. & TECH. 1 (2006).
131. TRIPS, art. 31(b).
132. *China–Enforcement*, at ¶¶ 7.216–7.225 and ¶¶ 7.236, 7.366, & 7.279.
133. *See, e.g., id.* at ¶¶ 7.223, 7.237, & 7.504.
134. *See, e.g.,* Richard A. Epstein & A. Scott Kieff, *Questioning the Frequency and Wisdom of Compulsory Licensing for Pharmaceutical Patents*, 78 U. CHI. L. REV. 71 (2011).
135. Graeme B. Dinwoodie & Rochelle Cooper Dreyfuss, *International Intellectual Property Law and the Public Domain of Science*, 7 J. INT'L ECON. L. 431, 445 (2004); *see also* SOCIAL SCIENCE RESEARCH COUNCIL, MEDIA PIRACY IN EMERGING ECONOMIES 11–18 (Joe Karaganis ed., SSRC Books 2011) (suggesting ways of calculating losses tied to local realities).
136. Ricketson, *supra* note 127, at 5.
137. eBay Inc. v. MercExchange, 547 U.S. 388 (2006).
138. *See, e.g.,* International Intellectual Property Alliance, Re: Anti-Counterfeiting Trade Agreement (ACTA): Request for Public Comments, 73 Fed. Reg. 8910 (February 10, 2008), *available at* http://www.iipa.com/pdf/IIPAACTAlettertoUSTRfinal03212008.pdf.
139. For example, in a recent case against a website distributing music without authorization, the recording industry demanded damages that exceeded the GDP of the entire world; Sarah Jacobsson Purewal, *RIAA Thinks LimeWire Owes $75 Trillion in Damages*, PC WORLD, March 26, 2011, *available at* http://www.pcworld.com/article/223431/riaa_thinks_limewire_owes_75_trillion_in_damages.html. *See also* Joe Karaganis, *Rethinking Piracy, in* MEDIA PIRACY IN EMERGING ECONOMIES, *supra* note 135, at 1.
140. *Havana Club*, at ¶ 216.
141. *Id.* at ¶¶ 225–226.
142. *See* Robert Howse, *Comment*—China—Measures Affecting the Protection and Enforcement of Intellectual Property Rights, 10 WORLD TRADE REV. 87, 91 (2011).
143. *US–110(5)*, at ¶¶ 6.108, 6.110, 6.112, 6.165, 6.166, 6.223 & 6.225.
144. Festo Corp. v. Shoketsu Kinzoku Kogyo Kabushiki Co., Ltd., 535 U.S. 722, 731 (2002).
145. *US–110(5)*, at ¶¶ 6.62–6.66 (concluding that TRIPS incorporated the Berne acquis).
146. *Cf. id.* at ¶ 6.59 (rejecting the argument that the minor exceptions doctrine should be frozen as immunizing only those exceptions in national laws at the time of its adoption in 1967).
147. *See* Leahy-Smith America Invents Act, Pub. L. No. 112–29, Sec. 14, 125 Stat. 284, 327 (2011).
148. *US–110(5)*, at ¶ 6.67 (citing the WIPO Copyright Treaty).
149. *See, e.g., Havana Club*, at ¶¶ 138 & 145; *US–110(5)*, at ¶¶ 6.53–6.54; *China–Enforcement*, at ¶ 7.126.

Chapter 4

1. Appellate Body Report, United States—Section 211 Omnibus Appropriations Act of 1998, WT/DS176/AB/R (August 6, 2001) [hereinafter *Havana Club*] (national treatment and MFN issues); Panel Report, European Communities—Protection of Trademarks and Geographical Indications for Agricultural Products and Foodstuffs, WT/DS174/R (March 15, 2005) [hereinafter *EC–GI*] (national treatment issue).
2. Panel Report, Canada—Patent Protection of Pharmaceutical Products, WT/DS114/R (March 17, 2000) [hereinafter *Canada–Pharmaceuticals*].

3. Directive 96/9/EC of the European Parliament and of the Council of March 11, 1996, on the Legal Protection of Databases, 1996 O.J. (L 77) 20 [hereinafter Database Directive].
4. eBay Inc. v. MercExchange, L.L.C., 547 U.S. 388, 396 (2006) (Kennedy, J., concurring).
5. JAMES BESSEN & MICHAEL J. MEURER, PATENT FAILURE: HOW JUDGES, BUREAUCRATS, AND LAWYERS PUT INNOVATORS AT RISK (Princeton University Press 2008); ADAM B. JAFFE & JOSH LERNER, INNOVATION AND ITS DISCONTENTS (Princeton University Press 2004).
6. UNITED STATES PATENT AND TRADEMARK OFFICE, PATENT TECHNOLOGY MONITORING TEAM, U.S. PATENT STATISTICS CHART, CALENDAR YEARS 1963–2009 (showing that the number of U.S. patent applications has quadrupled over a forty-six-year period, with foreign applications multiplying nearly twelvefold).
7. Paris Convention for the Protection of Industrial Property, July 14, 1967, art. 4, 21 U.S.T. 1583, 828 U.N.T.S. 305 [hereinafter Paris Convention].
8. Patent Cooperation Treaty, June 19, 1970, 28 U.S.T. 7645, 1160 U.N.T.S. 231.
9. *See* Trilateral (EPO, JPO, USPTO), Strategic Handling of Applications for Rapid Examination—SHARE, *available at* http://www.trilateral.net/projects/worksharing/share.html (last visited April 4, 2011). *See also* United States Patent and Trademark Office, Enhanced Examination Timing Control Initiative; Notice of Public Meeting, 75 Fed. Reg. 31763 (June 4, 2010); Lily J. Ackerman, *Prioritization: Addressing the Patent Application Backlog at the United States Patent and Trademark Office*, 26 BERKELEY TECH. L.J. 67 (2011) *available at* http://ssrn.com/abstract=1795408.
10. Todd R. Farnsworth & Michael A. Sartori, *USPTO Proposes Mandatory Examination Delay for Foreign Priority Applications*, 25 WORLD INTELL. PROP. REP. (BNA) No. 2 (December 21, 2010).
11. TRIPS, art. 3 & note 3 (providing that national treatment and MFN apply to the acquisition of rights, not merely their enjoyment). *See Havana Club*, at ¶ 243.
12. *See, e.g.*, Robert E. Hudec, *GATT/WTO Constraints on National Regulation: Requiem for an "Aim and Effects" Test*, 32 INT'L LAW. 619 (1998) (discussing adjudication under the General Agreement on Tariffs and Trade, October 30, 1947, 61 Stat. A-11, TIAS 1700, 55 UNTS. 194).
13. General Agreement on Tariffs and Trade 1994, April 15, 1994, arts. III & XX, Marrakesh Agreement Establishing the World Trade Organization, Annex 1A, LEGAL INSTRUMENTS—RESULTS OF THE URUGUAY ROUND, vol. 31, 1867 U.N.T.S. 187, 33 I.L.M. 1154 (1994) [hereinafter GATT].
14. *See Havana Club*; *EC–GI*. In addition, one case raised a national treatment claim under TRIPS, but it was somewhat peripheral to the principal dispute and barely addressed by the DSB. *See* Panel Report, Indonesia—Certain Measures Affecting the Automobile Industry, ¶¶ 14.264–14.279, WT/DS54/R, WT/DS55/R, WT/DS59/R, WT DS64R (July 2, 1998).
15. *See Havana Club*, at ¶ 253.
16. *Id.* at ¶ 241.
17. *Id.* at ¶¶ 256 & 268.
18. TRIPS, arts. 22–24 (permitting protection through trademark and unfair competition law).
19. *EC–GI*, at ¶ 7.406.
20. *Id.* at ¶ 7.428.
21. Presumably, this is one of the benefits of the one-year priority period that the Paris Convention, Article 4C(1), provides applicants filing successive applications.
22. Panel Report, United States—Section 337 of the Tariff Act of 1930, L/6439 (November 7, 1989) [hereinafter *US–337*].
23. Hudec, *supra note* 12, at 622–623 & 633–634.
24. *Id.* at 631; *see also* Henrik Horn & Petros C. Mavroidis, *Still Hazy After All These Years: The Interpretation of National Treatment in the GATT/WTO Case-Law on Tax Discrimination*, 15 EUR. J. INT'L L. 39, 40 (2004).

Notes to Pages 88–92

25. Hudec, *supra* note 12, at 631 (citing Appellate Body Report, Japan—Taxes on Alcoholic Beverages, WT/DS8/AB/R, WT/DS10/AB/R, WT/DS11/AB/R (October 4, 1996) (adopted November. 1, 1996)).
26. Appellate Body Report, Korea—Taxes on Alcoholic Beverages, at ¶ 150, WT/DS75/AB/R, WT/DS84/AB/R (January 18, 1999) [hereinafter *Korea-Taxes*].
27. *Havana Club*, at ¶¶ 242 & 262.
28. *See, e.g., EC–GI*, at ¶¶ 7.433–7.463.
29. *Id.* at ¶¶ 7.133 & 7.135. *See also Canada–Pharmaceuticals*, at ¶ 7.98 (applying these cases to the interpretation of TRIPS, art. 27.1).
30. GATT, art. XX(d).
31. Appellate Body Report, India—Patent Protection for Pharmaceutical and Agricultural Chemical Products, ¶ 59, WT/DS50/AB/R (December 19, 1997) [hereinafter *India–Pharmaceuticals*].
32. World Trade Organization, Ministerial Declaration of November 20, 2001, ¶ 17, WT/MIN(01)/DEC/1, 41 I.L.M. 746 (2002) [hereinafter Ministerial Declaration].
33. *Korea-Taxes*, at ¶ 150.
34. *EC–GI*, at ¶ 7.194 (emphasis added).
35. Indeed, the United States does not permit an applicant to file a foreign patent application on an invention made in the United States until six months after filing a U.S. application, unless the applicant receives authorization from the Commissioner (now Director) of Patents. *See* 35 U.S.C. § 184 (2000); 37 CFR § 5.11 (2005). An applicant must similarly acquire a license if no patent application is made in the United States. Furthermore, for U.S. inventions, a patent application is "considered to include a petition for a license," 37 CFR § 5.12 (2005), thus making it even more convenient for U.S. inventors to file first in the United States.
36. For example, John Allison and Mark Lemley examined 1,000 patents filed between 1996 and 1998. They found that of the 460 originating outside the United States, 394 claimed priority based on a foreign application. Thus, approximately one in seven foreigners filed first in the United States. *See* John R. Allison & Mark A. Lemley, *Who's Patenting What? An Empirical Exploration of Patent Prosecution*, 53 Vand. L. Rev. 2099, 2119–2120 (2000).
37. France, for example, appears to require domestic inventors to file first in France. *See* Code de la Propriété Intellectuelle [Intellectual Property Code], Livre VI: Protection des inventions et des connaissances techniques, arts. L.612-8 to L.612-10; L.614-2 and L.614-18 (Fr.).
38. *See, e.g.,* Joel P. Trachtman, *Regulatory Jurisdiction and the WTO*, 10 J. Int'l Econ. L. 631 (2007).
39. *Cf.* Belgian Family Allowances (Allocations Familiales), G/32-1S/59, at ¶ 3 (Report adopted November 7, 1952) (holding that Belgium could not make a tax exemption "dependent on certain conditions" of a foreign law); Appellate Body Report, United States—Import Prohibition of Certain Shrimp and Shrimp Products, Recourse to Article 21.5 of the DSU by Malaysia, ¶ 144, WT/DS58/AB/RW (October 22, 2001) (permitting the United States to "condition[] market access on the [complainant's] adoption of a programme comparable in effectiveness" to the U.S. regulatory regime for shrimp fishing).
40. *Cf.* Panel Report, China—Measures Affecting the Protection and Enforcement of Intellectual Property Rights, ¶ 7.513, WT/DS362/R (January 26, 2009) (giving China a margin of appreciation in how it structures remedies).
41. *See, e.g.,* TRIPS, arts. 66.2, 67, & 69.
42. *Cf.* 35 U.S.C. § 154(d); 35 U.S.C. § 154(c).
43. Paris Convention, arts. 4A(1) & C(1).
44. TRIPS, art. 65.
45. *India–Pharmaceuticals*, at ¶ 45. The AB suggested that the United States was effectively seeking to assimilate approaches to GATT non-violation complaints into the analysis of violation claims at a time when (as is still the case) TRIPS does not authorize the bringing of non-violation complaints. *See id.* at ¶ 42.

46. *Id.* at ¶ 59 (citing TRIPS, art. 1.1).
47. *Id.* at ¶ 66.
48. Paris Convention, art. 4B.
49. *See, e.g., In re* Hilmer, 359 F.2d 859 (CCPA 1966) (holding that the foreign priority date applies only to the question whether a patent can issue, not to whether it can be used as prior art).
50. 499 U.S. 340 (1991).
51. Commission of the European Communities, DG Internal Market and Services Working Paper, First Evaluation of Directive 96/9/EC on the Legal Protection of Databases, at 7 (December 12, 2005); Commission Proposal for a Directive of the Council on the Legal Protection of Databases, COM (92) 24 final, at ¶¶ 1.4, 2.1.3, 2.1.6, 2.1.23, and 2.3–2.3.5 (May 13, 1992).
52. Database Directive, *supra* note 3.
53. Paris Convention, art. 10bis(1).
54. *Id.* art. 10bis(2).
55. Jerome H. Reichman, *Universal Minimum Standards of Intellectual Property Protection Under the TRIPS Component of the WTO Agreement*, 29 INT'L LAW. 345, 350 (1995).
56. *Havana Club*, at ¶ 328.
57. *Id.* at ¶¶ 336 & 338.
58. *Id.* at ¶ 339.
59. *But see* Graeme B. Dinwoodie, *Copyright Lawmaking Authority: An (Inter)Nationalist Perspective on the Treaty Clause*, 30 COLUM. J. L. & ARTS, 355 (2007).
60. *EC–GI*, at ¶ 7.664.
61. *See, e.g.,* Steele v. Bulova Watch Co., 344 U.S. 280 (1952); Vanity Fair Mills, Inc. v. T. Eaton Co., 234 F.2d 633 (2d Cir. 1956); General Motors Corp. v. Ignacio Lopez de Arriortua, 948 F. Supp. 684 (E.D. Mich. 1996).
62. *See, e.g.,* Goldstein v. California, 412 U.S. 546 (1973) (copyright preemption); National Basketball Association v. Motorola, Inc., 105 F.3d 841(1997) (same); Bonito Boats, Inc. v. Thunder Craft Boats, Inc., 489 U.S. 141 (1989) (patent preemption).
63. *See, e.g.,* Joined Cases C-92/92 and C-326/92, Phil Collins v. Imtrat Handelsgesellschaft mbH v. EMI Electora GmbH, 1993 E.C.R. I-5145; Case 158/86, Warner Bros Inc. and Metronome Video ApS v. Erik Viuff Christiansen, 1988 E.C.R. 2605.
64. *India–Pharmaceuticals,* at ¶ 45.
65. *Cf.* DG Internal Market and Services Working Paper, *supra* note 51 (discussing implementation of the Database Directive within the European Union).
66. 17 U.S.C. §§ 901–914 (1994). Under §§ 902 and 914, countries merely had to make good faith efforts to adopt legislation on "substantially the same basis" as U.S. law.
67. Peter K. Yu, *Currents and Crosscurrents in the International Intellectual Property Regime,* 38 LOY. L.A. L. REV. 323, 377 (2004).
68. TRIPS, arts. 35–38.
69. *See, e.g.,* General Motors Corp. v. Ignacio Lopez de Arriortua, *supra* note 61.
70. Carlos M. Correa, *Protecting Test Data for Pharmaceutical and Agrochemical Products Under Free Trade Agreements, in* NEGOTIATING HEALTH: INTELLECTUAL PROPERTY AND ACCESS TO MEDICINES 81 (Pedro Roffe, Geoff Tansey & David Vivas-Eugui eds., Earthscan 2006).
71. DEV GANGJEE, RELOCATING THE LAW OF GEOGRAPHICAL INDICATIONS (Cambridge University Press. 2012) (forthcoming).
72. TRIPS, arts. 23.4 & 24.2.
73. *See* Diamond v. Chakrabarty, 447 U.S. 303 (1980).
74. *Id.* at 318; Bilski v. Kappos, 130 S.Ct. 3218 (2010).
75. *EC–GI,* at ¶ 7.130.
76. *See* Miriam Bitton, *Exploring European Union Copyright Policy Through the Lens of the Database Directive,* 23 BERKELEY TECH. L.J. 1411, 1468–1469 (2008).

77. It is possible that the Directive would be regarded as facially discriminatory for national treatment purposes based on the text of Article 11, but as nominally treating nationals of different foreign countries alike—prompting any MFN claim to be grounded in de facto discrimination. *See* Database Directive, *supra* note 3, art. 11.
78. *Cf.* Appellate Body Report, Canada—Certain Measures Affecting the Automotive Industry, ¶ 85, WT/DS139/AB/R, WT/DS142/AB/R (May 31, 2000).
79. *See, e.g.,* TRIPS, arts. 66, 67, & 69.
80. TRIPS, arts. 22 & 23.
81. *See, e.g.,* Frontiero v. Richardson, 411 U.S. 677 (1973); Theunis Roux, *Principle and Pragmatism on the Constitutional Court of South Africa*, 7 INT'L J. CONST. L. 106 (2009).
82. *See* Graeme B. Dinwoodie, *The Development and Incorporation of International Norms in the Formation of Copyright Law*, 62 OHIO ST. L.J. 733 (2001) (suggesting that panels consider whether challenged laws are a rational means, or a particularly appropriate, or a well-tailored means, or the least burdensome means, of achieving a particular goal).
83. *Havana Club*, at ¶ 132 (quoting Article 6.1 of the Paris Convention).
84. Council Regulation 510/2006 on the Protection of Geographical Indications and Designations of Origin for Agricultural Products and Foodstuffs, art. 5.9, 2006 O.J. (L 93) 12, 16.
85. In *Havana Club*, the AB did note that the discrimination was on the face of the measure, *Havana Club*, at ¶¶ 267 & 309; the panel in *EC–GI* similarly used that phrase, *see, e.g., EC–GI*, at ¶¶ 7.62, 7.114, & 7.151.
86. Hudec, *supra* note 12, at 621.
87. *Id.* at 633.
88. *See* Commission Proposal for a Directive of the Council on the Legal Protection of Databases, *supra* note 51, at 4.
89. *See, e.g.,* UNITED STATES PATENT AND TRADEMARK OFFICE, 2007–2012 STRATEGIC PLAN (May 1, 2007), *available at* http://www.uspto.gov/web/offices/com/strat2007/stratplan2007-2012.pdf.
90. *Havana Club*, at ¶ 297.
91. *Id.* at ¶¶ 304–308
92. *See, e.g.,* GATT, art. XXIV; General Agreement on Trade in Services, April 15, 1994, art. II.2, Marrakesh Agreement Establishing the World Trade Organization, Annex 1B, 1869 U.N.T.S. 183, 33 I.L.M. 1125, 1167 (1994) [hereinafter GATS].
93. Peter Sutherland et al., Report by the Consultative Board to the Director-General Supachai Panitchpakdi, *The Future of the WTO: Addressing Institutional Challenges in the New Millennium*, ¶ 60 (2004), *available at* http://www.wto.org/English/thewto_e/10anniv_e/future_wto_e.pdf.
94. Henrik Horn & Petros C. Mavroidis, *Economic and Legal Aspects of the Most-Favoured-Nation Clause*, 17 EUR. J. POL. ECON. 233, 234 (2001).
95. *Id.* at 265–268.
96. ALCIDE DARRAS, DU DROIT DES AUTEURS ET DES ARTISTES DANS LES RAPPORTS INTERNATIONAUX 555 (Paris 1887) ("un emprunt malheureux"), *cited in* 1 SAM RICKETSON & JANE C. GINSBURG, INTERNATIONAL COPYRIGHT AND NEIGHBOURING RIGHTS: THE BERNE CONVENTION AND BEYOND ¶ 1.42 at 38 (2d ed. Oxford University Press 2005).
97. Frederick M. Abbott, *Toward a New Era of Objective Assessment in the Field of TRIPS and Variable Geometry for the Preservation of Multilateralism*, 8 J. INT'L ECON. L. 77, 97 (2005).
98. We return to the question of MFN and bilaterals in Chapter 6.
99. *See* GATT, art. XXIV; TRIPS, art. 4(a)–(d). Subsections (b) and (d) of Article 4 are both grandfathering provisions.
100. *Canada–Pharmaceuticals*, at ¶ 7.91. *See also id.* at ¶ 7.98 (applying GATT Article III jurisprudence to the TRIPS Article 27.1 claim).
101. *Id.* at ¶ 4.6 n.27.
102. *See* Chapter 2.
103. *Canada–Pharmaceuticals*, at ¶¶ 7.94–7.105.

104. *Id.* at ¶ 7.98.
105. *Id.*
106. LIONEL A. BENTLY & BRAD SHERMAN, THE MAKING OF MODERN INTELLECTUAL PROPERTY LAW (Cambridge University Press 2008).
107. *Canada–Pharmaceuticals*, at ¶ 7.105.
108. Bilski v. Kappos, 130 S.Ct. 3218, 3258 (2010) (Breyer, J., concurring).
109. *Cf. Canada–Pharmaceuticals*, at ¶ 7.104. While we suggest that in national treatment cases, de jure discrimination is a per se violation, there are costs to invalidating these laws so quickly, especially with regard to rights that are covered by Article 3, but not the substantive provisions of the Agreement. If states are to be encouraged to serve as laboratories, there are benefits in allowing them to limit their exposure to the cost of mistakes. For example, many states are testing alternative forms of protection for folklore and traditional knowledge, *see* Daniel J. Gervais, *TRIPS, Doha, and Traditional Knowledge*, 6 J. WORLD INTELL. PROP. 403 (2003) (suggesting folklore and traditional knowledge are within the scope of "intellectual property" under Article 3); an argument could be made that even if they provide rights only to their own indigenous populations, they should be allowed to do so as a way to minimize the costs of experimentation.
110. WIPO Copyright Treaty, December 20, 1996, Preamble, 2186 U.N.T.S. 121, 36 I.L.M. 65 (1997).
111. *See* Ministerial Declaration; *see also* World Trade Organization, Declaration on the TRIPS Agreement and Public Health, WT/MIN(01)/DEC/2, November 20, 2001, 41 I.L.M. 755 (2002).
112. Ministerial Declaration ¶ 17 (on health) and ¶ 19 (providing that the TRIPS Council should be guided "by the objectives and principles set out in Articles 7 and 8").
113. *Canada–Pharmaceuticals*, at ¶¶ 7.25–7.26.
114. *See supra* notes 40 & 46.
115. *China–Enforcement*, at ¶ 7.513.
116. Paris Convention, art. 4bis (patents) and art. 6 (trademarks).
117. *See, e.g.*, Stephen P. Ladas, *The Position Against Adherence: The Madrid Agreement for the International Registration of Trademarks and the United States*, 56 TRADEMARK REP. 346 (1966) (discussing an attempt by France to impose its automatic registration system on a worldwide basis).
118. *Cf.* L'Oreal SA v. Bellure BV, [2006] E.C.D.R. 16 Cour d'Appel, Paris) (Fr.); Lancôme Parfums et Beauté et cie S.N.C. v. Kecofa BV, [2005] E.C.D.R. 5 (Ct. App., Den Bosch, 2004), *aff'd*, [2006] E.C.D.R. 26 (Supreme Court) (Neth.).
119. *But see* LAWRENCE LESSIG, FREE CULTURE 287–292 (Penguin 2004).
120. *See e.g.*, Knowledge Ecology International, General Statement to the Fifteenth Standing Committee on the Law of Patents (SCP) (October 12, 2010), *available at* http://keionline.org/node/975 ("Finally, KEI notes that the experts failed to distinguish between compulsory licenses that are granted under the procedures of Part II of the TRIPS, concerning patent rights, and those granted under Part III of the TRIPS, concerning the remedies for infringement of those rights.").
121. *See, e.g.*, Proposed Amendments to TRIPS, art. 8a(2), *in* INTELLECTUAL PROPERTY IN A FAIR WORLD TRADE SYSTEM: PROPOSALS FOR REFORMING THE TRIPS AGREEMENT (Annette Kur ed., Edward Elgar 2011).

Chapter 5

1. Jessica D. Litman, *Copyright, Compromise, and Legislative History*, 72 CORNELL L. REV. 857, 860–861 (1986–1987).
2. Panel Report, United States—Section 110(5) of the U.S. Copyright Act, WT/DS/160/R (June 15, 2000) [hereinafter *US–110(5)*].

3. Sonny Bono Copyright Term Extension Act, Pub. L. No. 105-298, 112 Stat. 2827 (1998).
4. 35 U.S.C. § 156 (2002).
5. 35 U.S.C. § 271(e) (2003).
6. Drug Price Competition and Patent Term Registration Act of 1984, Pub. L. No. 98-417, 98 Stat. 1585 (1984).
7. Panel Report, Canada—Patent Protection of Pharmaceutical Products, ¶¶ 7.78–7.79 & 7.82, WT/DS114/R (March 17, 2000) [hereinafter *Canada–Pharmaceuticals*].
8. Eldred v. Ashcroft, 537 U.S. 186, 205–206 (2003).
9. *Cf.* MARGARET E. KECK & KATHRYN SIKKINK, ACTIVISTS WITHOUT BORDERS: ADVOCACY NETWORKS IN INTERNATIONAL POLITICS (Cornell University Press 1998).
10. General Agreement on Tariffs and Trade, October 30, 1947, art. XX, 61 Stat A-11, TIAS 1700, 55 U.N.T.S. 194 (1947) [hereinafter GATT].
11. GATT, art. XXVIII.2 (providing, in part, that "the contracting parties concerned shall endeavour to maintain a general level of reciprocal and mutually advantageous concessions not less favourable to trade than that provided for in this Agreement prior to such negotiations."). The GATS Agreement, General Agreement on Trade in Services, April 15, 1994, Marrakesh Agreement Establishing the World Trade Organization, Annex 1B, 1869 U.N.T.S. 183, 33 I.L.M. 1125, 1168 (1994), has similar flexibilities: Article II.2 permits exemptions to MFN; Article X envisions negotiations over emergency safeguard provisions; and Article XIV contains general exceptions.
12. Warren F. Schwartz & Alan O. Sykes, *The Economic Structure of Renegotiation and Dispute Resolution in the World Trade Organization*, 31 J. LEGAL STUD. 179, 184 (2002).
13. *See* Kyle Bagwell, Petros C. Mavroidis & Robert W. Staiger, *It's a Question of Market Access*, 96 AM. J. INT'L L. 56 (2002).
14. Of course, if the TRIPS Agreement were modified to include substantive maxima, or users' rights, this analysis might change. We discuss the development of users' rights in Chapter 7.
15. *See* Laura J. Robinson, *Analysis of Recent Proposals to Reconfigure Hatch-Waxman*, 11 J. INTELL. PROP. L. 47 (2003).
16. Bilski v. Kappos, 130 S. Ct. 3218 (2010).
17. As we discuss later in the context of external trade-offs, it is not inconceivable that an expressio unius est exclusio alterius argument would be invoked to counter this line of reasoning, given instances in the Agreement where the text expressly allows members to choose the regime by which to implement specific obligations. However, we argue that there is a eusdem generis rebuttal to that: those instances highlight a context where such choice is most important, namely, where international protections are in flux. *See infra* text accompanying notes 24–28.
18. *See* Yochai Benkler, *A Political Economy of the Public Domain: Markets in Innovation Goods Versus the Marketplace of Ideas, in* EXPANDING THE BOUNDARIES OF INTELLECTUAL PROPERTY: INNOVATION POLICY FOR THE KNOWLEDGE SOCIETY 267, 291–292 (Rochelle Cooper Dreyfuss, Harry First & Diane L. Zimmerman eds., Oxford University Press 2001).
19. *See* 35 U.S.C. §§171–173.
20. *See* Ralph S. Brown, *Design Protection: An Overview*, 34 UCLA L. Rev. 1341, 1344–1357 (1987). Many commentators believe that the Federal Circuit's decision in *Egyptian Goddess, Inc. v. Swisa, Inc.*, 543 F.3d 665, 678–679 (Fed. Cir. 2008) (en banc) may have breathed new life into design patent protection. Taken with the reinvigoration of limits on trade dress protection effected by the U.S. Supreme Court in *Wal-Mart Stores, Inc. v. Samara Bros., Inc.*, 525 U.S. 205 (2000) and *TrafFix Devices, Inc. v. Marketing Displays, Inc.*, 532 U.S. 23 (2001), the question whether design patent or trade dress law may provide more effective protection may be closer than it has been for some time.
21. By "fresh investments," we do not mean to suggest that the need to make application to receive protection rather than receive automatic protection should of itself preclude the alternative form of protection from satisfying TRIPS obligations (unless the Agreement specifically mandated protection without formalities, such as the Berne Convention does for copyright).

22. The main provisions are in the Patent Act, 35 U.S.C. §§ 156 and 271(e). However, provisions regarding the way in which generic producers challenge patents are to receive compensation for such challenges are found in 21 U.S.C. § 355. *See generally* Alfred B. Engelberg, *Special Patent Provisions for Pharmaceuticals: Have They Outlived Their Usefulness?*, 39 IDEA 389 (1999).
23. Appellate Body Report, United States—Section 211 Omnibus Appropriations Act of 1998, WT/DS176/AB/R (August 6, 2001) [hereinafter *Havana Club*]. *See also* Panel Report, Indonesia—Certain Measures Affecting the Automobile Industry, WT/DS54/R, WT/DS55/R, WT/DS59/R, WT/DS64/R (July 2, 1998) (examining whether Indonesia's National Car Programme, which benefited only cars bearing Indonesian trademarks, violated Articles 3, 20, and 65 of the TRIPS Agreement).
24. *See* TRIPS, arts. 23 n.4, 27(3)(b).
25. *See, e.g.,* Thomas Pogge, *The Health Impact Fund: Better Pharmaceutical Innovations at Much Lower Prices, in* INCENTIVES FOR GLOBAL PUBLIC HEALTH: PATENT LAW AND ACCESS TO ESSENTIAL MEDICINES 135 (Thomas Pogge, Matthew Rimmer & Kim Rubenstein eds., Cambridge University Press 2010); Steven Shavell & Tanguy van Ypersele, *Rewards Versus Intellectual Property Rights*, 44 J. L. & ECON. 525 (2001).
26. *See, e.g.,* Clarisa Long, *Patent Signals*, 69 U. CHI. L. REV. 625 (2002); Robert P. Merges, *Contracting into Liability Rules: Intellectual Property Rights and Collective Rights Organizations*, 84 CAL. L. REV. 1293 (1996).
27. *See, e.g.,* TRIPS, art. 41.5.
28. *See id.* arts. 23.1 & 27.3.
29. *Canada–Pharmaceuticals*, at ¶ 4.41.
30. Understanding on Rules and Procedures Governing the Settlement of Disputes, April 15, 1994, art. 22, Marrakesh Agreement Establishing the World Trade Organization, Annex 2, LEGAL INSTRUMENTS—RESULTS OF THE URUGUAY ROUND, vol. 31, 1869 U.N.T.S. 401, 33 I.L.M. 1226 (1994); Report of Arbitrators, United States—Section 110(5) of the U.S. Copyright Act—Recourse to Arbitration under Article 25 of the DSU, WT/DS160/ARB25/1 (November 9, 2001); Report of Arbitrators, EC—Regime for the Importation, Sale and Distribution of Bananas—Recourse to Arbitration by the EC under Article 22.6 of the DSU, WT/DS27/ARB/ECU (March 24, 2000).
31. United States—Section 337 of the Tariff Act of 1930, L/6439-36S/345 (November 7, 1989) [hereinafter *US-337*].
32. *Id.* at ¶ 5.12.
33. *Id.* at ¶ 5.14.
34. *Havana Club*, at ¶¶ 294, 317.
35. *See supra* note 30.
36. *See* John H. Jackson, *International Law Status of WTO Dispute Settlement Reports: Obligation to Comply or Option to "Buy Out,"* 98 AM. J. INT'L L. 109 (2004).
37. Appellate Body Report, India—Patent Protection for Pharmaceutical and Agricultural Chemical Products, ¶ 45, WT/DS50/AB/R (December 19, 1997) [hereinafter *India–Pharmaceuticals*].
38. JOSEPH SCHUMPETER, CAPITALISM, SOCIALISM AND DEMOCRACY (HarperCollins 2008) (original publication 1942).
39. GATT, art. XIX.1(a) (providing, in part, that "[i]f, as a result of unforeseen developments and of the effect of the obligations incurred by a contracting party under this Agreement ... any product is being imported into the territory of that contracting party in such increased quantities and under such conditions as to cause or threaten serious injury to domestic producers ... the contracting party shall be free ... to suspend the obligation in whole or in part or to withdraw or modify the concession."). *See also* Agreement on Safeguards, April 15, 1994; WTO Agreement, Annex 1A, 33 I.L.M. 112 (1994) (intending to clarify the application of Article XIX).
40. Andrew T. Guzman, *Global Governance and the WTO*, 45 HARV. INT'L L.J. 303, 346–347 (2004).

41. See Chapter 4.
42. 17 U.S.C. § 111 (1999); see also 17 U.S.C. § 119 (2002) (covering satellite retransmissions).
43. For example, at the birth of cable television, broadcasters and content providers claimed that copyright incentives would be reduced if retransmission was permitted; see, e.g., STAFF OF HOUSE COMM. ON THE JUDICIARY, 89TH CONG., COPYRIGHT LAW REVISION PART 6: SUPPLEMENTARY REPORT OF THE REGISTER OF COPYRIGHTS ON THE GENERAL REVISION OF THE U.S. COPYRIGHT LAW: 1965 REVISION BILL (Comm. Print 1965), yet in a sense, cable would improve incentives by widening the markets for the protected works.
44. See, e.g., Memorandum Opinion and Order on Reconsideration of Cable Television Report and Order, FCC 72-108, 36 F.C.C.2d 143 (1972), reconsideration granted in part by FCC 72-530, 36 F.C.C.2d 326; Timothy Wu, Copyright's Communications Policy, 103 MICH. L. REV. 278 (2004).
45. See REPORT OF THE REGISTER OF COPYRIGHTS, SATELLITE HOME VIEWER EXTENSION AND REAUTHORIZATION ACT SECTION 109 REPORT, xiv (June 2008), available at http://www.copyright.gov/reports/section109-final-report.pdf.
46. See Directive 2001/29/EC on the Harmonisation of Certain Aspects of Copyright and Related Rights in the Information Society, art. 5.2(b), 2001 O.J. (L 167) 10.
47. See Gunnar Karnell, The Berne Convention Between Authors' Rights and Copyright Economics—An International Dilemma, 26 IIC 193, 212 (1995).
48. Canada–Pharmaceuticals, at ¶ 7.55 (analyzing the analogous provision in Article 30); US–110(5), at ¶ 6.183.
49. See 17 U.S.C. §§ 1201–1203 (2010); see also BRUCE A. LEHMAN, WORKING GROUP ON INTELLECTUAL PROP. RIGHTS, INFO. INFRASTRUCTURE TASK FORCE, INTELLECTUAL PROPERTY AND THE NATIONAL INFORMATION INFRASTRUCTURE 230 (1995), available at http://www.uspto.gov/web/offices/com/doc/ipnii/ipnii.pdf.
50. See City Studios, Inc. v. Corley, 273 F.3d 429 (2d Cir. 2001). But see Lexmark Int'l, Inc. v. Static Control Components, Inc., 387 F.3d 522 (6th Cir. 2004); Chamberlain Group, Inc. v. Skylink Techs., Inc., 381 F.3d 1178 (Fed. Cir. 2004).
51. See, e.g., Debra P. Steger, Afterword: The "Trade and . . . " Conundrum—A Commentary, 96 AM J. INT'L L. 135, 137–138 (2002).
52. Appellate Body Report, United States—Definitive Safeguard Measures on Imports of Certain Steel Products, WT/DS248/AB/R, WT/DS249/AB/R, WT/DS251/AB/R, WT/DS252/AB/R, WT/DS253/AB/R, WT/DS254/AB/R, WT/DS258/AB/R, WT/DS259/AB/R, AB-2003-3 (December 10, 2003) [hereinafter US–Steel Safeguard Measures].
53. See, e.g., Raj Bhala & David A Gantz, WTO Case Review 2003, 21 ARIZ. J. INT'L & COMP. L. 317, 401 (2004).
54. GATS Agreement, art. II.2; List of MFN Exemptions, available at http://tsdb.wto.org/selection.
55. US–Steel Safeguard Measures, at ¶ 340.
56. See Ruth L. Okediji, The International Relations of Intellectual Property: Narratives of Developing Country Participation in the Global Intellectual Property System, 7 SING. J. INT'L & COMP. L. 315, 374–375 (2003).
57. Maria Auxiliadora Oliveira et al., Has the Implementation of the TRIPS Agreement in Latin America and the Caribbean Produced Intellectual Property Legislation That Favours Public Health?, 82 BULL. WORLD HEALTH ORG. 813 (2004).
58. Margaret Chon, Intellectual Property "From Below": Copyright and Capability for Education, 40 U.C. DAVIS L. REV. 803, 829 (2007); Jillian C. Cohen-Kohler, The Morally Uncomfortable Global Drug Gap, 82 CLINICAL PHARMACOLOGY & THERAPEUTICS 610 (2007).
59. See generally Daniel Benoliel & Bruno Salama, Towards an Intellectual Property Bargaining Theory: The Post-WTO Era, 32 U. PA. J. INT'L L. 265 (2010); Gregory Shaffer, Michelle Ratton Sanchez & Barbara Rosenberg, The Trials of Winning at the WTO: What Lies Behind

Brazil's Success, 41 CORNELL INT'L L.J. 383 (2008); Peter K. Yu, *Access to Medicines, BRICS Alliances, and Collective Action*, 34 AM. J.L. & MED. 345 (2008).
60. See Jerome H. Reichman, *Intellectual Property in the Twenty-First Century: Will the Developing Countries Lead or Follow?*, 46 HOUS. L. REV. 1115 (2009).
61. See Amy Kapczynski, *Harmonization and Its Discontents: A Case Study of TRIPS Implementation in India's Pharmaceutical Sector*, 97 CALIF. L. REV. 1571, 1617–1622 (2009).
62. Kamal Saggi & Joel P. Trachtman, *Incomplete Harmonization Contracts in International Economic Law: Report of the Panel*, China—Measures Affecting Protection and Enforcement of Intellectual Property Rights, *WT/DS362/R, adopted March 20, 2009*, 10 WORLD TRADE REV. 1, 8 & 11 (2010).
63. *Cf.* Schwartz & Sykes, *supra* note 12, at 198 & 201 (noting that clarification of the WTO agreements through dispute resolution is an important public good, which must be paid for by the parties to the dispute).
64. Omnibus Trade and Competitiveness Act of 1989, Pub. L. No. 100–418, 102 Stat. 1176–1179; 19 U.S.C. § 2242.
65. See e.g., Peter Drahos, *BITs and BIPS: Bilateralism in Intellectual Property*, 4 J. WORLD INTELL. PROP. 791 (2001); MATTHIAS BUSSE, AXEL BORRMANN & HARALD GROSSMANN, THE IMPACT OF ACP/EU ECONOMIC PARTNERSHIP AGREEMENTS ON ECOWAS COUNTRIES: AN EMPIRICAL ANALYSIS OF THE TRADE AND BUDGET EFFECTS (2004), available at http://www.hubrural.org/pdf/hwwa_etude_ape_eng.pdf; Daniel Gervais, *Epilogue: A TRIPS Implementation Toolbox*, in INTELLECTUAL PROPERTY, TRADE AND DEVELOPMENT: STRATEGIES TO OPTIMIZE ECONOMIC DEVELOPMENT IN A TRIPS-PLUS ERA 527, 530–531 (Daniel Gervais ed., Oxford University Press 2007).
66. Panel Report, China—Measures Affecting the Protection and Enforcement of Intellectual Property Rights, ¶ 7.132, WT/DS362/R (January 26, 2009) [hereinafter *China–Enforcement*].
67. See, e.g., *id.* at ¶¶ 7.577, 7.595 & 7.602–7.606.
68. *Id.* at ¶¶ 7.512 & 7.594.
69. *Id.* at ¶ 7.139.
70. *India–Pharmaceuticals*, at ¶ 62.
71. *Id.* at ¶ 59.
72. *Id.* at ¶ 58.
73. *Id.* at ¶ 57.
74. *US–110(5)*, at ¶ 6.59.
75. See Laurence R. Helfer, *Adjudicating Copyright Claims Under the TRIPS Agreement: The Case for a European Human Rights Analogy*, 39 HARV. INT'L L.J. 357, 431 (1998); *see also* Pedro Roffe & Gina Vea, *The WIPO Development Agenda in Historical and Political Context*, in THE DEVELOPMENT AGENDA: GLOBAL INTELLECTUAL PROPERTY AND DEVELOPING COUNTRIES 79, 81–85, & 92–95 (Neil Weinstock Netanel ed., Oxford University Press 2009).
76. *See* Chapter 3.
77. DSU, art. 3.8.
78. *Cf.* DANIEL GERVAIS, THE TRIPS AGREEMENT: DRAFTING HISTORY AND ANALYSIS § 1.57 (3d ed. Sweet & Maxwell 2008) (reporting views voiced in the TRIPS Council).
79. See TRIPS, art. 64.2; World Trade Organization, TRIPS: Non-Violation" Complaints (Article 64.2): Background and the Current Situation, available at http://www.wto.org/english/tratop_e/trips_e/nonviolation_background_e.htm.
80. *India–Pharmaceuticals*, at ¶ 42.
81. Saggi & Trachtman, *supra* note 62, at 22–23.
82. Susy Frankel, *Challenging TRIPS-Plus Agreements: The Potential Utility of Non-violation Complaints*, 12 J. INT'L ECON. L. 1023 (2009).
83. Panel Report, United States—Sections 301–310 of the Trade Act of 1974, WT/DS152/R (December 22, 1999) [hereinafter *US-301*].
84. *Id.* at ¶ 7.109.

85. *See* Appellate Body Report, European Communities—Measures Affecting Asbestos and Asbestos-Containing Products, ¶¶ 50–57, WT/DS135/AB/R (March 12, 2001); *cf.* United States—Import Prohibition of Certain Shrimp and Shrimp Products, ¶ 110, WT/DS58/AB/R (October 12, 1998) (information from NGOs attached to government submissions); *see also* ANDREW T. GUZMAN & JOOST PAUWELYN, INTERNATIONAL TRADE LAW: CASES AND MATERIALS 158 (Aspen Publishers 2009) (noting limited acceptance of amicus briefs and even lesser regards paid to the content of such briefs).
86. Steve Charnovitz, *Opening the WTO to Nongovernmental Interests*, 24 FORDHAM L. REV. 173 (2000); Steve Charnovitz, *WTO Cosmopolitics*, 34 NYU J. INT'L L. & POL. 299 (2002).
87. JOSÉ E. ALVAREZ, INTERNATIONAL ORGANIZATIONS AS LAW-MAKERS 609 & 632–633 (Oxford University Press 2006).
88. Kal Raustiala, *Compliance and Effectiveness in International Regulatory Cooperation*, 32 CASE WEST. RES. J. INT'L L. 387 (2000).
89. Kapczynski, *supra* note 61, at 1634; Peter Drahos, *"Trust Me": Patent Offices in Developing Countries*, 34 AM. J.L. & MED. 151 (2008).
90. Agreement Between the World Intellectual Property Organization and the World Trade Organization, December 22, 1995, arts. 2 & 4, 35 I.L.M. 754 (1996).
91. Proposal by Argentina and Brazil for the Establishment of a Development Agenda for WIPO, WIPO Doc. WO/GA/31/11 (August 27, 2004), *available at* http://www.wipo.int/edocs/mdocs/govbody/en/wo_ga_31/wo_ga_31_11.doc.
92. *See* World Trade Organization, Decision of the Council for TRIPS of February 19, 2003, WTO Doc. No. IP/C/28, February 20, 2003.
93. *See, e.g.*, Laurence R. Helfer, *Toward a Human Rights Framework for Intellectual Property*, 40 U.C. Davis L. Rev. 971 (2007); World Health Organization, Commission on Intellectual Property Rights, Innovation and Public Health (CIPIH), Public Health, Innovation and Intellectual Property Rights (2006); Dwijen Rangnekar, UNCTAD/ICTSD Capacity Building Project, Resource Book on TRIPS and Development: An Authoritative and Practical Guide to the TRIPS Agreement (2004), *available at* http://www.iprsonline.org/unctadictsd/ResourceBookIndex.htm.

Chapter 6

1. The Doha Declaration includes the Doha Ministerial Declaration and the Declaration on the TRIPS Agreement and Public Health. *See* World Trade Organization, Ministerial Declaration of November 20, 2001, ¶ 17, WT/MIN(01)/DEC/1, 41 I.L.M. 746 (2002) [hereinafter Doha Ministerial Declaration]; World Trade Organization, Declaration on the TRIPS Agreement and Public Health, WT/MIN(01)/DEC/2, November 20, 2001, 41 I.L.M. 755 (2002) [hereinafter Declaration on Public Health].
2. Panel Report, China—Measures Affecting the Protection and Enforcement of Intellectual Property Rights, WT/DS362/R (January 26, 2009) [hereinafter *China–Enforcement*].
3. Panel Report, European Communities—Protection of Trademarks and Geographical Indications for Agricultural Products and Foodstuffs, WT/DS174/R (March 15, 2005) [hereinafter *EC–GI*].
4. *See generally* Laurence R. Helfer, *Regime Shifting: The TRIPS Agreement and New Dynamics of International Intellectual Property Lawmaking*, 29 YALE J. INT'L L.J. 1 (2004).
5. General Agreement on Tariffs and Trade 1994, April 15, 1994, Marrakesh Agreement Establishing the World Trade Organization, Annex 1A, LEGAL INSTRUMENTS—RESULTS OF THE URUGUAY ROUND, vol. 31, 1867 U.N.T.S. 187, 33 I.L.M. 1154 (1994) [hereinafter GATT].
6. *See* DUNCAN MATTHEWS, GLOBALISING PROPERTY RIGHTS: THE TRIPS AGREEMENT 9 (Routledge 2002) (discussing the introduction and treatment of counterfeiting and intellectual property during the Tokyo Round).

7. Margaret Chon, *A Rough Guide to Global Intellectual Property Pluralism*, in WORKING WITHIN THE BOUNDARIES OF INTELLECTUAL PROPERTY 445 (Rochelle Dreyfuss, Harry First & Diane Zimmerman eds., Oxford University Press 2010); Amy Kapczynski, *The Access to Knowledge Mobilization and the New Politics of Intellectual Property*, 117 YALE L.J. 804 (2008); Graeme Dinwoodie, *The WIPO Copyright Treaty: A Transition to the Future of International Copyright Lawmaking?*, 57 CASE WESTERN RES. L. REV. 751, 761–764 (2007).

8. Convention for the Protection of Human Rights and Fundamental Freedoms, November 4, 1950, 213 U.N.T.S. 222; Laurence R. Helfer, *The New Innovation Frontier? Intellectual Property and the European Court of Human Rights*, 49 HARV. INT'L L.J. 1 (2008). *See also* Universal Declaration of Human Rights, December 8, 1948, art. 27.2, G.A. Res. 217A(III), U.N. Doc. A/810, at 71 ("Everyone has the right to the protection of the moral and material interests resulting from any scientific, literary or artistic production of which he is the author."); International Covenant on Economic, Social and Cultural Rights, December 16, 1966, art. 15(1)(c), 993 U.N.T.S. 3, 5 ("The States Parties to the present Covenant recognize the right of everyone ... to benefit from the protection of the moral and material interests resulting from any scientific, literary or artistic production of which he is the author.").

9. Convention on Biological Diversity, June 5, 1992, 1760 U.N.T.S. 79 [hereinafter CBD]; Nagoya Protocol on Access to Genetic Resources and the Fair and Equitable Sharing of Benefits Arising From Their Utilization to the Convention on Biological Diversity, Conference of the Parties to the Convention on Biological Diversity (October 29, 2010) [hereinafter Nagoya Protocol], *available at* http://www.cbd.int/abs/text/.

10. *See, e.g.,* Beatrice Lindstrom, *Scaling Back TRIPS-Plus: An Analysis of Intellectual Property Provisions in Trade Agreements and Implications for Asia and the Pacific*, 42 N.Y.U. J. INT'L L. & POL. 917 (2010); Matthew Turk, *Bargaining and Intellectual Property Treaties: The Case for a Pro-development Interpretation of TRIPS but Not TRIPS-Plus*, 42 N.Y.U. J. INT'L L. & POL. 981 (2010).

11. Dominican Republic—Central America—United States Free Trade Agreement (August 5, 2004), *available at* http://www.ustr.gov/trade-agreements/free-trade-agreements/cafta-dr-dominican-republic-central-america-fta/final-text [hereinafter CAFTA]. For Europe, *see, e.g.,* Directive 98/44/EC of the European Parliament and of the Council of July 6, 1998, on the Legal Protection of Biotechnological Inventions, 1998 O.J. (L 213) 13 [hereinafter Biotech Directive].

12. *See, e.g.,* Anti-Counterfeiting Trade Agreement, March 31, 2011 Text, *available at* http://trade.ec.europa.eu/doclib/docs/2011/may/tradoc_147937.pdf [hereinafter ACTA]; Peter K. Yu, *Six Secret (and Now Open) Fears of ACTA*, 64 S.M.U. L. REV. ___ (2011) 975; Office of the United States Trade Representative, the Trans-Pacific Partnership (2011), *available at* http://www.ustr.gov/tpp.

13. WIPO Copyright Treaty, December 20, 1996, 2186 U.N.T.S. 121, 36 I.L.M. 65 [hereinafter WCT]; WIPO Performances and Phonograms Treaty, December 20, 1996, 2186 U.N.T.S. 203, 36 I.L.M. 76 [hereinafter WPPT]; World Intellectual Property Organization, Treaty for Improved Access for Blind, Visually Impaired and Other Reading Disabled Persons, Annex, WIPO Doc. SCCR/18/5 (May 25, 2009) (proposal put forward by Brazil, Ecuador, and Paraguay based on recommendations of the World Blind Union) [hereinafter Treaty for the Visually Impaired]; William New, *Proposed WIPO Treaty on Visually Impaired Access Gets Deeper Look*, INTELL. PROP. WATCH, May 29, 2009, *available at* http://www.ip-watch.org/weblog/2009/05/29/proposed-wipo-treaty-on-visually-impaired-access-gets-deeper-look.

14. World Health Organization, *Public Health, Innovation, and Intellectual Property*, *available at* http://www.who.int/phi/en/. *See, e.g.,* Ruth Bell, Sebastian Taylor & Michael Marmot, *Global Health Governance: Commission on Social Determinants of Health and the Imperative for Change*, 38 J. L. MED. & ETHICS 470 (2010).

15. *See, e.g.,* MOHAMMED K. EL SAID, A POLICY GUIDE FOR NEGOTIATORS AND IMPLEMENTERS IN THE WHO EASTERN MEDITERRANEAN REGION (World Health Organization

& International Center for Trade and Sustainable Development 2010), *available at* http://acp-eu-trade.org/library/files/E1%20Said:EN_170111_ICTSD_A%20policy%20guide%20.pdf

16. Documents on the Development Agenda are available at http://www.wipo.int/ip-development/en/agenda/.
17. *See, e.g.,* Joint Recommendation Concerning Provisions on the Protection of Marks, and Other Industrial Property Rights in Signs, on the Internet, WIPO Doc. 845E (2001) [hereinafter Internet Use Joint Recommendation].
18. The CBD, for example, establishes a Conference of the Parties, art. 23; a Secretariat, art. 24; and a Subsidiary Body on Scientific, Technical and Technological Advice, art. 25. Article 36 of ACTA creates the ACTA Committee to, among other things, review implementation and consider amendments.
19. CAFTA, art. 20. *See also, e.g.,* North American Free Trade Agreement, Chapter 20, December 8, 1993, 107 Stat. 2057, 32 I.L.M. 289, 605 (1993); Canada–United States: Free Trade Agreement, January 2, 1988, art. 1504, 27 I.L.M. 281 (1988); Australia-United States: Free Trade Agreement, May 18, 2004, art. 21, 43 ILM 1248 (2004) [hereinafter US-Australia FTA].
20. *See, e.g.,* Sabrina Safrin, *Chain Reaction: How Property Begets Property*, 82 NOTRE DAME L. REV. 1917 (2007). *See also* Rosemary J. Coombe, *The Recognition of Indigenous Peoples' and Community Traditional Knowledge in International Law*, 14 ST. THOMAS L. REV. 275 (2001); Nagoya Protocol, *supra* note 9.
21. *See, e.g.,* International Law Commission, *Fragmentation of International Law: Difficulties Arising from the Diversification and Expansion of International Law: Report of the Study Group on the Fragmentation of International Law*, Finalized by Martti Koskenniemi, ¶ 242, UN Doc. A/CN.4/L.682 (April 13, 2006) [hereinafter Koskenniemi]; Symposium: *The Interpretation of Treaties—A Re-examination*, 21 EUR. J. INT'L L. 507 (2010); Susan K. Sell, *The Quest for Global Governance in Intellectual Property and Public Health: Structural, Discursive, and Institutional Dimensions*, 77 TEMP. L. REV. 363 (2004). *See also* Eyal Benvenisti & George W. Downs, *The Empire's New Clothes: Political Economy and the Fragmentation of International Law*, 60 STAN. L. REV. 595 (2007).
22. *See, e.g.,* Anheuser-Busch v. Budejovicky Budvar NP, [1984] F.S.R. 413 (U.K.); Anheuser-Busch Inc. v. Portugal, App. No. 73049/01, 45 Eur. H.R. Rep. 36 [830] (Grand Chamber ECHR 2007); Anheuser-Busch Inc. v. Budejovicky Budvar, 2004 ECR I-10989 (ECJ 2004); Case T-225/06, Budějovický Budvar v. OHIM, [2009] E.T.M.R. 29 (CFI 2008); Case C-482/09, Budejovický Budvar v. Anheuser-Busch, Inc, [2012] E.T.M.R. 2 (CJEU 2011).
23. *Cf.* Golan v. Holder, 609 F.3d 1076 (10th Cir. 2010), *cert. granted*, 131 S.Ct. 1600 (2011) (claiming reliance interest in public domain status of works taken out of the public domain when the United States complied with its obligations under the Berne Convention).
24. *See, e.g.,* Joel P. Trachtman, *The International Law of Financial Crisis: Spillovers, Subsidiary, Fragmentation and Cooperation*, 13 J. INT'L ECON. L. 719 (2010); Daniel C. Esty, *Good Governance at the Supranational Scale: Globalizing Administrative Law*, 115 YALE L.J. 1490 (2006).
25. Dinwoodie, *supra* note 7, at 758–761.
26. Peter K. Yu, *The International Enclosure Movement*, 82 IND. L.J. 827, 867–868 (2007) (distinguishing between "TRIPS-plus," "TRIPS-extra," and "TRIPS-restrictive" provisions).
27. *See, e.g.,* Henning Grosse Ruse-Khan, *Protecting Intellectual Property Under BITs, FTAs, and TRIPS: Conflicting Regimes or Mutual Coherence, in* EVOLUTION IN INVESTMENT TREATY LAW AND ARBITRATION (Kate Miles & Chester Brown eds., Cambridge University Press 2011); Ruth L. Okediji, *Back to Bilateralism? Pendulum Swings in International Intellectual Property Protection*, 1 U. OTTAWA L. TECH. J. 125 (2004); Peter Drahos, *BITs and BIPS: Bilateralism in Intellectual Property*, 4 J. WORLD INTELL. PROP. 791 (2001).
28. Many of these are analyzed in Frederick M. Abbott, *Toward a New Era of Objective Assessment in the Field of TRIPS and Variable Geometry for the Preservation of Multilateralism*, 8 J. INT'L ECON. L. 77 (2005).

29. United States-Morocco Free Trade Agreement, Final Text, June 15, 2004, art. 15.9(4)(2004), *available at* http://www.ustr.gov/trade-agreements/free-trade-agreements/morocco-fta/final-text [hereinafter U.S.-Morocco FTA]. *See also* U.S.-Australia FTA, art. 17.9(4).
30. United States-Chile Free Trade Agreement, June 6, 2003, art. 17.2 (1), *available at* http://www.ustr.gov/trade-agreements/free-trade-agreements/chile-fta) [hereinafter U.S.-Chile FTA]. *Cf.* Case C-283/01, Shield Mark BV v Kist (t/a Memex), [2004] E.T.M.R. 33 (ECJ 2003) (sound marks are capable of graphic representation).
31. *See, e.g.,* Standing Committee on the Law of Trademarks, Industrial Designs and Geographical Indications, Grounds for Refusals of All Types of Marks, ¶ 12, WIPO Doc. SCT 22/2 (October 9, 2009) (comparative study).
32. EU-Central America FTA, Title VI, May 18, 2010, arts. 5–6 (2010), *available at* http://www.bilaterals.org/spip.php?article18220. *See also* Agreement Between the United States of America and the Hashemite Kingdom of Jordan on the Establishment of a Free Trade Area, October 4, 2000, art. 4, *available at* http://www.ustr.gov/trade-agreements/free-trade-agreements/jordan-fta/final-text [hereinafter U.S.-Jordan FTA].
33. *See, e.g.,* U.S.-Chile FTA, art. 17.1(3) and (4) (requiring ratification of a series of instruments) & art. 17.2(9) (requiring "recognition of the importance of the Joint Recommendation on the Protection of Well-Known Marks").
34. *Compare* United States-Singapore Free Trade Agreement, May 6, 2003, art. 16.4(7) (2003), *available at* http://www.ustr.gov/trade-agreements/free-trade-agreements/singapore-fta/final-text, *with* 17 U.S.C. §§ 1201(a) & (b).
35. U.S.-Morocco FTA, art. 15.9(2)(a); CAFTA, art. 15.9(2).
36. WIPO and Assembly of the Paris Union for the Protection of Industrial Property, Joint Recommendation Concerning Provisions on the Protection of Well-Known Marks, arts. 2 & 4, Pub'n 833, *available at* http://www.wipo.int/about-ip/en/development_iplaw/pub833.htm. *See, e.g.,* U.S.-Chile FTA, art. 17.2; U.S.-Jordan FTA, art. 17.2
37. *See, e.g.,* World Trade Organization, Council for TRIPS, Minutes of Meeting of October 4, 2010, IP/C/M/63, ¶ 7, *available at* http://www.wto.org/english/tratop_e/trips_e/intel6_e.htm (detailing previous attempts to raise enforcement issues) [hereinafter October 2010 Minutes of the TRIPS Council].
38. *China–Enforcement*, at ¶ 7.577 (whether infringement is of a commercial scale depends "on the magnitude or extent of typical or usual commercial activity").
39. ACTA, arts. 8–10, 11.
40. For the new institutions, see ACTA, arts. 36–37 (ACTA Committee) & art. 38 (consultations).
41. *Id.* art. 23.1.
42. *Id.* art. 9.3 (for copyright and trademark infringement).
43. *Id.* arts. 16–17; *see generally* Henning Grosse Ruse-Khan, *A Trade Agreement Creating Barriers to International Trade? ACTA Border Measures and Goods in Transit*, 26 AM. U. INT'L L. REV. 645 (2011). *See also* Joined Cases C-446/09 and C-495/09, Koninklijke Philips Electronics NV v. Lucheng Meijing Industrial Company Ltd, and Nokia v. Her Majesty's Comm'rs of Revenue and Customs, [2012] E.T.M.R. ___ (CJEU December 1, 2011).
44. ACTA, art. 27.
45. *See, e.g., id.* nn. 2 & 6.
46. *See, e.g., id.* Preamble (describing "the problem of infringement of intellectual property rights, including infringement taking place in the digital environment").
47. *See, e.g.,* Thomas Faunce & Ruth Townsend, *Public Health and Medicines Policies, in* NO ORDINARY DEAL: UNMASKING THE TRANS-PACIFIC PARTNERSHIP FREE TRADE AGREEMENT 149 (J. Kelsey ed., Allen & Unwin 2010).
48. Internet Use Joint Recommendation, *supra* note 17.
49. Dinwoodie, *supra* note 7, at 756–757.
50. *See, e.g.,* Biotech Directive, *supra* note 11.
51. ACTA, Preamble & art. 2.3. The Doha Declaration includes the Doha Ministerial Declaration and the Declaration on the TRIPS Agreement and Public Health. *See supra* note 1.

52. International Convention for the Protection of New Varieties of Plants, December 2, 1961, art. 15, 33 U.S.T. 2703, 815 U.N.T.S. 89.
53. *See, e.g.,* Maximiliano Santa Cruz, Counsellor, Permanent Mission of Chile to the WTO, *Intellectual Property Provisions in European Union Trade Agreements: Implications for Developing Countries,* ICTSD Programme on IPRs and Sustainable Development (June 2007), *available at* http://www.iprsonline.org/resources/docs/Santa-Cruz%20Blue20.pdf.
54. Carlos M. Correa, *Bilateralism in Intellectual Property: Defeating the WTO System for Access to Medicines,* 36 Case W. Res. J. Int'l L. 79, 88 (2004).
55. *See, e.g.,* Abbott, *supra* note 28, at 90.
56. *See* GATT, arts. III & XX; *see also* Request for Consultations by India, European Union and a Member State—Seizure of Generic Drugs, at 1, WT/DS408/1 (May 19, 2010).
57. Request for Consultations, European Union and a Member State—Seizure of Generic Drugs in Transit, WT/DS408/1 (May 11, 2010); *EU, India Drop Generics Dispute to Focus on FTA Talks,* FDAnews, January 24, 2011, *available at* http://fdanews.com/newsletter/article?issueId=14404&articleId=133690; *see also* Request for Consultations, European Union and a Member State—Seizure of Generic Drugs in Transit, WT/DS409/1 (May 12, 2010) (complaint by Brazil).
58. *Cf.* Quality King Distrib. v. L'Anza Research Int'l, Inc., 523 U.S. 135 (1998) (attempting to use the copyright on labeling information to stop importation of shampoo).
59. *See, e.g.,* Chee Yoke Ling, *Hope for an Anti-Biopiracy Treaty in 2010,* 231/232 TWN (Third World Network) (December 2009), *available at* http://www.twnside.org.sg/title2/res.urgence/2009/231-232/cover1.htm; Fritz Dolder, *Biopiracy and Patent Law: Implementing the Rio Convention (CBD) (2001), available at* http://www.evb.ch/en/p25000814.html.
60. *See, e.g.,* Molly Torsen & Jane Anderson, *Intellectual Property and the Safeguarding of Traditional Cultures: Legal Issues and Practical Options for Museums, Libraries and Archives* (World Intellectual Property Organization 2010), *available at* http://www.wipo.int/export/sites/www/tk/en/publications/1023.pdf. *See generally* World Intellectual Property Organization, Program Activities, Traditional Knowledge, Genetic Resources and Traditional Cultural Expressions/Folklore, *available at* http://www.wipo.int/tk/en/; Sedfrey M. Candelaria et al., The Road to Empowerment: Strengthening the Indigenous Peoples Rights Act, vol. I (International Labor Organization 2007), *available at* http://www.ilo.org/wcmsp5/groups/public/—ed_norm/—normes/documents/publication/wcms_100819.pdf.
61. For a general perspective on international organizations, see José E. Alvarez, International Organizations as Law-Makers (Oxford University Press 2006).
62. *See* UNCTAD's website, http://www.unctad.org/ United Nations Conference on Trade and Development, The Biotechnology Promise: Capacity-Building for Participation of Developing Countries in the Bioeconomy (2004), *available at* http://www.unctad.org/en/docs/iteipc20042_en.pdf.
63. *See, e.g.,* Dwijen Rangnekar, Resource Book on TRIPS and Development: An Authoritative and Practical Guide to the TRIPS Agreement (UNCTAD/ICTSD Capacity Building Project 2004), *available at* http://www.iprsonline.org/unctadictsd/ResourceBookIndex.htm.
64. *See also* Jerome H. Reichman with Catherine Hasenzahl, *Non-voluntary Licensing of Patented Inventions: Historical Perspective, Legal Framework Under TRIPS, and an Overview of the Practice in Canada and the United States of America* (UNCTAD/ICTSD Capacity Building Project on Intellectual Property and Sustainable Development 2003).
65. *See* WHO Agenda, *available at* http://www.who.int/about/agenda/en/index.html; Thomas Faunce, *Innovation and Insufficient Evidence: The Case for a WTO-WHO Agreement on Health Technology Safety and Cost-Effectiveness Evaluation, in* Incentives for Global Public Health: Patent Law and Access to Essential Medicines (Thomas Pogge, Matthew Rimmer & Kim Rubenstein eds., Cambridge University Press 2010).
66. El Said, *supra* note 15.

67. WORLD HEALTH ORGANIZATION, TRADE, INTELLECTUAL PROPERTY RIGHTS AND ACCESS TO MEDICINES, *available at* http://www.who.int/medicines/areas/policy/globtrade/en/index.html (2010). *See also* WORLD HEALTH ORGANIZATION, REPORT OF THE COMMISSION ON INTELLECTUAL PROPERTY RIGHTS, INNOVATION AND PUBLIC HEALTH (2006), *available at* http://www.who.int/intellectualproperty/documents/thereport/ENPublicHealthReport.pdf.
68. *Id.* at 20–21.
69. *See, e.g.,* Ilona Kickbusch et al., *Addressing Global Health Governance Challenges Through a New Mechanism: The Proposal for a Committee C of the World Health Assembly*, 38 J. L. MED. & ETHICS 550 (2010).
70. *See supra* note 8.
71. Universal Declaration on the Human Genome and Human Rights, November 11, 1997, U.N. Doc. No. C/RES/1997/16; *see also* G.A. Res. 152, U.N. GAOR, 53rd Sess., U.N. Doc. A/RES/53/152 (December 9, 1998), *available at* http://www2.ohchr.org/english/law/genome.htm.
72. Convention for the Protection of Human Rights and Dignity of the Human Being with Regard to the Application of Biology and Medicine: Convention on Human Rights and Biomedicine, April 4, 1997, *available at* http://conventions.coe.int/treaty/en/treaties/html/164.htm.
73. *See generally* Shira Pridan-Frank, *Human Genomics: A Challenge to the Rules of the Game of International Law*, 40 COLUM. J. TRANSNAT'L L. 619, 622–623 (2002).
74. *See, e.g.,* Audrey R. Chapman, *Approaching Intellectual Property as a Human Right: Obligations Related to Article 15(1)(c)*, 35 COPYRIGHT BULLETIN 4 (UNESCO Publishing, July–September 2001) (prepared as background resource for the UNESCO Committee on Economic, Social and Cultural Rights), *available at* http://unesdoc.unesco.org/images/0012/001255/125505e.pdf. *See generally* Margaret Chon, *Global Intellectual Property Governance (Under Construction)*, 12 THEORETICAL INQUIRIES L. 349 (2010).
75. LAURENCE R. HELFER & GRAEME W. AUSTIN, HUMAN RIGHTS AND INTELLECTUAL PROPERTY: MAPPING THE GLOBAL INTERFACE (Cambridge University Press 2011).
76. WIPO Arbitration and Mediation Center, *available at* http://www.wipo.int/amc/en/index.html; ICANN, Uniform Domain-Name Dispute-Resolution Policy, *available at* http://www.icann.org/en/udrp/udrp.htm.
77. Agreement Between the World Intellectual Property Organization and the World Trade Organization, December 22, 1995, Preamble, 35 I.L.M. 754 (1996) [hereinafter WIPO-WTO Agreement]; *see* TRIPS, arts. 63 & 68.
78. Dinwoodie, *supra* note 7, at 755. *See also* Pamela Samuelson, *The U.S. Digital Agenda at WIPO*, 37 VA. J. INT'L L. 369 (1997).
79. *See, e.g.,* Katherine J. Strandburg, *Accommodating User Innovation in the International Intellectual Property Regime: A Global Administrative Law Approach*, 2009 ACTA JURIDICA 283.
80. Proposal by Argentina and Brazil for the Establishment of a Development Agenda for WIPO, WO/GA/31/11 (August 27, 2004). The proposal was supported by other developing states, including Bolivia, Cuba, the Dominican Republic, Ecuador, Iran, Kenya, Sierra Leone, South Africa, Republic of Tanzania and Venezuela.
81. *See, e.g.,* Provisional Committee on Proposals Related to a WIPO Development Agenda (PCDA), Fourth Session (June 11–15, 2007), *available at* http://www.wipo.int/ip-development/en/agenda/pcda07_session4.html. For the Millennium Development Goals, see http://www.un.org/millenniumgoals/. *See also* Conference of NGOs in Consultative Relationship with the United Nations, *NGO Participation Arrangements at the UN and in Other Agencies of the UN System* 9 (March 2006), *available at* http://www.itu.int/council/groups/stakeholders/Resources/Non-Paper%20on%20NGO%20Participation%20in%20the%20UN%20System3%20_CONGO_.pdf.
82. World Intellectual Property Organization, Committee on Development and Intellectual Property (CDIP), Director General's Report on Implementation of the Development

Agenda, CDIP/7/2 (March 8, 2011), *available at* (with annexes) at http://www.wipo.int/edocs/mdocs/mdocs/en/cdip_7/cdip_7_2.pdf.

83. *See, e.g., id.* Annexes IX & XI.
84. *Id.* Annex X
85. *Id.* Annex XIII (mentioning, among others, WHO, UNITAID, and FAO).
86. *See, e.g.,* World Intellectual Property Organization, Limitations and Exceptions, *available at* http://www.wipo.int/copyright/en/limitations/.
87. *See* Treaty for the Visually Impaired *supra* note 13.
88. *See, e.g.,* Standing Committee on Copyright and Related Rights, Automated Rights Management Systems and Copyright Limitations and Exceptions, SCCR/14/5 (April 27, 2006). *See also* Standing Committee on Copyright and Related Rights, WIPO Study on Limitations and Exceptions of Copyright and Related Rights in the Digital Environment, SCCR/9/7(April 5, 2003) (prepared by Sam Ricketson).
89. *See* Standing Committee on Exclusions from Patentable Subject Matter and Exceptions and Limitations to the Rights, SCP/15/3 Annex I (September 2, 2010) (prepared by Lionel Bently, et al.).
90. *See, e.g.,* Gregory C. Shaffer & Mark A. Pollack, *Hard vs. Soft Law: Alternatives, Complements, and Antagonists in International Governance,* 94 MINN. L. REV. 906 (2010); Jyh-An Lee, *The Greenpeace of Cultural Environmentalism,* 16 WIDENER L. REV. 1 (2010); Chon, *supra* note 7; Amy Kapczynski, *The Access to Knowledge Mobilization and the New Politics of Intellectual Property,* 117 YALE L.J. 804 (2008).
91. *See, e.g.,* DOCTORS WITHOUT BORDERS, TRADING AWAY HEALTH: INTELLECTUAL PROPERTY AND ACCESS TO MEDICINES IN THE FREE TRADE AREA OF THE AMERICAS (FTAA) AGREEMENT (2003), *available at* http://www.doctorswithoutborders.org/publications/reports/2003/FTAA_Advocacy.pdf.
92. *See, e.g.,* ERIC VON HIPPEL, DEMOCRATIZING INNOVATION (MIT Press 2005); Creative Commons website, http://creativecommons.org/.
93. INTELLECTUAL PROPERTY IN A FAIR WORLD TRADE SYSTEM: PROPOSALS FOR REFORMING THE TRIPS AGREEMENT (Annette Kur ed., Edward Elgar 2011).
94. The Geneva Declaration on the Future of the World Intellectual Property Organization (promulgated in 2004), *available at* http://www.cptech.org/ip/wipo/genevadeclaration.html; The Washington Declaration on Intellectual Property and the Public Interest (August 2011), *available at* http://infojustice.org/washington-declaration.
95. *See supra* note 56.
96. CBD, art. 15.5; CBD, Annex II.
97. *See* Ruse-Khan, *supra* note 27.
98. *See generally* Brian Cimbolic, *The Impact of Regional Trade Areas on International Intellectual Property Rights,* 48 IDEA 53 (2007); Susy Frankel, *WTO Application of "The Customary Rules of Interpretation of Public International Law" to Intellectual Property,* 46 VA. J. INT'L L. 365, 417 (2006).
99. *See, e.g.,* Peter Drahos, *An Alternative Framework for the Global Regulation of Intellectual Property Rights,* 21 AUSTRALIAN J. DEV. STUD. 1, 7 (2005).
100. We provide a formal analysis of the application of MFN in Chapter 4.
101. For a detailed account of the use of exogenous hard law and soft law in the WTO, see Mary E. Footer, *The (Re)turn to "Soft Law" in Reconciling Antinomies in WTO Law,* 11 MELBOURNE J. INT'L L. 241 (2010).
102. *See, e.g.,* AMERICAN LAW INSTITUTE, INTELLECTUAL PROPERTY: PRINCIPLES GOVERNING JURISDICTION, CHOICE OF LAW, AND JUDGMENTS IN TRANSNATIONAL DISPUTES (2008).
103. *See* Understanding on Rules and Procedures Governing the Settlement of Disputes, April 15, 1994, arts. 1.1. 3.2, 7.1, Marrakesh Agreement Establishing the World Trade Organization, Annex 2, LEGAL INSTRUMENTS—RESULTS OF THE URUGUAY ROUND, vol. 31, 1869 U.N.T.S. 401, 33 I.L.M. 1226 (1994) [hereinafter DSU].

104. Vienna Convention on the Law of Treaties, May 23, 1969, 1155 U.N.T.S. 331, 8 I.L.M. 679 (1969); *see* Steven P. Croley & John H. Jackson, *WTO Dispute Procedures, Standard of Review, and Deference to National Governments*, 90 AM. J. INT'L L. 193, 200 (1996).
105. Koskenniemi, *supra* note 21. *See also* JOOST PAUWELYN, CONFLICT OF NORMS IN PUBLIC INTERNATIONAL LAW: HOW WTO LAW RELATES TO OTHER RULES OF INTERNATIONAL LAW (Cambridge University Press 2003).
106. *See, e.g.,* John O. McGinnis & Mark L. Movsesian, *The World Trade Constitution*, 114 HARV. L. REV. 511 (2000).
107. *See, e.g.,* Tomer Broude, *Principles of Normative Integration and the Allocation of International Authority: The WTO, the Vienna Convention on the Law of Treaties, and the Rio Declaration*, 6 LOY. L. REV. 173 (2009).
108. For the argument, see Koskenniemi, *supra* note 21, at ¶ 129 (defining "self-contained" in this way); *see also id.* at ¶¶ 166–167; McGinnis & Movsesian, *supra* note 106.
109. Appellate Body Report, United States—Standards of Reformulated and Conventional Gasoline, WT/DS2/AB/R, DSR 1996:I, at 17 (May 20, 1996).
110. DSU, art. 3.2.
111. Appellate Body Report, Mexico—Tax Measures on Soft Drinks and Other Beverages, WT/DS308/AB/R (March 6, 2006) [hereinafter *Mexico–Soft Drinks*].
112. Panel Report, European Communities—Measures Affecting the Approval and Marketing of Biotech Products, ¶ 7.68, WT/DS291/R, WT/DS292/R, WT/DS293/R (September 29, 2006) [hereinafter *EC–Biotech*]; *see also* PAUWELYN, *supra* note 105, at 257–263 (canvassing arguments and competing scholarship prior to the *EC–Biotech* ruling); *id.* at 258 (noting that as a result [of the reading ultimately adopted in *EC–Biotech*] it "would ... seem difficult to argue that, pursuant to Art. 31(3)(c), a bilateral agreement between the disputing parties concluded outside the WTO context can play a role in the interpretation of the WTO agreement.").
113. Koskenniemi, *supra* note 21, at ¶ 450 ("The panel buys what it calls the 'consistency' of its interpretation of the WTO Treaty at the cost of the consistency of the multilateral treaty system as a whole.").
114. Robert Howse, *The Use and Abuse of International Law in WTO Trade and Environment Litigation*, in THE WTO: GOVERNANCE, DISPUTE SETTLEMENT AND DEVELOPING COUNTRIES 635–670, at 656–659 (M. Janow, Victoria Donaldson & Alan Yanovich eds., Juris Publishing 2008); *cf.* PAUWELYN, *supra* note 105, at 260–263 (noting that failure of a treaty to satisfy the formal requirements of Article 31.3(c) does not preclude interpretative relevance to the dispute between the parties).
115. *See, e.g.,* Broude, *supra* note 107, at 198–199.
116. *See* Koskenniemi, *supra* note 21, at ¶¶ 168, 191–193 (citing Appellate Body Report, United States—Import Prohibition of Certain Shrimp and Shrimp Products WT/DS58/AB/R, DSR 1998:VII, at ¶¶ 127–131 (November 6, 1998)); Howse, *supra* note 114, at 639–648.
117. Panel Report, Canada—Patent Protection of Pharmaceutical Products, WT/DS114/R (March 17, 2000) [hereinafter *Canada–Pharmaceuticals*]; Panel Report, United States—Section 110(5) of the U.S. Copyright Act, WT/DS/160/R (June 15, 2000) [hereinafter *US–110(5)*]. *See* Chapter 3.
118. *See* Chapter 4.
119. *See generally* Lorand Bartels, *Applicable Law in WTO Dispute Settlement Proceedings*, 35 J. WORLD TRADE 499 (2001). *Cf.* José E. Alvarez & Joel P. Trachtman, *Institutional Linkage: Transcending "Trade and ...,"* 96 AM. J. INT'L L. 77, 88–89 (2002) (suggesting that the WTO treaty could be amended to incorporate other norms directly, along with other ways to apply norms across intergovernmental bodies).
120. *See, e.g.,* TRIPS Agreement, arts. 5, 9.1, 15, 22, 39 & 68; WIPO-WTO Agreement, *supra* note 77.
121. The only WTO members that are not officially in WIPO are the European Union, whose members joined WIPO individually, Hong Kong, Macao, and Taiwan, where there are

Notes to Pages 162–167

122. US–110(5), at ¶ 6.70.
123. Deborah J. Halbert, *The World Intellectual Property Organization: Past, Present and Future*, 54 J. COPYRIGHT SOC'Y 253, 262 (2007).
124. *See, e.g.,* Appellate Body Report, United States—Section 211 of the Omnibus Appropriations Act of 1998, ¶ 145, WT/DS176/AB/R (January 2, 2002) [hereinafter *Havana Club*]; US–110(5), at ¶ 6.53–6.54.
125. US–110(5), at ¶ 6.69.
126. *Id.* at ¶ 6.70.
127. Neil W. Netanel, *The Next Round: The Impact of the WIPO Copyright Treaty on TRIPS Dispute Settlement*, 37 VA. J. INT'L L. 441, 471–472 (1997).
128. WCT, art. 11.
129. *See* Dinwoodie, *supra* note 7, at 758–759.
130. *See* R. Anthony Reese, *Will Merging Access Controls and Rights Controls Undermine the Structure of Anti-circumvention Law?*, 18 BERKELEY TECH. L.J. 619 (2003). It could be argued that just as we advocated regard for the legislative packages that are enacted at the domestic level in Chapter 5, so too must the DSB take account of the packaging of international agreements. If that is true, then the failure to integrate the technological protection requirements might cast doubt on integrating the exceptions provisions. But we think inquiries into the validity of national legislation are substantially different from interpretive exercises involving international instruments.
131. US–110(5), at ¶ 6.68.
132. *See* Footer, *supra* note 101, at 262–264.
133. These values derive from work on global administrative law principles. *See* Benedict Kingsbury, Nico Krisch & Richard B. Stewart, *The Emergence of Global Administrative Law*, 68 LAW & CONTEMP. PROBS. 15 (2005).
134. *China–Enforcement*, at ¶ 7.562.
135. *Id.* at ¶ 7.567 (emphasis in original).
136. TRIPS, art. 16.3.
137. *See* World Intellectual Property Organization Memorandum of the Director on the Joint Recommendation, WIPO Doc. A/34/13 ¶ 8 (August 4, 1999), *available at* http://www.wipo.int/meetings/en/doc_details.jsp?doc_id=1101. *See also* Paul J. Heald, *Trademarks and Geographic Indications: Exploring the Contours of the TRIPS Agreement*, 29 VAND. J. TRANSN'L L. 635, 654 (1996). Another potential candidate for integration is the WIPO Model Provisions on Protection Against Unfair Competition, WIPO Publication No. 832 (Geneva 1996), which was based on a study by the Max Planck Institute and expands upon the meaning of Article 10bis of the Paris Convention. Although it has been criticized as exceeding the scope of WIPO's authority, *see* William R. Cornish, *Genevan Bootstraps*, 19 EUR. INTELL PROP. REV. 336 (1997) (discussing the impact of the Model Provisions on Protection Against Unfair Competition on the interpretation of the TRIPS Agreement), that critique could be taken into account in its utilization.
138. DSU, art. 3.2 (emphasis added). The argument here is somewhat analogous to the one made in Chapter 4 on whether the scope of the TRIPS Agreement should be read dynamically to encompass new forms of creativity.
139. Intergovernmental Committee on Intellectual Property and Genetic Resources, Traditional Knowledge and Folklore, *The Protection of Traditional Cultural Expressions/Expressions of Folklore: Draft Objectives and Principles*, Objective (xii), WIPO/GRTKF/IC/10/4 (October 2, 2006), Annex at 4, *available at* http://www.wipo.int/edocs/mdocs/tk/en/wipo_grtkf_ic_10/wipo_grtkf_ic_10_4.pdf.
140. TRIPS, art.1.1.
141. *See, e.g.,* International Centre for Trade and Sustainable Development, *EU Sued Over Secrecy Surrounding FTA Talks with India*, vol. 15, no. 5 (February 18, 2011), *available at* http://ictsd.org/i/news/bridgesweekly/101086/.

142. See Turk, *supra* note 10.
143. *See, e.g., SK—US Free Trade Deal Would Violate 169 Korean Laws: Critics*, The Hankyoreh, January 17, 2007, *available at* http://www.hani.co.kr/arti/english_edition/e_business/184691.html.
144. *See, e.g.,* Free Trade Agreement Between the EFTA States and the Republic of Korea, December 15, 2005, Annex XIII, art. 3; CAFTA, art. 15.9(5).
145. *Cf.* Koskenniemi, *supra* note 21, at ¶ 56.
146. See ACTA, arts. 8.1 &. 23.1 & note 9.
147. *See, e.g.,* Parliamentary Questions (October 28, 2010), *available at* http://www.europarl.europa.eu/sides/getDoc.do?pubRef=-//EP//TEXT+WQ+E-2010-8847+0+DOC+XML+V0//EN&;language=EN; Sean Flynn, *ACTA's Constitutional Problem: The Treaty That Is Not a Treaty*, 26 Am. Univ. Int'l L. Rev. 903 (2011).
148. *See, e.g.,* International Centre for Trade and Sustainable Development, *EU Parliament Criticises Secrecy of ACTA Negotiations in a Landslide Vote*, 14 Bridges Weekly Trade News Digest, March 17, 2010, *available at* http://ictsd.org/i/news/bridgesweekly/72497/.
149. See Helfer, *supra* note 8.
150. *Cf. Japan Trade Official Says ACTA Should Serve as a Model for WTO Rules*, Elec. Comm. & L. Rep. April 6, 2011 (quoting Japanese official stating that Japan would like ACTA brought into the WTO process once ACTA is ratified and becomes a treaty).
151. Kamal Saggi and Joel P. Trachtman, *Incomplete Harmonization Contracts in International Economic Law: Report of the Panel*, China—Measures Affecting Protection and Enforcement of Intellectual Property Rights, WT/DS362/R, *adopted March 20, 2009*, 10 World Trade Rev. 1–2 (2010).
152. *See, e.g.,* Claus-Dieter Ehlermann & Lothar Ehring, *The Authoritative Interpretation Under Article IX:2 of the Agreement Establishing the World Trade Organization: Current Law, Practice and Possible Improvements*, 8 J Int'l Econ. L. 803 (2005); Claus-Dieter Ehlermann & Lothar Ehring, *Decision-making in the World Trade Organization*, 8 J. Int'l Econ. L. 51 (2005); Esty, *supra* note 24; Claude E. Barfield, Free Trade, Sovereignty, Democracy: The Future of the World Trade Organization (AEI Press 2001); Tomer Broude, International Governance in the WTO: Judicial Boundaries and Political Capitulation (Cameron 2004).
153. *See, e.g.,* Oliver Ziegler, *EU-US Regulatory Coordination: A Two-Level Game Approach*, FRP Working Paper 04/2009, *available at* http://www.regensburger-politikwissenschaftler.de/frp_working_paper_04_2009.pdf ("Regulatory cooperation is a . . . way of achieving common standards. In contrast to harmonization, regulators do not negotiate already existing standards ex post but create the conditions for the development of new policies—or the prevention of harmful unilateral action—ex ante.").
154. TRIPS, arts. 23 & 24.
155. *Id.* art. 27.3(b). The charge concerning animals and plants has been expanded to include consideration of the patentability of living products produced by genetic manipulation. *See* Meir Perez Pugatch, The International Political Economy of Intellectual Property Rights 135 (Edward Elgar 2004).
156. TRIPS, art. 64.3.
157. *Id.* art. 66.
158. Ministerial Declaration on Global Electronic Commerce, WT/MIN(98)/DEC/2 (May 20, 1998); *see also* Doha Ministerial Declaration, ¶ 34.
159. Doha Ministerial Declaration, ¶¶ 17–19.
160. Declaration on Public Health, ¶¶ 6 & 7.
161. *See* http://www.wto.org/english/tratop_e/trips_e/intel6_e.htm.
162. *See, e.g.,* Annual Report, IP/C/56, ¶ 3 (November 10, 2010). *See generally* Kal Raustiala, *Compliance and Effectiveness in International Regulatory Cooperation*, 32 Case. W. Res. J. Int'l L. 387, 434–438 (2000).
163. October 2010 Minutes of the TRIPS Council, *supra* note 37, at ¶ 344.

164. *See* World Customs Organization website, http://www.wcoomd.org/home.htm.
165. *See* October 2010 Minutes of the TRIPS Council, *supra* note 37.
166. *See, e.g.,* Ernst-Ulrich Petersmann, *Challenges to the Legitimacy and Efficiency of the World Trading System: Democratic Governance and Competition Culture in the WTO,* 7 J. INT'L ECON. L. 585, 601 (2004).
167. *Cf.* Riccardo Pavoni, *Mutual Supportiveness as a Principle of Interpretation and Law-making: A Watershed for the "WTO-and-Competing-Regimes" Debate,* 21 EUR. J. INT'L L. 649 (2010).
168. *See generally* Joost Pauwelyn & Luiz Eduardo Salles, *Forum Shopping Before International Tribunals: (Real) Concerns, (Im)Possible Solutions,* 42 CORNELL INT'L L.J. 77 (2009).
169. Marrakesh Agreement Establishing the World Trade Organization, April 15, 1994, art. V, LEGAL INSTRUMENTS—RESULTS OF THE URUGUAY ROUND, vol. 1, 1867 U.N.T.S. 154, 33 I.L.M. 1144 (1994).
170. *See* PAUWELYN, *supra* note 105, at 348–350, citing Agreement on the Application of Sanitary and Phytosanitary Measures, April 15, 1994, art. 3.2, 1867 U.N.T.S. 493, which refers to standards established by the Codex Alimentarius Commission, the International Office of Epizootics, and the Secretariat of the International Plant Protection Convention; the Agreement on Subsidies and Countervailing Measures, April 15, 1994, 1867 U.N.T.S. 14, which refers implicitly to actions undertaken by the Organisation for Economic Co-operation and Development (OECD), and Agreement on Technical Barriers to Trade, April 12, 1979, arts. 2.4 & 2.5, GATT B.I.S.D. 26S/8 (1979), which make general references to standards developed by international organizations.
171. *See, e.g.,* TIM BÜTHE & WALTER MATTLI, THE NEW GLOBAL RULERS: THE PRIVATIZATION OF REGULATION IN THE WORLD ECONOMY (Princeton University Press 2011).
172. Private international law may also reduce inconsistencies, and various institutions are working on providing courts with guidance. *See* AMERICAN LAW INSTITUTE, INTELLECTUAL PROPERTY: PRINCIPLES GOVERNING JURISDICTION, CHOICE OF LAW, AND JUDGMENTS ON TRANSNATIONAL DISPUTES (2008); EUROPEAN MAX-PLANCK-GROUP ON CONFLICT OF LAWS IN INTELLECTUAL PROPERTY (CLIP), PRINCIPLES ON CONFLICT OF LAWS IN INTELLECTUAL PROPERTY LAW, Final Text, December 1, 2011, *available at* http://www.ip.mpg.de/ww/de/pub/mikroseiten/cl_ip_eu/en/pub/home.cfm. *See also* Internet Use Joint Recommendation, *supra* note 17, setting up principles on the meaning of "use" on the internet in ways that are helpful in resolving questions on jurisdiction and choice of law.
173. Decision by the Arbitrators, European Communities—Regime for the Importation, Sale and Distribution of Bananas—Recourse to Arbitration by the European Communities Under Article 22.6 of the DSU, ¶ 152, WT/DS27/ARB/ECU (March 24, 2000).
174. *Id.* at ¶ 161.
175. Each of these Conventions permits suit in the International Court of Justice; *see* Berne Convention for the Protection of Literary and Artistic Works, July 24, 1971, art. 33, 1161 U.N.T.S. 3; Rome Convention for the Protection of Performers, Producers of Phonograms and Broadcasting Organizations, 26 October 1961, art. 30, 496 UNTS 43; Paris Convention for the Protection of Industrial Property, March 20, 1883, as last revised at Stockholm, July 14, 1967, art. 28, 21 U.S.T. 1583, 828 U.N.T.S. 305, though no state has heretofore exercised this option.

Chapter 7

1. *See* R. Michael Gadbaw, *Systemic Regulation of Global Trade and Finance: A Tale of Two Systems,* 13 J. INT'L ECON. L. 551, 567 (2010).
2. Appellate Body Report, Japan—Taxes on Alcoholic Beverages, at 14, WT/DS8/AB/R, WT/DS10/AB/R, WT/DS11/AB/R (October 4, 1996).
3. *See* Petros C. Mavroidis, *No Outsourcing of Law? WTO Law as Practiced by WTO Courts,* 102 AM. J. INT'L L. 421, 465 (2008); Appellate Body Report, United States—Final

Anti-Dumping Measures on Stainless Steel from Mexico, WT/DS344/AB/R, p. 160 (April 30, 2008) (emphasizing "security and predictability"); Michael Wabwile, *Re-examining States' External Obligations to Implement Economic and Social Rights of Children*, 22 CAN. J.L. & JURIS. 407, 433 (2009) (noting gap-filling role).

4. Panel Report, United States—Section 110(5) of the U.S. Copyright Act, WT/DS/160/R (June 15, 2000) [hereinafter *US–110(5)*].

5. *See generally* Mary E. Footer, *The (Re)turn to "Soft Law" in Reconciling Antinomies in WTO Law*, 11 MELBOURNE J. INT'L L. 241 (2010).

6. *See* Peter Drahos, *BITs and BIPs—Bilateralism in Intellectual Property*, 4 J. WORLD INTELL. PROP. 791 (2001).

7. WIPO Copyright Treaty, December 20, 1996, 2186 U.N.T.S. 121, 36 I.L.M. 65 [hereinafter WCT]; WIPO Performances and Phonograms Treaty, December 20, 1996, 2186 U.N.T.S. 203, 36 I.L.M. 76; Anti-Counterfeiting Trade Agreement, March 31, 2011 Text, *available at* http://trade.ec.europa.eu/doclib/docs/2011/may/tradoc_147937.pdf [hereinafter ACTA]; Congressional Research Service, The Trans-Pacific Partnership Agreement (June 25, 2010), *available at* http://fpc.state.gov/documents/organization/145583.pdf; *see also* Public Knowledge, Rashmi Rangnath, *ACTA the Sequel: The Transpacific Partnership Agreement*, *available at* http://www.publicknowledge.org/blog/acta-sequel-transpacific-partnership-agreement; Thomas Faunce & Ruth Townsend, *Public Health and Medicines Policies*, *in* NO ORDINARY DEAL: UNMASKING THE TRANS-PACIFIC PARTNERSHIP FREE TRADE AGREEMENT 149 (J. Kelsey ed., Allen & Unwin 2010).

8. *See* TRIPS, art 31bis. *See also* World Trade Organization, Ministerial Declaration of November 20, 2001, ¶¶ 17 & 19, WT/MIN(01)/DEC/1, 41 I.L.M. 746 (2002) [hereinafter Doha Ministerial Declaration]; World Trade Organization, Declaration on the TRIPS Agreement and Public Health, ¶¶ 4, 5(a), WT/MIN(01)/DEC/2, November 20, 2001, 41 I.L.M. 755 (2002) [hereinafter Declaration on Public Health].

9. *See* Daniel J. Gervais, *The Protection of Databases*, 82 CHI.-KENT L. REV. 1109, 1119 (2007) (noting that the draft Database Treaty was "in limbo" eleven years after it was withdrawn from the Geneva Diplomatic Conference).

10. *See WIPO Members Fail to Agree on Performers' Rights for Audiovisual Treaty*, 61 PAT. TRADE. & COP. J (BNA) 231 (2001). *But see* World Intellectual Property Organization, *Agreement on Transfer of Rights Paves Way to Treaty on Performers' Rights*, Geneva, June 24, 2011, WIPO Doc. No. PR/2011/692 (noting that the General Assembly of WIPO would be asked to resume the Diplomatic Conference on the Protection of Audiovisual Performances).

11. *See* International Centre for Trade and Sustainable Development, *WIPO Broadcast Treaty Talks Collapse*, June 20, 2007, *available at* http://ictsd.org/i/ip/39618//; *see also* Shyamkrishna Balganesh, *The Social Costs of Property Rights in Broadcast (and Cable) Signals*, 22 BERKELEY TECH. L.J. 1303, 1314 (2007).

12. Documents on the Development Agenda are available at http://www.wipo.int/ip-development/en/agenda/; World Intellectual Property Organization, Program Activities, Traditional Knowledge, Genetic Resources and Traditional Cultural Expressions/Folklore, *available at* http://www.wipo.int/tk/en/; SEDFREY M. CANDELARIA ET AL., THE ROAD TO EMPOWERMENT: STRENGTHENING THE INDIGENOUS PEOPLES RIGHTS ACT, vol. I (International Labor Organization 2007), *available at* http://www.ilo.org/wcmsp5/groups/public/---asia/---ro-bangkok/---ilo-manila/documents/publication/wcms_124767.pdf.

13. *See, e.g.,* Margaret Chon, *A Rough Guide to Global Intellectual Property Pluralism*, *in* WORKING WITHIN THE BOUNDARIES OF INTELLECTUAL PROPERTY 445 (Rochelle Dreyfuss, Harry First & Diane Zimmerman eds., Oxford University Press 2010); Amy Kapczynski, *The Access to Knowledge Mobilization and the New Politics of Intellectual Property*, 117 YALE L.J. 804 (2008).

14. *See* Keith E. Maskus & Jerome H. Reichman, *The Globalization of Private Knowledge Goods and the Privatization of Global Public Goods*, *in* INTERNATIONAL PUBLIC GOODS AND

TRANSFER OF TECHNOLOGY UNDER A GLOBALIZED INTELLECTUAL PROPERTY REGIME 3, 37 (Keith E. Maskus & Jerome H. Reichman eds., Cambridge University Press 2005).
15. See Donald P. Harris, *Carrying a Good Joke Too Far: TRIPS and Treaties of Adhesion*, 27 U. PA. J. INT'L ECON. L. 681 (2006); Donald P. Harris, *TRIPS and Treaties of Adhesion Part II: Back to the Past or a Small Step Forward?*, 2007 MICH ST. L. REV. 185.
16. P. Bernt Hugenholtz & Ruth L. Okediji, *Conceiving an International Instrument on Limitations and Exceptions to Copyright* (2008), *available at* www.ivir.nl/publicaties/hugenholtz/finalreport2008.pdf.
17. The Washington Declaration on Intellectual Property and the Public Interest (August 2011), *available at* http://infojustice.org/washington-declaration.
18. INTELLECTUAL PROPERTY IN A FAIR WORLD TRADE SYSTEM: PROPOSALS FOR REFORMING THE TRIPS AGREEMENT (Annette Kur ed., Edward Elgar 2011) [hereinafter PROPOSALS FOR REFORMING THE TRIPS AGREEMENT].
19. *See, e.g.*, Hugenholtz and Okediji, *supra* note 16, at 4.
20. *See, e.g.*, ACTA; *see also* Chapter 6.
21. Benedict Kingsbury, Nico Krisch & Richard B. Stewart, *The Emergence of Global Administrative Law*, 68 LAW & CONTEMP. PROBS. 15 (2005).
22. *See, e.g.*, Christophe Geiger, *Trade Marks and Freedom of Expression: The Proportionality of Criticism*, 38 IIC 317 (2007); Boehringer Ingelheim Ltd v. VetPlus Ltd, [2007] E.T.M.R. 67 (UK); Ashdown v. Telegraph Group Ltd [2002] QB 546.
23. *See, e.g.*, Case C-324/09, L'Oreal SA v. eBay Int'l [2011] E.T.M.R. 52 (CJEU) at ¶ AG49 (Opinion of Advocate-General) ("It should not be forgotten that the listings uploaded by users to eBay's marketplace are communications protected by the fundamental rights of freedom of expression and information provided by Article 11 of Charter of Fundamental Rights of the EU and Article 10 of the European Convention on Human Rights."); Directive 2000/31/EC of the European Parliament and of the Council of 8 June 2000 on Certain Legal Aspects of Information Society Services, in Particular Electronic Commerce, in the Internal Market, recital 9, 2000 O.J. (L 178) 1 ("The free movement of information society services can in many cases be a specific reflection in Community law of a more general principle, namely freedom of expression as enshrined in Article 10(1) of the Convention for the Protection of Human Rights and Fundamental Freedoms, which has been ratified by all the Member States.... [T]his directive is not intended to affect national fundamental rules and principles relating to freedom of expression.").
24. *See* Anheuser-Busch Inc. v. Portugal, App. No. 73049/01, 45 Eur. H.R. Rep. 36 [830] (Grand Chamber ECHR 2007).
25. *See e.g.*, LAURENCE R. HELFER & GRAEME W. AUSTIN, HUMAN RIGHTS AND INTELLECTUAL PROPERTY: MAPPING THE GLOBAL INTERFACE (Cambridge University Press 2011).
26. Appellate Body Report, United States—Import Prohibition of Certain Shrimp and Shrimp Products, ¶¶ 127–131, WT/DS58/AB/R, DSR 1998:VII (November 6, 1998).
27. *US–110(5)*, at ¶ 6.55.
28. *See* Tomer Broude & Yuval Shany, *The International Law and Policy of Multi-sourced Equivalent Norms*, in MULTI-SOURCED EQUIVALENT NORMS IN INTERNATIONAL LAW 1 (Tomer Broude & Yuval Shany eds., Hart Publishing 2011); *cf.* Laurence R. Helfer, *Adjudicating Copyright Claims under the TRIPS Agreement: A Case for a European Human Rights Analogy*, 39 HARV. INT'L L.J. 357, 431 (1998) (arguing that any analysis of state practice should consciously look to the laws of states at every stage of development).
29. *See* J. H. Reichman, *Saving the Patent Law from Itself: Informal Remarks Concerning the Systemic Problems Afflicting Developed Intellectual Property Regimes*, in PERSPECTIVES ON THE PROPERTIES OF THE HUMAN GENOME PROJECT 289 (F. Scott Kieff ed., Elsevier/Academic Press 2003).
30. *See, e.g.*, Jessica Litman, *The Public Domain*, 39 EMORY L.J. 965 (1990).
31. *See, e.g.*, AMARTYA SEN, DEVELOPMENT AS FREEDOM (Oxford University Press 1999); Margaret Chon, *Intellectual Property and the Development Divide*, 27 CARDOZO L. REV. 2821 (2006).

32. Berne Convention for the Protection of Literary and Artistic Works, July 24, 1971, art. 2.8, 1161 U.N.T.S. 3 [hereinafter Berne Convention]. *See also* SAM RICKETSON & JANE C. GINSBURG, 1 INTERNATIONAL COPYRIGHT AND NEIGHBOURING RIGHTS: THE BERNE CONVENTION AND BEYOND, ¶ 6.111 at 331 (2d ed. Oxford University Press 2005).
33. TRIPS, art. 9.2; WCT, art. 2.
34. *See* WCT, art. 5 (noting that the protection afforded by copyright to compilations of data or other material "does not extend to the data or the material itself"); TRIPS, art. 10.2.
35. Paris Convention for the Protection of Industrial Property, July 14, 1967, art. 6ter, 21 U.S.T. 1583, 828 U.N.T.S. 305 [hereinafter Paris Convention]. There are also a number of provisions that limit protection, but do so primarily to protect other interests, such as Article 6bis of the Paris Convention's protection for well-known marks, which includes as an obligation to deny registration of certain conflicting marks; Article 5ter of Paris permits unlawful use of patented devices on vehicles in transit; and Article 37.1 of TRIPS, which protects the innocent incorporation of unlawfully produced circuit designs. *See also* Nairobi Treaty on the Protection of the Olympic Symbol, adopted September 26, 1981, art. 1, 1863 U.N.T.S. 367 (requiring states to deny registration to marks that unlawfully incorporate Olympic marks).
36. *See* Paris Convention, art. 6quinquiesB.
37. TRIPS, art. 15.1.
38. *Id.* art. 15.3
39. *Id.* art 27.1
40. *Id.* arts. 27.2–27.3.
41. SAS Institute Inc v World Programming Ltd, [2010] EWHC 1829 (Ch), ¶ 204; *see also* TRIPS, art. 9.2 ("Copyright protection shall extend to expressions and not to ideas, procedures, methods of operation or mathematical concepts as such.").
42. SAS Institute Inc v World Programming Ltd [2010] EWHC 1829 (Ch), ¶¶ 217–218; *see also* WCT, art. 2 ("Copyright protection extends to expressions and not to ideas, procedures, methods of operation or mathematical concepts as such.").
43. CCH Canadian v. Law Society of Upper Canada [2004] 1 SCR 339, ¶ 19 (McLachlan CJ) (Can S Ct) ("the idea of intellectual creation was implicit ... in the Berne Convention").
44. Daniel J. Gervais, Feist *Goes Global: A Comparative Analysis of the Notion of Originality in Copyright Law*, 49 J. COPYRIGHT SOC'Y 949, 971–973 (2002); SAM RICKETSON, THE BERNE CONVENTION FOR THE PROTECTION OF LITERARY AND ARTISTIC WORKS: 1886–1986, at 900-901 (Oxford University Press 1987) (suggesting that common law countries that adopt a sweat of the brow standard for originality depart from "the spirit if not the letter" of the Berne Convention). *But see* 1 RICKETSON & GINSBURG, *supra* note 32, ¶ 8.05 at 405–406 (noting that countries are "allowed to adopt differing interpretations of the minimum of 'intellectual creation' that is required" to be a work within Article 2.1 of the Berne Convention).
45. TrafFix Devices, Inc. v. Marketing Displays, Inc., 532 U.S. 23, 29 (2001); Philips Electronics NV v Remington Consumer Products Ltd [1998] RPC 283, [2002] ECR-I-5475 (ECJ).
46. Bilski v. Kappos, 130 S.Ct. 3218, 3225 (2010) (citations omitted).
47. *See, e.g.*, 17 U.S.C. § 102(b); Lotus Development Corp. v. Borland Int'l. Inc., 49 F.3d 807 (1st Cir. 1995).
48. *See, e.g.*, Council Regulation (EC) No. 207/2009 of February 26, 2009, on the Community Trade Mark (codified version), art. 15.1, 2009 O.J. (L 78) 1 (requiring mark owner to make genuine use of a mark within the European Union within five years of registration); *id.* art. 51.1(a) (listing non-use as ground for revocation).
49. European Patent Convention, October 5, 1973, arts. 52 & 53, 1065 U.N.T.S. 199 (as amended December 13, 2007), *available at* http://www.epo.org/law-practice/legal-texts/epc.html; Lionel Bently et al, *Exclusions from Patentability and Exceptions and Limitations to Patentees' Rights*, Standing Committee on Patents, WIPO Doc. SCP/15/3, Annex 1 (October 2010).

Notes to Pages 184–186   251

50. See Chapter 3.
51. See Directive 2009/24/EC of the European Parliament and of the Council of April 23, 2009, on the Legal Protection of Computer Programs (codified version), art. 1.3, 2009 O.J. (L 111) 16; Directive 96/9/EC of the European Parliament and of the Council of March 11, 1996, on the Legal Protection of Databases, art. 3.1, 1996 O.J. (L 77) 20; Directive 2006/116/EC of the European Parliament and of the Council of December 12, 2006, on the Term of Protection of Copyright and Certain Related Rights (codified version), art. 6, 2006 O.J. (L 372) 12.
52. See Wittem Group, European Copyright Code, art. 1.1(1), available at http://www.copyrightcode.eu/. Cf. Jane C. Ginsburg, International Copyright Law: From a "Bundle" of National Copyright Laws to a Supranational Code, 47 J. COPYRIGHT SOC'Y 265, 273–274 (2000) (making such a prediction, though not with reference to whether by further legislation or a process of interpretation). Of course, at least in the near term, a strict textual approach to interpretation by national courts might confine the evolving common standard to the works explicitly covered, allowing lower standards of originality to be applied to other works. Cf. Newspaper Licensing Agency v. Meltwater, [2011] EWCA Civ 890; Football Dataco Ltd v Brittens Pools Ltd, [2010] EWCA Civ. 1380.
53. BENJAMIN KAPLAN, AN UNHURRIED VIEW OF COPYRIGHT 46 (Columbia University Press 1967).
54. Berne Convention, art. 10.1. See also 1 RICKETSON & GINSBURG, supra note 32, ¶ 13.95 at 847 ("Under Article 9(1) [of TRIPS] it will be obligatory for members to provide for exceptions for quotations under article 10(1) [of Berne], this being the one mandatory exception under Berne.").
55. Berne Convention, arts. 10(2) & 10bis. For a fuller listing, see Hugenholtz and Okediji, supra note 16, Appendix A.
56. See 1 RICKETSON & GINSBURG, supra note 32, ¶ 14.49–14.106.
57. Berne Convention, art. 7.
58. TRIPS, arts. 19 & 21.
59. Id. arts. 24.4–24.9; 25.1; 37.
60. Id. arts. 31 & 31bis
61. Id. art. 33.
62. See, e.g., Panel Report, China—Measures Affecting the Protection and Enforcement of Intellectual Property Rights, WT/DS362/R (January 26, 2009) [hereinafter China–Enforcement]; see also TRIPS, arts. 31(b) & 44.2.
63. TRIPS, arts. 13, 17, 26, & 30.
64. WCT, art. 10.
65. U.S. CONSTITUTION, art. 1 §8 cl. 8; cf. Eldred v. Ashcroft, 537 U.S. 186 (2003).
66. See, e.g., 17 U.S.C. § 109(a); Trade Marks Act 1994, § 11 (UK); Prestonettes, Inc. v. Coty, 264 U.S. 359 (1924); Adams v. Burke, 84 U.S. 453 (1873).
67. See Directive 2001/29/EC on the Harmonisation of Certain Aspects of Copyright and Related Rights in the Information Society, arts. 5.2–5.3, 2001 O.J. (L 167) 10 [hereinafter Copyright Directive].
68. See id. art. 5.1.
69. See Software Directive, arts. 6 & 5.2. See also 17 U.S.C. § 117.
70. See Lisa P. Ramsey, Free Speech and International Obligations to Protect Trademarks, 35 YALE J. INT'L L. 405 (2010). See, e.g., Laugh It Off Promotions v. South African Breweries Int'l (Finance) BV, 2006 (1) SA 144 (Const. Ct.) (South Africa) (2005); Economic Partnership Agreement between the CARIFORUM states, of the one part, and the European Community and its member states, of the other part, October 15, 2008, art. 144.F, 2008 O.J. (L289) 3 ("The EC Party and the Signatory CARIFORUM States shall provide for the fair use of descriptive terms, including geographical indications, as a limited exception to the rights conferred by a trademark. Such limited exception shall take account of the legitimate interests of the owner of the trademark and of third parties.").

71. *See, e.g.,* Patents Act 1977, § 60(5)(b) (UK).
72. *See* Panel Report, Canada—Patent Protection of Pharmaceutical Products, WT/DS114/R (March 17, 2000) [hereinafter *Canada–Pharmaceuticals*].
73. Patents Act 1977, § 60(5)(g) (UK).
74. *Id.* § 60(5)(a).
75. *See, e.g.,* eBay Inc. v. MercExchange, L.L.C., 547 U.S. 388 (2006).
76. *See* Copyright Directive, art. 5.5; Jonathan Griffiths, *The "Three-Step Test" in European Copyright Law—Problems and Solutions*, [2009] INTELL. PROP. Q. 428.
77. *See Canada–Pharmaceuticals; US–110(5). See also* Chapter 3; Max Planck Institute for Intellectual Property, Competition and Tax Law, *Declaration: A Balanced Interpretation of the "Three-Step Test" in Copyright Law* (April 2010), *available at* http://www.ip.mpg.de/ww/en/pub/news/declaration_on_the_three_step_/declaration.cfm; Jane C. Ginsburg, *Toward Supranational Copyright Law? The WTO Panel Decision and the "Three Step Test" for Copyright Exemptions*, 187 REVUE INTERNATIONALE DU DROIT D'AUTEUR 3, 17 (2001); Griffiths, *supra* note 76; Robert Howse, *The Canadian Generic Medicines Panel—A Dangerous Precedent in Dangerous Times*, 5 J. WORLD INTELL. PROP. 493, 494 (2000) (criticizing the panel in *Canada–Pharmaceuticals* for failing to do "justice to the delicate balance of social and economic interests reflected in the stated purposes of [the TRIPS] Agreement").
78. *See* Annette Kur, *Of Oceans, Islands and Inland Water—How Much Room for Exceptions and Limitations under the Three-Step Test?*, 8 RICH. J. GLOBAL L. & BUS. 287, 331 (2008–2009) (discussing decision of the Barcelona Court of Appeals in *Google—Caching*, Audiencia Provincial de Barcelona, AC\2008\1773, September 17, 2008); *see also* Griffiths, *supra* note 76 (discussing same decision, *available* in Spanish at http://www.irpi.ccip.fr/upload/pdf/private/decisions/080917_Audencia_Barcelona_GoogleSpain.pdf).
79. 17 U.S.C. § 107.
80. Harper & Row Publishers, Inc. v. Nation Enters, 471 U.S. 539, 589–590 (1985).
81. Copyright, Designs and Patents Act 1988, § 29–30 (UK); *see also* Ashdown v. Telegraph Group Ltd., [2001] 3 WLR 1368.
82. LIONEL A. BENTLY AND BRAD SHERMAN, INTELLECTUAL PROPERTY LAW 202 (3d ed. Oxford University Press 2009).
83. *See* Ashdown v. Telegraph Group Ltd., [2001] 3 WLR 1368.
84. Paris Convention, art. 5. *See* Chapters 1 & 2.
85. TRIPS, art. 31
86. *Id.* arts. 8 & 40.
87. Thomas Dreier, *Balancing Proprietary and Public Domain Interests: Inside or Outside of Proprietary Rights?, in* EXPANDING THE BOUNDARIES OF INTELLECTUAL INTELLECTUAL PROPERTY: INNOVATION POLICY FOR THE KNOWLEDGE SOCIETY 316 (Rochelle Dreyfuss, Diane L. Zimmerman & Harry First eds., Oxford University Press 2001).
88. Joined Cases C-241/91P and C-242/91P, Telefis Eireann and Independent Television Publications Ltd v. Commission of the European Communities (*Magill*), 1995 ECR I-743 (ECJ) (constraining exercise of copyright).
89. *See* J. H. Reichman and Pamela Samuelson, *Intellectual Property Rights in Data?*, 50 VAND. L. REV. 51, 87 n.153 (1997).
90. *See, e.g.,* 15 U.S.C. §§ 1–7 & 12–27; CONSOLIDATED VERSION OF THE TREATY ON THE FUNCTIONING OF THE EUROPEAN UNION, September 5, 2008, arts. 101–102, 2008 O.J. (C 115) 47; *cf.* F. Hoffman-LaRoche Ltd. v. Empagran S.A., 542 U.S. 155 (2004) (attempting to utilize U.S. antitrust law extraterritorially to compensate for lack of local law).
91. WCT, Agreed Statement Concerning Article 10 ("It is understood that the provisions of Article 10 permit Contracting Parties to carry forward and appropriately extend into the digital environment limitations and exceptions in their national laws which have been considered acceptable under the Berne Convention. Similarly, these provisions should be understood to permit Contracting Parties to devise new exceptions and limitations that are appropriate in the digital network environment.").

92. TRIPS, art. 13; *US–110(5)*, at ¶¶ 6.59 & 6.187.
93. WCT, art. 11; Copyright Directive, art. 6.4.
94. *See, e.g.,* 17 U.S.C. § 117; Software Directive, art. 5.2; Copyright Directive, art. 5.1; Joined Cases C-236/08-C238/08, Google France v. Louis Vuitton Malletier, Centre National de Recherché en Relations Humaines, and Viaticum [2011] All E.R. (EC) 411 (CJEU) (holding out the possibility that Google may benefit from safe harbors in the E-Commerce Directive with respect to alleged liability for keyword advertising using marks of plaintiffs); L'Oreal SA v eBay International AG [2009] EWHC 1094 (Ch) (UK), Case C-324/09, [2011] E.T.M.R. 52 (CJEU) (same possibility with respect to provision of online auction services).
95. Directive 98/44/EC of the European Parliament and of the Council of July 6, 1998, on the Legal Protection of Biotechnological Inventions, 1998 O.J. (L 213) 13; Monsanto Technology LLC v. Cefetra BV, Case C-428/08, [2010] All ER (D) 65 (Jul) (CJEU 2010).
96. *See, e.g.,* Bernt Hugenholtz, *Why the Copyright Directive Is Unimportant, and Possibly Invalid*, 22 EUR. INTEL. PROP. REV. 501 (2000).
97. *See, e.g.,* Graeme B. Dinwoodie, *Private Ordering and the Creation of International Copyright Norms: The Role of Public Structuring*, 160 J. INST. AND THEORETICAL ECON. 161 (2004).
98. *See, e.g.,* Daniel J. Gervais, *Towards a New Core International Copyright Norm: The Reverse Three-Step Test*, 9 MARQ. INTELL. PROP. L. REV. 1, 8 (2005) ("The fact that private use is not expressly mentioned as an exception in a number of national laws or the Berne Convention is not surprising: it was of little interest to copyright holders until the invention of the VCR and double-deck cassette players, which only became popular in the 1970s.").
99. *See, e.g.,* Metro-Goldwyn-Mayer Studios Inc. v. Grokster, Ltd., 545 U.S. 913 (2005), which involved facts that were also litigated in the Netherlands; Computer Associates, Inc. v. Altai, Inc., 126 F.3d 365 (2d Cir. 1997), where the same case was litigated in France; Case C-593/03, Roche Nederland BV v. Primus, [2007] F.S.R. 5, which envisions successive infringement litigation against related defendants throughout Europe. *See also* International Association for the Protection of Intellectual Property, Resolution, Question Q174—Jurisdiction and Applicable Law in the Case of Cross-Border Infringement of Intellectual Property Rights (October 25–28, 2003), *available at* http://www.aippi.org/reports/resolutions/Q174_E.pdf.
100. 1 RICKETSON & GINSBURG, *supra* note 32, ¶¶ 2.07–2.09.
101. STEPHEN P. LADAS, PATENTS, TRADEMARKS, AND RELATED RIGHTS: NATIONAL AND INTERNATIONAL PROTECTION, § 44 at 59 (Harvard University Press 1975).
102. *See e.g.,* Metro-Goldwyn Mayer Studios, Inc. v. Grokster, Ltd., 545 U.S. 913 (2005) (claim against purveyors of peer-to-peer software); Sony Corp. v. Universal City Studios, 464 U.S. 417 (1984) (claim against manufacturers of videocassette recorders); A&M Records, Inc. v. Napster, Inc., 239 F.3d 1004, 1010–1011 (9th Cir. 2001) (claims against distributors of peer-to-peer software); Tiffany (NJ) Inc. v. eBay, Inc., 600 F.3d 93 (2d Cir. 2010) (rejecting Tiffany's attempt to hold auction site liable for sale of counterfeit items on its website); LVMH v. eBay, [2010] E.T.M.R. 10 (Tribunal de commerce, Paris 2008); Cartoon Network LP v. CSC Holdings, Inc., 536 F.3d 121, 123 (2d Cir. 2008) (considering whether defendant cable company's digital video recorder system, allowing home recording of cable broadcasts, infringed plaintiff's copyrights); L'Oreal SA v eBay International AG [2009] EWHC 1094 (Ch) (UK), Case C-324/09, [2011] E.T.M.R. 52 (CJEU); Twentieth Century Fox Film Corp v Newzbin Ltd [2010] EWHC 608 (Ch), (2010) ECC 13 (UK); Roadshow Films Pty Ltd v iiNet Ltd [2010] FCA 24, (2010) 83 IPR 430, *on appeal*, Roadshow Films Pty Limited v iiNet Limited [2011] FCAFC 23 (Australia).
103. *See, e.g.,* REBECCA GIBLIN, CODE WARS: 10 YEARS OF P2P SOFTWARE LITIGATION (Edward Elgar 2011).
104. *See* Jane C. Ginsburg & Sam Ricketson, *Inducers and Authorisers: A Comparison of the US Supreme Court's Grokster Decision and the Australian Federal Court's Kazaa Ruling*, 11 MEDIA & ARTS L. REV. 1 (2006); cases cited *supra* note 102.

105. See Peter K. Yu, *Six Secret (and Now Open) Fears of ACTA*, 64 SMU L. REV. 975(2011).
106. See, e.g., Copyright Directive, art. 6.4; NAT'L COMM'N ON NEW TECHNOLOGICAL USES OF COPYRIGHTED WORKS, FINAL REPORT (1978) (recommending what became 17 U.S.C. § 117); Carys J. Craig, *Digital Locks and the Fate of Fair Dealing in Canada: In Pursuit of "Prescriptive Parallelism,"* 13 J. WORLD INTELL. PROP. 503 (2010); Jerome H. Reichman, Graeme B. Dinwoodie & Pamela Samuelson, *Reverse Notice and Takedown Regime to Enable Public Interest Uses of Technically Protected Copyrighted Works*, 22 BERKELEY TECH. L.J. 981, 1042 (2007) (discussing the concept of prescriptive parallelism).
107. See Annemarie Bridy, *ACTA and the Specter of Graduated Response*, 26 AM. UNIV. INT'L L. REV. 559 (2011); Michael Geist, *The ACTA Guide, Part One: The Talks To-Date* (January 25, 2010), *available at* http://www.michaelgeist.ca/content/view/4725/125/.
108. See ACTA Communique, Washington University Conference on ACTA, June 24, 2010, *available at* http://www.wcl.american.edu/pijip/go/acta-communique ("ACTA would distort fundamental balances between the rights and interests of proprietors and users, including by ... introducing highly specific rights and remedies for rights holders without detailing correlative exceptions, limitations, and procedural safeguards for users.").
109. CC Decision No. 2009-580DC, July 10, 2009, J.O. 9675, *available at* http://www.conseil-constitutionnel.fr/decision.42666.html.
110. Graeme B. Dinwoodie, Rochelle C. Dreyfuss, & Annette Kur, *The Law Applicable to Secondary Liability in Intellectual Property Cases*, 42 N.Y.U. J. INT'L LAW & POL. 201, 227 (2009).
111. See, e.g., EUROPEAN MAX-PLANCK-GROUP ON CONFLICT OF LAWS IN INTELLECTUAL PROPERTY (CLIP), PRINCIPLES ON CONFLICT OF LAWS IN INTELLECTUAL PROPERTY LAW, December 1, 2011, art. § 3–604, *available at* http://www.ip.mpg.de/ww/de/pub/mikroseiten/cl_ip_eu/en/pub/home.cfm; *see also* Frederick W. Mostert & Martin B. Schwimmer, *Notice and Takedown for Trademarks*, 101 TRADEMARK REP. 249 (2011) (seeking to establish an "ius gentium" on trademark law applicable to trademark infringement online). The WIPO Standing Committee on Trademarks recently decided it was premature to consider developing a global standard for intermediary liability for online trademark infringement, deciding instead to convene a seminar to explore the issue. *See* Daniel Pruzin, *WIPO Panel Passes on Global Standards for ISP Liability for Trademark Violations*, 16 ELEC. COMM. L. REP. (BNA) 623 (April 13, 2011); *see also* World Intellectual Property Organization, Standing Committee on the Law of Trademarks, Industrial Designs and Geographical Indications Twenty-Fifth Session, Geneva, March 28 to April 1, 2011, Summary by the Chair, WIPO Doc. SCT/25/6, at ¶¶ 15–18 (April 1, 2011).
112. Request for Consultations by India, European Union and a Member State—Seizure of Generic Drugs, at 1, WT/DS408/1 (May 19, 2010); *EU, India Drop Generics Dispute to Focus on FTA Talks*, FDAnews, January 24, 2011, *available at* http://fdanews.com/newsletter/article?issueI d=14404&articleId=133690; *see also* Joined Cases C-446/09 and C-495/09, Koninklijke Philips Electronics NV v. Lucheng Meijing Industrial Company Ltd, and Nokia v. Her Majesty's Comm'rs of Revenue and Customs, [2012] E.T.M.R. __ (CJEU December 1, 2011).
113. TRIPS, art. 51.
114. ACTA, art. 16.1
115. AMERICAN LAW INSTITUTE, INTELLECTUAL PROPERTY: PRINCIPLES GOVERNING JURISDICTION, CHOICE OF LAW, AND JUDGMENTS IN TRANSNATIONAL DISPUTES (2008): CLIP, *supra* note 111. *See also* European Patent Office, Working Party on Litigation, Draft Agreement on the Establishment of a European Patent Litigation System (February 16, 2004), *available at* http://www.epo.org/law-practice/legislative-initiatives/epla.html.
116. See Internet Corporation for Assigned Names and Numbers, Uniform Domain Name Dispute Resolution Policy, ¶ 4 (October 24, 1999), *available at* http://www.icann.org/en/udrp/udrp-policy-24oct99.htm.
117. See Barcelona.com v. Excelentisimo Ayuntamiento De Barcelona, 330 F.3d 617 (4th Cir. 2003).

118. *See* Laurence R. Helfer & Graeme B. Dinwoodie, *Designing Non-national Systems: The Case of the Uniform Domain Name Dispute Resolution Policy*, 43 WM. & MARY L. REV. 141 (2001).
119. ACTA, recital 4.
120. *See* 1 RICKETSON & GINSBURG, *supra* note 32, ¶ 1.21, at 20.
121. Berne Convention, arts. 3 & 5. *See also* Rome Convention for the Protection of Performers, Producers of Phonograms and Broadcasting Organisations, October 26, 1961, arts. 2, 4–6, 496 U.N.T.S. 43.
122. Paris Convention, art. 2.1.
123. TRIPS, art. 3.1 & footnote 3 (emphasis added).
124. *See, e.g.,* Vera Franz, *Back to Balance: Limitations and Exceptions to Copyright*, in ACCESS TO KNOWLEDGE IN THE AGE OF INTELLECTUAL PROPERTY 517, 517 (Gaëlle Krikorian & Amy Kapczynski eds., Zone Books 2010) (giving the example of exceptions permitting reproduction for the visually impaired).
125. The first step of the copyright provision—Article 13—speaks of exceptions being confined to "certain, special cases," but the *US–110(5)* panel interpreted this phrase as requiring in part that the challenged measure be "limited in its field of application or exceptional in its scope." *US–110(5)*, at ¶¶ 6.107–6.110.
126. *See* World Intellectual Property Organization, The 45 Adopted Recommendations under the WIPO Development Agenda, ¶ 45, *available at* http://www.wipo.int/export/sites/www/ip-development/en/agenda/recommendations.pdf.
127. WCT, Preamble (noting the "balance between the rights of authors and the larger public interest, particularly education, research, and access to information.").
128. Doha Ministerial Declaration, ¶¶ 17 & 19; Declaration on Public Health, ¶¶ 4, 5(a).
129. ACTA, recital 6 ("Desiring to address the problem of infringement of intellectual property rights ... in a manner that balances the rights and interests of the relevant right holders, service providers, and users.").
130. *See* International Law Commission, *Fragmentation of International Law: Difficulties Arising from the Diversification and Expansion of International Law: Report of the Study Group on the Fragmentation of International Law*, Finalized by Martti Koskenniemi, UN Doc. A/CN.4/L.682 (April 13, 2006).
131. *See, e.g.,* Kamal Saggi & Joel P. Trachtman, *Incomplete Harmonization Contracts in International Economic Law: Report of the Panel*, China—Measures Affecting Protection and Enforcement of Intellectual Property Rights, *WT/DS362/R*, adopted March 20, 2009, 10 WORLD TRADE REV. 1–2, 23–24 (2010).
132. Understanding on Rules and Procedures Governing the Settlement of Disputes, April 15, 1994, art. 3.2, Marrakesh Agreement Establishing the World Trade Organization, Annex 2, LEGAL INSTRUMENTS—RESULTS OF THE URUGUAY ROUND, vol. 31, 1869 U.N.T.S. 401, 33 I.L.M. 1226 (1994).
133. UNITED NATIONS CONFERENCE ON TRADE AND DEVELOPMENT, BILATERAL INVESTMENT TREATIES 1995–2006: TRENDS IN INVESTMENT RULEMAKING 44–51 (United Nations 2007), *available at* http://www.unctad.org/en/docs/iteiia20065_en.pdf.
134. *Id.* at 8.
135. *See* Henning Grosse Ruse-Khan, *Protecting Intellectual Property Under BITS, FTAs, and TRIPS: Conflicting Regimes or Mutual Coherence?*, in EVOLUTION IN INVESTMENT TREATY LAW AND ARBITRATION (Kate Miles & Chester Brown eds., Cambridge University Press 2011).
136. *See* Ruth L. Okediji, *The Regulation of Creativity Under the Internet Treaties*, 77 FORDHAM L. REV. 2379, 2404–2408 (2009) (discussing the institutional capacity of developing countries to exercise effective design choices at the national level).
137. TRIPS, art. 1.1.
138. Jessica Litman, *Readers' Copyright*, at 22, 58 J. Copyright Soc'y 325, 345 (2011).

139. World Intellectual Property Organization, Treaty for Improved Access for Blind, Visually Impaired and Other Reading Disabled Persons, Annex, WIPO Doc. SCCR/18/5 (May 25, 2009); see also Graeme Dinwoodie, *The WIPO Copyright Treaty: A Transition to the Future of International Copyright Lawmaking?*, 57 CASE WESTERN RES. L. REV. 751, 760 (2007).
140. Hugenholtz & Okediji, *supra* note 16.
141. Annette Kur & Henning Grosse Ruse-Khan, *Enough Is Enough: The Notion of Binding Ceilings in International Intellectual Property Protection*, in PROPOSALS FOR REFORMING THE TRIPS AGREEMENT, *supra* note 18, at 359.
142. PROPOSALS FOR REFORMING THE TRIPS AGREEMENT, *supra* note 18, arts. 13.1(b) & 13.1(c)(v); 17.1(a) & 17.1(b)(iii); 30.1(a)-(d); see also Rochelle Cooper Dreyfuss, *TRIPS—Round II: Should Users Strike Back?*, 71 U. CHI. L. REV. 21 (2004); Graeme B. Dinwoodie, *The International Intellectual Property Law System: New Actors, New Institutions, New Sources*, 98 AM. SOC'Y INT'L L. PROC. 213 (2004). *Cf.* L. RAY PATTERSON & STANLEY W. LINDBERG, THE NATURE OF COPYRIGHT: A LAW OF USERS RIGHTS (University of Georgia Press 1991).
143. Proposed Treaty on Access to Knowledge (May 10, 2005), *available at* http://keionline.org/content/view/235/1.
144. *See, e.g.,* Jane C. Ginsburg, *Authors and Users in Copyright*, 45 J. COPYRIGHT SOCY'Y 1, 6–9 (1997); Justin Hughes, *Recoding Intellectual Property and Overlooked Audience Interests*, 77 TEX. L. REV. 923, 924–928 (1999).
145. *See* David Vaver, *Copyright and the Internet: From Owner Rights and User Duties to User Rights and Owner Duties?*, 57 CASE W. RES. L. REV. 731 (2007) ("If user rights were truly to be balanced against owner rights, one would expect to find a provision that owner rights should be enacted or enforced only in (1) certain special cases that (2) demonstrably encourage the production of the work, and that (3) do not unreasonably prejudice the legitimate interests of users. That feature of balance does not yet appear on any WIPO or TRIPS agenda. It should."). *See also* Gervais, *supra* note 98.
146. *Cf.* Litman, *supra* note 138, at 6.
147. *Cf.* BRUCE J. ACKERMAN, RECONSTRUCTING AMERICAN LAW (Harvard University Press 1984). Others have adopted this device in international law. *See, e.g.,* Anne-Marie Slaughter & William Burke-White, *An International Constitutional Moment*, 43 HARV. INT'L L.J. 1, 2 (2002); *see also* Michael P. Scharf, *Seizing the "Grotian Moment": Accelerated Formation of Customary International Law in Times of Fundamental Change*, 43 CORNELL INT'L L.J. 439, 445 (2010) (suggesting the alternative term of "Grotian moment" for such moves in international law).

INDEX

Access to medicines
  compulsory licences, 38, 191
  Council for TRIPS, attention to, 171
  data exclusivity, 103, 151, 153, 167, 172
  diagnostic exceptions, 17, 58–71
  Doha Declaration on the TRIPS Agreement and Public Health (*see* Doha Round)
  Doha Ministerial Declaration (*see* Doha Round)
  effect of gene patents on, 16–17
  exhaustion rules, 151
  generics, 31, 38, 52, 54, 57, 64, 70, 81, 103, 117, 151–152, 191, 201
  in-transit seizures, 191, 201 (*see also* In-transit seizures)
  neglected diseases, 53, 153
  and TRIPS-plus agreements, 151
  in Uruguay Round negotiations, 31
Acquis, 6, 20, 42, 139, 147, 176–203
  access-regarding principles, 182–189
  application in treaty interpretation, 194–201
  benefits of, 15, 42, 139, 147, 174, 176–177, 195–197
  emerging elements, 188–189
  global administrative law, parallels to, 180
  lawmaking, use in, 197–198
  need for an acquis, 178–181
  and neofederalism, 6
  principles reflecting interdependence of nations, 193–194
  principles protecting national autonomy, 192–193
  principles protecting proprietary interests, 189–192
  prior usage of concept in international law, 6, 176
  principles on scope of protection, 185–187
  principles to curb abuse of rights, 187–188
  sources of, 6, 20, 177, 181–182, 200
  subject-matter exclusions, 183–184
  treaty interpretation, use in, 194–197
  and user rights, 198–201
Agreement on Trade-Related Aspects of Intellectual Property. *See* TRIPS Agreement.
Anti-Counterfeiting Trade Agreement Act (ACTA), 42, 143
  compliance mechanism, 149, 158
  criminal provisions, 149
  export controls, 191
  and fragmentation, 156
  governance structures, 145
  integration in TRIPS dispute settlement, 168–170
  internet intermediaries, liability of, 150, 190
  in-transit seizures, 149–151, 169
  and MFN, 157
  motivation for, 46, 168, 178–179
  and national autonomy, 192
  negotiation of, 168–169, 197
  parties, 149, 178–179
  presumptions regarding damages, 149
  effect of regime shifting, 149
  scope of, 150, 168
  technological protection measures, 150
  and TRIPS, 150, 158, 168–170, 196
Antitrust law. *See* Competition law
Appellate Body. *See* Dispute Settlement Body
Auction sites. *See* Internet intermediaries
Audiovisual Performers' Treaty, 179

Berne Convention,
  acquis, 26, 37, 136, 166, 176, 195
  Association Littéraire et Artistique Internationale, 189
  administration of, 26
  adoption and evolution of, 4–5, 23, 189, 192

Berne Convention (*continued*)
Appendix, 29, 37, 133–134, 185
author, meaning of, 25
and censorship, 135
compulsory licences, 185
enforcement of, 26, 178, 186
exceptions and limitations, 185–187
formalities, prohibition of, 112–113
and human rights, 156
initial content, 24
minor exceptions doctrine, 163, 166, 177
news of the day, 183
moral rights, 25, 41
origins, 193
originality, 183–184
quotation right, 183, 185, 194, 198, 201
revision of, 26
subject-matter exclusions, 183
Stockholm Protocol (1967), 28–29
term of protection, 185
and TRIPS, 36, 133, 135, 163, 174
translation rights, 27, 133
Bilateral and regional agreements, 145–148, 197
EU-Central America Agreement, 148
in nineteenth century, 23
integration in TRIPS dispute settlement, 166–168
US-Chile, 148
US-Jordan, 148, 160
US-Korea, 167
US-Morocco, 103, 148
US-Singapore, 148
in advance of TRIPS, 30
Bilateral Investment Treaties (BITs), 42, 135, 145, 197
BRICS
effect of intellectual property rights on, 35
political economy of, 11–12, 133
TRIPS, view of, 14
Broadcasting treaty, 179

Capacity. *See* Developing countries
Central American Free Trade Agreement (CAFTA), 145
Codex Alimentarius Commission, 173
Commodification initiatives, 144, 148–152
Competition law
in the EU, 10, 187–188
innovation policy, as crucial part of, 15, 195
TRIPS and, 37, 111–112, 155, 161, 187–188
Convention on Biological Diversity (CBD), 145–146, 158
and capacity problems, 138
and gene patents, 156
integration into interpretation of TRIPS, 158–159

observer status of CBD Secretariat at Council for TRIPS, 172
and traditional knowledge, 143, 152, 171
and World Trade Organisation, 15
Convention for the Protection of New Varieties of Plants, 151
Copyright Directive
ephemeral copy exception, 185, 188
exceptions and limitations, 185, 188
mandatory exceptions, 185
private copy exception, 130, 185
technological protection measures, 188
Copyright law
authorship, 25–26
cable retransmission provisions, 129–130
compilations, protection for, 93
compulsory licences, 29, 77
and digital rights management, 130–131, 150, 164
exceptions and limitations, 26, 59–60, 155, 166, 179, 185, 188, 199
facts, non-protection of, 183
fair dealing defense, 186–187
fair use defense, 10, 26, 73, 186
homestyle exception, 60–62, 117–118, 120
idea/expression distinction, 160–161, 183
levy systems, 130
methods of operation, 184
moral rights, 25, 40
originality, 93, 183–184
orphan works, 12
parody exception, 185, 187, 199
private copy exception, 130, 189
public interest defense, 187
related rights, 95
reverse engineering exception, 187, 194, 199 (*see also* Software Directive)
secondary liability, 190–191, 194, 196
and technological protection measures, 12, 155, 188
term of protection, 11, 12, 117–118, 185
Council for TRIPS, 134, 144
access to medicines, 171
benefits of acquis to, 196
built-in agenda, 96, 171
as forum for declaratory judgment action, 138
electronic commerce, 171
and emergent issues, 178
discussion of enforcement provisions, 149
role in reducing fragmentation, 171, 173
geographical indications, 40, 96, 171
intellectual property and development, 171
least developed countries, extra assistance for, 171
living plants and animals, 171
nonviolation complaints, applicability to TRIPS, 171

and objectives and principles of TRIPS, 110
observer status at, 39, 171–173
relationship of TRIPS and CBD, 171
role of, 7, 21, 38
extension of transition period, 39
work of, 171–173
Counterfeiting
 ACTA (*see* Anti-Counterfeiting Trade Agreement Act)
 Council for TRIPS, 172
 secondary liability, 190–191
 Tokyo Round of the GATT, 29–30, 168
 and TRIPS, 73–74, 145, 149–152
Counternorms, 147, 152–156, 169–170, 202
Creative Commons, 155

Database Directive, 93–97
 and competition concerns, 188
 copyright protection, 93
 and Article 10bis of Paris, 93–95
 purpose of, 84, 101
 reciprocity provision, 93, 101, 104–105, 109
 and scope of TRIPS, 94
 sole source compulsory license, 187–188
 sui generis right, 93–97
 as protection against unfair competition, 198
Database treaty, 179
Design protection, 121–123
Development Agenda
 and balance, 196
 and fragmentation, 145
 and TRIPS, 14, 166
 and WIPO activities, 138, 154–155, 166
Developing countries
 and Berne Convention, 26–27
 Berne Convention Appendix (*see* Berne Convention)
 capacity, 34, 132–139, 145, 147–148, 152, 167, 177, 180, 189, 197–198
 diffusion, 116, 128–132
 and the Dispute Settlement Body, 135–138
 and the Dispute Settlement Understanding (Article 24, DSU), 134
 effects of intellectual property protection on, 10–11, 34–35, 111, 116
 and Paris Convention, 27–29
 political economy of, 133
 Stockholm Protocol to the Berne Convention, 28–29
 transition periods for TRIPS compliance, 37–39, 51, 91, 128, 133
 and TRIPS interpretation, 70–71, 78–79, 81
 and TRIPS negotiations, 30–39
 United Nations reports, 27
Digital Millennium Copyright Act
 anticircumvention provisions, 131, 148

Dispute Settlement Body
 Amicus briefs, 137
 Appellate Body, 50
 Appellate Body vs panel, 82
 benchmarks, use of, 56, 61, 64–65, 69, 80–81, 161, 202
 Canada-Pharmaceuticals, 40, 54–57, 59–71, 75, 78, 80–82, 84, 105–108, 111, 113, 117–118, 124, 161, 196
 cases brought, 75, 82, 170
 China-Enforcement, 39, 73–82, 112, 134–135, 144, 149, 164, 168, 192
 components of, 7, 170
 cumulative reading of Exception Provisions, 60–61, 69–70, 80, 195
 decisions to date, 8, 50
 declaratory judgment actions, 50, 136–137
 deference (*see* Dispute Settlement Body, levels of scrutiny of national laws)
 discretion, treatment of, 74–75, 78–79, 82, 135
 Dispute Settlement Understanding, 39, 134, 159, 165, 196
 EC-Bananas, 174
 EC-Biotech, 159–160, 162, 166
 EC-GI, 41, 60, 65, 69–70, 80–82, 86–89, 98–101, 107–109, 144, 146
 formalism of decisionmaking, 20, 67–68, 71, 78, 80, 122–123, 162
 fact-finding by, 124
 GATT cases, decisionmaking in, 88–89
 GATT jurisprudence, reliance on in TRIPS cases, 88, 106–107
 granularity of analysis, 53, 76, 80–81
 Havana Club, 79, 82, 86–89, 94–95, 98–104, 108, 122, 125, 163
 India-Pharmaceuticals, 39, 82, 91–92, 95, 112, 128, 135–136
 intention of parties, weight given to, 95–96
 integration of varied norms through adjudication (*see* Integration)
 Japan-Taxes on Alcoholic Beverages, 176
 levels of scrutiny of national laws, 8, 57, 73–75, 81–82, 84, 88, 91–92, 98, 100, 104, 107–109, 112–113, 118, 128
 Mexico-Soft Drinks, 159, 173
 nonviolation complaints, 136–137, 171
 operation of, 50–51
 proof in cases before, 54–55, 66, 74, 82, 125–126, 134
 relevance of effect on world trade, 70–71
 reliance on non-WTO materials, 159–161
 scope of jurisdiction, 158–159
 soft law, references to, 181
 state practices, references to, 56, 64–65, 69–70, 81, 136, 161, 166, 181

Index

Dispute Settlement Body (*continued*)
  taking account of packaging or tradeoffs, 117–128
  US-110(5), 41, 59–64, 66, 69–70, 75, 78, 80–82, 111, 117–118, 120, 124, 126, 134, 136, 161–164, 166, 176–177, 181, 188, 195
  US-301, 137
  US-337, 125
  US-Shrimp Turtle, 181
  WIPO materials, reliance on, 39, 81, 162–166
Dispute Settlement Understanding (DSU)
  Article 3.2, 39, 159, 165, 196
  Article 24, 134
Doha Round
  Article 31bis mechanism, operation of, 52, 57, 133–134
  Article 31bis and ACTA, 151–152
  Council for TRIPS, additional tasks, 171
  Doha Declaration on the TRIPS Agreement and Public Health, 38, 133, 150–151, 179
  Doha Ministerial Declaration, 8, 38, 51–52, 56, 57, 81, 89, 110–111, 144, 154, 160, 169, 196
  and Development Agenda, 154
  revision of TRIPS (Article 31bis), 52, 79, 133–134, 179, 201

Exhaustion of rights, 41, 98, 148, 151, 185, 187
European Court of Human Rights (ECHR), 145–146, 186
European Union (EU)
  acquis communautaire, 176
  Biotech Directive, 146, 156, 188
  Database directive, 84, 93–97, 101, 104–105, 109, 187–188
  Directives, adoption of, 145
  Geographical Indications regulation, 86–87, 98–100, 109
  vs. traditional international law regimes, 68–69
Experimentation
  and acquis, 189, 192
  and certainty, 176
  effect of DSB interpretation on, 67–69, 89, 96–97
  from enlarged international system, 11
  and gene patents, 18–19
  and in-transit seizures, 191
  and multiple lawmaking institutions 147
  in periods of assimilation, 116,
  in periods of technological change, 121
  effect of reciprocity on, 104
  and speed of international lawmaking, 164
  and structural provisions, 109–110
Export controls, 191

Federal Communications Commission (FCC), 129
Folklore, 146, 152, 165, 171–172, 179, 232n109
Food and Agriculture Organisation (FAO), 169–170
  and capacity problems, 138
  and human rights, 154
  and traditional knowledge, 143
  and World Trade Organisation, 15, 173
Flexibility (*see also* TRIPS Agreement, flexibilities)
  and acquis, 192
  stage of development and, 71
  and failure by DSB to consider legislative packaging, 118
  in Paris and Berne Conventions, 24, 26
  in period of assimilation, 116
  as feature of TRIPS, 111
  in WCT and WPPT, 150
Fragmentation, 42, 114, 146–156, 202
  cycling of disputes, 146, 158, 161, 165, 171–174
  thickets of rights, 146
  role of acquis in ameliorating, 177–178
  role of individual actors in ameliorating, 174

General Agreement on Tariffs and Trade (GATT)
  Agreement on Safeguards, 128–132
  Article XIX (*see* Agreement on Safeguards)
  compensatory concessions (Article XXVIII), 119, 126, 202
  General Exceptions (Article XX), 86, 89–90, 119, 202
  national treatment (*see also* National treatment)
  safeguards in, 16, 38, 119, 202
  Tokyo Round, 30, 145, 168
  Uruguay Round (*see* World Trade Organisation)
  weaknesses of GATT 1947, 29, 50
General Agreement on Trade in Services (GATS), 102, 132, 159
Gene patents, 3, 16–19, 58–71, 195
  and the CBD, 156
  exclusions from protection, 17
  effects on diagnostic testing, 17
  exceptions, 17, 107
  and human rights, 153
  infringing acts, 17–18
  and injunctive relief, 72–73
  scope of, 17
  Secretary's Advisory Committee on Genetics, Health, and Society (SACGHS), 16–17, 49, 58–71

Hatch-Waxman Act, 117, 120, 122, 126
Harmonisation, 10
  limits of, 15–16
  optional provisions as part of, 68, 189
  scope of, 41
Human rights
  access to knowledge as, 9, 153
  as source for content of acquis, 181
  balance of public and proprietary rights within system of, 9–10, 154
  Committee on Economic, Social and Cultural Rights, 154
  Council of Europe Convention for the Protection of Human Rights and Dignity, 153
  right to education, 10, 153
  free expression, 10, 153
  and graduated response, 190
  fora for post-TRIPS lawmaking, 145
  individual control over the genome, 153
  right to health, 10, 153
  protection of property, 10, 170
  rights of authors, 10, 153
  suggesting how to characterize user rights, 200
  United Nations Sub-Commission on the Promotion and Protection of Human Rights, 138, 143
  Universal Declaration on the Human Genome and Human Rights, 153
  Universal Declaration of Human Rights, 10, 153, 156
  and WTO, 15

Injunctive relief
  eBay v MercExchange, 49, 72–79, 107, 113
  and open innovation, 73
Intellectual property law
  adaptation of, 97, 115, 130–131, 179, 187–188, 192, 202
  balance, 9–10, 36–37, 42, 51, 68–69, 80–81, 102–103, 110–111, 114, 127, 146, 150, 175, 177, 180–181, 190, 195–196, 200
  complexity, 114
  and digital technologies, 12
  diversity and, 10–12, 51, 108, 114, 177, 181, 187
  enforcement of, 15, 143, 149–152, 168, 189–192
  and follow-on innovation, 9, 42, 53
  historical contingency of, 12–14, 55, 58, 64, 70, 84, 97, 108, 114, 130, 177
  normative underpinnings, 31, 95, 176, 187, 202
  political economy of, 11–12, 33, 79, 115–118, 124, 133, 170, 180, 194, 200
  territorial tradition, 4

Integration, 147, 156–174
  of ACTA in the WTO, 168–169
  of bilateral and regional trade agreements in the WTO, 166–168
  through DSB adjudication, 158–170
  in lawmaking, 170–174
  variables relevant to integration through interpretation, 162–170
  of WIPO materials, 162–166
Interdependence of nations, 177, 189, 193–194, 198, 200–201
International acquis. *See* Acquis
International Centre for Trade and Sustainable Development (ICTSD), 152
International constitutional moment, 202
International intellectual property law
  backwards-looking, 25
  enforcement of, 7, 21, 36, 178, 193
  expertise, harnessing of, 146, 161, 169–174, 177, 189
  and free expression, 10, 26, 187, 200
  resilience of, 51
  tailoring of national laws, 57–58, 91, 110–111, 133, 178–179, 189, 192, 195, 201
  and universality, 7, 23–24, 40, 84, 192
International Labour Organization (ILO), 152
International law
  fragmentation of (*see also* Fragmentation)
  integration-through-interpretation (*see also* Integration)
  soft law, 145, 162, 164, 181, 191–192, 199
International Law Commission. *See* Koskenniemi Report
International Monetary Fund, 173
International Organisation for Standardization, 173
Internet Corporation for Assigned Names and Numbers (ICANN), 154, 191–192
Internet intermediaries
  and ACTA, 190
  auction sites, 13, 190
  cooperation with rightholders, 143
  graduated response, 190
  international rule on secondary liability, 190–191, 193
  liability for keyword advertising, 188
  peer-to-peer file sharing, 196
  secondary liability actions against, 12–13
Internet service providers. *See* Internet intermediaries
In-transit seizures
  and ACTA, 151–152, 156, 169
  India complaint against the European Union, 151, 156, 191, 201
  under GATT, 191
  under TRIPS, 149–150, 156, 169, 191

Inventive step
  Glivac case, 49, 53
  height of, 10, 14, 51–58, 71, 133–134, 184
  Indian patent law, section 3(d), 52–59, 81, 134, 136
  U.S. standard, 56

Joint Recommendation on Internet Use, 150
Joint Recommendation on Well-Known Marks, 148–150, 165, 168
  definition of "well-known" contained in, 149, 165
  dilution protection required by, 149, 160, 165, 168

Knowledge Economy
  interoperable products, 13
  nature of, 3–4, 12, 71–72, 85, 92–93, 96, 121, 188
  open innovation, 73, 77, 189
  and patents, use of as signals, 13, 123
Koskenniemi Report, 158–162, 196

Madrid Protocol, 148
Magill v. Commission, 187–188
Moral rights. *See* Copyright law
Most Favoured Nation obligation (MFN),
  in early bilateral treaties, 103
  in GATS, 132
  in GATT, 102–104, 157
  in TRIPS, 7, 84, 86, 99, 102–110, 114, 157, 159–160, 202

National autonomy
  and acquis, 192–193, 203
  and code view of TRIPS, 201
  continuing pedigree of, 25
  and creation of counternorms, 152
  and domestic political pressures, 115
  and effect on third countries, 57
  as embodied in TRIPS Article 1.1, 75, 80, 89–90, 112, 135 (*see also* TRIPS Agreement, Implementation of)
  as embodied in TRIPS, Articles 7–8, 89–90, 111
  in enforcement of intellectual property, 75, 79–80
  expansive reading of Article 27 and, 106
  functional substitutes for GATT provisions and, 89, 202
  greater need for in period of diffusion, 129
  greater than contemplated by conventional wisdom, 20
  and in-transit seizures, 191
  and assessment of motivation for laws, 101, 123–124
  relationship with national treatment, 24, 84, 100, 125, 202
  as overarching principle of Paris and Berne Conventions, 24, 201
  and priority provisions, 91
  and reciprocity provisions, 109
  reflected in DSB reports, 39, 75, 101, 144
  reflected in exceptions provisions, 114
  reflected in TRIPS, 41–42
  relevance in identifying structural features of TRIPS, 110
  scope of, and relation to future shape of international system, 180
  theoretical vs. real, 200
  and user rights, 200
  and working requirement, 195
National treatment, 97–109, 125–126, 193–194, 198, 201–203
  as part of acquis, 193–194
  De facto claims (*see* Nondiscrimination, de facto vs. de iure)
  De iure claims. (*see* Nondiscrimination, de facto vs. de iure)
  difference between substantive provisions of TRIPS and national treatment, 100, 125
  in GATT, 86–89, 125
  reliance on GATT jurisprudence in TRIPS cases, 88–89
  under Paris and Berne Convention, 4, 24, 93, 193, 198
  TRIPS v. GATT, 86, 88–89
  application to TRIPS-plus protection, 97–98
  and national autonomy, 24, 84, 100, 125, 202
  and neofederalism, 108
  vs. other claims of discrimination, 108
  relevance of design, architecture and structure of challenged law, 88–89
  relevance of motivation for challenged law, 88, 101–102
  relevance of practical equality of treatment, 86–88, 125
  scope of guarantee, 97–98, 193–194, 200
  levels of scrutiny, 100–101, 202
  as structural feature of TRIPS, 98, 100, 108
  in TRIPS, 7, 84, 86–90, 93–109, 193–194
  applied to rights of users, 193–194
Neofederalism
  and acquis, 6, 20, 203
  and Article 1.1 of TRIPS, 112
  and Articles 7–8 of TRIPS, 111–112
  and balance, 68
  costs of, 15, 176
  and de iure/de facto distinction, 108

and diffusion strategies, 129
and experimentation, 19
and flexibility, 22
and gene patents, 16
reflected in DSB reports, 19–20, 39, 51, 79, 82
and national autonomy, 16, 39
and national treatment, 99–100, 108
and nonmarket values, 22, 111–112
and private international law, 16
and structural principles, 110–112
and TRIPS, 5–6, 14, 39, 42–43, 68, 79, 82, 115, 143–144
underlying values, 201–203
Nondiscrimination, de facto vs. de iure, 87–90, 98–109
Nongovernmental organisations (NGOs)
  Consumer Project on Technology, 199
  and Council for TRIPS, 171
  Creative Commons, 155
  cross-border operation, 118
  declarations of, 156
  Doctors Without Borders, 155
  Knowledge Ecology International, 199
  role in development of post-TRIPS instruments, 145, 155, 170
  role in fragmentation and production of counternorms, 147, 153, 179, 199
  role in WTO dispute settlement, 137
  and technical assistance, 198
  and WIPO (*see* World Intellectual Property Organisation)
Non-practicing entities (NPEs)
  eBay v. MercExchange, 72–73, 107–108
  and injunctive relief, 13, 72–80
  rise and function of, 71–76
Nonviolation complaints, 136–137, 171
  in the GATT, 136–137
  moratorium on, 136
  in TRIPS, 136–137, 171
North American Free Trade Agreement (NAFTA), 33
Nutrition, 9–10, 31, 37, 111, 169, 187, 198

Paris Convention
  administration of, 26
  adoption and evolution of, 4–5, 23, 189, 192
  and developing countries, 27–28
  enforcement of, 26, 178
  initial content, 24
  origins, 193
  priority rules, 4, 24, 85–86, 90–92, 109, 112–113
  revision of, 26, 28
  subject-matter of registrations, 183
  telle quelle provision (Article 6quinquies), 99
  trade names, protection of (Article 8), 94–95
  and TRIPS, 36, 44, 90, 94, 112, 174
  unfair competition (Article 10bis), 24, 25, 94–95, 198
  Vienna Exposition of 1873, 23, 189
  well-known marks (Article 6bis), 24
  working requirement, 24, 28, 187
Patent law
  and basic research, 13, 19, 58
  Bolar Exemption, 115, 117
  bounty system, as alternative, 123
  compulsory licences, 28, 45, 77–80, 133, 152, 161, 185, 187, 191, 197
  exclusion for diagnostic methods, 184
  exceptions and limitations in general under national law, 186, 199
  experimental use, 199 (*see also* research exception)
  farmers' rights to save seed, 151, 186, 198
  first-to-file vs. first-to-invent, 92
  gene patents (*see also* Gene patents)
  injunctive relief, 13, 72–80
  inventive step (*see also* Inventive step)
  laws and principles of nature, 182–184, 195, 200
  noncommercial use exception, 199
  protection for pharmaceuticals, 11, 38, 51–58, 91, 103, 117, 167
  regulatory review exception, 54, 59–71, 117, 120, 124, 186
  research exception, 10, 58–71, 186, 199 (*see also* experimental use)
  second use patents, 184
  software patents, 121
  term of protection, 185
  thresholds to protection, 184
  tax subsidies, as an alternative to, 123
  thickets, 17, 18
  universities, patenting by, 13, 58
Patent offices
  pressures on examination by, 13
  SHARE program, 84–92, 98–101, 105, 109, 111, 113
  sharing of workloads, 16, 84–92
Patent trolls. *See* Non-practicing entities (NPEs)
Peer-to-peer software. *See* Internet intermediaries
Pirate Party, 115–116
Priority rules. *See* Paris Convention
Private international law, 15, 16, 189–192
Private ordering, 189
Public health. *See also* Access to medicines
  and acquis, 187
  ACTA and recognition of concern for, 150
  effect of bilateral agreements on, 103, 151
  consideration by DSB, 55, 57, 65, 67
  data exclusivity (*see* Access to medicines)

Public health (*continued*)
  Doha Ministerial Declaration (*see* Doha Round)
  exclusions from protection to further, 65, 67–68
  exhaustion rules, 151
  effect of intellectual property law on, 9 (*see also* Patent law, protection of pharmaceuticals)
  in-transit seizures (*see also* In-transit seizures)
  role of NGOs, 155
  reflected in TRIPS, 37, 111
  revision of TRIPS to reflect, 38–39 (*see also* Doha Round)
  WHO (*see* World Health Organization)

Reciprocity
  in early bilateral treaties, 22
  in Database Directive, 84, 93–94, 97–99, 104–105, 109, 198
  and de facto discrimination, 104, 109
  as feature of the international intellectual property system, 96–98, 104–105, 109
  pernicious effect of, 98, 104–105
  purpose of reciprocity provisions, 84, 93
Regime shifting, 146, 149, 156, 175, 180, 202
  by North, 14, 29–30, 144
  by South, 152–156, 169
Regulatory competition, 146–147, 171 (*see also* Fragmentation)
Rome Convention, 174

Science
  changes in business of, 13, 58
  human genome, sequencing of, 12, 17
  Mertonian norms, 9
Secretary's Advisory Committee on Genetics, Health, and Society (SACGHS), 16–17, 49, 58–71
Semiconductor Chip Protection Act, 96, 109
Software Directive
  backup exception, 186, 188
  interoperability exception, 185, 194
  reverse engineering exception, 185, 194
Sonny Bono Copyright Term Extension Act, 115, 117–118, 120, 131
Sovereignty. *See* National autonomy
Strategic Handling of Applications for Rapid Examination (SHARE). *See* Patent offices
Substantive maxima (*see also* User rights)
  in Berne Convention, 198
  proposals for, 199
  reverse three-step test, 200
  in TRIPS, 198–201
Substantive minima
  undemanding in early treaties, 25
  ability to offer more protection than, 121, 150–151, 166, 192, 198–199
  and national autonomy, 193
  compared to national treatment, 126
  nature of, 25, 112, 118, 121, 150–151, 192–193, 198–199
  need to move beyond, 180, 193, 198–201
  and neofederalism, 112
  in Paris and Berne, 24, 182
  and TRIPS, 112, 118, 166, 192
  and code view of TRIPS, 112
  and user rights, 198–199

Technical assistance, 38–39, 138, 154, 163, 198
Technology Transfer, 11, 27–28, 35, 37, 38–39, 43, 133–134, 138, 152, 169
Territoriality, 4, 24
  vs. universality, 23
Three Track Examination. *See* Patent offices
Trademark law
  comparative advertising, 199
  descriptive fair use, 186–187 (*see also* TRIPS Agreement, exceptions under Article 17)
  dilution, 68, 149, 157, 160, 165 (*see also* Joint Recommendation on Well-Known Marks)
  and domain names, 13, 154, 191–192
  and e-commerce, 13, 188, 191–192
  functionality, 184
  generic terms, 183–185
  and geographical indications, 40, 61, 65
  Joint Recommendation on Well-Known Marks, 148–150, 160, 165, 168
  keyword advertising, 188
  noncommercial use, 199
  parodic uses, 186–187
  secondary liability, 190–191
  trade dress protection (*see* Design Protection)
  use requirement, 184–185
Trade law
  bilateral trade agreements (*see* Bilateral and regional agreements)
  borrowings from, 103, 108, 114, 202
  European Partnership Agreements (EPAs) (*see* Bilateral and regional agreements)
  European Union Trade Barriers Regulation, 29
  vs. intellectual property law, 8, 103–104, 118–119, 127, 202
  US Free Trade Agreements (*see* Bilateral and regional agreements)
  Trade Act, Special 301, 29–30, 33, 42, 53, 135
Trade secrets. *See* Undisclosed information, protection of.

Index

Trademark Law Treaty, 148
Traditional knowledge, 143, 146, 152, 165, 171
Transpacific Partnership Agreement (TPP), 145, 150, 178–179
Treaty on Access to Knowledge (A2K Treaty), 199
TRIPS Agreement (*see also* Dispute Settlement Body)
   abuse, regulation of, 43–44, 111–112, 155, 187 (*see also* Competition law)
   allocation of national resources, 80, 101, 123
   coercion narrative, 33–34
   comparative advantage and, 8, 43, 53, 127
   compensation for violations (*see* TRIPS Agreement, enforcement of member state obligations)
   compulsory licence provisions, 77–80, 106, 113, 191, 197
   compromise narrative, 34–41
   as a contract of adhesion, 42, 179
   copyright provisions, 36, 160–161
   counterfeiting, provisions on, 73–74, 149–152, 168
   design provisions, 36, 121–122
   dispute settlement (*see* Dispute Settlement Body)
   effect on domestic lawmaking, 106, 115–139, 202
   enforcement of member state obligations, 21, 36, 125–126, 134, 144, 174
   enforcement provisions, 36–37, 73–82, 109–110, 112–113, 135, 149–152, 168, 185, 192
   Exceptions Provisions, 19, 37, 60–65, 111, 113–114, 155–156, 161, 185, 194–195, 200
   exceptions under Article 13 (copyright), 59–63, 66, 69–70, 129–130, 136, 155, 163, 185, 188, 194–195 (*see also* Copyright law)
   exceptions under Article 17 (trademark), 60–61, 65, 161, 185 (*see also* Trademark Law)
   exceptions under Article 30 (patent), 18, 59–65, 69–71, 155, 194–195 (*see also* Patent law)
   exchange narrative, 32
   exclusions from patentability (Article 27.3(a)), 67, 155
   exhaustion of rights (Article 6), 41, 98, 148, 151 (*see also* Exhaustion of rights)
   export controls, 191
   flexibilities, 57–58, 75–76, 79, 111, 114, 115, 133–134, 138, 147, 152–156, 180, 186, 192
   functional substitutes of GATT provisions in, 86, 89–90, 119, 202

   geographical indications provisions, 40, 98–99, 112
   implementation of, 75–76, 79, 82, 109, 112, 116–117, 135–136, 192 (*see also* Substantive minima; National Autonomy)
   as an incomplete contract, 18, 41, 196, 201
   and injunctive relief, 73–80
   Intellectual Property Committee (IPC), role of, 33–34
   in-transit seizures, 149–152, 156, 169, 191 (*see also* In-transit seizures)
   moral rights, 41, 44
   most favoured nation obligation (*see also* Most Favoured Nation obligation (MFN))
   narratives of, 21–22, 32–39
   normative assessment by panels, 60–65, 69–70, 78–81, 100–101, 123–124, 161–162, 194–195
   nondiscrimination generally, 8, 71, 86–109
   nondiscrimination, justification for, 87–90, 102, 104, 107–108, 110, 112–113, 123–124, 161
   principle of nondiscrimination (Article 27), 7, 8, 13, 36, 53–58, 66–71, 84, 105–108
   North-North debate, 39–41
   North-South debate, 30–39
   objectives and principles of (Articles 7–8), 36–37, 38, 39, 42, 44, 55–56, 67–69, 81, 89–90, 107, 109–112, 138, 150–151, 154, 160, 162, 169, 194–196
   patent provisions of, 36–37, 160–161, 183, 185
   pipeline protection, 38, 51–52, 82, 91, 128, 135–136
   plant protection, 37, 123, 148, 151, 156, 171, 183
   ratchet-up dynamic, 8, 58, 117–118, 131, 157
   rental rights, 36, 40, 123, 161
   remedies, provisions on (*see* TRIPS Agreement, enforcement provisions)
   revision proposals, 155–156, 170, 179
   scope of the Agreement, 94–98
   software, copyright protection of, 121
   standards vs. rules, 123, 167
   structural principles of, 66, 71, 81, 83–114, 196
   subject-matter exclusions, 183–184
   as a supranational code, 5, 6–8, 15–16, 18, 22, 51, 82, 84, 99, 133, 143–144, 166, 178, 201
   technical assistance, 38, 138, 198
   topography rights, provisions on, 96
   trademark provisions of, 36, 82, 99–100, 148, 160–161, 183, 185
   transition provisions, 37–39, 51, 91, 128, 133
   undisclosed information, protection of, 36, 96, 123, 132, 151, 167, 172

TRIPS-plus agreements, 135, 137, 146, 148–152, 160, 178, 180, 194

Unfair competition, 24, 25, 40, 83, 94–97, 198
Uniform Domain Name Dispute Resolution Policy (UDRP), 154, 191–192
United International Bureaux for the Protection of Intellectual Property (BIRPI). *See* World Intellectual Property Organisation
United Nations
  General Assembly debate (1961), 27
  Human Rights Council, 154
  Report on patents and transfer of technology to developing countries, 27
  WIPO as specialised agency of, 5, 27–28
United Nations Conference on Trade and Development (UNCTAD), 152–153, 169, 179
  capacity building, 152, 198
  report on proposed revision of the Paris Convention, 27–28
  resource book on TRIPS and Development, 152
United Nations Educational, Scientific and Cultural Organisation (UNESCO), 169
  and human rights, 153
  and traditional knowledge, 143
  and World Trade Organisation, 15
User rights, 198–201 (*see also* Substantive maxima)
  characterization as rights, 200
  examples in the Berne Convention, 198
  enforceability, 200–201
  goals of, 174, 180
  and national autonomy, 200
  and national treatment, 194
  need for, 180
  proposals for, 199
  examples in TRIPS, 96
  implicit in TRIPS, 112, 175, 198–199
  raised at WCT, 199

Vienna Convention on the Law of Treaties, 92, 158–168

Washington Declaration on Intellectual Property and the Public Interest, 156n94, 179
Well-known marks, 24, 36. *See also* Joint Recommendation on Well-Known Marks
Working requirement
  as used by developing countries, 11, 133
  under the Paris Convention, 24, 28
  under TRIPS, 21, 43–45, 106, 195
  US-Brazil dispute, 45

World Blind Union, 199
World Customs Union, 172
World Health Organisation (WHO), 145, 153, 169–170, 172, 179
  and capacity problems, 138, 198
  global strategic plan on public health innovation and intellectual property, 145, 153
  and traditional knowledge, 143
  and TRIPS, 145
  and World Trade Organisation, 15, 146–147, 173
World Intellectual Property Organisation (WIPO)
  Arbitration and Mediation Centre, 154
  Committee of Experts on measures against counterfeiting and piracy, 164–165
  creation of, 5, 26
  Council for TRIPS, observer status at, 39, 171
  and development, 27
  Development Agenda, 14, 138, 145, 154–155, 166, 196
  expertise, 146, 154, 162–163, 168
  The Geneva Declaration on the Future of the World Intellectual Property Organization, 156n94
  mission, 154, 163
  NGOs, participation of, 155
  post-TRIPS instruments, 145, 150
  role in revision of Paris and Berne Conventions, 26, 154
  standing committees, 145, 148, 150, 155, 164, 166
  and technical assistance, 39, 138, 163, 198
  and traditional knowledge, 143, 152, 165
  World Trade Organisation, agreement with, 39, 138, 154, 162
WIPO Copyright Treaty (WCT), 162–166, 178
  anticircumvention provisions, 148, 164–165, 188
  balance, reference to, 110, 196
  and bilateral agreements, 148
  integration into TRIPS by DSB panels, 162–166
  exceptions in the digital environment, 164–165, 185, 188
  impulse behind, 146, 150
  development and negotiation of, 147, 164
  mandatory exceptions, 199
  subject-matter exclusions, 183
WIPO Performances and Phonograms Treaty (WPPT), 145, 148, 150, 178
WIPO Provisions for the Protection of Traditional Cultural Expressions/Expressions of Folklore, 165, 172
WIPO Treaty for the Visually Impaired, 145, 155, 199

Index

World Trade Organisation (WTO)
   and broader values, 14–15, 31–32, 38–39, 169, 173
   Council for TRIPS (*see also* Council for TRIPS)
   Declaration of Punta del Este, 32
   and democratic values, 126–128, 196–197
   Dispute Settlement Body (*see also* Dispute Settlement Body)
   Doha Declaration (*see* Doha Round)
   General Council, 7, 144, 173
   linkage, 126, 144–145, 160, 180
   membership, 162
   Ministerial Conference, 7, 96, 144
   Sutherland Report, 102
   Uruguay Round, 30–31
   and World Intellectual Property Organisation, 39, 138, 154, 162, 171